The Old Country School

Sixth-year reading class, Arbor Vitae Summit School, District 7, Oneida Township, Delaware County, Iowa. (State Historical Society of Iowa.)

The Old Country School

*The Story of Rural Education
in the Middle West*

Wayne E. Fuller

The University of Chicago Press

Chicago & London

WAYNE E. FULLER is professor of history
at the University of Texas, El Paso.

The University of Chicago Press, Chicago 60637
The University of Chicago Press. Ltd., London

©1982 by The University of Chicago
All rights reserved. Published 1982
Printed in the United States of America
89 88 87 86 85 84 83 82   5 4 3 2 1

Library of Congress Cataloging in Publication Data

Fuller, Wayne Edison, 1919–
  The old country school.

  Includes bibliographical references and index.
  1. Education, Rural—Middle West—History.
  2. Middle West—Rural conditions. I. Title.
LC5147.M55F84   370.19′346′0977   81-16069
ISBN 0-226-26882-9   AACR2

Contents

✻✻✻

For
Jamie, Douglas, Bryan
and for
Vicki and Annette

Preface

If you drive through the rural Midwest today for any reasonable distance, you are almost certain to come upon an abandoned one-room schoolhouse. Its single door that once protected country children from the winter wind is like to be missing, and its window panes broken. Gone, too, are the scholars' desks and the big stove that sat in the middle of the room. In the yard the old pump rusts beneath the sun; grass and weeds grow where children once played crack-the-whip and fox-and-geese; and the underbrush has all but obscured the tiny buildings at the far end of the school lot.

In such a schoolhouse, some seven generations or so of Midwestern farm children were educated, many of whom made outstanding contributions to the American civilization. Indeed, it is perhaps not too much to say that the majority of the Midwest's political and professional leaders near the turn of the century began their education in just such humble surroundings. Certainly it is true that in thousands of little rural school districts across that broad land, the one-room school had virtually eliminated illiteracy.

All of which raises interesting questions for modern Americans accustomed to large, magnificent schools and school budgets running into millions of dollars each year. How was it possible, we ask, to educate so many children in such rude circumstances? What kind of education did Midwestern farm children receive in such buildings? Who were their teachers and how were they trained? Who controlled the day-to-day affairs of the little school, and who determined what would be taught and what would not be? Who drew the blueprints for the schoolhouse and who built it? And why did it sit where it sat rather than someplace else?

To answer these and other questions, much has been written in the following pages about rural education, especially about the origins and operation of the one-room schools, the rise of professional educators, and the long conflict between them and the farmers over the adequacy of their schools. But this is not meant to be a book merely about rural education. Rather, it is intended to be a social history of Midwestern rural America, seen through the development of one of its most important institutions. What follows is an effort to say something about the everyday life of rural people on the Middle Border in the late nineteenth and early twentieth centuries, to show in some concrete ways how they felt about democracy and education and why they felt as they did, and above all to capture something of their spirit and values, and the hopes and dreams they had for their children.

The research for this study has led me through all but one of the state historical societies of the ten Midwestern states surveyed, and through a number of local historical societies as well, and I am deeply grateful for their generous help in locating and making available to me their source materials on country schools. I am particularly indebted to Katherine Thompson, reference librarian at the Wisconsin State Historical Society in Madison, who responded so cheerfully through the years to my many requests, and to Dr. Robert Warner, former director of the Michigan Historical Collections at the University of Michigan, and his staff for their unfailing help during my many visits there. I wish also to thank Ruth Hughes, a long-time friend at the Rock County Historical Society in Janesville, Wisconsin, who gave generously of her time and knowledge to my research, and Merton Dillon, professor of history at Ohio State University, who has taken so much interest in this study and made available some of his own manuscript material.

The Registers of Deeds, who now control the records of the country schools in Kansas, were universally kind and helpful in opening their records to me and in permitting me to use their offices for research, especially W. W. McDaneld in Osborne County, whose office I visited more than once and whose patience with my requests and questions was extraordinary. I am also indebted to James L. Murphy, reference librarian for the Ohio State Historical Society, for his part in tracing down one of the stories included in this study.

For the completion of this manuscript I also owe much to the encouragement given me by my colleagues in the Department of History at the University of Texas at El Paso, to grants-in-aid from the Research Institute at the university, and to the help of my graduate students, whose papers on rural eucation in the Midwest were more valuable than they knew.

Finally, I wish to acknowledge the help of my daughter, Jamie, who read the manuscript and suggested changes in it, and the indispensable support of my wife, Billie, who not only made several research trips with me to the Midwest when she would rather have gone elsewhere, but also typed the manuscript and helped immeasurably to put it in its final form.

1
Recollections

I

As the snows melted and the earth warmed across the Illinois farmland in the spring of 1947, the farmers in Jasper County in the eastern part of the state were gathering to decide the fate of their one-room schools and the small, independent school districts that supported them. As happened elsewhere across the state that spring, the majority of the county's farmers voted to abandon their one-room schools and to send their children to larger, consolidated schools in the fall.

By their votes they merged more than one hundred small school districts, many of them as old as the county itself, into eighteen. And throughout the county that summer auctioneers began to auction off the little schoolhouses, schoolhouses with names like Freeland, Round Prairie, and Sand Ridge, that had been so much a part of rural life for more than a century. The Baptist Church in Newton bought the old Richards schoolhouse; the Maple Grove and Greenwood schoolhouses were sold to farmers; and others were disposed of in similar fashion as the summer days went by. "The Little Red Schoolhouses that have dotted the countryside for many years will soon be things of the past . . . ," the local newspaper reported in July. "They may not all be red schoolhouses, but they symbolize the seats of early learning so often referred to in song and story and now, having outlived their usefulness for educational purposes, [they] will soon be converted to other practical purposes."[1]

Neither in this nor in subsequent newspaper stories on school consolidation was there a sense of loss at the sale of the one-room schoolhouses. Nor was any effort made to consider what the little schools had meant to generations of farm children who had passed through them in preparation for their life's work. Instead, the stories conveyed a sense of progress and a feeling of haste to get on with the process of consolidation. It was obviously time to look forward, not back.

But if the Jasper County newspaper reporters had no time to write about student life in the one-room schools, a number of Midwestern men and women who had attended them in the years following the Civil War did. From World War I when the novelist Hamlin Garland, whose literary career was launched from a one-room school in Iowa, wrote *A Son of the Middle Border,* through the next three decades and beyond, the alumni of the old district schools turned out a small but significant collection of autobiographies in which they wrote of the days of their youth in the rural Midwest and recorded in detail the events of their passage through their one-room schools.

By the time they wrote, the America of their youth, that "small world," as one of them called it in the title of her book, had all but vanished, and they looked back nostalgically on their days in the one-room schoolhouse. "There was the thrill of competition and the joy of achievement," one woman wrote, recalling her days at the Shady Grove School in Ottawa Township, Waukesha County, Wisconsin, "the hilarity of playtime antics, the embarrassment of classroom error, the tenseness of intrigue, the intimacy, and the awakening of youthful romance!"[2]

Still, the nostalgic memories of their school days did not prevent them from revealing the blemishes of their country-school education. Indeed, much of what they wrote seemed to confirm the long list of imperfections that critics of one-room-school education had complained of for so long: poorly trained teachers, poorly equipped schoolrooms, want of books, voluntaristic education, and insufficient time for recitation as teachers hurried from class to class.[3]

Indelibly etched on their minds, too, was a picture of the barren, isolated schoolhouse, so often condemned as unfit for children. "The school-house which was to be the center of our social life stood on the bare prairie about a mile to the southwest [of our home,]" Hamlin Garland wrote of the district school he attended in Mitchell County, Iowa, in the 1870s, "and like thousands of other similar buildings in the west, had not a leaf to shade it in summer nor a branch to break the winds of a savage winter.... It was a barren temple of arts even to the residents of Dry Run."[4]

Such descriptions were only a part of the general scene of poverty and toil of childhood days in the rural Midwest. Whether in the settled portions of Ohio, Indiana, or Illinois, or on the Kansas, Nebraska, or Iowa frontier, circumstances were much the same. Rude homes, scarcity of possessions, long days spent in the fields, these were what they wrote of, not complainingly for the most part, but matter-of-factly, as though such hardships were in the natural order of things.[5]

To be sure, there were compensations for the harshness of the life they lived on the Middle Border, and these, too, they remembered. They told of the joys of outdoor life, of fishing in streams, of the pleasure of riding across the prairies on horseback, of sleigh rides in the winter, and of pursuing wild animals to their lairs. They remarked upon the beauty of the prairies in spring and summer, and they recalled their days of rest and rural amusements, their Sundays filled with church and visiting, picnics in the community grove, Friday night affairs at the schoolhouse, and the Fourth of July, which was almost as eagerly awaited as Christmas.[6]

But the great reality in their life was work, and the men, especially, noted that by the time they were eleven they were needed on the farm to do a man's work, and could no longer attend the spring and summer terms of school. Only after the corn was harvested in the fall could they return to school for the winter term, which meant their schooling was limited to about four months each year. One Iowa resident reckoned he had spent altogether only six hundred days in his one-room school, a school which no one was forced to attend and which by modern standards lacked nearly every essential for good learning.[7]

Yet those who wrote their memoirs had emerged from their poverty and one-room schools to become reputable doctors, lawyers, ministers, scientists, writers, and even educators. "Notwithstanding the fact that most of these little urchins dressed in homespun, home-made clothing," one man wrote of his Indiana school, "and that some of them came from humble homes where instruction in manners and culture were almost unknown, it is surprising to know the large number from that school who in after years filled official positions in the professional world as teachers, preachers, doctors, lawyers, and even state and governmental positions."[8]

More precisely, in 1932, one man at the University of Nebraska discovered that of those students who attended a certain one-room school in Jefferson County, Nebraska, in the terrible 1890s, eleven graduated from college, and three from a conservatory of music.

Twelve became teachers, one an attorney, one an engineer, one a noted eye specialist, one a prominent artist, and two were widely known musicians. Several were successful farmers, and not one seems ever to have been involved in crime.[9]

How had they managed to go so far from such rude beginnings? Was there any connection between their success and their training in the one-room school? They tried to answer these questions as they traced their odyssey from farm to fortune, but why some are inspired to pursue education and others are not was as baffling to them as it is to modern educators. One of them, at least, a professional educator, who had risen from a poverty-stricken one-room school to take a Master's degree at Columbia University, fell back upon individuality as an explanation. "We are so smug and complacent with our better buildings, and teachers colleges and organizations," he wrote, as he thought about his one-room school and mused over the lack of incentive of those who attended fine modern schools, "that we almost forget that learning is a personal matter like dying and that each one in the last analysis has to do it for himself."[10]

Nevertheless, most of those who wrote about growing up in the rural Midwest did try to show what they believed had contributed to their own success at least, if not to that of others. In doing this a few implied, if they did not say so directly, that their escape from the farm to a higher station in life had been due primarily to the quickness of their minds. But even they never believed that this alone had been responsible for all they had achieved. Compelled by the writing of their memoirs to ponder the forces that had shaped their lives, most of them found the sources of their success in their schooling and in their rural environment. One factor in particular to which they all paid tribute was the interest their parents took in their education.[11]

II

Looking back at their childhood days, these alumni of the one-room school remembered how in the round of their frustrations and fears, their parents had encouraged them step by step. They recalled the times their mothers or fathers had read to them such literature as was in the house, and how their mothers, who had never heard of "reading readiness," taught them their ABC's and even to make out words, so that more than one of them knew how to read when they first entered school. One man wrote that his mother was so concerned about his education that she compelled him to spell through an entire spelling book before he was six years old, so that when he reached school, he was ready to begin the second reader.[12]

They remembered, too, that it had been their parents who, without laws forcing them to do so, saw to it that they attended school, insisting when at times they rebelled. One woman recalled that when she had once complained of illness to avoid school, her mother, a Swedish immigrant with great common sense, asked her if she would like some bread and cream, which was her favorite dish. When that was accepted and eaten, another was offered, and when that had gone the way of the other, her mother sent her off to school. And Enoch E. Byrum, editor and owner of the *Gospel Trumpet,* a Christian paper of the 1920s, met with the determined resistance of his mother when he begged to leave his district school in Indiana because his studies had become difficult. "No," he remembered her saying, "you must go to school, for when you are eighteen years of age, you will want to go to college as your older brothers have done." Further protests that he did not want to go to college, but to be a farmer for whom an education was not necessary, met with no success, and his respite from school lasted one day.[13]

Perhaps not many parents encouraged their children to pursue their educations beyond the district school like Byrum's mother, but, considering their own lack of education, it was surprising how many did. Herbert Quick, novelist and lawyer, who grew up on a pioneer farm in Iowa and began his career as a country schoolteacher, recalled how his mother had urged his father to sell their farm so they could move to a college town where their children might be better educated; and Hamlin Garland observed that his mother sympathized with his desire to improve his education and leave the farm.[14]

Some parents were, in fact, quite willing to make great sacrifices to educate their children beyond the country school. When James Crabtree, Nebraska educator and long-time secretary of the National Education Association, wanted desperately to attend a normal school but was reluctant to cause his parents any expense or to leave them short-handed on their poverty-ridden Nebraska homestead in 1878, it was his mother who learned that he might work for his board at the normal school at Peru and insisted that he go. "We will all work a little harder," he quoted her as saying. "We will get along somehow. When you get an education, perhaps you can help the other children about going to school."[15]

Many parents in those years, like Byrum's, were deeply religious; and though there were some notable exceptions—Clarence Darrow's for example—it was often the case that the more interested the parents were in religion, the more they stressed the importance of education. In such homes the Bible was omnipresent, and fathers read aloud from the King James Version, whose sonorous rhythms reverberated through the house. Presbyterian and Methodist discipline brooded over the homes in a never-to-be-forgotten presence. "My father and God, not then altogether distinguishable from each other," wrote Ray Stannard Baker of his awesome Presbyterian father, "filled the largest place in my boyhood." And a prominent Iowa educator, recalling the strict Presbyterianism in which he was raised, observed that "strict obedience or swift punishment" was virtually a household rule.[16]

The disciplined life, however, was shared by virtually all in the rural Midwest in the late nineteenth century, whether they came from religious homes or not, for the routine of the family farm demanded it. There were cows to milk, livestock to feed and water, eggs to gather, coal and wood to bring to the kitchen woodbox for the morning fire, and the cookstove reservoir to fill with water, to say nothing of the long days they had to spend in the fields doing a man's work at an early age. "For seventy days I walked behind my plow," wrote Hamlin Garland of his eleventh summer, "while my father finished the harvest on the rented farm and moved to the house on the knoll."[17]

These duties—which, incidentally, inspired many of them to improve their educations so they could leave the farm—imposed a discipline which they saw in later years as a source of strength. "I am not regretting that my father was so strict," one man wrote; "that I had only a trace of pleasure and a flood of toil in my boyhood days. . . . I see now that this early, hard, continuous work on the farm was building for me a constitution of unusual powers of resistance."[18]

Some of them understood, too, that in addition to their parents, they owed much to their school-district community for their interest in education and success in life. The community brought them their school, of course, but it did more than that. It helped them to define their place in society—often at the top of the heap since their community was small—which gave them a certain confidence they might otherwise have lacked. Hamlin Garland explained it well: "In all essentials my life was typical of the time and place. My father was counted a good and successful farmer. Our neighbors all lived in the same restricted fashion as ourselves, in barren little houses of wood or stone, owning few books, reading only weekly papers. It was a pure democracy wherein my father was a leader and my mother beloved by all who knew her. If anybody looked down upon us, we didn't know it, and in all the social affairs of the township we fully shared."[19]

Because they knew each family in the community—knew them so well, indeed, that after a lapse of fifty years they could still recall their names and the location of their farms along the roads that led to the schoolhouse—the Midwestern rural school community was like an enlarged family to them, and provided them with a sense of security and encouragement. The door of the schoolhouse opened to Catholic and Protestant, to the children of the richest families in the community and the poorest, to native born and immigrant. And though it was true, as Garland remembered, that there was sometimes bad feeling between the latter two groups and even fights on the way home from school, memoirs often noted how little animosity there was, especially where the mixture was even or nearly so. The school community did act as a melting pot in which Old World ways were soon given up or absorbed until there developed an American community. In a little school no one was merely a face in the crowd, and all knew one another so intimately that anyone, without invitation, might say to another on the playground: "I'm going home with you tonight. I have asked Ma."[20]

The familylike atmosphere of the school was enhanced by everyone's knowing that the members of the school board were their fathers or the fathers of their friends, and by the comfortable familiarity of a small world. The road to the schoolhouse ran past a neighbor's farm, and the fields they played in at recess likely belonged to their parents or their friends' parents. "Nobody heard of such a thing as trespass . . .," wrote Marshall Barber, the famous malariologist, of the places where he and his companions played at his one-room school in Kansas. "There was a hedge fence separating the schoolyard from the Baughman meadow, but we had a broad opening where we could duck through to the baseball ground. I never heard of Dwight Baughman's whacking a rubber ball any more lightly because he was on his father's land; I cannot imagine Mr. Baughman's objecting if the whole gang of us played ball on his grassland every day."[21]

They also perceived that the older people in the community, although largely uneducated, were sincerely interested in education, and passed on this interest partly by frequent visits to the school. To see their parents and other members of the community crowded into the little schoolroom on a Friday afternoon or evening as they recited the pieces they had learned, or sang songs, or spelled down their class, assured them of their parents' and the community's approval of their schoolwork and helped kindle their own interest in learning. Of these occasions they wrote warmly in the stories of their lives as if the exercises themselves had given purposefulness and importance to the material they had mastered.[22]

So they saw how much they were indebted to their parents and to their community for their schooling, but what they learned in the one-room school and how they learned it depended largely, as they saw, upon their teacher who "made the school," as the saying went.

III

Because they had no television, radio, theater, or museums, the Midwestern rural schoolchildren depended more heavily upon their teachers for information and direction than contemporary urban children do. For that reason, perhaps, country schoolteachers had more influence upon the lives of their students than modern teachers do, which may account for the fact that their pupils remembered them so well for so long a time. Whatever the reason, nearly all who wrote about their early schooling recalled many of their teachers by name, remembered minute details about them, and gave them credit for much of all they learned, from the three R's to the more advanced subjects to the harsher realities of life such as discipline.

Discipline, indeed, loomed large in their minds as they dredged up memories of their school days, possibly because discipline meant correction, and correction in the district schools was a drama in which the alleged offender was brought before the bar of justice, tried, convicted, and summarily punished before a hushed and expectant, and often uneasy, audience. They were, in any event, deeply impressed with their teachers' ingenious methods of bringing order to the classroom. As they remembered it, they were sometimes forced to sit apart from the other children, sit with the girls, stand on the floor, stand in a corner, or stand with one arm outstretched for a time. Often they had to stay in at recess or after school. One of them remembered a teacher whose practice was to hurl a ruler at the head of an offending whisperer, then order the guilty party to return the ruler to the teacher's seat.[23]

Even the seating arrangement in the little school was designed in part to produce order and rarely varied from school to school. As beginners they were seated at the front of the room, where the double desks in which everyone sat two-by-two were small. From there they gradually worked their way to the back, which they finally reached when they were fifteen or sixteen. For the sake of decorum as well as discipline, the girls were normally seated on one side of the room and the boys on the other, but an uneven number of boys or girls made a certain mixture, and often trouble, inevitable.[24]

But when neither the seating arrangement nor less severe methods of discipline brought order, the whip was used, and if their memories are reliable on this point, a small forest of willow whips was broken across their backs and bottoms.

Their teachers' punishments, though much like those administered at home, were sometimes cruel and unjust, and if their psyches were not disturbed by such discipline, some of them, at least, never forgot what they believed to be unfair treatment. Herbert Quick recalled how he had been whipped, unjustly he thought, for talking out loud when he had only whispered, and John Ise, professor of economics and the University of Kansas, who wrote so interestingly of his family's life on the Kansas plains, always remembered the teacher who wrestled him to the floor to wipe the chalk from his face and broke his shingle dart in the process.[25]

Both Quick and Ise had misbehaved and obviously merited some punishment, but more than one country-school student recounted how he or one of his classmates had been punished severely for not knowing their lessons. Mary Bradford, who followed the familiar path from country schoolgirl to professional educator in Wisconsin, recalled how her sister in the primer class had been forced to stand in a corner with her eyes on her book because she could not spell the word *does,* and Quick remembered how severely his first teacher had beaten a small girl about the arms and shoulders because the girl refused to spell *sky* correctly even when told how to spell it.[26]

On the other hand, it was clear that they did not respect those teachers who could not rule their schools. The good teacher, they often said, was one who maintained order, and with a sense of justice occasionally displayed by young children, they were sometimes most loyal to the teacher who had punished them justly. The teacher, for example, who whipped James Crabtree when he was seven or eight years old, then told him that he was not a bad boy, that she hated to use the whip, and who then began to cry because of the necessity of doing so won his lasting devotion. From that day on he arrived at the school early, lit the fires in the stove, and cleaned the blackboards, and even his parents noticed that he was a changed boy. For him that episode was a turning point in his life. "She made a man of me," he wrote.[27]

As vividly as he remembered the whipping his teacher gave him, Crabtree remembered the lessons she taught her students in morality. Her rendition of the story of the sticks, which when wrapped together could not be broken but separated could easily be snapped, made a lasting impression upon him, as did "Harry and the Guidepost," a poem she taught them on keeping up one's courage in the face of the unknown. This poem he once put to the test and acknowledged long afterward that it had given him both "conscious and unconscious support many times thereafter."[28]

The teaching of such lessons, gleaned from McGuffey's or other readers, which were usually copies of McGuffey's, was another more subtle form of disciplining country schoolchildren on the Middle Border, and their recollections confirm how effective the lessons were in teaching them not only to be honest and courageous but to be ambitious, to reach beyond themselves, to overcome obstacles, and not to be discouraged. More than half a century after they had read the stories and memorized the poems, children would still remember "Up, Up Lucy, Why Do You Lie in Bed!," "Meddlesome Mattie," the boy who stood on the burning deck, "Try, Try, Again" (an all-time favorite), and this little verse on the evils of smoking:

> Tobacco is a filthy weed,
> It was the Devil sowed the seed,
> It leaves a stench wher'er it goes,
> It makes a chimney of the nose.[29]

Even Clarence Darrow, who in his older years called McGuffey's ethical and religious stories "utterly impossible lies which average children should have easily seen through," was impressed in his youth by those readers, "so packed," as he wrote, "with love and righteousness."[30]

Not only did their teachers teach them lessons about adversity, but they helped them in various ways to leap the hurdles life placed in their way. Many remembered how as frightened beginners they had been comforted by their teachers and how their teachers' compliments had buoyed their spirits. All his life Herbert Quick remembered how thrilled he had been when his teacher complimented him on his arrangement of a bouquet of wild flowers he had given her. They recalled, too, how their teachers urged them to pursue their educations, and this, for some, was the greatest contribution their teachers made to their development. Some of them had only one such teacher, but that one had been enough to help them find a way to move up in the world. "Whatever success I have had I attribute first to this man," wrote one professional educator of the teacher "who . . . early impressed me with the necessity of doing things right and inspired me with confidence to attack any problem no matter how hard it appeared at the outset. He encouraged me to take the county teachers' examination, for he knew I must soon teach if I were to go away to school." Indeed, teaching in a country school was often the only avenue open to ambitious farm boys who wished to secure a better education and move on to the professions.[31]

If in writing of their experiences in the one-room school, they lingered long on the way they were disciplined, perhaps it was because discipline was so much a part of the learning process that when they tried to explain what they had learned and how they had learned it, they unconsciously linked the two together and felt that they could not explain one without the other. In any case, discipline was, indeed, firmly interwoven into the methods their teachers used to take them through the common branches of learning, which helps explain why they remembered so well so much of what they studied and how their teachers taught them.

IV

The common branches included, in the usual order of importance, reading, arithmetic, writing, and spelling; then, in no particular order, grammar, history, geography, literature, and physiology. Geography and physiology, the latter of which most of them were studying in the 1880s, were as close as they came to a study of science.[32]

Reading, of course, was the first subject they learned, and not all of them remembered how they learned it. But those who did explained that their teachers had first taught them the ABC's, then tried to show them how these letters were combined into words. It was a laborious process, requiring much self-discipline, for although textbooks offering the phonic and sight methods of teaching reading had been published as early as 1878, they remembered that they had to combine letters into words without reference to the sound of letters. Only those fortunate enough to have *McGuffey's Pictorial Eclectic Primer,* which contained pictures representing each letter, *a* for ax, for example, might learn to associate a letter with a sound.[33]

As for the rest of the common branches, these were taught largely by memorization, except for arithmetic and grammar, which could not be completely mastered by such a method. Day in and day out they recalled having to memorize something new. One day it might be the capitals of the states, or the names of the states that bordered upon one another; and the next day it might be a new reading, a poem, new spelling words, or the first five presidents in the order of their succession. This, too, required discipline, and often, they admitted, the process of learning was routine and tiresome with only the morning and afternoon recesses, the noon lunch hour, possibly a trip to the privy and one for a pail of water to break the monotony. But their days in the classroom were not always so dull, for they all remembered a variety of teaching methods their teachers used to make their lessons interesting and rewarding.[34]

One educator wrote perceptively of two excellent history teachers he had had in his Ohio district school. One had a way of summarizing the important events in a given period, so that the era could be easily understood and remembered as a whole; the other paid less attention to details but emphasized the causes of important events and the contributions great men had made to the nation's history. And in geography, the memorization of states and their capitals was made easy for some when the teacher had them chant their lessons. "Maine, Maine, Augusta, on the Kennebec River," they would chant as the teacher pointed on the map to the place they named. "New Hampshire, Concord, on the Merrimac River," and so on through the list. Better still they were sometimes allowed, or ordered, to go to the blackboard and draw a map of a nation or a continent with all its prominent topographical features. "Map-making was a favorite part of geography for us," one man wrote; "perhaps all children like to study with their hands. I was not good at maps, but I used to gaze by the hour at the wonderful accomplishments of my schoolmates as outlined on the blackboard. The continents were impressive, for they had a definite personality."[35]

To vary the daily routine as well as to see if they understood how words function in a sentence, teachers also sent them to the blackboard to diagram sentences. In this exercise, instead of using straight lines to mark off words, they sometimes drew rings around subjects and predicates and objects on a horizontal line until their work looked, as one person described it, "like loaves of bread on a baker's counter." Perpendicular to the horizontal line ran other oval links surrounding prepositional phrases and modifiers of one kind or another, so that when the sentence was completely diagrammed it looked like a work of art and fascinated smaller children. "To watch some big girl go to the board and draw this intricate picture of links," one woman wrote, "furnished me a fascinating occupation; and I looked forward to the time when I, too, should study grammar, and use my hands in this diverting way."[36]

Another way teachers had of accomplishing the same purpose but without sending them to the blackboard was to have them stand at their desks and parse a sentence. "We will parse 'cow' in the following sentence," wrote one man as he explained how he and his companions were taught to do it. " 'Hasten, the naughty cow is eating our melon.' Cow, noun, common, third person, singular number, feminine gender, nominative case, subject of the verb 'is eating' and modified by the definitite article 'the' and the adjective 'naughty.' Then followed all the other words in the sentence, if there were time enough in the recitation period to parse them."[37]

To make arithmetic—a difficult subject for most of them—more interesting, teachers used the competitive method. Sometimes they did this by sending them to the board to see who could solve a given problem first and thereby "cipher down" their opponents. Or, they would give them problems to be worked in their heads while seated at their desks. "Take two, add two, add six," their teacher would say, "subtract eight, add ten, divide by six, add ninety-eight, divide by ten, subtract eight, multiply by ten, add ten, and how many have you."[38]

This method of teaching was also used in spelling, of course, and no one who wrote at any length about schooling in the one-room schoolhouse failed to mention the Friday afternoon or evening spelldowns, when they had stood in a line across the schoolroom as the teacher called out the words they had spent hours memorizing. When one of them missed a word, the next in line would try to spell it and, if successful, move ahead of the one who had missed it, or "turn him down," as they said. The one who stood at the head of the line when time ran out won what they called the "head mark" for the day, and automatically went to the foot of the line for the next spelldown. Sometimes, in the evening spelldowns when parents and neighbors filled the little schoolhouse to watch the contest, there would be team competition. For this they chose sides and stood before the audience in two lines behind the leaders while words were given first to one side, then the other. One by one as they missed a word they went to their seats until at last there was only one student, the winner, left standing.[39]

In debates too there was keen competition and excitement. One man recalled a debate in his district school on the question "Are Horses More Useful Than Edged Tools?" in which one participant became so excited that he actually swore.[40]

Advanced reading, often a favorite subject, could not be taught by such games, but it was remembered by some that an element of competition did exist even in their reading classes, for each tried to outdo his classmates in the skill and emotion with which he read or recited chosen passages.

Readers were filled with poems, essays, and orations, and many of these were either memorized or read, usually for reading classes, but sometimes for a larger audience—the children from a visiting school, perhaps, or the Friday evening crowd that so often gathered at the schoolhouse. However it was, when they performed they had to do more than merely recite or read their selections. In their readers were dozens of rules on articulation and inflection, on how to stand, and even on how to breathe properly, and teachers somehow found time to instruct them in these rules, so that, like Hamlin Garland, they all had "a high ideal of the way in which these grand selections should be read."[41]

With this in mind, they stretched themselves to read or declaim with the proper diction and voice modulation in order to perform better than their companions. "In reading," one of them wrote, "we were limited to one series—the McGuffey.... The result was that we read the books over and over. The reading was oral. We vied with each other in intonation, in inflection, in interpretation. We thundered Rienzi's address to the Romans, Spartacus to the Gladiators, Webster's Reply to Hayne, and all the fine selections that characterized these choice readers. We committed to memory and 'spoke' dozens of the pieces we liked.... McGuffey was our all, and constituted the only study of English literature open to us."[42]

Because all their classes were held in one room, they learned many selections from the readers simply by listening to the class ahead of them recite, which, in fact, was the way they picked up much of what they knew. Avis Carlson, for example, who grew up on a farm in Chautauqua County in southeastern Kansas, and became a writer and civic leader in St. Louis, remembered this aspect of her education vividly. "The easy stuff in my 'reader' was soon gulped down and the sums laid out," she wrote. "Then I was ready to listen to the older students 'recite.' By the time I got to geography or history, I already knew what was in the textbooks." And Hamlin Garland wrote that he soon knew not only his fourth reader but selections from the fifth and sixth: "I could follow word for word the recitations of the older pupils."[43]

V

This, then was what teachers taught and the way they taught in the one-room school as the children remembered it. So well had they grasped the fundamentals of the common branches that few of them had difficulty moving to the normals or high schools or whatever schools they later attended. Carl Seashore, for example, who became professor of psychology at the University of Iowa, was able to go directly from his one-room school in Boone County, Iowa, to the academy in town and complete his work there in two years on the strength of an entrance examination he passed upon leaving the country school. This examination, he explained, "was directed to United States history, advanced arithmetic, advanced geography, and advanced grammar, and the type of instruction I had had in the district school proved very effective in facilitating my passing it." And when Carl Becker, the famous Cornell University historian who wrote with "the urbanity of a Lord Chesterfield and the pithiness of a Benjamin Franklin," moved at the age of eleven with his family from their Iowa farm to Waterloo, he was placed in the class above boys of his own age.[44]

But did this education not clutter up their minds with an excessive number of facts, poems, and orations, memorized but not fully understand, as was so often charged at the turn of the century? And had not the discipline involved in this rigorous memorization stifled their interest in learning and wasted their time? Clarence Darrow, reflecting upon his district-school education in Kinsman, Ohio, thought so. "As I look back at my days at the district school...," he wrote, "I cannot avoid a feeling of the appalling waste of time. Never since those days have I had occasion to use much of the arithmetic that I learned.... I began grammar in the grades and continued it in high school, but it was a total loss.... For my part, I never could learn grammar, at either the primary or the high school. I have used language extensively all my life, and no doubt have misused it, too; ... but I am convinced that I was rather hindered than helped in this direction by the public schools."[45]

But this was not the way most of them saw it as they looked back upon their experiences in the one-room school. To be sure, they remembered the monotonous hours spent in learning, and the many repetitions that grew tiresome. Yet few believed that the drills they endured, the memorization that had been forced upon them, and the discipline involved in it all had been harmful or in any sense a waste of time. Some, in fact, would have welcomed more of it than they received. "I may be accused of overloading the youthful mind with too much memory work," wrote Marshall Barber as he thought of his own work as a teacher and reflected upon his days in the district school. "But my adolescent memory was like a sturdy horse; the more one asked of it the more it would do—within reasonable limits. In my youth it was considered meritorious to learn the multiplication table up to fifteen times fifteen. That we thought an unreasonable limit; and I still think so."[46]

Even those who became professional educators, and might have been expected to agree with the new theories of their colleagues, often compared the new education, which favored less discipline and memorization, unfavorably with the way they had been taught in the country school. "There was necessarily much repetition of the text year by year," one of them wrote of his early schooling. "I know that I 'went through' Pinneo's Grammar four times. I knew every rule, exception and sentence in it from 'Aaron Burr was a traitor' to 'Hail, Holy Light.' I could analyze every sentence and parse every word in the book. . . . Measured in terms of modern teaching it was a great waste of time. Not so then. These studies afforded endless opportunities for discussion as to the real meaning of words and sentences, and incidentally we acquired a power of analysis that later was very valuable."[47]

But even when they did not explore the meaning of the words or analyze the sentences in many of the selections they memorized, what they had stored in their minds took on meaning that greatly enriched their lives as they grew older. "The moral import of many of the classic selections," wrote another professional educator who had spent his early years in a one-room school, "of course, did not dawn upon the learner until much later in life. Then one often found himself repeating the lines in the light of an entirely new view whose implications were realized for the first time."[48]

That they found so much of what they had memorized to be worth repeating and thinking about as they grew older was due, as nearly all of them recognized, to the excellence of the readers from which the selections had been drawn. The first edition of the readers most used in the 1870s and 1880s, particularly, had been written before the war by an Ohio professor, William McGuffey. He had been admirably prepared by his pioneer origins in Pennsylvania and his Calvinistic training to write the kind of textbook that would appeal to rural Midwesterners, and it is doubtful if there has ever been a set of textbooks so well suited to the times and the needs of the people as the McGuffey Readers. Certainly none has ever had more influence on people's lives, and, indeed, it might almost be said that the Midwestern mind of the late nineteenth century was the McGuffey Reader mind.[49]

The McGuffey Readers taught moral and religious lessons, to be sure, but they did more than that. They acquainted literally thousands of poor, provincial Midwestern country schoolchildren who often had no books but these with the best writing in the English language. "From the pages of his readers," wrote Hamlin Garland, "I learned to know and love the poems of Scott, Byron, Southey, Wordsworth and a long line of English masters. I got my first taste of Shakespeare from the selected scenes which I read in these books."[50]

What they got, of course, were only excerpts of Shakespeare's plays and bits and pieces from other writings. But no matter. Because they read them over and over, and memorized much of their contents, long passages stayed with them throughout their lives. Coming across the English classics years after he had left his little school in District 9, Herbert Quick felt as if he were meeting someone he already had an acquaintance with. "I could say," he wrote, "as I opened my Shakespeare, my Milton, or my Byron, 'Why, don't you remember our meeting away back on the farm in that old book with the front cover off? Here's this passage in which the little prince appeals to Hubert de Burgh not to burn out his eyes with those hot irons! I haven't read it yet, but I'll just repeat it from memory. You're no stranger to me. I don't know much of you, but what I do know I know well!' "[51]

Like Quick, one after another of those who went to the district schools in the Midwest noted how the readers had touched their lives, fed their imaginations, nurtured their aspirations. As they read through the pages or listened to the older classes recite, they sometimes forgot the drab little schoolhouses in which they sat, and, like Hamlin Garland, "Became imaginatively a page in the train of Ivanhoe, or a bowman in the army of Richard the Lion Heart battling the Saracen in the Holy Land."[52]

For those whose imaginations were not roused by stirring passages, memorizing the selections the teachers imposed may have been an arduous task indeed. But for those who could hear the roll of thunder in a verse, or stand with Logan, the noble Indian chief, when he said, "I appeal to any white man to say, if ever he entered Logan's cabin hungry . . .," as Herbert Quick did, memorizing such speeches was not a chore; it was a passion. They spoke them in the fields when they plowed or harrowed, or when they brought the cows from the pasture in the evening. "Carefully hiding in a place where no one could hear me," wrote Marshall Barber, "I used to practice the notable speech of Regulus to the Carthaginians. How I strove to drop the voice to the sepulchral tone indicated where Regulus quotes the ghost, 'Roman, I bid thee curse with thy dying breath this fated city;' and then how I tried to lift the voice above the tomb as the orator continues, 'And now go bring your sharpest torments. The woes I see impending o'er this guilty realm will be enough to sweeten death though every nerve be a shooting pang.'"[53]

Such speeches stirred the desire to be great orators or great men; and perhaps it was easier for country schoolchildren to aspire to greatness than for their counterparts in the cities, for had not most of the nation's great men risen from just such backgrounds? Had not Elihu Burritt, the poor blacksmith, whose writings appeared in the Fifth Reader, gone to a district school? In any case the first ambition some of them had when they thought of leaving the farm was to become orators, and their recollections of those ambitions suggest how oratory was stressed in the late nineteenth century.[54]

Their enthusiasm for oratory must have derived in part, at least, from the speeches which they had memorized and which had been given by famous men on historical occasions. But the patriotism that was kindled by the coming of the Civil War also had much to do with it."As the war between the states came on, it affected our school life," wrote one northern Iowa man. "It inspired patriotic sentiment and quickened our joyous pride of nationality. It ruled our tastes and our selections for declamation." And, as the years passed, reminders of the war lingered on, deepening their sense of history and their love of country. The veterans of the war were all around them filling them with awe. Here was a neighbor, now grown portly, who had been but a skeleton, they heard, when he had returned from a Confederate prison. And there was the cemetery near the schoolhouse where a number of veterans were buried, upon whose graves they placed flags. Memorial Day, too, brought its reminders as they watched the men who were their neighbors don their uniforms and march in the procession to the cemetery.[55]

For children such as these, Patrick Henry's address to the Virginia Convention or Daniel Webster's reply to Hayne in the famous debate of 1830 had meaning even if some of the words in them did not, and to memorize such speeches was, in their view, no waste of time. Indeed, they had little misgiving about the reliance their teachers had placed upon memorization. Rather, they regarded it as a positive force in their education, just as they did the competitive method their teachers had used to stimulate their interest in learning.

How much they owed to competition as a spur to their learning was abundantly clear. Time and again they recalled how hard they had worked to excel in their school contests. One man told of the many nights he had lain before the fireplace in his home memorizing words for the next day's spelldown, and another of how he had learned McGuffey's Speller by heart, so that "I can yet see just how the pages looked, and repeat column after column in order."[56]

Yet another indication of the efficacy of the competitive method was the eagerness with which they looked forward to those Friday afternoon contests when they could put to the test what they had learned. Avis Carlson, for whom the studies in the one-room school were easy, recalled that the only time in the week she was "fully engaged," as she put it, "was the last period on Friday when we had a spelling or a 'ciphering match.'" In these contests, she remembered especially the spirited rivalry between herself and an older male student who cared nothing at all about history, grammar, or geography, but everything for the contests in arithmetic and spelling: "He would crouch with one foot braced against the blackboard wall and the other well back, his eyes like slits, his eraser hand poised as his chalk hand moved up one column and down the next." Usually she lost the ciphering match, but in spelling when the contest had narrowed to her and Bill, as it usually did, "the whole room became quiet and intensely partisan."[57]

Victory, of course, meant much, for it gave them confidence and a feeling of accomplishment. The number was kept of the head marks each student received in spelling, and a reward sometimes given to the person who had the most at the end of the term. But whether prizes were given or not, all recalled the joy they felt in winning, and particularly in "turning down" children older than themselves. Their parents, too, took pride in their accomplishments, and one man remembered that the first question he was asked when he returned home after school was, "Did you miss any words today, and did you get any head marks today?"[58]

Competition, however, was not reserved for the classroom. It was also a part of their life on the playground, where learning was continued informally, away from the watchful eye of the teacher.

VI

Midwestern country schoolchildren had, of course, no physical education instructor, no organized teams, and not even playground equipment for the most part. No one wrote of having a slide in the schoolyear or a merry-go-round, and probably not one in a thousand, or even two thousand, district schools on the Middle Border had such luxuries in the late nineteenth century. In play, as in so

19

much of life, country schoolchildren were left to "make do," as the expression went, with what they had in hand or could invent.

What they had in hand, they all remembered, were games like dare-base, Andy-over, hide-and-seek, crack-the-whip, and drop-the-handkerchief, which apparently had been passed down through generations of farm children; and if by good fortune someone had a ball and bat and there were enough students to form at least the skeleton of two teams, they played ball. But, as one of them remarked, much of their time was spent in games they themselves manufactured, and there were no limitations on their inventiveness. Their gymnasium was not only the schoolyard but the adjoining fields, and these they roamed over during their recesses or in the noon hour chasing rabbits, killing snakes, or drowning gophers in their holes. They made whistles of willow twigs they found along the streams, and they strung various kinds of vegetation on horsehairs to make beads. They built wigwams from grass and shrubs and pressed the flowering grasses to make bookmarks.[59]

The girls, some recalled, had their own games and the boys theirs, but there were no separate physical education classes, and they often played together. In schools so small, this was more or less forced upon them if they wished to play in any organized way, for, as one of them pointed out, "how could we do without girls when numbers were so few that we could not make up two baseball teams without them?" So they joined forces in simple democratic fashion, and thought of each other, for a time at least, as teammates and equals rather than as members of opposing sexes. Still, in some games, the girls did have special roles. Their part in drowning gophers, for example, was to carry pails of water to pour down the holes while the boys stood ready, in great anticipation, to slaughter the animals if they surfaced from their watery holes.[60]

Winter games were apparently as enjoyable to them as those they played in the spring and fall. After a great snow, the schoolyard became a vast fox-and-geese circle, in which they played rigorously until the bell called them to more serious endeavors. Or sometimes they built snowmen, engaged in furious snowball fights, skated on a nearby pond, or simply skidded over icy patches of snow to see how far they could go. Those whose schoolhouses stood upon a hill remembered the thrill of sliding down its snow-covered back on improvised sleds.[61]

Oddly, they played such games in the wintry outdoors, even after they had suffered much from the cold in merely reaching the schoolhouse in the early morning. Rarely did their parents take them to school or go after them even on the coldest day, and often one of their most vivid memories was that of making their way to school through huge snowdrifts in the bitter cold. Though many remembered it, no one captured the experience quite as well as Hamlin Garland. "Facing the cutting wind," he wrote of those winter days when he and his sister and brother had walked to school, "wallowing through drifts, battling like some small intrepid animals, we often arrived at the door [of the schoolhouse] moaning with pain yet unsubdued, our ears frosted, our toes numb in our boots, to meet others in similar case around the roaring stove."[62]

Then came the pain of thawing out, during which their fingers and toes ached, then itched almost unbearably, so that they were forced to tap their feet upon the floor, filling the room with a drumming noise, which the teacher usually understood and forgave. Sometimes, one man remembered, the only relief from the pain and itching was to leave the schoolhouse and plunge a bare foot through the ice-covered stream and into the water. Yet, once warmed, they were outdoors again at recess playing in the snow.[63]

No wonder, then, that so many of them remembered the big stove the best of all their schoolhouse's furnishings and described it most fully in their memoirs. One called it "the black monster which either scorched the unfortunate near it or froze the unfortunate in far corners." And yet on a winter day they crowded around it as quickly as they could, and at noon put their frozen lunches on it to thaw them out. And sometimes the girls heated water on it so they could wash their hands after lunch.[64]

On the playground, too, as in the classroom, they were enmeshed in that first love affair, which in its own way was a learning experience and disturbing enough to remain in their memories through all the passing years. One man looked back across the span of more than half a century to recall how as punishment he had been sent to the girls' side of the room and wound up seated directly behind his "beloved Martha," whose auburn curls "trailed over the McGuffey page at 'Abhor, annul, construct,'" and with his pocketknife he clipped a ringlet, put it in an envelope, and hid it in the barn where it became a priceless treasure to be secretly kissed from time to time.[65]

Other affairs were less secret. Notes passed saying "I love you" and asking "Do you love me" and the rising emotions, the sudden loss of interest, and the flaring jealousies were the common lot of all those who recorded their memories of the country schools. When he entered a school in a new district, one man recalled that three girls immediately had a crush on him. One, whose father owned a store, brought him a sack of candy much to the chagrin of the other two. But, alas, "the affair was soon over," and he became "just another boy."[66]

In these affairs, as in the games they played, competition was a constant presence, as it was in the classroom. For in love as in the classroom, some won and some lost. For many of the games they played they chose sides, as they did in spelling matches, and this, more clearly than most lessons, taught them their standing in relation to their classmates. "The 'choosing up' was a wholesome exercise for us," one person wrote of this process, "whether for intellectual or athletic contests, for it gave one a clear idea of his standing in the estimation of his peers—there could be no favoritism shown by leaders if they were going to win."[67]

This, of course, was true, and doubtless those who looked upon the system as a "wholesome exercise" did so because they were usually winners. But there were those who did not always win and for whom "choosing up" was painful. Several of those who remembered the agony of it all were cripples or simply had no athletic skills, and were, naturally, always chosen last if they were chosen at all. "I was always kept out of games," one man remarked. "Limpy was not wanted." And Avis Carlson, who was short, and unable to bat or catch a ball or even throw it over the schoolhouse in Andy-over, was "never chosen until far down the list, no matter what the game. . . . In school I was a real outsider, never allowed to forget it and forever assuring myself that I really didn't mind."[68]

Carlson, however, and those like Herbert Quick, who was crippled, could compensate in the classroom for the games they could not play on the playground. "Now I had something of which to be proud," Quick wrote when he discovered how quickly he could learn. "I had bad legs and feet, and I was always caught first when playing black man; but in this little domain of learning, I was the wonder of the school, and grew to be the possessor of something like celebrity."[69]

But for those who had neither athletic nor intellectual skills, "choosing up" could be a humiliating, always-remembered experience. Indeed, the Midwestern one-room schools, in spite of their smallness and their students' easy familiarity with one another were, like the lives of the people they served, stern schools in some ways, and many of those who attended them never forgot the painful moments they suffered there.

For children who rarely saw anyone but the members of their own families in their early years—hermit children, Herbert Quick called them—shyness was a major problem, and the first days in a new school were occasionally unrelieved torment. At the outset of his schooling in Iowa, Carl Seashore, unable to speak a word of English and terrified by the appearance of the teacher at the school door, fled from the schoolhouse on two successive mornings. Only when his mother found neighbor children to take him to school did his formal education begin.[70]

And Herbert Quick, entering the schoolyard of District 9 with his sister for the first time, remembered it as one of his most dreadful experiences: "Not one of the children spoke to us; they simply sheared off from us and stared. I felt a strange sense of being insulted and humiliated....These little fellow-beings, it seemed to me, not only despised me, but were actively hostile." When at last he reached the schoolroom and was given a seat, he wept uncontrollably until the teacher comforted him. "The world has placed me in many trying positions since that day in 1869, but never through any contact with my fellow human beings have I suffered as I did then."[71]

Perhaps even more painful were the times when as beginners they misjudged their need and failed to leave the room in time, or the humiliation that came with being too poor to buy books, or the temporary hurt that followed a failed love affair. Words passed among them, too, that cut deeply. One woman remembered being called "homely" as she entered a new school, and though she did not know what it meant, she sensed it was uncomplimentary, and still remembered it at the age of ninety-four when she wrote her memoirs.[72]

They recalled, too, the embarrassment that came from not being able to solve a problem on the blackboard. Mary Bradford told how she had once gone to the blackboard to diagram a sentence, knowing nothing about the function of words in a sentence: "Having something of an eye for symmetry," she wrote, "and some skill in drawing and writing, I arranged a beautiful series of links and appendages, and proceeded to write in these the words of the sentence, with due regard to length and order. I shall never forget what followed. The older pupils snickered, and the teacher, unable to conceal her amusement, came to me and quietly suggested that I erase my work. The ridicule left a scar on my sensitive soul."[73]

Reading was another source of trouble, not only for the poor reader, but for the good reader as well. When he first read an excerpt from Lyman Beecher on "The Necessity of Education," Quick was thrilled with the words: "We must educate, we must educate, or we shall perish in our own prosperity." But the words soon lost their flavor for him when time after time they were so poorly read: "We—must— I can't pernounce that, teacher." "Well, spell it, Johnny." "E-d-u-c-a-t-e." "Or we purrish—in our own—our own— our own—"[74]

But if there was pain as well as joy in their one-room schools, so was there in life itself. The district schools that emerge from the pages of the memoirs confronted life as it was. Few evasions were possible, and little effort was made to shield them from the realities of life. Daily they had to face the fact that there were no substitutes for learning to read, write, figure, and spell; that mastering the fundamentals could be done only through toil, discipline, and repetition; that disappointments were inevitable; and that some would win and others fail.

Even so, most of those who told about their country schools looked back at them fondly, and perhaps never again will Americans who write their memoirs remember so well what they had read in their readers or devote so many pages to their elementary school experience. Yet it was not their intention to write a history of education, and for all they wrote, they omitted much. They never really discussed the origins of their school system or the sacrifices and controversies that lay behind the building of their schoolhouses; neither did they examine very closely the way their schools were governed. Moreover, they had little to say about the training of their teachers and even less about the part professional educators and county superintendents played in their education. And only a few of those who became professional educators themselves understood the forces that swept through educational circles at the turn of the century and threatened to alter drastically the way they had been educated. To complete the picture was left to those who try to follow Hamlin Garland's trail across the Middle Border.

2

Free Schools for Farm Children

꽃꽃

I

THE MIDDLE BORDER BEGINS WHERE THE OHIO RIVER COMES RUSH-
ing from the Appalachian Mountains to touch the eastern border of
Ohio, and it stretches westward across the Mississippi and Missouri
rivers to the plains of Kansas and Nebraska. On the south its boundary is the Ohio River and the southern boundary of Missouri, and on
the north, the Great Lakes and northern boundaries of Minnesota
and North Dakota. In 1800, scarcely more than fifty thousand white
people lived within its boundaries, and no states had yet been carved
from its wilderness. Seven decades later, the region contained nearly
thirteen million inhabitants, ten states, and one territory, and formed
what Lord Bryce called in his *American Commonwealth* "the most dis-
tinctively American part of America."[1]

The Midwest was a land of contrasts. It was the meeting place between Yankees and Southerners who occupied the northern and
southern portions of Ohio, Indiana, and Illinois in the years following
the War of 1812. It was home, too, for thousands of immigrants—
German, Scandinavian, and others—people with unpronounceable
names, odd customs, and strange languages. From east to west,
moisture fell unevenly upon its soils, and its landscape changed from
wooded hills and rich, watered plains to semiarid prairies. Still, by
1887 the United States commissioner of education found enough .
similarities among the people and the institutions of the states there to
lump them together into what was thereafter called the North Central
Division, and observers believed they could discern in the common
outlook of the people a common Midwestern mind.[2]

25

If there was a common Midwestern mind, it was surely shaped in large measure by the country school in which so many Midwesterners had learned life's lessons and around which their community life had centered.

The system of free public education that nourished the country schools had been established throughout most of the area before the Civil War. Organized originally to bring free schools primarily to farm children, it had been so successful that the nation's commissioner of education, noting the difficulty of educating children in rural areas where the population was sparse, paused in 1887 to pay tribute to the people who had supported it: "It is a notable circumstance that while the density of the population in the North Central States is less than one-third of that in the North Atlantic States . . . the people of the former group have nearly equalled, and in some cases surpassed, those of the latter in the development of their public schools. The fact that this is so forms a high encomium upon the enterprise and intelligence of the people of the North Central States."[3]

But there had been a time, not many years before the commissioner wrote, when almost no one would have believed such an achievement possible. Hardly more than a generation before, thousands of Midwestern children were without schooling and illiteracy flourished. In 1850, the controversy, largely between educators and farmers, over whether or not to establish free education had disturbed the Midwest for two decades and was still going on.

Education was the Midwest's birthright. "Religion, morality, and knowledge, being necessary to good government, and the happiness of mankind," ran the famous Ordinance of 1787 that established government in the area, "schools and the means of education shall forever be preserved." Warmed by this ideal, every Midwestern state, with the exception of Illinois, had incorporated similar sentiments in its constitution. But these provisions were more pledges for the future than promises of immediate action, and, as it turned out, the first schools on the Middle Border were private, subscription schools, not free public schools.[4]

Subscription schools, organized and paid for by associations of parents, were established in nearly all the region's towns and villages almost as soon as those towns and villages were founded. Timothy Flint, the peripatetic missionary to the region in the 1820s, saw a number of them in Indiana, and noted that "among the first works in an incipient village, is a school house, and among the first associations, that for establishing a school." President Grant attended such a school in Georgetown, Ohio, in the 1830s, and recalled years later that in his youth in his part of Ohio there were no free schools.[5]

Grant's observations would have applied equally well to most parts of Ohio as well as the rest of the region at the time, for outside the towns and villages throughout the Middle Border there were virtually no schools. Here and there an itinerant schoolmaster wandered through the forest and began a school for whatever impoverished parents might pay. In one such school near Pigeon Creek, Indiana, Abraham Lincoln received all his formal education of less than a year, and this was, in fact, more than many pioneer children received.[6]

The legislatures of the various Midwestern states, it was true, had enacted public education laws in the 1820s and '30s to redeem the pledges in their constitutions. Ohio in 1821, Indiana in 1824, and Illinois the following year had passed such laws. Missouri, too, had a major public school law by 1839, but the most important of all these early laws was that passed by the Michigan legislature in 1837. This law, which had a strong New England flavor, was written by John Pierce, Michigan's first state superintendent of public instruction, and served as a model school law for other states in the region.[7]

These laws were much alike. They authorized the creation of school districts throughout the states, permitted the settlers to build schoolhouses, and allowed them to tax themselves for the upkeep of their schools. But there was no compulsion. The settlers could establish schools or not just as they chose, and since there was no compulsion, neither was there much education. By the 1830s only a few district schools, as opposed to subscription schools, had been built in the forest clearings and at farm corners across the land. There was one in the corner of Mrs. Abram Garfield's farm in Cuyohoga County, Ohio, where another future president spent his first school days, and a report from an eastern Indiana township boasted of the progress district schools had made there: "Our township is laid off into 9 school districts," the report related, "each containing 4 sections of land. In addition to our former schoolhouses, our people erected 9 new ones last fall, seven of them of hewn logs, and furnished in such a way as to cost from $30.00 to $50.00 for the inside work, exclusive of materials. Nos. 1 and 2 are brick."[8]

But these schools were open only a short time each year, and many would not have been open that long or at all had it not been for the

27

Land Ordinance of 1785, which, even before the adoption of the Constitution, had laid the foundation for the national government's aid to education.

This famous law had provided that the land of the old Northwest be surveyed and broken into townships six miles square. Every township was to contain thirty-six sections, and each section, measuring one square mile, was to have within it 640 acres of land. Section 16 of every township, according to the law, was to be set aside for educational purposes. Congress first applied this provision to Ohio when it became a state in 1803, and then to the other Middle Border territories as they became states, and from the sale or lease of these lands each state created a permanent school fund.[9]

Corruption and mismanagement, which was to haunt so many of the national government's benevolent enterprises, began with the school land program, and some states were cheated of much of their inheritance designated for schools. Still, the permanent school funds did provide little communities across the area with enough money at least to begin a school. The trouble was that when the income from the permanent funds was divided among all the district schools in the state, each school's share was too small to do more than keep school for two or three weeks a year. In Indiana, for example, a committee reporting to the state legislature in 1847 noted that if the permanent funds were divided evenly among all district schools, each district would receive only $17. This was scarcely enough to open a school's doors, but the settlers, generally, were unwilling to tax themselves to keep their schools open longer. Thus the schools usually closed when the money from the permanent funds ran out unless, as was done in most states, the people resorted to the rate system after the depletion of the permanent funds.[10]

The rate system allowed parents to pay at a specified rate for every day each of their children attended school beyond the date when the permanent funds were exhausted, but regulations were stringent enough to make the farmers wary of its use. In the rate bills of the 1840s and '50s, the farmers' property was jeopardized if for some reason they could not pay their rate bills when they were due. In Michigan, where the rate system was used effectively, rate bills were turned over to the district school assessor with the following instructions: "You are hereby commanded to collect from each of the persons in the annexed rate bills named the several sums set opposite their respective names ... and within sixty days after receiving this warrant, to pay over the amount so collected by you, retaining five per cent for your fees . . .; and in case any person therein named, shall neglect or refuse to pay the amount set opposite his name aforesaid, you are to collect the same by distress and sale of the goods and chattels of such persons."[11]

By today's reckoning the parent's rate bill was never very much. In 1850 William Hicks, a Michigan farmer in Calhoun County, was assessed only $1.41 plus a six-cent assessor's fee for the thirty-eight days he sent his children to school. Still, in those pre–Civil War years, dollars were scarce on the Middle Border, and many a farmer, often with much embarrassment, withdrew his children from school when the public funds ran out rather than run the risk of jeopardizing his property if he could not afford to pay the rate bill. "How often," wrote one Michigan pioneer, "has a good teacher seen the good scholars leave, his classes broken up, and his school dwindle in numbers, as the term drew to a close."[12]

Nevertheless, individualistic Midwesterners, accustomed to paying their own way, seemed to believe that the rate system was the fairest method of raising money for education, for it taxed only those who used the schools. But whether they thought it equitable or not, not many of them wanted to exchange it for a general system of compulsory taxation. Time and again through the years of settlement on the Middle Border, the state legislatures, feeling pressure from now this side and now that, wrote new school laws and rewrote the old, often taking one step forward and two back. The Illinois law of 1825, providing for the taxation of property for educational purposes, would have almost assured free public education there far in advance of the other Midwestern states. But the protests against the law were so overwhelming that the next legislature not only repealed the law but made it next to impossible for even those communities who wished to tax themselves for education to do so. In Ohio, in 1838, the state legislature strengthened the position of the state superintendent of public instruction—an office created only the year before—and permitted the counties to tax themselves as much as two mills on every dollar's worth of taxable property for education. Yet within two years, the legislature had been forced to reduce the maximum county tax for education to one mill on the dollar and to combine the office of superintendent of public instruction with that of the secretary of state.[13]

What happened in Ohio happened also in Indiana, Michigan, and Missouri, the only other states in the region in the early 1840s. School laws were regularly passed and numerous changes were made. But no law forced the people to tax themselves for education. After more than twenty years of statehood, after all the glowing tributes to education made in the state constitutions, and after numerous amendments to the school laws, no state on the Middle Border had yet provided free public education for its children by 1850.[14]

This meant that for many children on the Middle Border there was no school at all. "A large minority of the rising generation," declared a committee investigating conditions in Indiana in 1833, "are destitute of any privilege of education." A similar study in Illinois in the same period, showed that scarcely one-fourth of the children of school age attended school. And in Ohio, the oldest state in the region, conditions were little better. In 1837, Samuel Lewis, the newly appointed state superintendent of public instruction, toured the state, traveling over twelve hundred miles on horseback and visiting some forty county seats and three hundred schools. What he found appalled him. Outside of Cincinnati, there were no schools worthy of the name that were open to rich and poor alike. Nearly half of the organized school districts had no schoolhouses, and not one-third of the schoolhouses standing, he thought, were worth more than $50 apiece.[15]

In human terms this want of education meant the growth of barbarism across the Middle Border which was noticeable to many travelers who visited the area in the 1830s. "There is a school at Harmony [Indiana]," wrote Prince Maximilian of Wiede, "where the children learn to read and write . . .; but in the country the young people grow up without education, and are, probably, no better than the Indians." Henry Schoolcraft, explorer and Indian agent, saw much the same thing in Missouri. Schools, he noted, were generally confined to the village, and country children went largely uneducated: "Thus situated without moral restraint, brought up in the uncontrolled indulgence of every passion, and without regard for religion, the state of society among the rising generation of this region is truly deplorable," he wrote. "In their childish disputes the boys frequently stab each other with knives, two instances of which occurred since our residence here. No correction was administered in either case, the act being looked upon as a promising trait."[16]

All told, it was a dismal picture, yet even as Samuel Lewis rode about the Ohio countryside in the summer of 1838 and into the autumn when the leaves were beginning to turn into vivid reds and yellows, a handful of men, not only in the Midwest but in New England and along the Atlantic coast, were already engaged, as was Lewis himself, in a campaign for free public education.

II

The origins of the free public education movement, particularly in the East, were rooted in the great changes that had come to the booming, bustling nation in the aftermath of the War of 1812. While thousands of Americans in these years were crossing the Appalachian Mountains to the promised land of the West, along the eastern seaboard industry was rapidly becoming the handmaiden of agriculture. New manufacturing towns were rising where only farms had stood, and older cities, fed by a rising river of immigrants as well as native Americans, were coming face to face with poverty, crime, and despair for the first time in any large way; the accompanying growth of illiteracy, less noticeable in an agrarian society, seemed suddenly a portent of danger to the democratic republic.[17]

These changes coincided with, or perhaps prompted, a resurgence of the old Puritan zeal to reform mankind, but unlike early Puritanism, this urge to reform was accompanied by a romantic, optimistic belief in the equality and perfectibility of men. In the 1830s, almost suddenly it seemed, the new spirit transfixed scores of Americans and pushed them into a sea of humanitarian reforms designed to improve the human condition. By no means the least of these was the movement to establish free public education.

In a sophisticated and cynical age it is almost impossible fully to comprehend the enthusiasm with which this little band of men set about their campaign for free public education. In that era of hope and optimism, when so many believed that all men are equal and equally capable of learning, education loomed as a panacea for all the nation's ills, and so well did the reformers present their case for education that they persuaded not only their own generation but succeeding ones as well of its remarkable power to solve human problems.

Through education democracy was to be saved, poverty and crime eliminated, mankind improved, and the growing disparity between rich and poor ameliorated. "If ever there was a cause . . . worthy to be upheld by all of toil and sacrifice that the human heart can endure," wrote Horace Mann, the great educational reformer who became secretary of the board of education in Massachusetts the same year Samuel Lewis became superintendent of public instruction in Ohio, "it is the cause of Education. It has intrinsic and indestructible merits. It holds the welfare of mankind in its embrace, as the protecting arms of a mother holds her infant to her bosom. The very ignorance and selfishness which obstruct its path are the strongest arguments for its promotion, for it furnishes the only adequate means for their removal."[18]

While Horace Mann and like-minded men campaigned for improved education in the East, another group of men were doing the same on the Middle Border, and if there was a difference between them, it was perhaps that the Midwesterners, like the people of the region as a whole, were more cosmopolitan than the Easterners. The Midwestern reformers came originally from New England, the Middle Atlantic states, and the South, and from a variety of occupations. Some were professors in the Midwest's new little colleges and seminaries, and some were schoolteachers in the private and public elementary schools. A number were ministers as well as educators, and others were lawyers, newspaper editors, and even politicians. They were not professional educators in the sense in which that term was later used, but a significant number had been educated in New England colleges and universities, were Whigs in politics, and participants in the temperance and antislavery crusades. The New England influence, in fact, was everywhere apparent in the movement.[19]

But whether they came from New England, New York, Pennsylvania, or Kentucky, the reformers had much in common. They were educated, either formally or informally, well-read for their day, and for the most part strong supporters of the Protestant view of the Christian faith. They were usually the most articulate men in their communities, and, in short, were what the people of the period would have thought of as the "best people." For the most part they lived in the Middle Border's rising towns and cities, and the center of their activities, at least in the 1830s, was Cincinnati, where they had established the Western Literary Institute. For nearly a decade this institute was the region's most important association in the struggle for free public education.[20]

Like the Eastern reformers, Midwesterners were practical idealists who hoped to preserve liberty and democracy through education, eliminate crime and poverty, and lift men to their own standards of conduct. Over and over in the late 1830s and '40s, in teachers' meetings, at conventions, and in the press, they would argue that free schools would wipe out distinctions between rich and poor, moderate class feeling, and give every child an equal chance in life. They would attack private schools and academies as rich men's schools, and plead for free public schools where the children of rich and poor alike would meet on equal terms, share the same seats, use the same books, and learn the same lessons. In the schools they sought, a poor man's son, ragged and barefoot, would be able to rise above the son of the community's richest man. What happpened would depend not on some artificial distinction but on the child's natural ability and diligence. "Where on earth is there such a practical demonstration of the doctrine that 'all men are born free and equal,'" argued a supporter of free schools in 1850, "as in the school house under a free school system."[21]

Yet idealism alone had not inspired these men to lift their banner of reform on the Middle Border. Fear, too, had been a motive. As they watched the passing scene from their homes in Cincinnati, Chicago, or St. Louis, and saw thousands upon thousands of settlers, many of them not only foreigners but Catholics too, moving into the region, and observed the rising rate of illiteracy, they could not help but wonder what would happen to their own values, to liberty, to democracy itself in the years to come if they failed to establish free public education.

In an older America they had been accustomed to a benign class structure in which it was understood that the educated men led the way. Now in the 1830s and '40s they saw rising on the Middle Border a rough, classless, contentious, independent, and turbulent society, and in the new age when all men had the right to vote and every citizen was king, it seemed certain to them that without education their own standards and all they held dear would be engulfed in a tidal wave of an illiterate majority. Nor did it seem likely to them that the settlers could bear their advancing prosperity without corruption if they had no education.

Lyman Beecher, graduate of Yale University, who had given up an imposing ministry in Boston in 1832 to head the Lane Theological Seminary in Cincinnati to help save the West, saw the danger early and warned Easterners of the situation in 1834 in an impassioned plea for help for the West. "But what will become of the West," he asked, "if her prosperity rushes up to such a majesty of power, while those great institutions linger which are necessary to form the mind, and the conscience and the heart of that vast world? It must not be permitted. And yet what is done must be done quickly; for population will not wait, and commerce will not cast anchor, and manufactures will not shut off steam...and agriculture, pushed by millions of freemen on their fertile soil, will not withhold her corrupting abundance. We must educate! we must educate! or we must perish by our own prosperity."[22]

This same fear of impending doom was shared by another Ohio

educator, William McGuffey, and by Beecher's son-in-law, Calvin Stowe.

If an archetype of the Midwestern education reformers were to be chosen, it might well be Calvin Stowe. He was born the son of a poor Massachusetts baker, made his way through Bowdoin College and Andover Theological Seminary, and came to Lane Seminary as professor of Biblical litrature in 1833. There he met and married Beecher's daughter, Harriet, and plunged into the fight for free public education with all the fervor of a man warding off imminent disaster. He was a member of the Western Literary Institute, and, after a visit to Europe in 1836, wrote a report for the Ohio legislature on European education which was to be quoted repeatedly through the years by educational reformers.[23]

Steeped in Biblical literature and foreign languages, and devoted to Protestant values, Stowe was profoundly disturbed by the Midwest's burgeoning foreign population that knew neither the English language nor the Puritan ideals he valued, and in an address on the education of the foreign population given in 1836, he reduced the reformers' motives for educating the people to pragmatic considerations. "Let us be reminded," he said, "that unless we educate our immigrants they will be our ruin. It is no longer a question of mere benevolence, of duty, or even enlightened self-interest but the intellectual and religious training of our foreign population has become essential to our own safety; we are prompted to it by the instinct of self-preservation."[24]

Years later when men looked at the Midwest's stable society, its rich farms and tranquil life, they would marvel at the reformers' terrible anxieties in the 1840s. Yet the reformers' fears of being overwhelmed by illiteracy and barbarism were not groundless. In Indiana, in 1847, so it was said, only 129,500 out of an estimated 350,000 children of school age were attending school, and in that state between 1840 and 1850, the number of those unable to read and write had increased by one hundred per cent, which was double the rate of increase of the population. And in Illinois, an editorial in the *Prairie Farmer* in 1842 noted that one in seventeen of the present population over twenty was illiterate. "To say nothing of our native population," the editor wrote as he pleaded for free public education, "what shall be done for the benefit of the thousands of foreigners coming among us annually?"[25]

It was statistics like these and the apparent decline of civilization they saw on every hand in the villages and on the farms of the Middle

Border that accounted for the educators' prophecies of doom and gave their movement its sense of urgency.

In the East the reformers drew support for free public education and better schools from the aristocrats, the businessmen, and laborers in the cities. Each group was convinced that its own special interests would be served by improved education. But on the Middle Border there were few aristocrats, few businessmen with large manufacturing plants, few urban workmen, and no large cities. Cincinnati, of course, Chicago, and St. Louis, whose well-organized school systems furnished models for the reformers, did have influential people whose support for free public education had to be won. But no city on the Middle Border was larger than 120,000 in 1850, and reformers were always aware that it was the farm children, whose families composed some eighty-nine per cent of the population of the area, for whom free public education was to be obtained and farmers who must support it.[26]

No one saw this more clearly than John Wright, Illinois newspaperman, who had arrived in Chicago from Massachusetts at an early age, had prospered, and founded the *Prairie Farmer*, which he dedicated to "Western Agriculture, Mechanics, and Education." "It is the farmers—the people at large—," he wrote in one of his many columns on the necessity for free public education, "who need to be reached and aroused to that exertion which is required of them in consideration of the vast importance of furnishing their children with a good common school education."[27]

But how to reach the farmers? Caleb Mills, graduate of Dartmouth College and Andover Theological Seminary, pondering the problem in 1833, thought that it would be "the work of years." He had just come west to head what was to be Wabash College in Indiana, but already he seemed to understand that if men like himself feared a future controlled by the uneducated and illiterate, the Midwestern farmers also had their fears of free public education.[28]

III

The farmers of the Middle West held a special place in the American imagination. In the minds of congressmen, senators, poets, and artists, they were simple, virtuous men, inhabiting a land flowing with milk and honey and building a democratic society where no man had too much yet all had enough. Far removed from the corrupting influences of the city, they tilled their own soil, owned their own farms, and produced enough for their necessities, and because they looked neither to a landlord nor to customers but only to heaven for their living, they were independent, honest, religious, and fiercely loyal to the government from whom they had obtained their land and in which they had a personal interest. They were, in the words of an Indiana congressman who spoke for them in 1841, "of the best *blood*, and noblest spirits in your land," and through most of the nineteenth century scarcely a debate in Congress relating to the Midwest or an article written about the farmers there failed to allude to this vision of the virtuous husbandman. "On each occurring season he sows his fields," wrote a journalist of the Middle Border in 1841, "with the calm reliance upon the bounty of an all-wise Providence, that in due time sunshine and shower will ripen them to harvest. . . . He possesses a free-hold—a tract of land which, under ordinary circumstances will yield him the means of subsistence; and, with this conviction, if he sows his crop with labor, he reaps with joy. He looks out upon his domain, and feels that he has an interest at stake in his country, for his own freehold is a part of its territory. Should the market for his products be contracted, he experiences no alarm, for the profits of his sales would only be required to furnish a few additional articles of taste. He feels, in fact, as a freeman should feel, lord of his creation."[29]

Like a Currier and Ives lithograph, this romanticized view of the Midwestern farmers was immensely appealing to the American people, perhaps because it was, in fact, not altogether fanciful. By the 1840s many of these farmers were just emerging from the pioneer period. They had built their homes, cleared their lands, sowed and harvested through the seasons. They had lost members of their families to the plagues and fevers and their crops to unseasonal weather. Yet they had endured, and what they had done, they had done virtually alone. In the process they had learned, better than many men, how to improvise, to get along with little, to "make do," as they said, "to front only the essential facts of life," as Henry Thoreau would have said.

Life on the land had made them individualistic, independent, and resourceful, traits that had made their conquest of the wilderness possible. Ownership of land had given them status and dignity, made them proud, even haughty perhaps, raised them to the equal of any man, and strengthened their nationalism. But the very isolation that helped make them independent and resourceful had also narrowed their intellectual horizons. On their isolated farms, with their days and years full of work, they had little time for intellectual exercises or the contemplation of fine art or even a flower garden. When opportunity afforded they were more likely to buy more land than to build a new home or plant shrubs for beauty's sake. What mattered most to them were the immediate things of life, how a man worked, and what he produced in material things. "A well-ploughed lot is more satisfactory to their eye than the most exquisite painting of a Raphael or a Claude," a Midwestern observer wrote in 1840. "They would prefer seeing a gristmill working on their own stream, to the sight of the sculptured marble of the Venus or the Apollo!"[30]

Most of what the farmers on the Middle Border knew in those years before the Civil War they had learned by experience. Nature was their teacher, the outdoors their classroom. They had plowed their fields as experience and common sense had taught them, had planted and harvested the same way, and their very success had given them confidence in their own judgment and made them reluctant to substitute experience for theory. They were, in fact, very often opinionated, boastful, and stubborn. Even a man who admired them in many ways, Lord Bryce, who visited them in the 1880s, wrote that they were "obstinate, tenacious of . . . habits, not readily accessible to argument."[31]

In the years to come, historians would find in all these traits the source of an antiintellectual strain that not only marked the American people generally, but led the farmers themselves to look with contempt upon "book-farming," as they called scientific farming, and made them apathetic if not hostile to education and to free public education in particular.[32]

There was truth in this. Crumbling log schoolhouses in numerous neighborhoods, short school terms, poor school attendance records, and in some communities no schools at all did suggest a low regard for education in the pre–Civil War days; and it is apparently true that in some districts, at least, the farmers' apathy and even opposition to the reformers' drive for free public education sprang, in some instances, from the wellspring of antiintellectuality.[33]

The farmers were not without reasons for their skepticism toward education and the educated. Knowing how hard farm life was, how lonely, and, in many ways, unrewarding, they could scarcely help feeling that educating their sons and daughters would either lure them away from the farm, where their labor was needed, or make them discontented with a life in which the monotony of morning and evening chores was broken mainly by bone-wearying work beneath a summer sun. But their apprehensions ran more deeply than this. They seemed instinctively to fear that education, at least too much education, went hand in hand with wealth, luxury, and leisure and ended in corruption and decadence.

Life's trials seemed to support their fears. One can only guess at the experience that prompted some farmers to tell an Indiana reformer that education's only tendency was to "make scoundrels of men," but it could easily have been an unhappy encounter with a smooth-talking, educated tree peddler or a corrupt lawyer. Or it may have been their dislike of the "professor," a term they used for both the medicine man with his elixir of life and the learned theorist, both of whom seemed fraudulent to them.[34]

Such apprehensions from which some opposition to free public education grew were to be found among farmers everywhere across the Middle Border, but they were particularly strong among those who had come from the South. For Southerners had had no tradition of public education as had those from New England and New York, and were surely more apathetic about education and more wary of free public education for that reason. Beyond this, their reservations about free public education were strengthened by the fact that it appeared to be a "Yankee notion," and by the observation that so many reformers campaigning for it were not only haughty, educated Yankees but members of the Whig party and antislavery people as well. Edward Eggleston's description in the *Hoosier Schoolmaster* of the ludicrous quality of education in Flat Crick, a school district apparently populated by Southerners, and of Squire Hawkins, the "poar Yankee schoolmaster, that said 'pail' instid of bucket, and that called a cow a 'caow,' and that couldn't tell to save his gizzard what we meant by *low* and *right smart*," suggests the Southerner's attitude toward education and his contempt for the Yankee.[35]

Still, as real as the farmer's antiintellectual attitudes seemed to be, they were usually applicable only to those matters beyond his experience. Shown the practical value of scientific farming or a new farm machine, and given proof that the expert was right, Midwestern farmers were quick to adopt new ways of farming and new machines. Had they not been, there would have been no revolution in agriculture in the nineteenth century. So it was with education. Certainly most, if not all, Midwestern farmers wanted their children to have at least an elementary education, and no doubt a significant number of them, in the usual American tradition, even hoped that their sons would go beyond reading, writing, and arithmetic, get a better education than they had had, and even leave the farm and go into the professions. There was much evidence, too, in the rate bills that so many of them paid to keep their children in school a bit longer each term and in the new frame schoolhouses they were building as the pioneer period drew to a close, that they were willing to sacrifice for their children's education. Indeed, one historian's observation that "no people ever built so many schools...on such a slender margin above the necessities of existence" was probably close to the truth.[36]

Again, it was a practical matter. Perhaps because of their own limited education and the sheer necessity of being able to read the Bible or figure their profits and losses, they understood as well as more educated people the need for their children to read, write, and cipher, and they would have looked askance at anyone who might have suggested that reading was unimportant. That is why rural mothers taught their children to read before they went to school, and many a rural child who could not read still appeared at the schoolhouse door for the first time knowing his ABC's.[37]

If, then, they hesitated to support free public education, it was not purely because of an antiintellectual bias against elementary education but in part because of a feeling that it was a new idea supported by strange arguments that seemed to lack common sense. Why, they might wonder, should a man who had no children in school be taxed to support those who had? And what were they to make of the argument that their children were the property of the state and the property of the state must be taxed for their support? Such an idea might be applicable in Prussia, but it was a strange doctrine to many Middle Border farmers who thought of their children as their own responsibility, and who would have resented any implication of government control of their children.[38]

But neither the novelty of the idea nor the new arguments used to support it would have delayed the establishment of free public education on the Middle Border had it not meant that all property owners would have to be taxed to pay for it whether they wished to pay or not. This was the stumbling block to all educational reform bills, and the farmer's fear of it was suggested by John Wright and his committee when they presented a plan promising free public education to every Illinois school child. Wright confessed that they had deliberately tried to make it sound attractive in order to "draw the people into the grasp of this awful monster—taxation."[39]

To most farmers on the Middle Border in the 1840s, compulsory tax for education was a monster, and time and again state legislators had taken extraordinary precautions in writing school legislation to make certain no one would be taxed against his will. Farmers, as a group, were probably no stingier than most men, or less willing to give what they felt they could to education. But compulsory taxation was a step into the unknown, an experiment that would remove their right to determine how much they could afford to pay for education, and they had no idea how this would affect them.[40]

Their life on the Middle Border in those antebellum years was always uncertain. Here and there the effects of the panic of 1837 lingered on. Some states were still in debt as a result of it, and dollars were always scarce even in good times. Each farmer had to weigh the problem of compulsory taxation carefully. How much was the tax likely to be each year? If the corn crop failed or a valuable horse died, would he be able to pay his tax and the money he owed on his farm too? What if there were sickness in the family, always a distinct possibility in that land of supposed miasmas? Could he afford both a doctor for his children and a schoolteacher too? And if in the end he could not pay the compulsory tax, would he lose his farm or some of his property?[41]

The reformers may have vaguely understood all these things, but if they did, they gave the farmers no respite because of them. For wherever the farmers went in these years, the county fair, an institute meeting, or even a Fourth of July picnic, there were the reformers to give speeches on the need for free public education. Year in and out, like reformers everywhere in these years, they argued, scolded, and irritated their targets. They formed organizations, held conventions, and passed resolutions for their legislatures. And in their journals and reports dark columns of figures enumerating the rising number of illiterates and unschooled children marched side by side with their vision of the good society that would flow from the establishment of free public education.

It was frustrating work. They had little money for their campaign and only a few journals to spread the word. They had to compete for the farmers' attention with the antislavery and temperance crusades, with the Western fever that excited farmers and lured them westward, the Mexican War, and the California gold rush at mid-century. Sometimes, it seemed, no argument, not even the lengthening shadow of illiteracy, would advance their cause, and as the years went on their writings took on a waspish edge revealing exaggeration. "No other interest of the State [but education] has been so shamefully neglected," wrote Ohio's state superintendent of public instruction in 1845; "any other treated with the same chilling indifference would have perished."[42]

But gradually their message got across. Laws were passed in the 1840s improving education step by step. Here was a law establishing the office of superintendent of public instruction and there another allowing, but not requiring, communities to tax themselves for the upkeep of their schools. Here was one providing for the education of black children, and yet another authorizing additional township taxes for education.[43]

At last, beginning in the late 1840s, the Middle Border states began providing for the establishment of free public education by passing laws requiring school districts to keep their schools open a certain number of months of the year and to tax themselves for this if need be. Wisconsin, profiting from the struggle that had gone on for so long in the older Midwestern states, provided for free public education in her constitution as she entered the Union in 1848 and implemented this by law the same year. Iowa and Minnesota too, new states in 1846 and 1858, made early provision for free public education, as did Kansas after it entered the Union in 1861 and Nebraska in 1867. And in the older states, the reformers had their victory in the early 1850s. Indiana established free public education in 1852, Ohio in 1854, and Illinois in 1855.[44]

Of the older states only Missouri and Michigan failed to have free public education before the Civil War. Missouri, the most southern of all the North Central states, had far too many obstacles to overcome to accomplish this before the war. But it was ironic that Michigan, filled primarily with settlers from New England and New York, and having the best school system of all Midwestern states until the late 1850s, waited until 1869 to eliminate its cherished rate system and establish a complete system of free public education.[45]

Nevertheless, the victory for free public education was largely won on the Middle Border in the 1850s. But it is virtually certain that it would not have come, even then, had farmers not been confident that they could still control school matters through the district school system with which they were familiar.

3

The School District

❧❧

I

ONE DAY IN JULY 1855, THE SUPERINTENDENT OF SCHOOLS OF
La Prairie Township, Rock County, Wisconsin, with a lofty disregard
for punctuation, scratched a letter to the township clerk. "I have this
day," he wrote, "formed a new school district in the town of La Prairie
to be called school district No 2 of the town of La Prairie of which the
following is a description Commencing with the W 1/2 of section 3 the
whole of sect 4 & 5 E 1/2 of sec 6 NE 1/4 of sec . . .," and so on until the
area bounded covered seven sections of land.[1]

The new school district lay just east of Janesville, the county seat of
Rock County. It was connected to town by a road that penetrated the
district's northwest corner and stretched in an easterly direction
through the township. On a hill near the place where the road crossed
the eastern boundary of section five, the district's farmers built a
one-room schoolhouse. Eventually it was called the Gravel Hill
School, and in the years to come, the Chicago, Milwaukee, and St.
Paul Railroad would run nearby, while across the road to the east of
the building would be an orchard through which the children would
make their way to get water for the school. For nearly a hundred
years, three generations of farm children, lunch pails in hand,
trudged along dirt roads and across fields, often a mile or more,
through snow and rain and in the summer's sun, to that small knoll
for their education.[2]

When it was built, Gravel Hill was not really the second school in the
township as its number implied. Four others had already been built
there. But the nearest one to Gravel Hill was about three miles away,

too far, some parents thought, for their children to walk to and from night and morning. And because there was no public transportation—no wagon or buggy—to take children to a school that far from home, the school was brought to the children simply by reorganizing the township's school districts and creating a new independent school district.[3]

Creating new school districts, to bring schools to children instead of taking children to schools, was the Midwestern farmers' solution to the problem of educating their scattered, isolated children in the nineteenth century and the foundation of that cherished American institution, the neighborhood school. But it was no Midwestern invention. Like the town meeting and the Congregational Church, the small independent school district was something the early settlers brought with them from New England as they poured into the old Northwest in the years following the War of 1812, and its origins could be traced back as far as 1647 when the Massachusetts General Court ordered all towns of fifty or more families to establish schools for their children.[4]

This law was passed just seventeen years after Boston was founded in the wilderness of the New World. But even at that early date, the Puritan settlers were able to establish schools their children could attend because, unlike other English colonists in America, they had at first settled in villages. But the villages did not long accommodate all settlers. As the population increased, farm families drifted to the fringes of their towns until the distance between them and the village was so great that their children could no longer attend the school there. When this happened the farmers in the isolated communities asked their town governments for permission to use their school tax money to build schools in their own areas and to discontinue paying taxes for the upkeep of the village school they could no longer use.[5]

Permission to do this was usually granted, though sometimes grudgingly, and for years Massachusetts farmers in remote areas built and managed their little schools with no more than an informal understanding regulating their relations with their town government. In 1789, however, and again in 1800, the General Court passed laws that authorized farmers to establish independent districts and gave those districts corporate powers so that residents could legally build, own, and manage their own schools.[6]

This was the origin of the small independent school districts the settlers organized on the Middle Border. The Ohio legislature introduced the system in 1821. From Ohio it moved across the Middle

Border, and wherever the plows furrowed the earth and settlements appeared, the land would be divided again and again into little patches of ground like that of La Prairie, District 2—a section here, a half-section there, and a quarter-section beyond—until by 1900 the process of division had virtually run its course, and the area was covered with thousands of little white one-room schoolhouses planted near the centers of as many independent school districts.[7]

These school districts varied greatly in size and shape throughout the Midwest. Their boundary lines were drawn to match as nearly as possible the farmers' frequently changing whims and the state laws, and were likely to be mapped along section or half-section lines, down the middle of country roads, and around creeks, sloughs, and lakes, so that some districts were oblong and some square, and some simply defied easy description.

For purposes of easy identification all districts were numbered, usually in order of their establishment in the township or county, and when it became necessary to create a school district partly in one township or county and partly in another so that all children would have a school within reach, fractional or joint districts were laid out. How complicated this could sometimes become was illustrated by Joint District 1 of Koshkonong Township, Jefferson County, Wisconson. This small district was located at the corner of Jefferson, Rock, and Walworth counties, and children from those counties and four townships—Koshkonong, Cold Spring, Whitewater, and Lima—attended the little school at the intersection of the road running north into the town of Whitewater and the road running east-west dividing Rock and Jefferson counties. For obvious reasons it was called the Tri-County School.[8]

In spite of the variations among them, the Midwestern school districts in the 1880s and '90s followed a general pattern that could be seen from the location of the schoolhouses. "It must be remembered," wrote an observer in Illinois in 1883, "that the township is exactly six miles square. It is the custom to divide it into nine districts, two miles square, and to erect a schoolhouse near the centre of each. As the county roads are in most instances, constructed along section lines— and therefore run north and south, east and west, at intervals of a mile—the traveller expects to find a schoolhouse at every alternate crossing."[9]

Actually, the Midwestern district pattern was rarely as orderly as this. Schoolhouses were not always at alternate crossroads, and although there might be more than nine schools in a heavily populated township, usually there were fewer. Nevertheless, those tiny markers denoting schoolhouses that appear on every third section or so in those remarkable Midwestern county atlases of the 1890s suggest how closely the school districts did resemble the pattern the observer described.[10]

It would be as difficult to exaggerate the contributions these small school districts made to the education of rural children and to the political and social life of Midwestern farm communities in the nineteenth and early twentieth centuries as to imagine rural America of that period without them. Besides making possible the schooling of countless children who otherwise would have gone uneducated, they brought scattered families together in a common effort, provided a community where none existed, and gave the people who lived among the empty stretches of hills and plains a sense of belonging to a place.

They were invaluable laboratories of democracy in which rural Americans learned the importance of their vote, how to make laws, and how to govern themselves. Here many Americans learned parliamentary procedures—how to make motions, how to reconsider action already taken, and how to support their motions with arguments. They wrestled with such intricacies as bond issues, taxes, and contingency funds, and if they had greater confidence in democracy than other groups of Americans, it was because democracy was no abstraction to them. In their school districts they learned that their vote made a difference, that they could change what they did not like, and that democracy actually worked.

Beyond all this, the little independent school districts made it possible for the government and parents to cooperate in the education of children, yet gave the parents almost complete control of that education in ways that would be virtually incomprehensible to later generations.

The Prussians, whose centralized system of education was so greatly prized by American educators in the nineteenth century, would never have appreciated the American independent school districts or understood the reasons for them. But for rural Americans, who were not much given to theory, the small school districts represented a commonsense compromise between the Prussian idea that the state should control the education of children and the long American tradition that the parents themselves were responsible for what their children learned or did not learn. To the Midwestern farmers the system was as practical as arithmetic, and if it had not already existed when the fight for free public education on the Middle Border was taking place, free schools would never have come to the area when they did. Only the farmers' realization that they would be in charge of everything, from the building of a schoolhouse to the hiring of a teacher to the raising of money to pay for it all, made free public education acceptable to them.[11]

For their part of the compromise, state governments gave the school districts corporate powers and required them to have school so many months of the year if they wished to secure state funds. They imposed general rules regulating district boundaries, annual school meetings, elections of school officials, and district indebtedness. They demanded that district teachers be licensed, and they apportioned money from state educational funds to each district according to the number of children attending its school. But almost everything else they left to the districts themselves.[12]

This meant that in nearly all the Middle Border states, the farmers themselves had to elect the members of the school board, purchase a building site, and build their own schoolhouse. It was up to them to decide how many months of school they would have, the amount of fuel they would need, the cost of the teacher, and how much they would raise through taxation to pay for it all. But that was not all. They decided whether or not the school would pay for textbooks and determined when the schoolhouse would be repaired, the grounds improved, a well dug, and new privies built. They directed the schoolboard in the employment of a teacher and drew up regulations for the school. Even the duty of informing farm families in a given locality that a new school district had been created there and that a school meeting was to be held was the responsibility of some taxable farmer living in the new district.[13]

II

The heart of the little independent school district was its annual school meeting, for it was here that the taxable farmers met to elect the members of their school board and make provision for the year's operation of their school.

The date of the annual meeting was fixed by state law. Usually the day fell in the summer or fall, as in Minnesota and Michigan, or in the spring, as was the case in Nebraska and Illinois. Advance notices of the time and place of the meeting were posted throughout the district, in the general store perhaps, and almost always on the schoolhouse door. And then on a warm summer evening, or on a rainy spring afternoon, perhaps, farmers throughout the state walked across fields or drove their buggies and wagons along narrow country roads to their one-room schoolhouses where the meetings were usually held. There, in the small, familiar room with its faintly musty odor of chalk and paper, sometimes surrounded by their children's paper work on the walls and their writings on the blackboard, they greeted their neighbors, talked about the spring planting or the recent harvest, complained about the rain or lack of it, and gradually arranged themselves at their children's desks, or huddled about the room's big stove if the day was cold, to make laws for the next year's operation of their schools.[14]

The exercise in participatory democracy that followed in this smallest self-governing political division in the nation showed how thoroughly the farmers controlled the most important aspects of their children's education. Talk was subdued by the call to order. The minutes of the last meeting and the treasurer's report were read and accepted, and the election of at least one school board member was held. Then it was time to consider matters that cost money. "On motion," they would write into the minutes, "that we have seven months school for the ensuing year, four months winter and three months summer, carried." Or: "It was moved supported and carried that we have 5 months of winter school & 3 months summer school for the ensuing year."[15]

For them there was no state bureaucracy to order children throughout the state to begin and end school on certain days. So complete was the Midwestern farmers' control over their school system that they determined not only the number of months they would have school beyond that required by the state, but also the dates when the school terms would start and finish. "Motion that we have seven months of school," the clerk of one little Wisconsin school district wrote in 1881, "four months for the winter term commencing on the second Monday of Nov. & three months for the summer term commencing on the first Monday of May, carried."[16]

Like farm life itself, these dates as well as the school terms were regulated by the passage of the seasons. The winter term usually began in late September or even as late as November, when the harvest was in and the farmers had turned to winter chores. The spring or summer term began about the time the farmers began to plow their fields and plant their crops, which might be as early as March or sometimes as late as May. But so tractable was the rural school system that Middle Border farmers could adjust their school terms for any eventuality, and often they would have three terms—winter, spring, and summer. One year the farmers at the Tri-County School voted to have nine months of school, but only if the weather was favorable; otherwise they would have eight months. And in the 1880s, the farmers in District 40 in Saunders County, Nebraska, adjusted their school terms to the harvest.[17]

District 40, the Eureka District, as the farmers called it, lay just to the west of the village of Ceresco, and from the hilltop schoolyard one could look south across the rolling hills and farms to the state's capital. To the north was Rock Creek, which flowed around the schoolhouse on the east and under the bridge that crossed the road at the bottom of the hill. It was homestead country and corn country as well, and when the farmers met for their annual school meeting in 1886, they were thinking as much about the corn harvest as about education. "Moved and seconded that we have nine months of school," the minutes read, "to begin about the first of Sept. Continuing 3 months unless the weather gets good for husking corn, if so have a vacation for husking corn."[18]

Once they had decided on the number of months of winter and summer school and calculated how much money they were to receive from the state's permanent education fund and from other sources, they knew how much they would have to raise in local taxes for fuel, teacher's wages, and other funds to operate the school, and more motions were in order. "It has been voted," ran the minutes of a school district in Michigan in 1883, "to raise $147.50 . . . to defray the expenses for the following year as follows: Wood—7.50, Cleaning house (twice)—4.00, Contingent fund—15.00, Officers salary—11.00, teachers wages—110.00"[19]

After this they would consider the problem of their school's fuel supply for the winter term. Once, about the time of the Civil War, Midwestern farmers had merely required that each family in the district furnish a cord or so of wood for each one of its children attending school. But by the 1870s they had developed a more sophisticated and businesslike approach to the problem. Taking into consideration the length of the winter term they had decided upon and the amount of wood they had on hand, they estimated their needs for the coming year. Then they offered the contract for securing the wood to the lowest bidder, and frequently, but not always, specified precisely what kind of wood was required, how it was to be cut, and when it was to be delivered.

The wood contract, which might vary from only a few dollars to as much as forty or fifty, was an important source of income for people who had as little ready cash each year as the Midwestern farmers, and no doubt many farmers attended the annual meeting merely to bid on the fuel contract. And because it was so important, it was a potential source of trouble in the community unless it was properly monitored.

From the village of Belleville in Dane County, Wisconsin, a county road runs due north. Not far from the village, it passes a cemetery and what was once the Willoughby Grand Springs Farm on the right. Farther on it rises above the Sugar River and fertile farms on the left to a point nearly two miles from the village, where it makes a sharp turn to the right and where the Illinois Central Railroad crosses it. There, wedged into a corner formed by the turn of the road, the railroad, and an intruding section line road, stood the little school-house for District 3, Montrose Township.

Through the 1880s District 3's farmers had been careless about their fuel contract. They never let the contract at their annual meet-ings and never estimated the amount of wood they would need. In-stead they permitted the school board to use money from the contin-gency fund to buy wood and apparently trusted the school board to get the wood at the cheapest possible price.

Diplomatically the board did pass the fuel contract around among the district farmers and even gave it once to a member of the school board. But this arrangement did not please all the farmers, either because they thought the school board's friends were getting the lion's share of the contracts or because they felt the district was not getting the wood at the cheapest price. The result was that at the annual meeting of 1892 someone moved that they give the fuel contract to the lowest bidder.

How the school board reacted to this reflection upon its manage-ment of the fuel problem, the minutes of the meeting do not say, but very likely the motion provoked a lively discussion. In any case, the dispute ended in a victory for the reformers, and from that time on through the early 1900s District 3 nearly always awarded the fuel contract at the annual meeting.[20]

If all this business proceeded without trouble, the farmers might complete their annual school business within an hour or so. But as often as not it took longer, for the course of democracy ran no more smoothly in rural America in the nineteenth century than it did elsewhere. First, there was always the possibility that not enough farmers would attend the annual meeting to conduct the district's business. If this happened the school's business was postponed and the meeting adjourned to another day.

Democracy in rural America's little school districts was carried on, as it was everywhere, by the concerned and the responsible, and those concerned in any district depended partly on the matters to be discussed at any given meeting and partly on the spirit of the community. Let the business before the meeting be the building of a new schoolhouse, the repair of the privies, or the digging of a well—whatever cost more than an ordinary amount of money—and the little schoolhouse would bulge with farmers anxious to have their say. On the other hand, if the business before them were merely routine, and the district's public spirit poor, some of the district's farmers were inclined to "let John do it."

District 3 of Blooming Grove Township in Dane County, Wisconsin, whose schoolhouse sat on the line between sections seventeen and twenty, a mile east of Lake Monono and within sight of Madison, was a case in point. In August of 1863, only a month after the battle of Gettysburg, fifteen farmers attended a specially called school district meeting and voted down a proposal to build a new schoolhouse. Having done that, however, nearly half of them apparently lost interest in school affairs. for only eight showed up for the district's annual meeting one month later. Nor can it be said that the farmers' interest in education in this particular district improved much as the years went by. Between 1878 and 1866, District 3's annual meeting had to be postponed six times, and once, in 1885, it was necessary to adjourn twice before enough farmers were present to conduct the school's business.[21]

Some onlookers in the nineteenth century concluded that what was happening in Blooming Grove, District 3, was happening all over the Middle Border and proved the failure of democracy in the small independent districts and the farmers' lack of interest in education. This was a hasty conclusion that took no account of the great variations among the school districts, which were as individualistic as the farmers themselves. There were, in fact, thousands of little school districts across the Midwest in which an adjourned meeting was a rarity.

There was District 1, of Pennfield Township, Calhoun County, Michigan, for example. Its boundaries had just been carved out of the wilderness through which Wanondoger Creek flowed down to meet Battle Creek, when Henry Parsons, taxable resident and sometime farmer and schoolteacher, tramped through the area in 1849 informing his neighbors of the time and place of the district's first school meeting. In 1870, after more than twenty years of schooling in the district's first schoolhouse, a special meeting was called to consider building another. Thirty-five farmers attended that meeting and voted to build the district's second schoolhouse at the southeast corner of section 16 on property once owned by William Hicks, and such was the interest of the farmers associated with the Hicks School that not once in twenty years, from 1870 to 1890, did the district have an adjourned meeting.[22]

Neither was it correct to assume that a small attendance at an annual meeting reflected the farmers' lack of interest in what was going on in the district school. Most Midwestern school districts were very small, and if only six or seven farmers appeared at the annual meeting, they might easily represent all the taxable residents of the district, or at least all those who had children in the school. Only seven farmers gathered on the afternoon of July 27, 1893, for the annual meeting at the little Ise School, which stood just a mile and a half northwest of Downs, Kansas, in District 37 of Osborne County. Yet these seven represented seven of the eight families who had children in the school.[23]

So it went in district after district throughout the Middle Border, and so far from proving the weakness of the little independent school districts, the farmers' record of attendance at their annual meetings rather suggested the strength of the system that allowed and even forced them to manage their own affairs. The minutes of the annual school district meetings, filled with names of thousands of farmers who found time each year to attend to their school's affairs, testify to the vigor of the system, and it is doubtful that there was a better example anywhere of the effectiveness of democracy than the Midwestern rural independent school districts.[24]

Of course, not all those who faithfully attended their district's annual school meeting did so out of a consuming interest in education. Some came merely to see that less, not more, was spent on education, and the wrangles between them and those who were determined to develop the best school possible sometimes tore the district meetings apart. Once a Wisconsin farmer broke up his school's meeting because, as he confided in his diary, "they did not proceed lawful." And, apparently in a fit of exasperation, a school director in Blooming Grove, District 3, abruptly ended the 1882 annual meeting in the face of the farmers who voted not to adjourn. The fact that the education laws of some states had provisions for removing disorderly people from school meetings suggests the fervor with which farmers sometimes supported their arguments at the annual meeting. Indeed, democracy's problem in the independent school districts was not really the farmers' failure to attend their meetings so much as their difficulty in reaching an agreement on the issues once they had assembled.[25]

III

No people in the land were more individualistic nor more cautious of spending money than the Midwestern farmers who gathered year after year to legislate for their school. Tempered by hard work, accustomed to living with nature's uncertainties, and taught by experience to hope for the best, expect the worst, and keep something in reserve for a rainy day, they felt it necessary to weigh carefully the effect each dollar spent on education would have upon them personally. So it was not to be expected that when such men deliberated upon their school's affairs there would be no arguments, no raised voices, no serious disagreements. Quite the contrary.

The farmers recorded the minutes of their meetings as sparingly as they spent money, but they wrote enough to make plain the problems they had in reaching agreement. They argued over almost every issue that came before them, over the building or repair of the schoolhouse, the improvement of the school grounds, the privies, textbooks, the treasurer's report, even over spilled ink. "Then after a lengthy wrangle . . . and talk over a Broken bottle of ink . . .," the clerk of a Rock County school district recorded in the minutes of the annual meeting in 1891, "the question whether the Dist Should furnish Ink for the pupels was finally setled by the vote of hands up a Majority said no." And once in 1889, in Fractional District 1 in Tecumseh Township, some three miles northeast of Tecumseh in Lenawee County, Michigan, the amount of wood in the woodpile became a bone of contention. The farmers were so obviously suspicious of one another that they appointed a committee of two, presumably one for each side, to appraise the woodpile and report back to the annual meeting before a vote could be taken on the fuel issue.[26]

But mostly they argued over the number of months of school they should have for the year, and when that was settled they argued over whether to have a longer winter than summer term or the other way around. Frequently, as happened in Blooming Grove's District 3 in 1875, a number of motions were required to settle such problems. In that year the farmers rejected one motion to have a seven-month school, rejected another to have a six-and-a-half-month school, and finally settled on holding school for six months that year. Even more complicated had been the voting in nearby Joint District 9 of Dunn Township in Dane County, Wisconsin. There the farmers voted for an eight-month school but rejected a motion to have a continuous school for four months in the spring. Instead they voted to have four months in the winter, two in the spring, and two in the summer, only to reconsider this, and accept another motion to have a fall term of two months, a winter term of four months, and a spring term of two. Finally, this too was reexamined, and the farmers wound up their business by reconsidering the eight months of school and voting to have school only seven months.[27]

Invariably their problem was money. The longer the school, the more costly, of course; and the longer the winter term, the more expensive, for not only was there a fuel bill for the winter school, but the male teacher, whom most districts preferred for the winter term when the older boys attended school, cost more than the female teacher. So they argued, and hard-pressed farmers, who thought they could not spend another dollar for education, tried to reduce the total number of months school was to be held, or voted to have a shorter winter than summer term of school; or they would support motions to direct the school board to employ a female teacher for all school terms. Failing all this, they would try to set the maximum monthly salary the school board could pay a teacher.

The farmers in District 40 in Saunders County, Nebraksa, went through this cycle in 1879. That year, when the more conservative among them lost a motion to have a shorter winter than spring term, they moved to order the directors to pay no more than thirty dollars a month for a teacher for both summer and winter school. And when this motion, too, was lost, they had to be content with another directing the school board to pay no more than thirty dollars a month for the spring-term teacher.[28]

From these efforts to employ cheap teachers, and reduce the length of their school terms, came the impression of the antiintellectual, miserly farmer, who prized a new plow more than he did the education of his children. And there were those farmers, perhaps some in every district, who did put the plow before the boy. There was Joshua Webb, for example, in District 11 of Pennfield Township in Calhoun County, Michigan. He had had almost no formal education and had learned to write scribbling on the back of an almanac. He had come to Pennfield Township virtually penniless and had raised himself from a sexton in the Hicks cemetery to a large landholder. But his principal contribution to the annual school meetings in the late 1880s was to try to reduce the length of the school term from eight to seven months.[29]

But there were nearly always as many and sometimes even more in each district who opposed such reductions. Only once in the years between 1885 and 1890 did the farmers in District 11 vote with Webb, and in other districts, even when the advocates of shorter school terms won out, victory came only after a prolonged fight with those who wanted more schooling for their children.[30]

After what must have been a particularly bitter fight over the issue of employing a cheap teacher and a proposal to reduce the number of months of school, the clerk of a little school in Grant County, Wisconsin, in 1872, obviously on the losing side of the battle, registered his contempt for the outcome when he recorded the adoption of the motion to have a six-month school. "Determined," he wrote with homespun irony, "that six months school is exactly right for our district—a three months term in Summer at ordinary wages by a female teacher and a three months term in winter by—(Biger [sic] the fool, Cheaper he'l [sic] teach School) Or a better rule if one can possibly be found."[31]

In nearly every district across the Middle Border, there were those like the Grant County school clerk, who opposed the cheap teacher, the short school term, and the dilapidated schoolhouse. For all those who year after year voted merely to repair the old schoolhouse, there were others who wanted to build a new one; for every one who wanted a cheap teacher, another wanted the best the district could employ; and for the cautious, thrifty farmers who voted against long school terms, there were the concerned who voted for them and did not hesitate to take matters in their own hands when opportunity offered. In District 40 in Saunders County, in 1884, a group of farmers, miffed because the voters had reduced the length of the school term at the annual meeting that year, petitioned the school board to call a special meeting in order to vote on a proposal to add one month of school, "or as much as we *shall have money* to pay for," to what had been voted on at the annual meeting. Probably the proponents of the longer school term had rounded up a contingent of like-minded people to vote for their proposal, as they sometimes did, and, in the end, the farmers did vote for a longer school term.[32]

By today's standards, of course, the budgets of the little Midwestern country schools and the amount the farmers taxed themselves to support those budgets seem ridiculously small. Throughout the 1890s, the average annual revenue taken in by the Gravel Hill School, District 2, La Prairie Township, was only $349.79, and of this amount the farmers had raised an average each year of only $196.63 by direct taxation in their district. But many times this had to be collected in the face of livestock epidemics, plagues of locusts and grasshoppers, drouths, appreciating currency, falling prices, and the uncertainties of life rarely experienced in the cities, and the farmers' willingness to tax themselves even as much as $200.00 a year indicated a commitment to education worthy of more educated people. So, too, did their determination to keep their schools in session as long as possible even under adverse conditions.[33]

In the 1880s, in Dodge County, Wisconsin, in section 16 of Elba Township, not far to the southeast of Danville village, stood the one-room schoolhouse for District 2. Facing north on an east-west road that crossed the Crawfish River a quarter of a mile to the east, it sat diagonally across the road from the Catholic cemetery where some of the district's directors from those years now lie buried. Looking east from the schoolyard, the children could see, just at the brow of the hill, the big red barn belonging to the Austin family for whom the school was named. Lush farms on rolling hills surrounded the little school, and for a number of years previous to 1886 the district's farmers had voted to have an eight-month school, which was three more months than required by state law.

But the summer of 1886 was unusually dry, and early in July the temperature in the county reached 108°. "If we don't get rain soon our crops will hardly be worth harvesting," the county newspaper reported. "All vegetation is completely wilting down under the scorching rays of the sun in a cloudless sky. Barley is withering and whitening very fast. . . . Dry pastures are turned brown and even sheep cannot live on them."[34]

Faced with the uncertainty of their harvest as they met that July for their annual school meeting, the farmers of Elba, District 2, did reduce the length of their school. But it was some indication of the value they placed on education that they shortened the school term by only one month rather than three as they might have done. And the next year, the farmers voted to return to an eight-month school.[35]

But it was not always the prospect of a catastrophic harvest or a little group of stingy men that prompted the farmers to reduce the length of their school terms or employ a cheap teacher. Sometimes the district had built a new schoolhouse or rebuilt the privies or dug a well, so that taxes were so high they were compelled to reduce their operating expenses until indebtedness was diminished.

Just west of the Devil's Lake post office and not far to the northeast of the village of Addison in Lenawee County, Michigan, resting on a gentle slope beside a tree-lined road, was the one-room schoolhouse, always known as the Sanford School, that belonged to District 5 of Woodstock Township. Many of the farms in this district were partially covered with timber, and the farmers there were apparently not particularly prosperous. Whatever their wealth, or lack of it, when they assembled at their schoolhouse on the evening of September 7, 1885, for their annual meeting, they were in no mood to employ an expensive teacher or extend the length of their school sessions.

The district had just built a new schoolhouse, and only the year before, after the building had begun, the farmers had authorized their school board to borrow money to complete it. Shortly after this, at a special meeting, they had directed the building committee to raise money to erect a fence, and out of the several choices a salesman had apparently offered them, they had voted to purchase "the ten dollar bell" for their school.

So when the meeting in the new schoolhouse was called to order that evening and the preliminaries were out of the way, the farmers voted "that the board be authorized to raise as little money as possible," for the ensuing year, and followed this with a motion to have only a six-month school and to employ a female teacher for the year.

Since 1871, longer than some of those present could remember, District 5 had been an eight-month school, and it came, perhaps, as a shock to some that the district was forced to reduce the length of its school terms by two months. But the building program had obviously stretched the farmers' pocketbooks thin, and there was general agreement that they had no choice but to shorten the time school was kept and employ the cheapest teacher possible.

But if there were those in the district who hoped to continue this austerity program, as they might with good reason have wished to do, they were not allowed. For although the district was still in debt in 1886 and forced to raise $140 merely to pay on their bonded indebtedness, the farmers voted nonetheless to return to an eight-month school and to employ a male teacher for the winter term.[36]

IV

District 5's experience illustrated once more the flexibility of the small independent school district system that allowed the farmers to steer their own bark in the education of their children. Without the right to reduce the length of their school terms and juggle their finances, the district's farmers might never have been able to build their new schoolhouse. But unfortunately, the system did not always work so well everywhere across the Middle Border. For the same laws that allowed District 5 to make adjustments to build a new schoolhouse allowed others to get along with an old dilapidated one, with a six-month school, and the cheapest teacher money could buy.

This was the essence of democracy, surely, and of the doctrine of self-help so revered in rural America. And for better or worse, the result of the evolution of both principles was sometimes visible in the contrast between a freshly painted, trim little schoolhouse in one district, bounded by trees and a fence, and another, two or three miles down the road, with peeling paint and sagging roof, sitting in a treeless, weed-filled yard, the victim of the farmers' unconcern or perhaps some bitter dispute that had blocked efforts to improve the school.

As the nation moved into the 1890s, however, those disputes that had wracked the annual school meetings in many Middle Border districts through the years seemed less bitter and the meetings less rancorous than they once had been. Perhaps this was because the farmers had grown more prosperous, at least in the older part of the region; or perhaps it was because their school districts' boundary lines had become reasonably well established, their schoolhouses had been built, and there were fewer matters to quarrel about. Whatever the reason, the farmers in many districts seemed mellower and more willing to turn more of the schools' business over to their school directors than they had been when their districts were newer.

The corn cutters were again on the swing across Woodstock Township, a cider mill was running in the area on Thursday each week, oats were being thrashed, and the fair at Morenci, a little town in the southern part of Lenawee County, was only a week away when the farmers of District 5 met on September 7, 1891, for their annual meeting. By this time the little Sanford schoolhouse was nearly seven years old and needed painting, and it was a mark of the more relaxed mood of the district's farmers that they simply voted to direct the school board to have it painted without specifying the limits of how much it was to cost. Nor did they feel it necessary to direct the school board to employ a male or a female teacher. The choice was left to the school directors, as was the amount of money to be raised for the teacher's wages.[37]

But this did not mean that the farmers were giving up control of their schools to the school boards. The farmers in District 5 still set the length of their school term and the price of wood, and here and there throughout the Middle Border, the farmers were still concerned even about little things in their schools. As late as 1911 in a school district in Dane County, Wisconsin, they voted to have the children fill their cups with the dipper rather than dipping their cups in the water pail, and five years later, they voted to hire an "older scholar," to carry the water to the school. Nor did it mean that the Midwestern farmers had given up disagreeing with one another over school matters.[38]

As long as the small independent districts and the one-room schoolhouses lasted on the Middle Border, so did the differences between those who wanted the best possible schools and those who wanted something less, and the quarrels that raged over this and other school matters left scars that passed from one generation to another. And perhaps there was no district anywhere in that vast region whose inhabitants could not remember some quarrel that had once divided the district, or some personal slight to themselves that had left its wound.

But the district was a community as well as a school district. Within the section lines that bounded it lived neighbors who exchanged their work, borrowed one another's plow, did the chores for those who were sick, and brought food and comfort to the bereaved, and sometimes in the shared life of the community, old animosities were softened. Agreement could often be reached in school meetings as the years passed, even among old enemies, for the sake of the community if not for education. For the school was a reflection of the community, and sometimes pride in their community, as well as the spirit of competition with an adjoining district—both powerful forces on the Middle Border in the nineteenth century—were enough to compel them to lay old grudges aside and vote to have a longer school term, better teachers, or build a new schoolhouse. Indeed, the degree to which old district quarrels had or had not been put aside for the common good, and "to some extent the aspiration of the neighborhood," as one educator remarked in 1897, was many times reflected in the district's schoolhouse.[39]

4

The Schoolhouse

꙰

I

READING THROUGH THEIR COPIES OF THE *Wisconsin State Journal*
on the morning of September 17, 1890, the residents of Madison saw
on page two a sketch of a one-room country schoolhouse. The American flag flew from its belfry and smoke poured from its chimney.
"DISTRICT SCHOOL" was painted just above the door, and written
across the roof was the inscription "THE LITTLE SCHOOLHOUSE."
Just below the picture in even larger letters was the command:
"STAND BY IT!"[1]

The accompanying article explained that this was the beginning of
a political campaign to elect Republicans William D. Hoard and
Lorenzo Dow Harvey to the offices of governor and superintendent
of public instruction and so prevent the Democrats from repealing, as
they had promised to do, a recently enacted law that made both the
teaching of the English language and school attendance compulsory
in all Wisconsin elementary schools. Buttons, badges, and additional
sketches of the little schoolhouse were to be sent to newspapers across
the state. "Hoard and the Little School House," the article said, "will
be the watchword of the campaign which will be the most memorable
in the history of Wisconsin."[2]

No one could truthfully say that Republican superintendents of
public instruction had always looked as benignly upon the little one-
room schoolhouse as the picture implied. Quite the opposite, in fact.
But there was nothing more likely to capture the attention of the
Wisconsin voters or to induce them to vote Republican than the suggestion that a vote for the Republicans was a vote for the little schoolhouse.

Among those city residents were many for whom that sketch evoked hallowed memories of their own days in the country school. In that picture they could see themselves once more playing fox-and-geese in the schoolyard on a winter's day or sleighing down the long schoolhouse hill; and they could remember first loves, spelldowns, poems memorized, and books read. But beyond that, the "little schoolhouse" was a symbol of so much that Midwesterners held dear—individualism, democracy, and their faith in the power of education to improve their children's lives and even to take them to the White House. "Who can pass a district school," wrote Vachel Lindsay, the quintessential Midwestern poet,

> Without the hope that there may wait
> Some baby-heart the books shall flame
> With zeal to make his playmates great,
> To make the whole wide village gleam
> A strangely carved celestial gem,
> Eternal in its beauty-light,
> The Artist's town of Bethlehem![3]

Moreover, in all America there was, perhaps, no better symbol of the shared community life people remembered than the one-room schoolhouse standing in the center of an independent school district on the Middle Border. From first to last that schoolhouse represented a community enterprise. The people of the district had voted for its construction, picked the place where it would stand, and controlled its use when it was completed. At one stage or another of this process, they had, in most cases, even fought over it as families fight; yet it belonged to all the district's families, and because it was their own, most people in the community were interested in what took place there.

At the first school meeting of any newly formed district on the Middle Border, the first order of business was to elect officers; the second was to approve the building of a schoolhouse; and the third was to choose the site where the new schoolhouse would sit.

For this last the farmers had reams of advice, composed in the course of a day's work by public school men. The site should slope gently toward the road for natural drainage, they said; it should be healthy and convenient; it should have a sunny exposure and natural beauty; and it should be large—an acre or so—and so situated that none of the district's children should have to walk more than a mile and a half to school.[4]

But it is doubtful that many farmers ever read any of the learned essays on the subject before they chose the place where they would build their school. They were far more likely to be governed by practical than by theoretical considerations.

Common sense dictated that the schoolhouse should be built as near the district's center as possible, and, if there were no extenuating circumstances, the farmers did build their schoolhouses there. But in the vast majority of Midwestern school districts in the 1870s and '80s, when thousands of schoolhouses were being built, many a small schoolhouse came to sit where it sat not because it was centrally located but because of other considerations, which frequently delayed the building and led to community fights that left bitter memories long afterward.

There were problems in selecting schoolhouse sites in the rural Midwest that the theorists never thought of as they wrote their pamphlets in the quiet of their studies. What could be done, for example, with the influential farmer who demanded that the schoolhouse be built close to his farm? If the district yielded to his request, it might mean that the location of the schoolhouse would be skewed to one side of the district or the other. But if his demands were ignored he might petition for a new district, leave the old, and take with him a large amount of taxable property the district could ill afford to lose.

There was also the problem of choosing a school site for a district that lay between two townships, a joint or fractional district, as it was called. Because each township wanted the schoolhouse to sit within its boundaries, township rivalries were added to personal rivalries to bring confusion and delay to the site selection. And finally, the cost had to be considered. The good school sites located in the heart of the district and recommended by the experts were often priced beyond the reach of the farmers, and the location of the little schoolhouses Lord Bryce saw as he toured the Midwest in the 1880s probably had more to do with the price of the site than the desire of the farmers to put one at each crossroads.[5]

Repeatedly the educational experts warned the farmers against selecting a site merely because it was cheap. But the farmers, not the experts, had to pay for their schoolhouse grounds, and hundreds of little one-room schoolhouses were built upon rocky hills or swampy bottoms, which were useless for farming, because such sites were all the farmers thought they could afford.[6]

Joint District 9 of Dunn Township in Dane County, Wisconsin, was no exception to the usual practice of expediency in selecting a schoolhouse site. This little district lay half in Dunn and half in Blooming Grove townships, and the first district meeting was at a farmhouse near the border of the two townships one October evening in 1868. They immediately elected a school board and then voted to build a schoolhouse on a plot of ground in Blooming Grove Township. But there were objections, apparently from the Dunn Township farmers, and the vote for the Blooming Grove site was quickly reconsidered. But when another vote was taken and that, too, resulted in the selection of the Blooming Grove site, the farmers agreed to suspend the meeting and to inspect a nearby site in Dunn Township that belonged to a prominent farmer named Cristian Uphoff. The newly elected school board was ordered to report its findings to the meeting.

So the farmers, or at least a part of them, tramped out into the night to look at Uphoff's land, and when they returned, the school board declared Uphoff's property to be suitable. Whereupon the farmers once again reconsidered their selection of the Blooming Grove site and voted to build their schoolhouse in Dunn Township on the Uphoff land, where it was to remain through the years.

What had happened out there in the darkness to cause the school board to recommend and the farmers to accept the Dunn Township site when they had twice voted for the Blooming Grove location? Very likely it was the discovery that Uphoff was willing to give his half-acre of ground to the district for virtually nothing. It was an offer, typical of many, that had something in it for everyone. The cheap land reduced the cost of the schoolhouse and lightened the district's burden; the site did happen to be near the center of the district; and for his generosity, Uphoff got a schoolhouse near his farm, which would thereafter be known as the Uphoff School.[7]

Locating the site of a school district's first schoolhouse was usually troublesome, but it was less so than choosing another site for the second schoolhouse when that became necessary, as it usually did.

By the 1880s, many of the little schools that had been standing since the 1850s were wearing out and had to be either repaired or abandoned. Besides this, many changes had taken place in the districts that made the old schools unsuitable. Until well into the 1880s and even into the '90s in most states of the area, farmers kept moving into the small school districts, either taking up new land or buying portions of the larger farms there and building new homes. This altered the pattern of homes in the districts, so that the old schoolhouses were no longer either in the center of population or large enough to take care of the increased number of children.

When this happened, a group of farmers, usually the more enter-prising, or perhaps those most injured by the changes, petitioned the school board to call a special meeting. Forced to act, the school board would post notices. "'Notice is hereby given," the sign would read, "to voters of School District No. 2 that a Special meeting is hereby called at the school house, Monday, July 15th at 7 o'clock for the purpose of voting on building a new schoolhouse."[8]

Such notices stirred heated controversies in the small independent school districts. Supporters and opponents of the proposal quickly took sides, and the fight over the question of whether or not to build a new schoolhouse on another site could last for months and even years.

Very often those who opposed the plan did so more because it called for a change of school sites rather than because it proposed the building of a new schoolhouse, and much more than nostalgia for the old site lay behind their objections. For some parents, at least, the change of sites meant not only that their children would have to walk farther to school, but also suggested in a subtle way their loss of prestige in the community. So the new site became an emotional issue, and opponents of the change attended the special school meetings grimly determined to prevent the change of sites by whatever means were available to them.

In the early 1860s a few farmers in District 3, Blooming Grove, began trying to rouse interest in building a new schoolhouse. The need was obvious, for the old building had been built in 1853 and measured only 16 by 18 feet. But the majority of the farmers rejected the proposal in 1863, and the idea was largely forgotten. Then, in 1868, apparently after thinking the matter over for five years, the farmers approved a proposal to build a new schoolhouse on a site a quarter of a mile to the west of where the old school stood.

But even though the majority had approved and the new site was not far from the old, there were objections to the change and nothing was immediately done. Finally, after another year had passed, the opponents of the new site called for a special meeting and attempted to reverse the decision. But they were too late. The majority had made up their minds. They rejected the motion to reverse the decision and then voted all over again to build a schoolhouse on the new site and to raise $700 for the project. This decision, like that in Joint District 9, Dunn Township, was made palatable, and probably possible, when George M. Nichols, whose two-hundred-acre farm lay along the shore of Lake Monona, and for whom the school was named, offered to donate the land for the new schoolhouse.[9]

The special school meetings in which farmers hammered out their disagreements over the building of a new schoolhouse and a change of site were protracted long beyond the farmers' bedtime, for every man must have his say. When the farmers at the Hicks School in District 1, Pennfield Township, met on January 3, 1870, to consider building a new schoolhouse on a new site, they had to listen to interminable arguments over the merits of the proposition and even to reminiscences by one of the pioneers about how the old school had been built twenty years earlier. Finally, "after much talk from everybody," as the clerk reported, the farmers did vote to build a new schoolhouse on property owned by William Hicks. For one acre of ground that included a well, the district had to pay only $100.[10]

The land was a bargain at that price, but eight of the twenty-five farmers present objected to the change of sites, and even though they were in an obvious minority, they continued to oppose the plan through two more special meetings. In the last of these, as a final effort, they forced the farmers to vote again on the change of sites on the grounds that the ballot taken at the first meeting was illegal. But those who favored the change were out in force and overwhelmed the opposition by a vote of twenty-eight to seven.[11]

II

The change in school sites, however, was only one of two major problems that troubled the farmers who contemplated building a second schoolhouse. The other, of course, was the cost of the new building.

In some parts of the broad Middle West, particularly in the flourishing counties in Nebraska and Kansas in the late 1860s and early '70s, the farmers sometimes rushed into their building programs with less caution than was generally characteristic of them. Optimism on the plains was high in those years, and country schoolhouses were rising like sunflowers on the prairie as the farmers in the most prosperous areas vied with one another to build the finest schoolhouse. "Surrounded, as we are, with States deeply in earnest in the cause of education," the Nebraska state superintendent wrote in 1872, "and under the inspiration of a salubrious climate, and the heritage of a soil of inexhaustible fertility, the people in many parts of our State, with an enthusiasm almost amounting to a phrensy, are bending all their energies toward erecting school houses, many of which would do honor to any city in our country. There is, at present, an intensity of feeling on this subject that has seldom, if ever, been witnessed in any other state."[12]

Unfortunately, some of the building programs, like that in District 40, in Saunders County, turned out to be more than the eager farmers had bargained for.

In a euphoric mood, the farmers at the Eureka School in District 40 voted unanimously in 1873 to raise $700 to build their schoolhouse and promised to pay off the debt over a five-year period. But then came the panic of 1873, followed by several bad years. This left the little district in such bad financial straits that when in their annual meeting of April, 1875, those present approved a tax of twenty-two mills on the dollar in order to keep up the payments on the debt, there was an instant protest. The new tax was more than the debt-ridden farmers could bear, and one month later, at a specially called meeting, the majority in the district voted to rescind the tax set at the annual meeting and to raise a tax of only three mills. For two years after this the district paid nothing on its loan, and only after 1877, when another special meeting was called, partly at the instigation of the creditor, did the farmers again begin paying on their indebtedness.[13]

But District 40's case was exceptional, not so much perhaps because of its default, but because of the amount they were willing to spend for their school at the time and because of the unanimity of the decision to build a new schoolhouse. Almost never did the farmers of any independent school district agree unanimously about anything, to say nothing of a building program that was to cost a great amount of money. Normally, even supporters of a new schoolhouse worried about its cost.

Most farmers knew, of course, that they could not pay for a new schoolhouse all at once and that they would have to sell bonds, or "bond the district," as they said, to raise the money. Their natural fear was that the district would go so deeply in debt and taxes would be so high that in the event of some calamity—a crop failure, perhaps, or low farm prices, realities with which they always lived—they would not be able to pay their taxes and their property would be in jeopardy.

Moreover, the debt they were asked to assume was very real to them. Unlike their urban descendants, whose community debt was shared by thousands of unknown people and arranged for by a nameless bureaucrat, the farmers' school debt was neither remote nor impersonal. When they voted to give the school board the right to sell bonds, the debt resulting was more like a personal obligation, the cost of which they could almost figure in their heads. So it was not surprising that when the time came to vote for or against the building of a new schoolhouse, there would inevitably be those who would oppose it; nor is it hard to understand their reasons.

On the other hand, the motives of those who were willing to incur a debt to build a new schoolhouse when the old one might have been repaired are more difficult to fathom. Some, of course, would be helped by the change of sites; and community pressure to vote "for progress" might have influenced others to go along. Competition with other districts and community pride were both factors which must have had some bearing on their decision. Their debates were not recorded, but in the motions they supported and the procedures they followed to push their program, there was a confident, upbeat spirit that reflected a faith in the value of education and a determination to give their children the best they could.

Whatever the motives of the two groups, those who chose to fight the building program were formidable antagonists. They could, with some reason, argue that the second schoolhouse, unlike the first, was a luxury, not a necessity; that the old schoolhouse was adequate for their needs; and that if it were not, it could be repaired. Often they were well versed in the school law and knew how to delay matters by asking for special meetings or by challenging the legality of meetings as they did in Elba Township, Dodge County, Wisconsin, at the Austin School in the summer of 1889.

The early summer there that year had been extremely wet. By late June the grain was already beginning to lodge, and the weeds were getting a head start on the farmers because the ground was too wet to work. But the weather was not bad enough to prevent a group of farmers from considering the district's need to do something about their schoolhouse. Early in July they asked the school board to call a special meeting to vote on whether to repair the old school-house or build a new one, and on July 15, just as the wheat harvest was beginning, the busy farmers met at the old schoolhouse to decide the issue.

As the evening meeting progressed, however, it was clear that the sponsors of the meeting fully intended to build a new schoolhouse instead of repairing the old one, for they had come with a set of plans for the new building in hand. And when their proposal was approved, the plans for the new building were also agreed upon, and a building committee was elected.

But not all the district's farmers approved this somewhat hasty action. District 2 was divided between Catholics and Protestants, a fact which may have been related in some way to the ensuing disagreement. Protestants had apparently been the ones to petition the school board for the meeting. But the opposition seemed principally to be to the decision to build a new schoolhouse rather than to repair the old, and possibly came from the realization that those behind the call for the special meeting had never really intended asking the meeting merely to repair the building.

For whatever reason, there were hard feelings in the little community, and another special meeting, called in early September to discuss the project further, ended in failure when the enemies of the building program charged that the notice of the meeting had been incorrectly given and that the meeting was illegal. Besides that, a member of the school board, Edward Murphy, who had just been elected for a three-year term a month and a half before, resigned, apparently in anger, as did the building committee without giving any reason for doing so. Finally, as a kind of footnote to the rising tempers, a motion to adjourn without setting a date for another meeting was not voted upon, and the meeting simply disintegrated, leaving the disgruntled farmers to go home and ponder the problem.

The supporters of the plan to build the new schoolhouse were so upset by this turn of events that they carried the notice of the next special meeting around the entire district. Back and forth across the Crawfish River and up toward Danville they went through the early part of September, asking the farmers and their families to sign their names to the notice as proof that they had seen it. All together, some sixty-eight names were attached to the notice, so that when the farmers gathered at the old schoolhouse on the evening of September 16, no one could challenge the legality of the meeting by charging that notice of it had not been given.

This was the end of the line for those who had opposed building the new schoolhouse. By secret ballot, twenty-two of the twenty-eight farmers present voted to borrow $550 for the new schoolhouse and to authorize the school board to pay six per cent interest on the loan. They also agreed to raise $150 in taxes to pay on the loan that year and another $150 each year until the loan was paid.[14]

The farmers in the Austin district had decided rather quickly to build a new schoolhouse, but, generally speaking, Midwestern farmers could not be rushed into building a second schoolhouse. Sometimes it was said of them that their first reaction to any new proposition was to say no, and that was usually their response to the first suggestion that the district build a new schoolhouse. That had been the answer the farmers had given to the proposition in Blooming Grove, District 3, in 1863, and it was the same reaction the farmers in Michigan gave when the subject was first approached at the Sanford School in District 5 in Woodstock Township.

Near the close of the annual meeting in September of 1880 in District 5, almost casually it seemed, a motion was passed to call a special meeting in November to vote on raising money for a new schoolhouse. Obviously this surprised many of the district's farmers, most of whom had probably not attended the meeting and heard of the proposal only from neighbors as the news spread quickly through the community. Their reaction, in any case, was direct and prompt. They demanded a special meeting, and within eight days following the annual meeting, they had met, overturned the decision to consider building a new schoolhouse in November, and voted to raise $10.00 to repair the old one. Two years later they were still trying to repair their schoolhouse and had paid Schooley Wilgus, whose farm lay nearby, $24.75 to do the work.[15]

Throughout the Middle Border this was often the reaction of the thrifty hard-pressed farmers to proposals to build a new schoolhouse, and very often as far as some districts ever went. Year after year in the 1870s the farmers at the Tri-County School in Joint District 1 of Koshkonong Township voted a little here and a little there to repair their schoolhouse, and once, in 1881, voted $200 for major repairs. But they would not build a new schoolhouse.[16]

It was different in Woodstock District 5, however. In December of 1883, after taking two years to get used to the idea, the farmers there did vote to build a new schoolhouse on a new site "as near the centre of the District" as they could find the ground.[17]

Normally a vote to build a new schoolhouse and select another site touched off a series of motions to provide for financing the construction, adopting building plans, selling the old schoolhouse and privies, setting the dates for the beginning and completion of the building, and appointing or electing a building committee to take charge of the project, and the farmers in District 5 followed that pattern. "Voted that all the material be on the ground by the first day of April, 1884," ran the minutes of their special meeting. "Said house to be completed by the first of October 1884. . . . Voted that the Building Committee be composed of Lewis Sanford, F. R. Pearson and J. L. Lewis," and so on until all, or nearly all, eventualities, including the financing, had been provided for in writing.[18]

Ultimately, of course, the project rested upon the district's ability to sell its bonds and raise the money for the building, and many a farmer, knowing how hard it was for him to borrow money and the exorbitant interest he must pay, must have wondered even as he voted for a new schoolhouse where the district could get the money it needed at the rate of interest it could afford. Surprisingly, in view of the apparent poverty of the farmers in so many of the little school districts, the money was usually borrowed from the people living within the districts themselves. At the Eureka School in Nebraska the money was obtained from a member of the school board, and in both the Sanford School in Michigan and the Austin School in Wisconsin, it was borrowed from women whose families lived in the district. Generally the money was borrowed, as it was in the Austin School, for six per cent interest, and the district usually agreed to pay it back within three or four years.[19]

In the 1880s, when so many schoolhouses were being built, the amount the farmers borrowed usually ranged from five to seven hundred dollars, but this, of course, depended upon their building plans, and these, too, were often approved at the same special meeting in which they voted to build the new schoolhouse.

III

To design their schoolhouse the farmers had at their disposal an enormous amount of information churned out by the educational specialists. Even before the Civil War, James Johonnot, a Missouri educator, had written a widely known book on the building and architecture of one-room schoolhouses, and for three decades or more following the Civil War, the reports of the Midwestern state superintendents were filled with information on the subject. In 1880 the commissioner of education added to the literature by commissioning a prominent Boston architect to write a treatise on rural school architecture. This document, published in that year, came complete with sketches of beautiful schools that had two or three doors, decorated cornices, spires, and elaborate ventilating systems. There were even plans for utilizing a gardener to take care of the grounds![20]

But nearly all such plans, although beautifully drawn and expertly explained, were so out of touch with the plain life of the Midwestern farmers and so far beyond their means that they were ignored as completely as the information on site selection.

The farmers of the Middle West were builders themselves after a fashion and had their own ideas of what schoolhouses should look like and what they could afford. So they drew their own plans or copied one another's, which was probably the reason for the similarity of their schoolhouses. Enthusiasts among them often came to the special meetings with the plans in hand, ready to present them the moment the project was approved.

They had no blueprints, of course. Their plans were simply scribbled on a piece of paper. But they could be elaborate nonetheless. The plans for the schoolhouse in Subdistrict 1 of Scott Township in Henry County, Iowa, ran to six legal-size pages. But regardless of their length, when they were read and the specifications given for the upper and lower joists, studs, box sills, window lights, shingles that stood five inches to the weather, rafter plates, and posts so many feet high, the farmers seemed to know exactly what was meant, and they would vote on the plans step by step, as they did at Woodstock, District 5. "Voted to Build new School house," began the minutes of their special meeting in 1883. "Voted that said house shall be 24 by 34 outside with 12 foot ceiling. . . . Voted that the house shall be seated with patent seats. Voted that the said house be ceiled [sic] as high as the bottom windows & plaster the rest. Voted that the building committee put in such an entry as they see fit. Voted that the floor shall be of hard wood."[21]

Many of the procedures were prescribed by law, but much was left to the common sense of the farmers themselves, and how they managed depended more on the community than upon the laws. Some districts turned many of the details of construction over to their building committees. In others, such as Woodstock, District 5, the farmers controlled the construction so tightly that when the building committee ran into difficulty over the school entry, another special meeting had to be called and a vote taken to reduce the length of the building by four feet in order to build "such an entry on the outside as presented in the plans drawn at this meeting."[22]

Such changes in plans frequently had to be made, and as the project progressed there were other decisions to make. Was a well to be dug at the new site? Should a fence be built around the new schoolhouse? And should they build new privies, or move the old ones from the old site to the new? All these matters had to be discussed and voted upon in specially called meetings, and some districts might call the farmers to four or five such meetings before the schoolhouse was completed. But few building committees or school boards in the Midwestern country districts would dare make important decisions without consulting their constituencies. Often there was trouble enough, particularly between the building committees and the school boards who were sometimes jealous of one another's prerogatives, without running the risk of creating additional unpleasantness by making decisions without the consent of the district.

In the meantime, the actual construction of the building would be under way. This might take only a month or as long as six months and even longer. In Osborne County, Kansas, District 65 began building its schoolhouse in May of 1883 and finished in early June. And above Wisconsin's Sugar River in District 3 of Montrose Township, when the farmers voted in late August of 1878 to build a new schoolhouse, they specified that it should be completed in time for the winter term of school, which would mean that they were allotting about two months for the construction.

But it often took longer than this to build the country schoolhouse on the Middle Border, for construction was frequently more complicated than might have appeared to an observer who happened to pass the building site on a summer's afternoon. Excavations had to be made for the foundation, and a small armada of wagons had to carry the building material to the site, often from a considerable distance. In the winter of 1884 all the building material and all the rock needed to build the schoolhouse in Subdistrict 1, Scott Township, had to be carried either from the depot at Winfield, Iowa, or from the quarry near that town over a lengthy route to the building site. And during the spring of 1884, nearly $360 worth of lumber, shingles, nails, flooring, windows, and paint were carted out to the hollow on Jennie Sanford's farm where the new schoolhouse for District 5, Woodstock, was to sit. Much of this material had to be brought from Brooklyn, some fifteen miles from the site.[23]

Furthermore, construction itself was a slow, laborious process in that handicraft age and was usually undertaken by only two or three men. The district farmers in the 1880s did not normally build their schoolhouses themselves, as they had built the log schools before the Civil War. Instead they gave this job to the lowest bidder. The contractor who received the bid might be a farmer as well as a builder, and he might or might not live in the district. Whatever the case, it was his responsibility to build in a "substantial and workmanlike manner," as his contract said, and to finish the building within the time specified in his contract.[24]

Usually the work lasted through the summer months, and the farmers coming and going in their fields and along the road could see their schoolhouse taking shape day by day. But when it was finally completed it resembled only coincidentally the plans and recommendations worked out so carefully by school officials.

IV

The typical Midwestern one-room schoolhouse looked very much like a child's drawing of a house. Except in Indiana, where there were a large number of brick schoolhouses, it was a rectangular frame structure, almost invariably painted white, with three windows on each of its longer sides, one door squarely in the middle of its shorter side, and a small belfry directly above the door.

Ideally, it was supposed to sit with its windowless front wall to the west so the light streaming through the windows from the north and south would strike the children's desks at the proper angle. But the direction the schoolhouse actually faced depended less on this ideal arrangement than on the direction of the road that ran past the building. If it sat on the west side of a north-south road, then, indeed, the schoolhouse might face west. But if the road that ran by it was an east-west road, the building probably faced north or south, whichever way would allow its door to open on the road, for it was almost a natural law in the rural Midwest that the schoolhouse door open upon the road.[25]

Then there was the problem of ventilation. A Midwestern school official once suggested that the farmer's knowledge of lighting and ventilating was limited to the rule that fire produces heat and windows give light, and the one-room schoolhouse seemed to confirm the charge. The usual three windows on each side of the building gave light and also cross-ventilation in the warm months. But in spite of pleas of specialists, the farmers rarely provided a system that would ventilate their school in winter by bringing fresh air in through the stove, and in thousands of one-room schools students soon exhausted the good air when the schoolhouse was buttoned up against the winter. Of the 12,859 schoolhouses reported on in Illinois between 1884 and 1886, eighty per cent had no other means of ventilation than by the doors and windows.[26]

Nor was the schoolhouse stove in the prescribed position. According to one theorist, if the schoolhouse were properly located with its solid front wall to the west, the schoolhouse chimney should be built into the northwest part of the front wall, and the stove should sit near the chimney at the front of the room near the north wall. This would eliminate the necessity of having a long stovepipe to connect with a stove sitting in another part of the room and would warm the building's coldest wall.[27]

But the farmers seldom tested this theory, which, in fact, may not have been very good. Most often the chimneys were built into that end of the building opposite the door, and the stove, connected to the chimney by a long stovepipe that ran along the ceiling, stood in the center of the room, where the farmers supposed it would heat the room most evenly, or near the back, where the fuel box was.

Occasionally the farmers did add a few ornamental designs to the outside. The contract for the schoolhouse in Subdistrict 1 in Scott Township, for example, called for the construction of elaborate cornices and a "crown mould and bud mould frieze." But this was somewhat pretentious for most country-school districts, and the customary exterior was as plain as the people who planned it.[28]

So the country schoolhouse on the Middle Border was no architect's dream, but it was a monument to community enterprise, or lack of it, and its appearance was one measure of the district's interest in education. Built with the participation of all the people, it had cost the farmers their time and money and sometimes friendships, but it had also forced them to consider the problem of education and measure its worth in ways not possible for succeeding generations of Americans.

Standing there beside a country road, the Midwestern country schoolhouse presented an honest, unpretentious, but durable face to the world, as though it could stand the worst that weather, children, and farmers could do to it. Perhaps, in some remote way, it owed something architecturally to the Greek Revival in building that spread across the Middle Border in company with the struggle for free public education before the Civil War. In any case, it was a model of symmetry. If there were three eight-pane windows on one side of the building, there must be three eight-pane windows on the other. And not until the early twentieth century, when the third generation of country schools was being built, could the architects persuade the farmers to move the door to one corner of the building or the other in order to take advantage of the sunlight. The schoolhouse door had to be directly opposite the front wall. Any other arrangement would have not only cost more, but ruined the symmetry the farmers seemed to prize.[29]

Those more sophisticated might have called the little one-room schoolhouse "functional," so well adapted was it to the farmers' needs and to the life style of Midwestern farm families. It was no threatening, prisonlike building spreading two or three stories tall across a city block. In some ways it was merely an extension of the rural child's home. It was not large enough to intimidate shy farm children who were attending school for the first time, and the familiarity of its appointments helped make them feel comfortable and secure. The wainscoting around the walls up to the window sills, the plastered walls above the wainscoting, and the clothes closets with hooks for coats and caps were not much different from what the children were likely to see in their homes. The four straight rows of patented seats, which had replaced the homemade variety in most schools by the 1880s and were a proud sign of progress, were unfamiliar to the newcomers, of course, as were the teacher's desk upon its platform and the blackboards around the room. But the quiet mixture of the familiar with the new, and older brothers and sisters seated about the room, helped subdue the anxieties of the first day in school and provided a better learning situation for beginners than might have been supposed.[30]

V

On the Middle Border, the one-room country schoolhouse was more than a school. Often the only public building in the neighborhood, it gave the community its identity, so that farmers might say they lived in the Gravel Hill District, or the Eureka District, or whatever the name of their schoolhouse might be.

More than that, it served as a social center. On Sunday it was likely to be a church, on Wednesday evening the Grange hall, on election day the polling place, and so on. "Last night there was a Pop meeting at the school house," wrote a reporter in Osborne County, Kansas, in 1894, when Populism was on the rise, "and was attended by a fair sized audience.... They [the speakers] told us that the rich were getting richer and the poor, poorer, and Smith talked about the fall of Babylon, Rome, etc. until the audience was about to fall—asleep." And at Gravel Hill, La Prairie, District 2, they tethered their horses in the big barn below the schoolhouse and hurried up the hill to the warm room before the curtains, which were only bedsheets, opened on the Christmas play. Again and again during the year, the one-room building was filled with farm people who had come to watch a spelldown or participate in those frequently staged debates that made shambles of the myth about inarticulate farmers.[31]

Sometimes the crowds at such functions were larger than the little schools could accommodate. "The debate in the stone schoolhouse last evening was attended by more people than could be seated," the reporter from Convis Township in Calhoun County, Michigan, wrote in 1886. "The question for decision was, 'Resolved that the horse is of more benefit to makind than steam.' The decision was in favor of the affirmative. Next Saturday evening the question discussed will be 'Resolved that the term of the office for the President of the United States should be extended to six years and no person be allowed to hold the office but one term.' "[32]

Requests to use the schoolhouse for events unrelated to school activities were usually made to members of the school board who had been given the authority to decide upon such matters at the annual meetings. Usually the use of the schoolhouse could be had for any public function, for it was, after all, a community hall. But this was not always so. In this as in all things related to their school, the district farmers had the final say, and it was not unusual for someone to question the use of the schoolhouse for a particular purpose, thereby leading to a wild dispute over who could and could not use the building.

Should the Democrats be allowed to have a political meeting in the schoolhouse? The Republicans? Or the Populists? And should the Baptists be allowed to hold church services there? Or the Presbyterians? The debate on such questions could last for weeks, and in the end there might have to be a special school meeting where it might be decided that neither a political party nor a church group could use the schoolhouse. Such decisions limited the use of the schoolhouse as a community center, of course, but that was the price some communities had to pay for peace and participatory democracy.[33]

As the years passed the farmers improved their schoolhouses in ways that marked not only their advancing prosperity but their civilization as well. For one thing, they began to pay more attention to the privy problem.

One of the peculiarities of the farmers in many of the small Midwestern independent school districts was their apparent indifference to toilet facilities. In his reminiscences, a California educator recalled that in neither of the two country schools in Ohio in which he had received most of his early education had there been a toilet. There was, he remembered, a general understanding, never violated to his knowledge, that the boys should use one part of the nearby woods and the girls another. Similar accommodations must have prevailed at the Uphoff School in its early years, for not until 1875, some six years after the beginning of the school, did the farmers provide privies for their children.[34]

Quite often the farmers supplied their schools with one privy but not two, which was in some ways worse than having none at all, for it offered a tempting opportunity to the larger boys to commandeer it at

75

recess time and allow no one else to use it. In the 1884–86 survey of country schools in Illinois there were 1,740 schools that had but one outhouse, and 1,180 that had none at all.[35]

Possibly this apathy toward building a "place of retirement," as it was delicately referred to, was left over from the primitive frontier conditions when for the most part there were no outdoor toilets. But even in later years, farmers had only one privy on their farms, and perhaps they could not see, until the state superintendents of public instruction pointed them out, the immoral consequences rising from the fact that boys and girls used the same privy or had none at all.

But by the 1890s much time was being spent on building privies or repairing old ones, making certain that there were two and these at respectable distances from each other. Efforts were also being made to clean them periodically and to provide screens of one kind or another, which was perhaps the final acknowledgment of the victory of Victorian morals.[36]

The school grounds, too, came in for their share of attention as the farmers' fortunes improved, and district after district voted to fence in their schoolyards and beautify them with shade trees. This beautification program received a tremendous assist from the Arbor Day movement that began in Nebraska in 1872 and made its way east across the Middle Border until every North Central state had made some provision for its schoolchildren to plant a tree on their school ground on Arbor Day. Usually the planting was accompanied by a program, for it was a learning as well as a physical exercise, and many a country schoolchild had to memorize the words to "Woodman, Spare That Tree," or "What do we plant when we plant a tree? / We plant the ship that will cross the sea," as the price of the outdoor festivities.[37]

The rising tide of nationalism that swept the country in the 1890s also had an effect on the appearance of the country school and the schoolyard. In 1892 Francis Bellamy, Baptist minister and editor of the *Youth's Companion,* wrote the pledge of allegiance and set off a flurry of flag buying and flagpole raisings in thousands of little districts across the Middle Border, so that for a time the minutes of the annual meetings ran black with motions to purchase a flag and flagpole. In 1896 in the little school of District 3, Montrose Township, south of Belleville in Dane County, Wisconsin, the farmers were able to restrain their enthusiasm and voted to purchase a flag no larger than three by five feet; but the year before, at the Uphoff School in the same county, the farmers voted not only to buy a "six foot bunting flag staff," but to invite Cristian Uphoff to raise the flag for the first time.[38]

In these years the flag was also being moved inside the schoolroom, which increasingly was being decorated to teach patriotism, history, and the middle-class virtues of perseverance and success. The interior of the Maple Grove School, District 8 in Berrien Township, Berrien County, Michigan, in 1887, was a typical example of how the schoolroom itself could be made to support the Midwesterners' values. On the front wall, visible to all as they entered, hung George Washington's picture, and next to it a huge "welcome" sign. On the left wall, written in large letters above the draped American flag, was the assurance that "Punctuality Brings Its Own Rewards," and prominently displayed behind the teacher's desk was the Ordinance of 1787.[39]

Besides adding pictures and mottoes, the farmers took more time as the years went by to clean their schoolhouses, and this, too, was done in part to teach a lesson. "There is scarcely a sounder principle of pedagogy," a committee studying country schools in the 1890s reported, "than that care begets care; order, order; cleanliness, cleanliness; and beauty, beauty." So as cleanliness began to be taught along with the three R's, the farmers not only spruced up their schoolhouses, but purchased toilet articles for the children. "We have everything very convenient," an eleven-year-old Kansas girl wrote in 1893. "We have a mirror, comb, towels, and a washbasin."[40]

And there were other additions that suggested that the old days of uneasy poverty were disappearing. Shades for the windows were purchased, and rope bells to ring out across the countryside calling the children to school were raised to newly constructed belfries. Sometimes new bracket kerosene lamps of the kind that sold at Montgomery Ward for $2.75 in the 1890s were bought for the schoolroom walls. Here and there organs were donated by the wealthier farmers. In the early 1890s some families at the Hicks School took up a collection to buy a ninety-dollar Victrola.[41]

More and more frequently, interested people were holding entertainments at the schools to raise money for those things the people had always been too poor, or too saving, to buy. A box social held at the Tri-County School in 1918 netted $17.60, which was used to buy a bubbler or a water fountain, a foot scraper and brush, and even a burlap curtain.[42]

Perhaps more significantly, greater attention was paid to the school libraries, too, as the old century moved toward the new. For years most Middle Border states had encouraged school districts and townships alike to have libraries. Wisconsin even had a provision in her constitution providing for the encouragement of libraries, and her first school law made it possible for township officers to establish library funds. But neither this law nor those that followed it could force the districts to buy books, and, poor as they were, so little was done that in 1878 the state superintendent of schools wrote that only 328 districts had reported having libraries that year. "It is fearful to think," he wrote, "how many thousands of our young people are growing up without the means at hand to become acquainted with our living works in history, biography, travel, science, and practical arts, and the great themes of life."[43]

But even in the 1880s times were changing on the Middle Border. The little Sanford School, District 5, Woodstock, had a library by 1882 and at the annual meeting that year began appointing librarians to take charge of it. This library was left in the homes of the librarians and for years moved about from home to home as the different librarians were appointed. But in 1897 there was a vote to leave the library in the schoolhouse, and in the late 1890s the library money began to be used for the purpose for which it was intended instead of for operating expenses, as had been done for so long. By the end of the century the school had among its books one on temperance called *Disenthralled: A Story of My Life;* Fleetwood's *Life of Christ,* which cost the district $1.50 and which the librarian thought was "just splendid"; and *The Life and Travels of General Grant.*[44]

In some schools, such as the Uphoff School, the libraries outgrew their shelf space, and new bookcases had to be built for them. In District 9, Fulton Township, Rock County, Wisconsin, the little library was so popular that the librarian began an elaborate system of checking books in and out, and in other rural communities of the Midwest as well, the small one-room schoolhouse served as the town library, just as it had served as a church and community center.[45]

By the end of the nineteenth century some districts were building their third generation of one-room schoolhouses, and now at last the architects were able the alter the building style. But for the most part the first and second schoolhouses continued to be used. Many of them were in need of repair, and in the late 1890s and early 1900s much of the time of the annual meetings was spent debating motions to raise the money. As usual, there were differences of opinion. But the arguments seemed less heated than they once had been, and much that had formerly been worked out in detail in the annual meeting was left up to those pillars in the community whom the farmers had elected to their school boards.

5
Educators in Overalls

❦

I

ON THE AFTERNOON OF THURSDAY, JULY 27, 1893, IN THE SOLOMON
River country in Osborne County, Kansas, a little group of homesteaders assembled at their schoolhouse in District 37 for their annual
school meeting. Outside the air was fresh and clear. The rain that had
fallen on Tuesday night and early Wednesday morning had
brightened the pasture that lay to the west of the schoolhouse, and the
weeds along the road had taken on a new life from the night's wetting.
A mile to the east of the schoolhouse the little village of Downs over-
flowed with some five thousand people who had come there to cele-
brate the town's fourteenth anniversary. But along the dirt road that
ran in front of the little schoolhouse and stretched south to meet the
main road running east into Downs, there was little to distract the
homesteaders as the meeting was called to order, the reports were
read and accepted, and the farmers prepared to elect a district treasurer for the next three years.[1]

The first ballot made it clear that there would be a struggle for the
position among three neighbors—Henry Ise, Albert Worley, and
August Juencke. The second ballot was indecisive, and so was the third.
Finally, when the contest had narrowed to Ise and Juencke, Henry
Ise, for whom the school was named and whose farmhouse lay across
the pasture a quarter of a mile or so to the northwest of the schoolhouse, was elected.[2]

For Ise and the other farmers gathered there that day, the future
looked especially grim. The summer had been hot and dry and
whether Tuesday's rain would be enough to save what was left of the
corn crop was a question. Worse still, the stock market had collapsed

79

in May, the nation had plunged into a financial panic, and farm prices were tumbling. The market price for number 2 wheat was quoted in Downs that day at fifty cents a bushel and corn at twenty-five cents. With good reason, the farmers in the little Ise schoolhouse voted to have only six months of school that year.[3]

But the farmers here and across the Middle Border had been through it all before, and no matter the panic or crop failure, annual school meetings, like the one in District 37, were held on schedule throughout the region that spring and summer. For even if they must reduce their school budgets, it went without saying that their children must go to school and that they must elect men to run the schools.

As if there were some magic in the number three, all Midwestern states except Indiana and parts of Iowa provided for the election of district school boards composed of three men, one elected each year for a three-year term. The titles of these officials varied from state to state, but whatever they were called, their duties were much the same. Each board had a clerk to record the minutes of the annual school meetings and to make various reports, a moderator to chair the meetings, and a treasurer to collect and disburse the district's money and to make a financial report at the annual district meeting.

But these were only their more conspicuous duties. Most of their work, which was done throughout the year, was little noticed by the people in the community. Did the schoolhouse and privies need cleaning or repair? The school board must see to it. Were globes, maps, charts, erasers, chalk, and standardized textbooks needed for the school? The members of the school board must supply them. They must employ the teacher, discipline those students the teacher could not, draw up regulations for the school, and visit the schools to offer encouragement to the teacher and to make certain the school was being properly conducted. They must account for every penny of school funds received and spent, and they must take the yearly census of the district's children.[4]

In short, the men the farmers elected to run their schools had many of the same responsibilities the professional school administrators had in the large urban schools, and it was always said that much of the success or failure of the country school depended upon them. And though they would never have thought of themselves as such, they were, in a sense, educators—educators in overalls—who provided the leadership for their small schools and whose backgrounds were varied enough to make generalizations about them difficult.

In the early days of any school district, those chosen to be school directors were, of course, the pioneers. They were men like William Hicks and Lewis Sanford, who had both arrived in Michigan before the Civil War. Hicks had settled in Pennfield Township in Calhoun County, where he helped found the school that bore his name, while Lewis Sanford had ended up in Woodstock Township in Lenawee County, where the Sanford School, District 5, had been established. Both were men with large land holdings. Sanford owned six hundred acres, was a Congregational minister, and had been a justice of the peace in his community for years. And on another frontier, where the process of building schools had to be done all over, men like Henry Ise, a German immigrant and Civil War veteran, who had moved from Iowa in 1873 to take up a homestead in Osborne County, Kansas, would be selected to help manage the district school.[5]

Later, when the pioneer days were over, the farmers often elected the sons of pioneers who had remained in the district and who had the prestige of being "old family"; or, they might choose men of wealth lately settled in the district, or men who led active political lives for whom a district school office was only one of a number they held.

All such men were likely to have biographical sketches and even pictures of themselves in their county's Autobiographical Albums, so that future generations might know them as men of affairs who served righteous causes and owned large farms and expensive barns and houses that were sometimes elegantly sketched in the pictorial atlases published in the 1870s and '80s.[6]

But as often as not, the farmers elected men who had no pioneer names and little wealth. Schooley Wilgus, for example, owned a modest forty-acre farm not far from the Sanford schoolhouse in District 5, Woodstock, in 1886, when he was elected moderator of the district school board. That year he lost a valuable cow to the ravages of an overdose of corn. "It was a hard blow to Mr. Wilgus," the *Adrian Weekly Times and Expositor* reported sympathetically, "as he is in poor circumstances."[7]

That was the condition of many of those elected to the Midwestern country-school boards. Unlike those board members who were "doing well," men like Wilgus were too poor to buy space for themselves in the Autobiographical Albums, and nearly all that remains in print to mark their passing are the county atlases showing where their farms lay and the country-school records proving they had once been prominent enough in their communities to have been elected to their district school boards.

Whatever their backgrounds, the men chosen to serve on the district school boards were usually elected again and again, and normally to the same position. Between 1866 and 1902, eighteen different men were elected to the school board at the Sanford School, and of these, eleven were reelected. Most of the eleven were returned to office more than twice, and one was reelected five times in that thirty-six-year period and always to the post of treasurer. In Montrose Township, District 3, thirteen men were chosen to be school board members between 1870 and 1900, and all except four served more than once.[8]

Possibly a greater proportion of those reelected to office through the years were men with wealth or old family names in their communities, but the results of hundreds of school elections do not show that they were elected merely because of their wealth or family name. Frequently men from influential families were not reelected to the board, and some were never elected at all. Nor did the farmers with less wealth or influence in the little districts necessarily stand in awe of those with more. Once, in 1885, in a stormy election in the Hicks School, Pennfield, District 1, it took eight ballots to reelect Ephraim Hicks director even though he was the son of old William Hicks, and his prominence was attested to by the fact that, according to the Autobiographical Album, he owned a barn worth $1,000 and a house that cost $1,800. Moreover, his election came only after one ballot had been challenged and a motion had been adopted directing all voters to go to the desk to cast their votes![9]

The country-school elections showed, too, that although the farmers tended to reelect their school board members, neither wealth nor family nor long service assured a person of reelection at the annual school meeting.

Not infrequently the Midwestern school districts were like disturbed beehives at annual meeting time, largely because of the farmers' discontent with their school board. "Perhaps more than one-half of all district broils and difficulties originate with district officers in some way," wrote one school administrator in the 1870s, and possibly this estimate was too low.[10]

The farmers might be dissatisfied over the teacher the school board had employed, or the way the members of the board repaired or did not repair the schoolhouse, or even the arrogant way in which they conducted themselves. In 1890 in District 33 of Russell County, Kansas, it was the apparent misconduct of the district treasurer, who allegedly did not know "how much [district] money he had paid out nor how much he got," who caused the trouble. "In all our school meetings, there appears to be a kind of enmity," wrote an aggrieved farmer to the county superintendent as he attempted to explain how, in the attempt to elect a new treasurer, harsh words had been exchanged, motions from the floor had gone unrecognized, the incumbent treasurer had left the meeting in a huff, and the remaining farmers were so divided that no business had been conducted. On occasions such as these, whatever the source of the trouble, men who had held office for years and served the district faithfully were swept aside at the annual election in the farmers' rage over what they believed to be their directors' misdoing, whether it was real or only the product of a rumor that had gathered strength as it circulated through the neighborhood.[11]

In retrospect, the school elections through the years suggest that the farmers tended to choose the natural leaders that had surfaced among them. Those who were elected were a cross-section of the community, ranging from the wealthy, influential farmers to those with little of this world's goods, which indicated that it was leadership, not wealth, that was important. Unlike urban school elections in which the school board candidates were largely unknown to the average voter, the farmers knew the people they voted for extremely well. They saw them in their daily life, visited with them after church, watched them farm, heard them speak at Grange, which was a kind of training ground for farm leaders, and had a reasonably good idea of who the most capable among them were; and though they could not always induce the best men to stand for election, over the long run it was probably true that they chose the best men they had for their school boards.[12]

But even the best men among them often seemed unlikely prospects for directing the education of children. For the most part they had only a country-school education, and some were even illiterate. Their writing betrayed their uncertainty over periods, commas, and capitalization, and their tendency toward creative spelling; and somehow their subjects and verbs were less likely to agree than disagree. They wrote as they spoke, in rural accents and directly to the point. "Annual School Meeting Sept 5th 1887," ran one clerk's account of the opening of an annual school meeting, "Was Called to order by the Moderator J L Boyce Minits of the last Meeting called for & was Read and Eccepted."[13]

They had no training in school administration, of course, and their philosophy of education was no more involved than that the school's purpose was to teach their children to read, write, figure, and spell.

They had never read a textbook on school administration and very likely would have scoffed at the necessity for one.

In the course of years they committed innumerable blunders, and sometimes had to be removed. Some of them never completely learned what it was they were to do. Their reports to the county superintendents were often inaccurate and even illegible. Now and then they quarreled among themselves and tried to usurp one another's authority, particularly when it came to employing teachers. More than once a director tried to employ a teacher without the approval of his colleagues and had to be shown the error of his ways. "Miss Libbie Williams will teach the spring term of school at the station," a local reporter in Burlington, Michigan, announced in 1886. "After some difficulty she was hired. It seems the director had hired a young lady without consulting the other officers, and as Miss Williams had taught there before and given satisfaction the other two wished to hire as they had agreed to."[14]

Sometimes, too, they were so carried away with their own importance and ability to get things done that they ignored the law. Once, in the spring of 1886, a correspondent from the little neighborhood around Newton, Michigan, lashed out at the school board in District 8 that had done just that. "In their endeavor to show each other their individual importance," wrote the reporter, "and to get a contract that would compel the teacher to keep the school property in repair and suppress all profanity in the neighborhood, the school board of school district 8, have so far neglected the legal points . . . as to leave themselves individually liable for the teacher's wages."[15]

Worse still, some of those elected made little effort to improve their schools.

The Midwestern independent school districts took their direction and their tone in some measure from the men who directed them. Because they were the chosen leaders and because the farmers were inclined to follow their recommendations, the school board members were in a position to build up their schools. At the annual meetings they could urge the farmers to have longer school terms, employ better teachers, and fix up their schoolhouses. "If the director will . . . he can do very much to awaken a proper interst in the cause of education in his district," the Nebraska state superintendent wrote in the 1870s, "or he can do much to injure the cause, and hinder laudable efforts to sustain a good school."[16]

Unfortunately, there were those who did the latter. Some were apathetic about the school and for that reason made no effort to improve it. But others, possibly because they themselves did not want to be taxed to pay for improvements, worked actively for shorter school terms and cheaper teachers. They objected to the purchase of school apparatus, the improvement of the schoolyard, and even neglected to have the school cleaned before the first day of school. Some were like the retired Midwestern farmer who recalled that when he had been a member of the school board he had always hired the cheapest teacher, purchased the cheapest blackboard and the cheapest crayons, painted the schoolhouse merely to preserve it, not to make it attractive, and even bought a small dictionary when the teacher had asked for a large one.[17]

II

It was easy to pass such men off as country bumpkins, and, unfortunately, the numerous complaints lodged against them through the years drew a portrait of miserly, apathetic, uneducated educators leading their little schools into educational bankruptcy. But this was a distorted picture that exaggerated their power to influence the direction of their schools, took no account of the restrictions that bound them, and overlooked completely both their accomplishments and their considerable talent.

The most that can be known about the Midwestern country-school directors is to be found in the accounts of "their doings," as their book of records called them, and these, considered as a whole, show them to have been conscientious, earnest men, who tried to improve their schools and who displayed a considerable amount of common sense and business ability in managing their schools' affairs.

With no more than the school law and sometimes a copy of Oliver Adams's book of school records containing school meeting procedures before them, they ran their school meeting with a surprising degree of self-assurance. They moved from item to item as if they had a prepared agenda and used parliamentary language one might not have expected to hear in a one-room country schoolhouse. Sometimes they elected their officers by "acclamation," or by "*viva voce*," and when they voted they often used both informal and formal ballots with tellers appointed to count them. And somehow they maneuvered their way through the most complicated array of motions and reconsiderations of motions involving taxes, school terms, and school budgets, to bring their school's business to a successful conclusion and make it possible for the school to operate through the year.[18]

Just as they learned to conduct their annual district meetings according to parliamentary procedures, so, too, did they learn to keep accurate school records and to make the necessary reports for their district.

One of these was the clerk's report. Each year the clerk of the school district, or director, as he was called in Michigan, was responsible for reporting to the proper officials the number of children of school age—those between four and twenty in some states—in his district. He must also include in his report, among other things, the number of children enrolled in school, the total number of days school was taught by a duly qualified teacher, the whole number of days attended by the students in the school, and the average daily attendance of the school.[19]

These reports were important because the amount of money the district received from the state and county depended in part on the number of children within its boundaries attending school. But in the 1870s and '80s there was much complaint about the way these reports were filed, and it was true that some clerks, either because they could not calculate the items requested, such as the average daily attendance at the school, or because they thought anything beyond the number of children attending school was unnecessary information, turned in incomplete reports. In 1890 the clerk in District 62 in Russell County, Kansas, ignored all the requested items except the names and ages of all the children attending school and did not even bother to sign his name to the report.

But this was the exception, not the rule. Most clerks took the annual census of their districts and laboriously worked out the desired information even when they might, like the clerk in District 62, have gotten by with less work. In 1890, for example, George Baldwin, clerk in District 63 in Russell County, Kansas, gave all the desired information for his district, and the seriousness with which some clerks undertook this duty can also be seen in the reports of William J. McIntyre, at the Tri-County School in Wisconsin.[20]

Teacher, farmer, and politician, McIntyre was clerk of that small, oddly shaped district off and on in the 1870s and through most of the '80s. He wrote the minutes of the annual meeting in a neat Spencerian hand and in excellent English, and his report to the county superintendent was a model of clarity that gave a vignette of his district in numbers. On May 31, 1882, he noted that there were fifty-one children between the ages of four and twenty in the district, twenty-seven male and twenty-four female. Twenty-nine children, none under four or over twenty, had been taught by a duly qualified teacher. School had been taught for 118 days, and the total number of days attended by the students was 1,485. The average attendance each day, however, was not quite thirteen.[21]

Much more interesting to the farmers than the clerk's report, however, was the treasurer's report, which told them where their money had gone and why. Year in and year out these records were meticulously kept and examined with care both by the treasurer and by the other two members of the board, and though an error was occasionally made and here and there a treasurer embezzled the district's funds, these were rare occurrences on the Middle Border in spite of the thousands of men who served as district treasurer throughout the one-room school's existence.[22]

The district treasurer had only a homemade bookkeeping system and kept his school's financial records much as he kept his own. There were pages in Oliver Adams's district record book to record the income and expenditures of the district; but many districts did not have these, and even when they did, the treasurer often made his report in his own way on a single sheet of paper. Near the top of the page were the amounts received from the county and the state, and from local taxes. Below these figures was a long list of items for which the school's money had been spent, together with the amount each item cost. All of these the treasurer, sitting perhaps at his kitchen table in the light of a kerosene lamp, had faithfully recorded, totaled, then subtracted from the amount of money received to come up with the balance on hand.

For obvious reasons the treasurer was the most important of the three school board members. He was the bonded member of the group, had the greatest responsibility, and required the greatest amount of business ability. The farmers obviously realized this, for they reelected their treasurer to office more often than any other member of the board. Sometimes it was said that he was always the wealthiest farmer in the district and the most interested in reducing school expenditures to keep taxes low, but there is little in the records to prove this.

In the 1890s, in District 3 of Montrose Township, at the place where the road from Belleville rose above the Sugar River and joined another a quarter of a mile or so southwest of the schoolhouse, sat the substantial home of William Morehead. Morehead had come to Dane County in 1845 and had been among the first to farm along the openings of the Sugar River bottoms. In the course of years he had become a prominent man. He was once the justice of the peace, once the chairman of his township board, and for thirteen consecutive terms he had been elected treasurer of District 3. In 1902, when he resigned at the age of eighty-four, the clerk noted that "Mr. Morehead Served as Treasur[er] of School dist No (3) for Forty years."[23]

Like many district treasurers, Morehad was a large landowner, and he may have been largely responsible for the fact that in the last fourteen years of the century the local school tax averaged only $128 a year, which was somewhat less than a number of other Dane County districts raised. But his years of faithful service belie the supposition that his principal interest in the school was to keep the tax structure low. Countless are the drafts he must have drawn to pay teachers' salaries, the district bills he must have paid, or the times he must have traipsed up the hill from his home to the little schoolhouse on some district business. Sometimes when he fixed the well or repaired the schoolhouse or did some other chore, he was paid for his trouble. Once, in 1887, after the district had voted to spend $25 to repair the schoolhouse, Morehead worked six days on the project for $3. But most of his work—the lengthy, detailed reports he made each year, the accounts he kept, the board meetings he attended, the times he was interrupted to pay the district's bills—was done for virtually nothing.[24] The treasurer's financial reports with their long lists of expenditures indicated how involved and time-consuming were the chores the school directors had to perform to keep their small schools in business. For here were the records of the many details they had to take care of: the people they had employed to repair the school house and privies; how they had managed to whitewash the schoolhouse and clean the schoolyard before the school opened; what they had done to get the pump and the well back into operation; when the wood for the winter school had been brought to the schoolhouse; and the list of school supplies purchased for the year.

In one year, from September 1896 to May 1897, an average year, the school board at the Sanford School had made certain that Lewis Sanford, who had the contract, brought the wood for the stove to the schoolhouse in time for the winter school; employed Anna Wilgus to clean the schoolhouse for $2.00; hired Fred Parker to fix the fence for $2.50 and George Whitten to clean the schoolyard for $0.50. Besides that, one of the board members had purchased for the school that year a key ring, a stovepipe elbow, towels, blackboard erasers, a broom, tablets, and maps.[25]

Not recorded in all this, however, were the trips to town the members of the school board had had to make to take care of this business, or the times they had gone to the schoolhouse to see that the work there was progressing, or the visits they had made around the neighborhood to find someone to work at the schoolhouse.

Sometimes the jobs that had to be done were given to specific persons at the annual school meeting. Otherwise the directors were free to employ anyone they wished. The pay for the work was small—two dollars for cleaning the schoolhouse, for example. But since one dollar would buy a lady's ready-made wrapper or a shirtwaist and two would buy a pair of shoes at Montgomery Ward in 1895, the wages paid for the odd jobs around the schoolhouse did not seem out of line, and people seemed eager to do them, possibly because the pay was certain and immediate.[26]

If given a choice the directors usually passed the jobs around among the various people of the district who wanted them, but the nepotism in District 3, Montrose, in the late 1880s and early '90s was by no means unique.

The clerk in District 3 in the 1890s was William W. Chatterton, apparently a well-educated man who kept the minutes of the annual meetings in a remarkably legible and literate form. Like Morehead, Chatterton had been reelected to office several times, and throughout the decade of the 1880s these two men seemed to be completely in charge of the school's affairs.

During his years in office Chatterton performed numerous services for the district, and there was no reason to believe he was not interested in improving education there. In 1884, to take but one year, he secured two new blackboards for the schoolhouse, took the school census, and purchased numerous school supplies, including new chairs. All this would have required hours of his time—travel to Belleville or Paoli, perhaps, visits to the farms in the district, and trips to the schoolhouse—for which the three dollars the district paid him for "time spent for Dist," as Morehead put it, was scarcely adequate compensation.[27]

But unfortunately for him as it turned out, Chatterton had a tendency to employ members of his family to do the jobs around the school, and each year more and more Chattertons appeared on the district payroll. Between 1885 and 1890 they had been employed to clean the schoolhouse, saw wood, fix the pump, build fires in the schoolhouse, and, in 1896, Rose Chatterton was employed to teach the school at thirty dollars a month.[28]

Signs of the farmers' discontent over the employment of so many members of one family to do the work that had previously been done by others surfaced in 1894 when they adopted the practice of awarding the district's jobs to specific individuals at the annual meetings. Then, in 1896, at the annual meeting following the winter and spring that Rose Chatterton had taught school in the district, as if to emphasize their disapproval of what had been taking place, the farmers turned Chatterton out of office, giving him only three votes on the first ballot in the election of that year and none on the second and third.[29]

III

Chatterton may have been defeated in part, at least, because Rose Chatterton had been employed to teach the spring and summer school in the district, but it was not at all uncommon in the life of the Midwestern country schools for the school boards to employ a daughter of a close relative of one of their members or the daughter of a neighbor who lived down the road from them. So universal was this practice, in fact, that the legend grew that country-school boards did not know a good teacher from a poor one and that they were more anxious to employ their relatives or relatives of friends to teach than to find an effective teacher. But like so many charges made against them, this one, too, was at least only partially true.[30]

Employing the teacher was the most important responsibility Midwestern country-school directors had. More than any of their other duties this one enhanced their prestige and gave them a sense of power; and generally they tried to get the best teacher they could. Often in the late 1880s and '90s they attended the county teacher institutes to find their teacher from among those who were completing their teacher-training course there. Or they asked the county superintendent to recommend a good teacher. They also considered and were perhaps impressed with well-written applications like the one Lillie Gasman sent to a member of the school board in District 2, Redwood County, Minnesota, in 1896. "I write to put in an application to teach your school again for the coming year," she wrote in a neat, clear hand. "I liked the school very much last year and would like to teach it again. I have a good second grade certificate. I have attended two summer training schools for teachers and will attend the one in Redwood this summer. I will teach for $30. per month. Hoping that you will consider my application, I remain yours respectfully . . ."[31]

Very often, of course, the school boards simply hired a person who had come to their farms to apply for the job. This applicant might or might not be the daughter of a school board member or a local young woman whom everyone knew and whom the board might be predisposed to employ. But even if she were the daughter of the district treasurer or the niece of the most influential farmer in the district, the school board could not automatically hire her, for in employing teachers, as in many of the other duties they were charged with, they were bound by a number of restrictions which often prevented them from employing the person of their choice.

In the first place they were accountable to the district for their actions and, like Chatterton, they could be replaced if they failed to heed the wishes of the community. Next, they were often directed by the annual meeting to hire only a male or only a female. Or the amount of money the annual meeting had set aside for the teacher's salary might require that they engage the cheapest teacher possible.

Besides this, the directors were bound by the state law to hire no teacher who did not have at least a third-grade teaching certificate. Such a person was usually the most poorly trained and the cheapest teacher available, and school directors who wished to improve their schools tried, when circumstances permitted, to employ someone who had passed more advanced examination and possessed a second-grade certificate. In some instances, indeed, the farmers at their annual meeting instructed the board, as they did at the Eureka School in Saunders County, Nebraska, in 1876, to employ no teacher who did not have the second-grade certificate.[32]

So the school board members had to work within these restrictions, and the difficulties these restrictions posed for them in their attempts to employ good teachers can be seen in the deliberations of the school board at the Austin School, Elba, District 2, in 1894.

Since 1889, when the schoolhouse was built, the farmers there had been struggling with their school budget, and at their annual meeting in July 1893, they had voted as they had for three years previously to have only a seven-month school and to let the board decide whether to employ a male or a female teacher. But after voting to spend $33.15 for wood, $10.00 to build a fence on three sides of the schoolhouse, $5.00 for the clerk's salary, $15.00 to build a new privy and repair the old one, and $10.00 for incidentals, they could raise no more than $100.00 for their teacher's wages for the year.

All this the school board members had in mind when they met one winter day in February to consider the employment of a teacher for the summer school. Some additional money, they knew, would be coming from the state and county to help with their budget, but they also knew that the teacher they had employed for the winter school, and who was just then completing her term, had cost $35 a month, and this had so depleted the teachers' fund that even under the best of circumstances there would be little left for the summer teacher.

But it happened that Tessie Cullen, whose family lived not far from Danville village and about a mile and a half northwest of the school-house, had applied to teach the summer school, and after pondering the problem, the school board decided to hire her if she would teach for $20 a month and if she had received her teaching certificate be-fore the term began.

As it turned out, Tessie did receive her certificate in early April, two weeks before the summer term was to begin, but her performance on the examinations at the county superintendent's office was disap-pointing. Her highest grade was 77 in Constitution, and her lowest was 57 in geography. But the 58 she received in the basic subjects—mental arithmetic, written arithmetic, English grammar, and even orthoepy—coupled with a 61 in reading, did not make for a promis-ing beginning.

Still the school board hired her according to their agreement, not necessarily because they wanted to employ a cheap teacher or because they did not understand that her low grades suggested that she might be a poor teacher. Indeed, school boards across the Middle Border were usually not so stupid that they did not know the difference a teacher's grades might make or so obtuse they did not know a good teacher from a poor one. Often in their records they commented be-side their teacher's name "good teacher," or "splendid teacher," and sometimes they would also write "not very good satisfaction," or more kindly, "nothing to say." No, the school board employed Tessie be-cause they had no choice in the matter.[33]

Actually, when they could, the Austin School directors had em-ployed teachers with good credentials. Just before they employed Tessie Cullen, they had hired Ella Burns, who had had not only a second-grade teaching certificate but grades that ran from a high of 95 in United States history to a low of 78 in orthography. And when they could no longer employ her, they turned to Mary Roche.

Mary was another young woman from the district whose family lived not much more than half a mile north of the schoolhouse, and perhaps she herself had gone to the little school across from the Catholic church. Like Ella Burns she was a good student. She had a second-grade certificate and an average of 84 in twelve subjects in-cluding algebra and the theory and art of teaching, and it was indicative of the school board's interest in having a good teacher that, contrary to tradition, they employed her for three years both summer and winter. Their decision to hire her for both summer and winter terms, however, had been made with the provision that it would be done "if the district was satisfied," which suggested the board's recognition that the ultimate authority in employing teachers lay with the people of the district.[34]

Just as the educators in overalls were restricted in various ways in the employment of a teacher for their school, so were they limited in their control over the school curriculum and the adoption of textbooks, both of which were their responsibilities in most states. About the curriculum the school directors never really bothered themselves. Everyone knew that the eight common branches, with heavy emphasis upon reading, writing, arithmetic, and spelling, were the subjects children studied, and it would never have occurred to them that anyone could think that the essence of education was learning to relate to others. Besides, most states required that the eight branches be taught, and the principal role of the school directors was reduced to seeing that they were taught well.

But the textbook question was another matter.

The textbook problem was a lingering malady on the Middle Border through most of the late nineteenth century. For years after the Civil War, children went to school taking the textbooks their brothers or sisters or even their parents had used, so that in any one-room school there might be as many different arithmetics, geographies, spellers, and readers as there were students. This meant that the teacher ended each day making individual assignments in perhaps as many as twenty different textbooks after having listened to recitations drawn from as many sources. Individualized instruction could be carried no further, and most people who thought about it very much agreed upon the desirability of having uniform textbooks adopted in the schools.[35]

But efforts to standardize the textbooks in the country schools on the Middle Border in those years raised serious questions. Were the state legislatures to force the school districts to adopt uniform textbooks? If so, who was to pay for them? And who was to select the books to be adopted?

These were questions most Midwestern state legislatures were not anxious to answer, and in time they shifted the burden of solving the problem to the local school directors. The laws passed on the subject varied from state to state, but, in general, they required the local school boards to adopt uniform textbooks. At the same time, except in Indiana, Missouri, and Kansas, where state commissions picked the books that were to be used, the legislatures also gave the responsibility of book selection to the school boards. But by the end of the nineteenth century, of the ten Middle Border state legislatures, only Nebraska's had been bold enough to require the local districts to supply the children with free textbooks—that is, free to use, not to have. Others merely asked the districts to vote at their annual meetings on whether they wished to supply free textbooks or not.[36]

These were the laws, but there was no way the state legislatures could force the school boards to adopt uniform textbooks without causing an upheaval in the countryside, and whether the school boards did as the law required was, in effect, up to them. It was not an easy decision. Standardized textbooks would mean that each farmer would have to buy new books for all his children, at least the first year, and although the books were cheap by today's standards—sometimes twenty cents or so—if he had several children the expense would be burdensome when corn was selling for only twenty-five cents a bushel. Moreover, it would be especially onerous to the parents who kept moving into the districts in Kansas and Nebraska as the western plains filled up to be confronted with the necessity of buying new books the moment their children entered school.[37]

In view of this, many Midwestern school boards were slow to act. But gradually most of them did adopt standardized textbooks, books which they themselves had selected. Occasionally they would select books all of one company. At the Sanford School in 1881, the directors chose Scribner's complete set, everything from arithmetic to history. But in the Tri-County School in Wisconsin a year later, the board was more selective. It chose Appleton's Readers, Robinson's Arithmetic, Spencer's Penmanship, and Swinton's Spellers, Geographies, Grammars, and Histories.[38]

How three farmers, who may have gone no further in school than McGuffey's *Third Eclectic Reader* and had certainly never had a course in curriculum, concluded that Appleton's Reader was better than Swinton's, or that Swinton's Speller was better than Appleton's, was a puzzle. They may have found something in one or the other they did not like, or they may have merely followed the county or state superintendent's recommendations. Probably the price of the books had something to do with their decision, and so very likely did the book agent.

At certain seasons of the year book agents descended on the rural

Midwest like a plague of locusts. They rode about the countryside in their buggies, called on the school directors at their farms, attended their meetings, flattered them, and promised them this or that if they would buy their particular books. One book agent noted that he had once got an adoption of his Speller when he convinced the township supervisor to build a bridge in the district where one of the school board members had been opposed to buying his book. "If you take my speller," the agent told the hesitant school director, "I've got your bridge."[39]

The book agents had numerous stories to tell about how they were able to maneuver the school directors into buying their books, and likely many of them were true. But unlike the slippery salesmen of useless academic charts who often infested the region selling their worthless goods by deceitful means to the unsuspecting school directors, the book agents sold good books published by established firms, and they were probably the most important single force in getting school boards to adopt standardized textbooks in the country schools in late-nineteenth-century America.[40]

Once the school boards had adopted a standard set of books, they could not, according to the laws of most states, change them again for four or five years. But the laws were unnecessary, for most school directors, for obvious reasons, were so reluctant to make changes that they kept the same books year after year until they were tattered and torn and sometimes pasted together with flour-and-water paste. And through the years other books were brought into the school either by new students or by teachers, so that in time there would be no more uniformity of books than there had been before standardized books had been adopted. Seeing this, the book agents would once more swoop down upon the rural districts and try to persuade the school directors once again to adopt a new set of standard books. "We have not escaped the importunities of irrepressible representatives of several school book publishing houses," a Wisconsin public school official wrote in 1880. "However, they came none too soon; and, although they were successful to a considerable degree in their efforts, we have no reason to regret their coming."[41]

Usually the farmers accepted their school board's selection, but when there was a dispute, they made the final decision, as they did at the Nichols School, District 3, Blooming Grove, in 1878. There in August a special meeting had been called just for the purpose of selecting textbooks, and after listening to one book salesman, who apparently did not please them, they twice voted down a resolution to adopt Appleton's series of textbooks. But after more discussion, they ended their meeting by voting to let the school board make the decision after all. A short time later the board adopted Appleton's Readers, but at the annual school meeting, as if they meant to have the last word in the matter, the farmers themselves selected Ray's Arithmetic and Sanders's Spellers.[42]

But the county school boards' inability to bring change where change was unwanted was clear in hundreds of those Midwestern country-school districts, for no more than the state legislatures could they force the parents in their school districts to buy the books they had adopted, and any attempt to do so would have ruined the school. "Notwithstanding an explicit law for uniformity," the Illinois state superintendent complained in 1883, "many schools do not prescribe the books for use within their districts and in many other cases the books prescribed are not used because of the opposition of parents unable or unwilling to procure them."[43]

Furthermore, to have their districts provide free books often violated the farmers' most enduring principles. Some thought the idea was paternalistic, even communistic. It would nurture in the young, they said, a lack of appreciation of books, spread disease from family to family as the books were passed around year after year from one child to another, and make getting an education too easy. Besides, those families that had more children than others would derive more benefit from the system than others, yet all would be taxed alike to pay for it.[44]

In a word, the principle of free textbooks, in the view of many Midwesterners, would undermine the doctrine of self-help, and for years throughout the 1880s and '90s, in district after district where they were asked to vote on the matter, the answer usually given was that recorded by the director of District 5, Woodstock, in 1889: "Voted on the Free text Book question No."[45]

All things considered, the Midwestern country-school directors as a group probably did as well as anyone could have done in standardizing textbooks, employing teachers, and handling the business affairs of their schools. They were as close to the people as it was possible to be. They knew what was possible and what was not. They pushed when it was timely and held back when it was not, and their schools did improve under their leadership. Even a little school like Montrose, District 3, that in the 1870s was sometimes a five- and sometimes a seven-month school, rose in the '80s to an eight- and in the '90s to a nine-month school, and after 1887 had teachers with second-grade certificates and good grades. And the Nichols School, Blooming Grove, District 3, whose school terms had wavered so long in the 1870s and '80s between five and seven months, had become a nine-month school by 1894.[46]

If the educators in overalls were remiss in any of their duties, it was in their failure to visit their school, supervise their teacher, and draw up written rules and regulations as the state laws generally required them to do.[47]

It was not that they never visited their schools. Each school term the visitors' register of the little schools throughout the Middle Border usually contained the names of one or more members of the board who had visited the school and pronounced it good or left little verses like the following, which said much about their Midwestern values:

> Had I this tough old world to rule
> My common sword and mallet
> Should be the dear old district school,
> God's Bible and the ballot.[48]

But they did not visit school as often as they might or perhaps should have. No doubt they were often too busy to do so, but more than that they may have felt uncomfortable in the presence of small children and thought of school visitation as woman's work. It was possible, too, that they were afraid they might be asked questions they could not answer. One other important reason for their hesitancy in visiting school very likely was their fear of having to speak to the teacher and to instruct her in some way. This, too, was one of their duties but one which they were probably not at all comfortable with and could avoid if they did not visit school.

Whatever the reason, the visitors' records of the Midwest's one-room schools as well as the testimony of interested observers indicate that school visitation and teacher supervision were two aspects of their jobs they neglected. So was the requirement that they draw up written rules and regulations.

Here and there school boards did draw up interesting rules for their schools. At the Tri-County School in Joint District 1, Koshkonong, the board decided in 1882, "if no cases of tardiness occur, neither morning nor noon of each week, that the teacher be authorized to close school on Fridays at half past 3 P.M." But at least until after the turn of the century, the Midwestern school boards rarely bothered to compose a set of written rules for their schools. Perhaps they thought that the set of rules found in their school record books was enough; or they may have supposed that everyone had enough common sense to know what rules had to be followed to have a successful school. And probably some school boards felt that to post written rules in the schoolhouse would be only one more source of trouble in the district.[49]

But even without such rules, school directors did not hesitate to act when the commonly understood rules were broken. "School boards do not show much interest in the matter of visitations," wrote a school official in Walworth County, Wisconsin, in 1888, "but they are always willing to cooperate with the teacher in the enforcement of all needed rules and regulations for the maintenance of a successful school." They did not hesitate to dismiss the teacher when they thought it necessary, but neither did they hesitate to support the teacher when she was right in her discipline of the children. In 1894, for example, in District 4, La Prairie Township, in Rock County, Wisconsin, when William Kirkpatrick complained to the school board because his son had been sent home from school, the board met promptly at ten o'clock one morning, listened to the complaint, and ruled forthrightly that the teacher had acted, in their belief, "in accordance with the School Laws on all such cases." The board went further and directed "the teacher to dismiss any and all pupels [sic] [who] knowingly willfully and persistently disobeys [sic] the lawful Rules of the School."[50]

Such decisions were not easy to make, and, in fact, it was rarely easy to be a member of a school board of a one-room school in the rural Middle West in the late nineteenth century. The people they served were so set in their ways, so individualistic, and so concerned about their schools, which were so much a part of their lives, that no school board could hope to please everyone in the district, and for some farmers one term on the school board was enough.

Yet many men were eager to be elected to the board, and the heated elections that frequently occurred at the annual school meetings suggest not only the desire of the candidates to be chosen but also the interest the people had in their schools. In District 4, La Prairie Township, in 1897, for example, it took six ballots for six men to choose one of their number for the board!

The candidates did not run for school board positions in any formal way or campaign across the district. But no doubt they had understandings among themselves about who was to run, and year after year, probably most often by prearrangement, they let their names go before the annual meeting as a candidate for one position or another.

Sometimes they won, of course, but often they suffered humiliating defeats as the ballots were counted before their eyes in the little schoolhouse. Yet they would often try again the following year, and the question naturally arises as to why they would subject themselves to such contests. Why, for example, would William J. McIntyre in the Tri-County school district in Wisconsin, after receiving only one vote in his bid for reelection as district clerk in 1888, run for director the next year with the same results, and run once again for treasurer in 1890 with still only one vote in his favor, which in fact, may have been his own?[51]

Sometimes it was said that they ran because of the money they received as clerk or treasurer of the district, but this scarcely seems plausible. The amount they received each year was usually no set sum but whatever the annual meeting voted to give them, and this amount did little more than cover their expenses. Nor is it probable that most of those who served on their district school boards thought of it as a steppingstone to a political career. More likely they ran for the office for more ordinary reasons.

Some no doubt entered the lists because they were discontented with something the school board had done, or because of some school dispute that had erupted in the community. Others were probably motivated merely by their desire to control their district's affairs. And probably almost everyone who ran for school board positions did so in part for the personal satisfaction of being known about the district as a school official. "The honor of serving in these positions," one observer wrote in 1914, "is sweet to them and given up reluctantly."[52]

But none of these reasons can really be separated from the environment in which Midwestern farmers lived, and this, in the long run, may have had as much to do with their eagerness to serve on the school board as anything else.

In their small world it was both a duty and a privilege to be elected to their school boards. "We wish to call your attention to the greater probability of a farmer being called upon to act upon a school board over a resident of a city," the education committee of the Illinois State Grange reported in 1891. A laborer in the city, the committee noted, could never expect to be asked to serve on the school board and would spend his life knowing no more about school affairs than what he remembered from his own school days or what he heard from his children. "But the farmer," the report continued, "being one of twenty in his district is very certain to serve his neighbors in that position," and in that capacity he had the opportunity of "shaping the future of the brightest, most practical boys and girls of our land."[53]

Moreover, rural Americans on the Middle Border in the late nineteenth and early twentieth centuries were far more politically oriented than are their descendants. Politics, indeed, surrounded them. No year passed when the people there were not called to the polls several times, for the ballot box was the great arbiter of disputes. Even the post office in their midst and the postmaster behind the counter were reminders of their political environment. In this world it was as natural as life itself to run for office, which explains, in part, why men who did not do so felt it necessary to have it said of them in their biographical sketches that they had never cared for "political preferment."

In large measure, then, it was this environment with its opportunities for service and its emphasis on the political process, rather than on bureaucracy, as a way of getting things done that moved men, even those who did not care for political preferment on a grander scale, to stand for election to their school boards. Theirs was a simple, democratic, political, and decentralized society, in which men could still control the education of their children and felt responsible for doing so.

Yet as the nineteenth century rolled on to its end, this simple school system was being vigorously attacked by the rising class of professional educators who objected to it largely because it was controlled by the farmers themselves.

6

The Professionals

✿

A FEW DAYS BEFORE THANKSGIVING IN 1896, A GROUP OF PUBLIC
school men met at the Auditorium Hotel in Chicago to put the finish-
ing touches on a study of the nation's rural schools, which they had
been working on for more than a year. For four days, from nine o'clock
in the morning until noon, and from three to six in the afternoon, while
dark clouds hovered over the city and rains fell and snow threatened,
they labored over the reports of the three subcommittees that had
studied separate aspects of rural education, and in the end, adopted
them all.[1]

Like so many such committees, the Committee of Twelve, as it was
called, discovered what its members already believed and had been
saying for more than twenty-five years: country schools were poor
schools.

The committee's general attitude toward the country schools was
fairly summarized in the report of the subcommittee on school maintenance, written by Burke A. Hinsdale, chairman of the subcommittee and the man who, next to Henry Sabin, Iowa's superintendent of public instruction, was most responsible for organizing the
Committee of Twelve. "No doubt there are many excellent schools in
the country," Hinsdale wrote; "but, on the whole, it may well be
doubted whether any money that is expended in the people's interest
is expended more wastefully than what goes to the country schools.
No doubt the country school has points of advantage over the city
schools . . . but on the whole it is inferior. The typical 'little red school-

101

house,' so invested with sentiment, is a costly and unsatisfactory institution of education."[2]

When he wrote this report Hinsdale was nearly sixty years old. Born and raised on a pioneer farm in Ohio, he had himself received his early education in a country school where he had at least learned enough to enable him to enroll at the age of sixteen in what would later be Hiram College. For seven years, alternating between teaching country schools in winter and farming in summer, he attended classes at Hiram. During the Civil War he stayed on there as an instructor, left for a time when the war was over, and returned in 1869, to become professor, then president of the institution in 1870. In 1882 he became superintendent of schools in Cleveland, and when he failed to be reelected to that post in 1886, he was appointed professor of the science and art of teaching at the University of Michigan in Ann Arbor.[3]

Like Hinsdale, most of the Midwesterners who helped draft the Committee of Twelve's report had rural backgrounds, were well educated for the time, and were or had been superintendents of urban school systems, or, like Henry Sabin, state superintendents of public instruction. But their most important common characteristic was that they belonged to a new class of professional educators that was rising on the Middle Border following the Civil War.

In some ways these professionals were little different from the older generation of educators that had fought the battle for free education in the antebellum days. Just as the older group had so often had New England, Whiggish, and Republican backgrounds, so their successors tended to have roots in New England and to be Republican, often of the Mugwump, reform mentality in politics. Almost certainly they would be Protestant, and in their efforts to stamp their Protestant values on the people of the Midwest, they were as zealous as even a Calvin Stowe had been. "In the name of the living God it must be proclaimed," wrote Newton Bateman, state superintendent of public instruction in Illinois in the 1870s and one of the professional group, "that licentiousness shall be the liberty—violence and chicanery shall be the law—superstition and craft shall be the religion—and self-destructive indulgence of all sensual and unhallowed passions shall be the happiness of that people who neglect the education of their children." Lyman Beecher could have said it no better.[4]

But the younger men lived in an age of centralization and specialization, and this made a difference. All about them villages were growing into towns and towns into cities. New industries were everywhere, and gigantic corporations that limited older areas of competition were spreading their tentacles even across the Middle Border. With every passing day American life, especially in the cities, was becoming more highly organized and the old American individualism more circumscribed. "From a handful of individuals we have become a nation of institutions," one observer noted as he charted the greatest changes that had occurred in the country since 1800. "The individual counts for less and less, organizations for more and more."[5]

And, while big business was imposing a new order on the American economy, the intellectuals were attempting to organize American intellectual life, to raise intellectual standards, and to professionalize their disciplines. Historians, writing in accordance with new scientific methods, came increasingly to think of themselves as professionals and to draw distinctions between themselves and amateurs. So, too, did the economists, who founded a professional organization, the American Economic Association, in 1885. Meanwhile, the physicians, lawyers, and clergymen, the three old and respected professions, were raising their standards and increasing the prestige of their orders.[6]

In this environment the educators, openly envious of the three traditional professions, longed to cross over the line that separated them from the professions. To William Payne, one-time country schoolboy, once superintendent of schools at Adrian, Michigan, in Lenawee County and the first to occupy the chair of pedagogy at the University of Michigan in 1879, the professions were like "an enclosed and fortified camp." Inside were those with rights, privileges, and prerogatives, which the educators coveted but which they were "half-conscious," as Payne wrote, that they did not deserve because they lacked the proper credentials.[7]

The mark of the professional, Payne observed, was not only that he was licensed, but that he had a special body of knowledge only a few possessed. "The body of knowledge needed for professional ends consists of principles, rules, maxims," he wrote, "which the logical faculty employs for the solution of specific problems that occur in the course of professional practice. It is not merely knowledge of processes and methods but of the principles which underlies [sic] them and give them their validity and efficiency. It is scientific knowledge."[8]

Physicians had this kind of knowledge, but teachers were not so fortunate. For although they were licensed to practice as physicians were, they had only a general knowledge that was shared by thousands, so that the approaches to their fortified camp, Payne noted, were open to the multitudes on all sides. Clearly, then, if they wished to enter the golden circle of the professions, the educators must develop a specialized body of knowledge that only a few would master, and these, and these alone, could then become professional. "Only a few," Professor Payne said, "will...study their art in its scientific aspects.... Out of the large number who teach, a few will be master-workmen, and these will know their art, both as a series of processes and a philosophy. With the teaching of educational science, men of talent and culture will there find a field for the exercise of their best powers, and the professional body of teachers will be reinforced."[9]

II

Even as Payne's essay on professionalism appeared in 1882, American educators were already preparing the kind of special knowledge he had called for, and it was in doing this that they began to speak and to write of the science of education, partly, it must be supposed, to gain respect for their discipline. For in the late nineteenth century, science reigned supreme among the intellectuals, and any body of knowledge worthy of recognition by the intellectual community must be based on science.

The idea that education was a science did not go unchallenged even by educators themselves. "Since education is capable of no such exact definitions of its principle and no such logical treatment as other sciences," one critic wrote, "the treatises written upon it abound in shallowness more than those of any other literature. Short-sightedness and arrogance find in it a most congenial atmosphere, and uncritical methods and declamatory bombast flourish as nowhere else."[10]

Such criticism forced the educators through the years to defend the proposition that education was a science, and much ink was shed in behalf of this idea. In 1881, one year before Payne had written on what educators must do to enter the professional ranks, another educator, stung by the denial that education was a science, wrote to explore the question. "Is There a Science of Education?" he asked. His answer was no, not yet, but contrary to the views of skeptics, he believed that education was capable of becoming a science. "The phenomena of mental growth take place," he wrote, "under the control of fixed and known or knowable laws," so that in time, when these laws were worked out, education would indeed become a science.[11]

The doubts that education was a science were never really dispelled, but in time most professional educators, perhaps on the theory that saying so would make it so, simply wrote and spoke as if it were a settled matter. In his book, *The History of Pedagogy*, which was translated by Professor Payne in 1886, the famous French educator Gabriel Compayre brushed off the controversy by noting that "the science of education is no longer an empty term, an object of vague aspirations for philosophers, of easy ridicule for critics. Doubtless," he continued, "it is far from being definitely established; but it no longer concedes its name and its pretensions; it defines its purposes and its methods; and manifests its youthful vitality in all directions."[12]

The last, at least, was true, for the new class of American professional educators did show tremendous vitality in all directions. In 1870, fourteen years before American historians got around to it, they formed a professional organization, the National Education Association, which became the vehicle for developing their profession. The educators attended their organization's meetings religiously, read innumerable papers on a variety of educational topics, and served on the association's various committees, like the Committee of Twelve, which were organized to study one or another aspect of American education. They also established professional journals, such as the *Proceedings of the National Education Association,* and in these they published scholarly articles on learning theory, psychology, the theory and practice of teaching, the philosophy and history of education, and a host of other topics with which the older generation of educators had not been much concerned.[13]

On the whole, the professional educators were good, decent, well-meaning men. True, their growing accumulation of theories about education made them arrogant and overconfident of their ability to prescribe solutions for all educational problems. But they stretched their energies to the utmost to raise the nation's educational and moral standards. And if their attempt to impose their Protestant moral standards upon an increasingly heterogeneous people was an affront to those with different values, the educators could scarcely be blamed for trying to preserve those standards which were common to the people when the nation was founded and which had served the country so well.

The professional educators were immensely impressed with the organization and apparent efficiency of the business enterprises they saw about them, and by the 1890s they had been working for nearly half a century to make the schools, especially the urban schools, as efficient as factories. By that time in the large city schools they had segregated students of the same age into separate classes—first, second, third, and so on; given each class its own teacher; and built huge schoolhouses with numerous classrooms so that each class might have its own room. They had standardized the course of study, textbooks, and examinations for each class in order that students in the same class would study the same subject, read the same books, and be passed, machinelike, on to the next grade, all at the same time. Finally, in the 1890s, in keeping with the age of centralization, they were in the process of removing the schools from the people, reducing the participation of school boards in the management of the schools, and concentrating the power to make crucial educational decisions in their own expert hands.[14]

By 1896, when the Committee of Twelve met to discuss the rural schools, virtually all the nation's large urban schools bore the professional educators' imprint. They appeared to be models of efficiency and order as thousands upon thousands of urban schoolchildren with diverse backgrounds marched through them and out into life. Everything considered, this was no small achievement, and it had been accomplished only after vigorous struggles with those whose interests had been adversely affected.[15]

But in the rural areas of the Middle Border where nearly seventy per cent of the region's population still lived in 1890 and where the majority of the area's schoolchildren remained, the professional educators' efforts to centralize, bureaucratize, and systematize the schools had stumbled over the stubborn resistance of individualistic and democratic farmers. This resistance was, of course, one reason for Hinsdale's gloomy report on the condition of rural schools and the source of the educators' greatest frustration in the late nineteenth century.

III

Anyone who read their long reports in the last thirty years of the nineteenth century could easily understand the reasons for the professionals' frustration over what was referred to as "the country school problem." For a generation they had spent the greater part of their energies trying to improve the Midwestern country schools, yet, compared with the apparent efficiency and standardization of the urban schools, the rural schools at the turn of the century were as individualistic, inefficient, and chaotic as ever. By the 1890s the educators' professional advice on rural school improvement had been repeatedly spurned by both the farmers and the state legislatures. This was reason enough for them to believe rural schools were poor schools, and almost to a man they had come to the conclusion that the source of the country-school problem on the Middle Border was the small, independent school district system.

Like some of the founding fathers at the Constitutional Convention in 1787 who believed that the nation's troubles sprang from an "excess of democracy," the professional educators thought that the independent school districts with their pure democracy were far too democratic to produce good schools and as outmoded in the late nineteenth century as the "blabb school." Long before the Committee of Twelve had met, Burke Hinsdale had pointed out that the democratic theory upon which the district system was based had been replaced by the representative system everywhere in the nation except in education. "The district system is very dear to the hearts of very many people," he wrote despairingly. "But anyone who will inquire into the facts can hardly avoid . . . the conclusion that . . . it is an absurdity."[16]

The truth was, of course, that the educators, partly because of their newly discovered expertise, had developed strong antidemocratic tendencies, like other professionals in that age. Knowing so much about education, they became convinced that the people as a whole, and farmers in particular, knew nothing about it, not even what was best for their own children. "Parents," wrote the Nebraska superintendent of public instruction in 1873, "are often very poor judges of what a school should be." Practical experience, too, their daily dealings with country-school matters, and their almost obsessive passion for efficiency also taught the educators that pure democracy was an unmanageable form of government for a school system.[17]

There were simply too many people involved in operating the country schools to suit the professional educators. In 1873 Newton Bateman, the Illinois state superintendent whom Lincoln called "my little friend, the big schoolmaster of Illinois" on account of his short stature, poured out his wrath against the independent district system in his widely read Tenth Biennial Annual Report. Illinois, he lamented, had about two thousand townships, each of which contained an average of six school districts or twelve thousand in all. Each township had four elected officials and each school district had three. Altogether, then, there were forty-four thousand officers to manage the affairs of the school system, or one for every twenty children of school age in the entire state![18]

Bateman believed, as did most Midwestern educators, that schools were businesses, and perhaps it was asking too much of such professionally oriented men, even those with rural backgrounds, to see that the little one-room school in the small independent district was no business but a vital part of community life to which rural people were deeply attached by ties of tradition and personal interest. In any case, it disturbed Bateman that the small army of school officials in his state made it impossible to run the schools in a businesslike manner. "Such a needless reduplication of agents," he wrote, "is at war with all sound maxims and established usages in relation to business affairs. . . . It is in conflict with the familiar principle that the more a business can be centralized, the fewer minds and hands essentially concerned in its management, the better."[19]

Besides this, there was the great waste involved in electing to office all these men who managed the country schools. Bateman estimated that the people of rural Illinois had to be called out some five times a year to vote on school matters and that there were as many as thirty-seven thousand elections annually across the state. Surely this, the educators believed, was an excess of democracy.[20]

All these elections might have been more bearable to the educators had they approved the kind of men the farmers chose to run their schools. But they did not, and few aspects of the independent district system annoyed them more than those educators in overalls who managed the country schools.

No matter that those country-school board members along the Middle Border were the people the farmers wanted to direct their school. And no matter the effort the directors made to keep their schools open, often under trying circumstances, or that they had demonstrated a certain amount of expertise of their own in running their schools. As a rule, the professionals were contemptuous of them, and demanded more of them than they had any right to expect. "They should be choice men," wrote Bateman, "picked men, men of large hearts, of comprehensive views, of high character, of considerable intellectual grasp and culture, of much reading and general intelligence; they should be men who know what education is and the value of it to the state and nation; men who can tell the genuine from the counterfeit, whether in books, methods, or men; who have judgment, taste, refinement, public spirit, integrity, and honor."[21]

Instead, according to the educators, the country-school directors were uneducated, sometimes illiterate, men with no grasp of school procedures, no theory of education, and no understanding of what made a good school. Bumbling and inefficient, they were often selfishly motivated and prone to run the cheapest school possible. They did not know a good teacher from a poor one, and, in any event, never employed a teacher more than one term, so that efficiency was utterly impossible. Worst of all, they were careless—careless in making out school reports, careless about the physical condition of their schools, and careless about the kind of school they had. "And, for indifference in discharge of his duties," wrote an Illinois educator in the *Illinois Schoolmaster* in 1875, "the average director is probably unexcelled by any other officer with whom the *Schoolmaster*'s readers ever come in contact. Such an official seems to regard his election as a call to the discharge of duties of little importance and responsibility."[22]

In the course of years, it was true, the educators sometimes softened their criticism of the country-school directors and at times even praised them. But such praise was usually merely a prelude to a discussion of their inadequacies. The Committee of Twelve, for example, acknowledged that the rural school board members were eager to learn, then noted at the same time that they were ignorant of their duties.[23]

Too many officers, too many elections, incompetent school directors—these were the problems flowing from the independent school districts. But they were not the only ones, and perhaps Midwestern educators would have written less about the shortcomings of the system had these shortcomings not been so often called to their attention by the most irritating problem of all: the eternal disputes that arose among the stubborn farmers who wanted to run the schools their way.

IV

In all the Midwest there was scarcely a school district that had not at one time or another been wracked by some wrangle that divided the district. Often the origin of the trouble was unrelated to the school itself. It might have started as a quarrel between two neighbors over a borrowed piece of machinery that was never returned, or over a cow that had broken through a fence. But in those little communities where lives were so intimately tied together and where the school was the nerve center of society, a quarrel that began in one place, like a running sore, was likely to break out in the school. In District 37, for example, at the Ise School in Kansas in the 1880s, a feud over the building of a county road was carried into the school, where it divided the children into warring camps.[24]

What bothered the professionals most, however, were those disputes that could not be settled at either the district or the county level but must go all the way to the state superintendent's office, where their adjudication occupied hours of his time. On any given day the disputes the superintendent might have to settle could range from the dismissal of a teacher to the problem of a schoolhouse site to the location of a district boundary line, and on to innumerable smaller problems. What should be done about a retarded eighteen-year-old pupil who continued to enroll in school against the wishes of most of the district's families? Could the Bible be read in school? And what if a school board member were elected to office but neglected to swear in? Could the other two members declare his office vacant?[25]

Occasionally some lesser school official saw the district quarrels as "the outward manifestation of vigor and life, and preferable by far to a state of apathy and stagnation." And perhaps they were. "I know of scarcely any instance," the county superintendent of Fond Du Lac County, Wisconsin, once wrote, "in which a smart district quarrel had not been followed by a better state of things in the district; and, although for the time being they may not have been deemed altogether joyous, yet experience teaches that it is oftentimes only through great tribulations that communities as well as individuals are to be lifted to a higher plain of civilization. Alive as most men are to all matters pertaining to their individual and worldly interests yet for some unaccountable reason, it seems that nothing less than an earthquake or the shocks of discord can arouse some men to the educational wants of their district."[26]

But few professionals agreed with such homespun philosophy. They much preferred those more apathetic school districts where everyone agreed and where matters ran as smoothly as they did in those urban schools the educators controlled. The country-school disputes tried their patience and required the wisdom of Solomon to solve in a way both sides would accept. And many times there was no satisfactory solution. In such cases the farmers who had not gotten what they wanted often petitioned for a new school district for themselves, and weary school officials agreed to their request as the best way to solve an otherwise unsolvable problem.

The result of the continual division of school districts, however, was the small school. By 1873 hundreds of school districts had been organized in Illinois for no more than four families and some for no more than two or three, and similar conditions existed everywhere across the Middle Border. Nor did matters improve much over the years.

Twenty years later, the superintendent of public instruction in Wisconsin reported that school districts were so small that 183 schools had no more than five students each, 853 no more than ten, and 3,523, almost three-fifths of the whole, had an average attendance of no more than twenty children.[27]

To most Midwestern professional educators the small school was ipso facto a poor school. Supported by only a handful of taxpayers it was too poor to employ a good teacher, to build a good schoolhouse, to buy school apparatus, and to stay open longer than the minimum number of days required by state law. Equally important, it had too few students to provide the competition necessary for good instruction.[28]

Their assessment of the little one-room school was confirmed by their own days in country schools, their teaching experience there, their routine visits, their professional training, and thousands of pages of statistics. Even the natural order of things was against the small school. In the Darwinian world of the educators, institutions, like animal life, moved from the simple to the complex, from the lower to the higher, from the small to the large, and this was progress. "Fitness," they would argue, "means adaptation.... Any change that makes a better adaptation to the environment is progress." The big school was a better adaptation to the environment than a small school. With its many fine classrooms, its graded classes, its wonderful apparatus so necessary for the innovative object-lesson teaching, the big school was the good school. The little school was the poor school.[29]

Yet some little schools were poorer than other little schools, and the unquestionable fact that good and bad district schools, or, in the educators' view, poor and poorer schools, often did lie side by side gave them one of their best arguments against the independent system.

This phenomenon was partly the inevitable result of that doctrine of self-help so valued in rural America. Some communities cared more about education than others and taxed themselves more to provide better teachers, longer school terms, and better school buildings. Throughout the Midwest it was not difficult to find the people in one poor, small district taxing themselves to the utmost and producing a good school, and others in a nearby wealthier district employing the cheapest teacher money could buy and allowing their schoolhouse to go unrepaired because they wanted to keep their taxes low.[30]

Unfortunately, individual effort was not the only reason for the financial discrepancies among the districts. Some districts were populous and could easily afford a good school, while others, sparsely populated, could not, even with the greatest effort. In 1878 the Wisconsin superintendent noted that the assessed valuation of property per school district in the state ran all the way from $2,300 in one district to $1,979,708 in another. Even in the same township the assessed valuation of the property of various school districts ranged from less than $3,000 in one district to $40,000 in another![31]

Obviously, then, the tax burden fell more heavily on some communities than it did on others, and poor communities that really wanted a good school had to make sacrifices others would not make. The Wisconsin figures, for example, indicated that district school taxes varied so dramatically from district to district that a person living in one district might pay only half a mill on the dollar in school taxes, while another might have to pay as much as fifty-five mills, and Wisconsin was no exception among the Midwestern states in this respect. "It is hard to see," Burke Hinsdale wrote in his report for the Committee of Twelve, "how or why the people have so long borne such inequalities—inequalities so contrary to the cherished principle that the property of the state should educate the youth of the state."[32]

All in all, in the view of the professional educators, "the wretched condition of the [country-school] district," as one of them put it, was "*not a question*." It was "an admitted fact," and so deplorable did the situation of the country schools appear in the reports the educators wrote, they seemed beyond redemption. "I have been in despair in regard to the improvement of the rural schools since 1870," wrote the United States commissioner of education near the turn of the century, "and up to the time of writing my part of the report of the committee of twelve."[33]

But perhaps it was not so much the condition of the rural schools that caused some educators to despair as the fact that no one had listened to or acted upon their solution to the problem, which they had proposed to their state legislatures year after year through the last decades of the century.

7

The Township Solution

꽃

I

"THE ONLY WAY I SEE TO BETTER THE CONDITION OF THE [COUNTRY] schools," one Michigan educator said to a group of professionals in 1879, "is to take just as much of their control out of the hands of the people as is possible. The people do not know the needs of the schools. They have been educated in these poor schools, and until the schools are better the people will be ignorant.... Centralization is what we need in school management."[1]

Centralization! Concentrating the control over the country schools into as few hands as possible, as was done in city schools! That was the solution to the country-school problem as the Midwestern professional educators viewed it in the last years of the nineteenth century, and their method of bringing this about was to replace the small independent school district with the township district system.

By this system, the districts that served the single, one-room schools would give up their corporate powers to the township. The township would thus become the school district for all the little schools within its boundaries. The township meeting would be the important school meeting where school taxes would be determined and township school officials elected. The old independent district, emasculated by its loss of corporate powers, would become a subdistrict.

This was the educators' consummate solution to the country-school problem. By this plan they would in one stroke broaden the school district's tax base to include the entire township, equalize the education of all the children within one township, eliminate the old disputes that consumed the little independent districts, diminish the prolifera-

113

tion of small schools, provide improved supervision of the schools, and, happiest thought, wipe out thousands of rural school board members, those educators in overalls who, the educators believed, had stood in the way of greater efficiency in the schools for so long.

If this was not the perfect system for country schools, it was very nearly so in the minds of the professional educators. All through the Middle West, from the Civil War to the century's end, one state superintendent after another recommended its adoption, lesser school officials and professors of pedagogy in the normal schools supported it, and finally in 1896, the Committee of Twelve recommended it. "The first proposition," ran a portion of the committee's report, "is that the township-unit system is far superior to the district system, and should be substituted, if practicable, for that system wherever it exists."[2]

The township system was not a new idea on the Middle Border in the post–Civil War years. Midwestern educators had inherited the scheme from Horace Mann, who, before the Civil War, had denounced the old Massachusetts law establishing the independent district system as "the most unfortunate law on the subject of Common Schools, ever enacted in the State," and advocated the township district. He argued that the township system would provide better teachers for the school, better supervision, and better schools all around than the old independent district system.[3]

As long as he lived Mann was never able to convince the people of his own state of Massachusetts of the wisdom of his township district system, but the idea had a more favorable reception in some areas of the Middle Border where frontier conditions made experimentation easier. Indiana adopted the township district plan in 1852, and Ohio in 1853. Five years later, Iowa, too, with the help of Horace Mann himself, established the new system. But the consequences were scarcely what the educators had expected.[4]

In Ohio the change to the township system was little more than a change of name. Corporate powers were, it was true, transferred from the local districts to a township board composed of one school director elected from each of the new subdistricts in the township. But the people of the subdistricts—the old independent districts—continued, except for the raising of taxes, to manage their schools the way they always had. They still had their annual school meetings, elected three-member school boards, and employed their own teacher. The Ohio law, as one Ohio commissioner of schools noted, was simply "a compromise between the independent subdistrict system...and a system in which each township becomes a school district."[5]

In Iowa and Indiana, however, the new laws did revolutionize the educational systems. In 1858, six years after the law had gone into effect in Indiana, the state superintendent told what had happened. "By this law," he wrote, "a system entirely new to the people of the State was attempted to be introduced. The management of the School was removed far from the people, and placed, in theory at least, in the hands of township, county, and State officers. School districts were abolished; whole townships were thrown into corporate organizations for School purposes. The number and location of schoolhouses, the employment of teachers, the furnishings of fuel and schoolhouse furniture, and the whole management of the educational interests of the township were confided to the township trustees."[6]

This process was repeated in Iowa. There, throughout 1859, the reorganization of school districts proceeded swiftly. In little more than a year's time more than three thousand independent school districts were replaced with 933 township districts, while within the townships themselves old district boundaries were erased and new subdistricts created to equalize the schools. Simultaneously, the property, assets, and liabilities of the old, independent districts were turned over to township school boards similar to those organized in Ohio.[7]

When they established the township district systems, the state legislators in Indiana and Iowa apparently had not bothered to ask what the farmers thought. They seemed to believe that the farmers were really not interested in the way their educational system was organized or that if they had objections to the new plan these would pass. But they learned soon enough that the farmers cared greatly about their one-room schools, for the establishment of the new township districts touched off a struggle between the Midwestern educators and farmers that lasted for years and left its mark upon the educational systems of both states.

II

The struggle rose, as so often happens when new ideas are proposed, out of a conflict of values. On the one side were the educators, supremely sure of their superior wisdom, determined to rule the schools, and wedded to the principles of centralization, efficiency, and the equalization of education for all the children in a township; on the other were the farmers, stubborn, independent, conservative, opposed to centralization, unwilling to give up the control of their schools and their right to tax themselves for education, and deeply committed to the principle of self-help.[8]

When the township plan went into effect in Iowa, it became necessary to create a number of new subdistricts in many townships in order to bring the schoolhouses closer to all the children, thereby equalizing educational facilities. But many of the new subdistricts were built in areas of sparse population, and the farmers complained that these subdistricts represented territory, not people, which made little sense to them. More to the point, each new subdistrict must have a new schoolhouse for which the entire township must pay. To those farmers who had struggled to build their own schoolhouses, it seemed unfair that they should now be taxed for a schoolhouse for which there seemed little use and which their children would not use. It made a mockery of the rule that people should pay for what they use.

Nor did it seem reasonable to them that in the effort to equalize education throughout a township, all the teachers in that township must be paid the same. In all walks of life some people performed better than others and received more for doing so. Teaching was no different as the farmers saw it. Yet if they wanted to employ a first-rate teacher, they could not do so unless she was willing to accept the same salary all the teachers in the township received.

What was true of teachers was also true of the schoolhouse, school terms, and every aspect of the school's operation. In Iowa's township system the township board, meeting in some village or town far removed from most of the township farmers, determined what taxes the farmers would pay for the upkeep of the schools for the year. If a majority of the board cared little for educational improvements and consequently set a low tax rate, those in any subdistrict of the township who wanted a better school could not have it, because they had no control over the raising of the money to pay for it.

This undermined the principle of self-help which was so ingrained in rural thinking, and, in the end, meant that if the township system made the weak schools stronger, it also made the strong schools weaker. This was so obvious that even some educators saw it. "It frequently happens," wrote the Iowa superintendent in 1872, "the people of one portion of a district township are fully alive to the value of good schools, while the people of another and larger part are less liberal and prefer the log schoolhouse, the cheap teacher, and the short term of school: and who are able to out-vote and prevent the former from thus providing such schools as they want to see established."[9]

To say that the township district system undermined the doctrine of self-help, however, was only another way of saying that it deprived the farmers of the control of their schools, and it was this that so aroused the farmers in both Iowa and Indiana. "The masses," wrote an Iowa county superintendent in 1859, "are opposed to the present Township-District system, and ask for the power to build houses and manage their own affairs." And a resolution submitted that year to the Iowa Board of Education echoed the theme: "An independent district system by which the people of every single district may elect their own officers, build their own school houses, and do all other acts concerning the affairs of the district, fully recommends itself to this Board as preferable to the complex and vexatious [township] school system."[10]

The persistence with which Midwestern farmers tried to regain control of their school affairs in Indiana and Iowa over the next few years, in the face of the educators' opposition, reflected their reluctance to accept the centralization that was steadily depriving Americans of control over their affairs, and their disdain of professional educators as well. They could not see that education was as complicated as the educators made it out to be. To them education was a commonsense matter; its primary purpose was simply to teach their children how to read, write, spell, and figure, and these objectives, they thought, could be accomplished better under the old system than under the new.

So they pushed vigorously for the restoration of the old system, and, in time, forced both the Indiana and Iowa legislatures to modify the township systems they had established. In 1855, only three years after it had provided for the new organizations of its schools, the Indiana legislature partially restored the old system, as the state superintendent noted, without, however, actually abolishing the township system. But in Iowa the legislature was forced to make a more drastic revision of the new system.[11]

There the fight against the township district system continued through the Civil War, dispelling any hope the educators may have had that the farmers would accept the new system in time. Throughout the 1860s, while the Iowa state superintendents fought to save the township system, the farmers continued their agitation against it. Finally in 1872, wearied by fifteen years of agitation, and "against an unbroken array of testimony from the ablest educators of the State and nation that small districts were objectionable," as one Iowa superintendent later recalled, the state legislature changed the law. And, unlike the Indiana legislature, which had not gone so far, the Iowa assembly made it possible for any township to return to the independent district system if a majority of voters in the township desired it.[12]

With the celerity that emphasized their contempt for the educators' system and their desire to control their own affairs, the Iowa farmers moved to take advantage of the new law. Within the first year and a half after the law had been changed, 119 out of the 1,700 Iowa townships had returned to the old independent district system; and so rapid was the shift away from the township system in the early 1870s that the state superintendent, looking back on what had taken place in those years, wrote in 1882 that "had the formation of these districts been allowed to go on as they had from 1872 to 1875, we should have had not less than six or seven thousand independent districts at the present time."[13]

As it was, the number of independent districts had already reached three thousand in 1876, when the state legislature repealed the statute permitting subdistricts of the township to become independent. This repeal, however, was so weakly drawn—a reflection no doubt of the legislature's fear of the farmers—that it did not completely stop the growth of independent districts. Not until 1888, when the legislature finally decided that no townships could be carved into smaller independent districts unless a majority of the voters of each subdistrict, as opposed to the majority of voters in the township district, agreed, was the conversion from the township to the small independent district system virtually ended.[14]

Still this did not destroy those independent district systems that had already been established, and Iowa ended the century with her independent and township districts operating side by side. In this, her situation was much like that of Ohio, where the original law establishing the township system had, in effect, created a double-headed system. Moreover, it was a matter of some significance that, in Iowa as in Ohio, in order to establish the township system, the educators had been forced to allow the people to elect a school director in each subdistrict who would represent the farmers' interests on the township school board.[15]

In neither state was this compromise between the township and independent district systems acceptable to the professional educators. Year by year they lamented their two-headed systems and urged their state legislatures to eliminate the independent school districts. By the late 1880s, as the cult of efficiency spread, their recommendations took on a note of urgency. In 1889 the Ohio commissioner of education called attention to that state's wasteful school system, which was "nowhere more strikingly exhibited than in the 'double-headed system' for township schools." That same year Henry Sabin was writing in his biennial report in Iowa that "if the people of the State could be made to understand how much time, and money, and strength is wasted in carrying the present complex system into effect, and how much the efficiency of the school could be increased by the adoption of the civil township as the unit [for a school district], they would demand that the legislature take immediate steps toward accomplishing that result."[16]

But in neither state could the farmers or state legislatures be made to understand this, and the century ended with the double-headed system in both states still intact. True, the Ohio legislature did enact a law in 1892 that eliminated the three-member school boards in each subdistrict and theoretically transferred the entire management of the township schools to the township board. But in many places the farmers paid no attention to the law, and by 1898 they had forced the legislature to return the management of the local schools to the school director in each subdistrict, as had been done in subdistricts in the township system in Iowa at an earlier date.[17]

III

Only in Indiana of all the Middle Border states was there a general acceptance of the township district system as the century waned. There in 1855 the legislature had been forced to modify its township plan to the extent of permitting the people in each subdistrict to hold a meeting to designate the teacher they wanted. But it had not at the same time deprived the township trustee, who was originally given the responsibility for employing the teacher, of having a voice in the teacher's selection. The result was that for nearly twenty years vast confusion prevailed, and the state superintendents spent their days trying to unravel the disputes that arose between the people and the trustee over the hiring of a teacher. "The old law has given rise to more trouble in school-matters," remarked one state superintendent, "than almost all other things combined."[18]

Nevertheless, Indiana maintained its township system and gradually ironed out its problems. With a nod to the experience of both Iowa and Ohio, the Indiana state superintendent wrote in 1888 that

119

because of the vision of those who planned the school system, Indiana never found it necessary to "go back and re-establish the system upon a new basis or upon a different plan. But whenever," he continued, "it has been found that an improvement could be made, there has been no hesitancy in adopting it. Thus, the old district system has given way to the more efficient township system."[19]

This was, indeed, what had happened. The township trustee, who was elected for a two-year term, gradually exercised the power that had been given him to establish and locate new schools in the township, to build a new schoolhouse and provide it with furniture and school apparatus, and to establish graded schools if they seemed desirable. In addition to this, even the right to designate the teacher was taken from the people in 1873 and given to the trustee, who now became the sole employer of all the teachers in the township.[20]

Thus, the management of the country schools in every township in Indiana had been concentrated in the hands of one person, and thousands of school officials had been eliminated. The tax money had been evened out so that the poorer areas of the township received as much as the richer; a more uniform system of schools had developed; and instruction was so regularized that a reporter, analyzing Indiana's rural schools in the early 1900s, observed that the work given in them had become completely standardized. "If the pupils make salt-boxes and read *The Children's Hour* in the southern montains," she wrote, "salt-boxes and *The Children's Hour* are occupying the schools on the northern plains."[21]

Furthermore, the great turnover of teachers that occurred each term in most country schools and seemed endemic to the independent district system had been significantly reduced in Indiana as early as the 1880s. In 1887 Indiana would have needed 13,500 teachers to supply her classrooms, if every teacher had been employed for the entire year. That she employed 14,006 made the turnover of her teachers for the various school terms only 3.42 per cent for the year, a record far superior to that in most Midwestern states. By comparison, Iowa, with its rapid turnover of teachers, employed 24,232 teachers that year to fill 14,747 positions, which made the percentage of change in her teaching corps 64.32 per cent for the year.[22]

By the 1890s, then, Indiana's township district system seemed to have fulfilled the professional educators' expectations and to have produced the most efficient rural school system in the Midwest. "Our school system is very efficient," the Indiana state superintendent boasted in 1892. "It approaches the ideal system." This good opinion of Indiana's country-school system was shared by William T. Harris, United States commissioner of education and perhaps the nation's most noted professional educator, and by most Midwestern educators, who regarded Indiana's township system as a model for their own states to follow.[23]

But, alas, not everything was as it seemed, and in retrospect it appears that Indiana's township system retarded the state's educational development more than it helped.

Throughout the last three decades of the nineteenth century the National Bureau of Education gathered a mass of statistics to show the progress of education in the nation. Admittedly the statistics were suspect, and what they really showed was uncertain. The commissioner of education himself wrote in 1887 that "few circumstances . . . that affect the educational life of a State can be subjected to quantitative measurements." Still, the statistics make it possible to compare Indiana's educational system in certain ways with those of the other Middle Border states and to draw some inferences about the effectiveness of the township system as it worked out in Indiana.[24]

If everything the professional educators had been saying for twenty years about the superiority of the township system over the independent district system was true, we would expect that Indiana would have led all the Middle Border states in some, if not all, of those characteristics which indicate a vigorous school system—the length of the school term, for example. Yet she rarely ranked first in any one of them in any single year, and averaged first in none of them.

For the period 1892–1900, when the statistics had become reasonably well standardized, Indiana was only seventh among the states in the amount spent per pupil. Through three decades, she fell far below most of her sister states in average length of school term: seventh in 1870; sixth in 1880; eighth in 1890; tied for sixth in 1900. Only Missouri, lowest ranking of the Midwestern states in most of the measurements made, consistently ranked below Indiana in the amount spent per pupil and length of school term.

Indiana did, it was true, rank among the leaders of the North Central states in certain important categories. She was third and fourth, respectively, in amount paid female and male teachers, and she was third in the percentage of school population enrolled in school. Finally, even though her school terms were short, in the number of days of schooling for every child five to eighteen years of age, a category which the commissioner of education called "the best single quantity for determining the extent and prevalence of school education in one community as compared with another," Indiana ranked third among the states.[25]

Indiana's figures, however, were based on the records of the city and town schools as well as the country schools, and most of the gains registered were the result of improvements in the urban schools, which had grown rapidly during the 1890s, when Indiana's urban population had increased faster than that of any Midwestern state except Illinois. In the rural areas, where the township school system held sway, there was little improvement in the schools.[26]

This was apparent in the statistics on the number of days school was kept in Indiana in 1900. That year, the average number of days school was held for the entire state was 144, but in the cities the average was 180 days, in the towns 143, and in the township country schools 125. "Again the figures show, apparently," the Indiana state superintendent commented, "an increase in the length of school terms, but the majority of pupils are not affected by this increase. The wonderful development of the town and city schools with nine or ten months of school is responsible for the increase in the average of 144 days."[27]

Indiana was not the wealthiest of the Midwestern states, to be sure. She was fourth in the true valuation of her real and personal property in 1880, fifth in 1890, and sixth in 1900. But this fact alone does not adequately explain why she did not do better in the statistics, and a finer sifting of the evidence and comparisons with other states support the conclusion that it was the township system itself that was largely responsible for the state's short school terms and for her inability to raise as much money for education as did other Midwestern states whose wealth was comparable.[28]

In important ways Indiana's township school system was a victim of the triumph of the doctrine of centralization and efficiency over the doctrine of self-help. For years the rapid progress of education in the Midwest had made that area a showcase for the principle of self-help, and even professional educators praised the doctrine. "In education as in other departments of human activity," Commissioner Harris wrote in 1890, "it is self-help that stimulates the healthiest and most vigorous growth and leads to the most enduring results." The Committee of Twelve, which so energetically supported the township system, paradoxically warned against removing the responsibility of education from the people. "It is a great mistake," the committee reported, "to remove the burdens of public education so far from the people that they forget . . . their existence. The principle is a vital one.

History shows conclusively that popular education has flourished most in those States of our Union where government is most democratic."[29]

Here and there an occasional county superintendent saw that to establish a township school system, thereby removing the schools one step from the people, might cause the farmers "to lose interest and consider it [education] a burden." The county superintendent of Mills· County, Iowa, who supervised both systems, candidly expressed his preference for the district system. It appeared to him that farmers in the independent districts were more interested in education. "I am partial to the independent system," he wrote in 1879. "The business of the independent system is accompanied by less 'red tape,' they pay better wages; appreciate a good teacher; are more particular about the grade of certificate held by an applicant; and more inclined to retain the teacher who had done good work. Somehow the independent system brings the school and patrons more together."[30]

But these were voices in the wilderness. Blinded by their eagerness to get rid of those squabbling little school districts and opinionated school directors and make their own work easier, most Midwestern professional educators apparently could not see that to take the management of the schools away from the farmers and give it to one trustee, and to shift the taxing power from the local to the township level, would encroach upon the doctrine of self-help and diminish the individual farmer's interest in his school.

Or, if they did understand this, they justified the township system on the grounds that it was equalizing the education of children throughout the township.

In Indiana, where the township trustee set the tax rate for the township, it was true that the money raised at the township level was spread evenly across the township, and that education, insofar as money was concerned, was equalized throughout the area. But the result was almost certainly a reduction in the total amount of money raised for education in the township. The people in those communities in the township that could have afforded to pay more for education made little effort in that direction because they knew that any additional money raised would be spent throughout the township and not on their particular school. Furthermore, by removing the management of the schools from the people and equalizing education across the township, Indiana's system dampened the farmers' interest in their schools and destroyed the competitive spirit that existed among the small independent districts where taxes were spent where they were collected and where farmers often voted for higher taxes than they might have otherwise in order to have a better school than their neighboring district.[31]

That the township district system had reduced the amount of money for education raised at the township level in Indiana was supported by the fact that the state's school system had to rely heavily on state taxes for its operation.

William T. Harris had written that "the amount of local tax [collected] measures in a general way the amount of local interest taken in the schools," and if this was true, then Indiana farmers were far more apathetic about their schools than were the farmers in other Midwestern states. Through the last two decades of the nineteenth century Indiana received a lesser percentage of her school money from local taxes and a greater percentage from state taxes than any other North Central state. In 1890, an average year, she received almost 26.00 per cent of her education money from state taxes and raised only 55.25 per cent locally. Ohio, which ranked next to her in this, received only 16.65 per cent of her school money from state taxes and raised 78.50 per cent locally, while Iowa and Kansas received nothing from state taxes and raised more than 80.00 per cent of all their school money from local taxes.[32]

The township district system may also have been largely to blame for Indiana's short school terms. Again, the lack of money, which itself was at least partly attributable to the Indiana farmers' refusal to tax themselves more, was partially responsible for the short school terms, but only partially. In 1900 Indiana was spending virtually the same amount of money on education as other states, yet they had longer school terms than Indiana. The difference was in the way the money was spent.[33]

Indiana spent more money on teachers' salaries and school buildings than most other Midwestern states, and possibly Indiana officials deliberately decided to do this rather than to spend the money for longer school terms. Very likely, however, the township district itself, like the tail wagging the dog, largely determined how the money should be spent. That system demanded uniformity, and if one subdistrict in the township had a fine brick schoolhouse, then other subdistricts must have fine brick schoolhouses; and if a male teacher was paid $63.40 a month—the average for Indiana in 1900—then all male teachers must receive the same regardless of their qualifications. By the same rule, if there was money for only 123 days of school for the year in the township, then all schools in the township must have only

123 days even though some subdistricts if left to govern themselves might have opted for more. Perhaps justice was served in this way, but improved education was not.

Moreover, the price Indiana had to pay for this uniformity and for the elimination of the country-school boards was not just in reduced school terms or diminished school taxes. The arrogant and corrupt township trustee was also a part of the cost. With no one to control him during his two-year term of office, the trustee frequently ran his township schools in a politically partisan manner. He not only appointed political favorites to teach the schools, but sometimes refused to remove them when they proved unsatisfactory. A trustee in Kosciusko County, for example, in 1884, when confronted with charges that two of his teachers had been involved in bastardy suits, were drunkards, and were "known to practice licentiousness among their students," refused to remove them and was alleged to have said that "he did not care a G— D— how much a man drank or how licentious he was as he had a license."[34]

Corruption among the township trustees, which surfaced in the 1880s on a scale unseen in any other Midwestern state, was an even more serious problem.

Stories of the trustees' mishandling of school funds, which they had sole control over, first attracted attention in 1885, and by the next year the state superintendent had been forced to investigate the situation. That he felt compelled to send questionnaires to farmers asking if there had been monetary losses in their townships, if their trustees had abused their power to select teachers by appointing favorites, if the trustees had been wasteful in the purchase of school apparatus, and if they visited the schools, all suggested the problems Indiana was encountering with its township district system.

The answers, when they came according to the state superintendent who was trying to put the best light possible on the scandal, were not so bad in view of the fact that out of more than a thousand trustees with "inadequate pay, with great temptations and abundant opportunities" for making money, only a few were actually guilty of criminal activity. Still, this was bad enough. Nearly thirty township trustees—and no one knows how many more escaped detection— were found to have had their hands in the till in one way or another, and the losses to the township ran into the thousands of dollars. The trouble was serious enough, at least, for the state superintendent to recommend to the state legislature that supervision of the trustees was needed.[35]

IV

The final test of Indiana's school system, however, was not in the amount of money spent on education, or in the number of days school was kept, or in the fine brick schoolhouses, but in the provisions of an education for its entire population. And in this, Indiana's system, whether because of its township districts or for some other reason, did poorly in comparison with most of the other Midwestern states, when judged by the standard of number of illiterate people.

In the last three decades of the nineteenth century, Indiana had the largest percentage of native-born and the smallest percentage of foreign-born whites of all North Central states. Her Negro population, although large for a Midwestern state, composed only 2.3 per cent of the total. Indiana's population, in fact, was made up of over 90.0 per cent native-born whites. Yet she had, with the exception of Missouri, the highest percentage of illiterate people ten years of age and over of any of the ten states in the Midwest in 1870 and 1880, and was surpassed in 1890 and 1900 only by Missouri and by Wisconsin, whose foreign-born white population had the highest illiteracy rate of any of the North Central states. Indiana had the highest native-white illiteracy rate of all ten states except Missouri throughout the entire period.[36]

Nor was Indiana's record of reducing her illiteracy rate all that might have been expected of a very efficient educational system. The number of blacks in Kansas and Indiana, for example, from 1870 to 1900 was roughly equal. But Kansas reduced the percentage of illiteracy among her Negro population by sixty per cent in those thirty years, while Indiana lowered hers by only fifty per cent. Similarly, in those last three decades of the old century, Indiana reduced the percentage of her illiterate native white population by sixty-four per cent at the same time that Missouri decreased hers by seventy per cent, Kansas by eighty per cent, and Nebraska by eighty-five per cent.[37]

In the last ten years of the nineteenth century Indiana did reduce the number of her illiterate schoolchildren between the ages of ten and fourteen from 20.5 per 1,000 to 5.5 per 1,000, which was a remarkable achievement to be sure. But the very fact that she had so many illiterates of school age in 1890, more than any of the ten states except Missouri, cast a shadow over the notion that her township system was as efficient as the professional educators liked to believe.[38]

Somehow the life seemed to have gone out of Indiana's school system. It appeared to lack the vigor other Midwestern state systems possessed, and this was particularly noticeable when Indiana was measured against a comparable state like Iowa.

Iowa and Indiana had much in common insofar as education was concerned in 1900. They had approximately the same number of schoolchildren, and they were spending roughly the same amount. And though Iowa had more than three thousand small independent school districts she also had a large number of township districts. But Iowa's township district system was never heralded by the professional educators as a model system, for, like the independent district system, it involved too many farmers in school affairs.[39]

Unlike the Indiana plan, the township system in Iowa was not controlled by a single township trustee but by a township board composed of one school director elected annually from each subdistrict of the township. Each year at the board's first meeting the directors had to certify that they had been duly elected at the annual school election in their subdistrict. The certified board then elected its officers for the following year and proceeded to conduct the school business for the township.

The board met several times each year and in one meeting or another set the school tax rate for the township, determined the salary to be paid the teachers, fixed the length of the school term, and paid the claims the directors had for the school supplies they had purchased in their subdistricts. When the need arose they created a new subdistrict, picked the schoolhouse site, and built the new schoolhouse. They also considered requests the directors made for the major projects that had to be done in their subdistricts. For example, in 1887 the director from Subdistrict 2, Fairview Township, Jones County, Iowa, informed the board that his school had neither a stove nor privies. The board considered the matter, and, according to the minutes of their meeting, authorized "J. S. Joslin Sub-director to Build two Privies and purchase a stove for said sub-district No 2 & report the expense to this Board."[40]

The township school board, then, did everything that was done by the farmers or their school boards under the independent district system except to employ the teachers. Actually, the township board had this power too, but it usually delegated this sensitive responsibility to the directors of the subdistricts who were closer to the people.

In essence, the Iowa township district was a compromise between the democratic independent district and Indiana's autocratic township district. It was not what the educators wanted, but it was the best they could get in Iowa, and, in truth, it was difficult to see in what ways the state's township districts were more efficient than the independent districts.

Perhaps the township system helped to equalize education among the six or seven little schools in the township, but it did not end those quarrels over school matters that always troubled the farmers in the independent districts. It merely transferred these to the township school board members, who fought over the same issues the farmers did in their annual meetings. The Fairview Township board's debates about how much to pay the township teachers frequently ended with a divided vote and, no doubt, hard feelings. Once in 1887, the board could not even accept the contractor's bill for a schoolhouse it had built for Subdistrict 5 without an argument and a divided vote because some board member felt the contractor had not fulfilled his contract.[41]

Neither did it make the farmers in the subdistricts happy to have the township board determine where their schoolhouses were to sit, and they often challenged the board's decision. When the Sugar Grove Township board in Dallas County, for example, established the site for the schoolhouse for Subdistrict 5 in 1870, the farmers appealed to the county superintendent to change it, and when that failed, they took their case to the state superintendent.[42]

The annual elections in the subdistricts for the school directors were also troublesome. In the spring of 1887 in Subdistrict 6 of Fairview Township, the election for the director had ended in a tie between Luke Weatherson and Charles Porter. But apparently the election had been irregular, and at its March meeting, the township board spent most of its morning session listening to angry farmers from Subdistrict 6 explain "the whole cause of the trouble in its true light," as the township secretary put it, before it decided to settle the matter by having the contestants draw straws. The secretary then recorded this scene: "the president of the Board procured a Broom straw cut it in two parts, one part longer than the other and placed them in his hand so that the ends protruded about 1/2 inch, & it was impossible for a person to see which was the longer. By request Weatherson & Porter now appeared in front of the president, who informed them in a distinct and audible voice, that the one drawing the longer would be director. Weatherson then put forth his hand and drew rather a short piece of straw. Porter then reached forth and drew a much longer piece, and according to the terms of the drawing C. F. Porter was the successful candidate, and immediately qualified as sub-director for Sub-dist No. 6."[43]

Finally, even though it handled the affairs of all the schools within the township, the township board found it hard to equalize education throughout the township as it was supposed to do. In the autumn of 1886, when the Fairview board declared that all the township teachers were to be paid thirty dollars a month for the winter school term, the director from Subdistrict 9 complained that he could not hire a teacher for that amount and was authorized to pay as much as thirty-seven dollars. And in 1899, a group of farmers petitioned the board to create a new subdistrict to eliminate the unequal situation that forced some fifteen students in one neighborhood to walk more than two miles to school, but in this case the board rejected the petition with the argument that the unequal situation had been exaggerated and that the people who requested the new subdistrict were merely transients anyway.[44]

So Iowa's township system, compared with Indiana's, was chaotic and inefficient and far too democratic to suit the professional educators. With its substantial number of independent districts standing side by side with the township districts to add confusion and, incidentally, provide competition for the township districts, Iowa's country-school system violated nearly all the dicta the educators had established for building good country schools. She often paid her teachers less than did any other Midwestern state. And instead of building larger and fewer schools, as the educators advocated, Iowa had built more and smaller schoolhouses until she had nearly fourteen thousand in 1900, more than twenty-five hundred of which had an average daily attendance of fewer than ten students each. She had the most schoolhouses of all Midwestern states, more even than Ohio and Illinois, although her school population was scarcely half that of those states! Nor had she spent a great amount of money on them or on school apparatus. The total value of all of Iowa's schoolhouses and school property amounted to little more than $18 million in 1900, while the value of Indiana's ten thousand schoolhouses and school property totaled $25 million.[45]

Measured, then, against the educators' standards, Iowa's school system should have been noticeably inferior to Indiana's. Yet there was a certain energy in Iowa's system that was lacking in Indiana's, and this was reflected in the statistics. Iowa ranked near the top of all Midwestern states in almost every measurement used to evaluate school systems and surpassed Indiana in virtually all categories measured by the Bureau of Education except teachers' salaries. Her school terms were longer than those in Indiana; she enrolled a greater proportion of her school-age children in school; and she surpassed Indiana in average number of days of schooling. She raised all of her school taxes locally, and, even without state aid, spent more per capita of school population on education than Indiana did. And finally, along with Nebraska, a state whose little independent districts mushroomed in the last three decades of the century, Iowa had the fifth highest literacy rate of all states in the Union in 1870; was second only to Nebraska in 1880; came in third in 1890; and tied with Nebraska for first in 1900![46]

Intangible and immeasurable factors such as the character of the population no doubt had much to do with making Iowa the most literate state in the nation, and it may have been that the kind of school system a state had counted for less than the professional educators supposed. But it is probable that Iowa's double-headed township and independent district system was one major reason for its educational progress. Contrary to the educators' expert opinion, the small school situation, the farmers' control of education, and even the competition between the two systems seem almost certainly to have made effective teaching possible and stimulated the farmers' interest in their schools. On the other hand, in Indiana, the transfer of control from the people to the township trustees seems to have reduced the farmers' concern for their schools, and in the name of efficiency, merely rigidified the school system.

If this was the lesson to be drawn from the comparison between a democratic, decentralized school system and one that was highly centralized and autocratic, it was a lesson the Midwestern professional educators never learned. True, an occasional professional did seem to understand the advantages of a decentralized educational structure. In 1896 the Ohio commissioner of education argued that Ohio's loosely organized educational system was one of its greatest strengths. And in 1911 the Nebraska state superintendent admitted that the independent district system was best where the people were progressive, for their school would not be held back by its attachment to a larger educational unit.[47]

But such praise for the old independent district system was rare as the nineteenth century closed. For the most part the professionals on the Middle Border continued to wage war on the small rural independent districts with increasing stridency. As year by year the farmers and state legislators rejected recommendations for a township system, the Michigan state superintendent issued this ill-tempered statement in 1900:

"He [the farmer] attends the farmers' picnic," the superintendent wrote, "the meetings of the farmers' clubs and the grange, listens to the speeches of agricultural-political quacks, and then signs a petition to the legislature protesting against centralization of school management. He is told that he must oppose the idea of making the district larger, for that would be the 'entering-wedge for the adoption of the township unit system.' He is exhorted to beware of centralization, for that would be a blow to the 'little red school house' for which his orator has such reverence. The school must be kept 'near the people,' and therefore he often votes for the most ignorant man in the district as school officer, and opposes every movement to bring the school up to the standard of the one his children are attending in a village five or six miles distant. The little red school house—we cherish it—becomes in many places a miserable structure on a bleak hillside, with dingy walls and battered desks within. No shade, no enclosure, and no encouragement to the poorly paid teacher and her handful of pupils—a standing mockery to the narrow misguided policy of those who in years past have been the leaders of our agriculture classes."[48]

But not even such outbursts as these could move the state legislators or farmers to abandon the independent district system throughout the Midwest. By the 1890s, it is true, the farmers in Wisconsin, Minnesota, and in the Upper Peninsula of Michigan had been given the right to establish the township district system if they wished. But when the choice was left to them, the farmers rarely chose to change from their independent districts. Indeed, it was more frequent to change the state superintendents who wanted to change the school system than it was to change the system, and throughout the last part of the nineteenth century, such superintendents had a job expectancy of one term.[49]

So, in 1900, almost everywhere across the Middle Border, the small, independent school districts—contentious, individualistic, democratic—pushed on into the twentieth century as small outposts of grass-roots democracy in a nation hurrying on toward centralization; and such centralization as there was in those little districts was brought about only by the county superintendents, who, through the years, tried to hold the systems together with a loose kind of supervision.

8

The Educator-Politician
on the Middle Border

❦

I

EARLY IN THE MORNING OF NOVEMBER 7, 1865, ANSON BUTTLES hurried from his little farm in Milwaukee Township, Wisconsin, to his polling place. Hardly more than a week previously he had been nominated to run for county superintendent of Milwaukee County, and he was anxious to vote and to determine if he could how the election was going. That evening he learned that he had received all the votes in his immediate area, and the next day when he drove down to the Green Bay Road, he found that he had also won all the votes in Granville, a nearby town, and that he had been elected for two years beginning the first of January. With his inauguration day in mind, he drove into Milwaukee on December 30 and bought a new suit of clothes.[1]

Buttles was an unusual man for his day. He was well educated and an avid reader who kept a record of the number of pages he read each year. No stranger to politics, he had been at one time or another town clerk, justice of the peace, county surveyor, and for years on end a director of the little district school near his farm. Now he would be one of the new county officials who, along with the township district system, were the professional educators' best hope for standardizing and centralizing the Midwestern country schools in the late nineteenth century.[2]

Very early, even before the Civil War, a few educators on the Middle Border had seen the necessity for establishing some kind of administrative link between the small, independent schools and the township, county, and state governments. For it was obvious to them that someone was needed to lay out school districts and apportion the money from the state's permanent school fund among the various district schools. Beyond that, human nature being what it was, they thought it prudent to have a township official supervise the small districts if for no other reason than to see that the state's money was not wasted.

One man who saw all this was John Pierce, the far-sighted minister-educator who wrote the law establishing Michigan's educational system. In this famous old law, so widely copied through the Midwest, Pierce had provided for a school inspector for each township. His duties were to establish school districts, examine teachers, visit schools, and to make such recommendations for improving the schools as he thought necessary. Although the law was modified somewhat over the years, its basic provisions remained, and for more than a quarter of a century the township inspectors provided whatever supervision there was over Michigan's country schools.[3]

Elsewhere, however, the supervision of country schools was taking a different turn. In 1854 Pennsylvania had placed much of the supervision of her rural schools in the hands of a county superintendent, and Iowa followed Pennsylvania's lead in 1858, the same year she adopted the township district system. Three years later the idea of having a county superintendent of schools had become so familiar that the people of Kansas provided for such an office in their state constitution, and through the 1860s most of the Middle Border states amended their school laws to make room for this official who, it was thought, could do so much to tidy up the freewheeling ways of the country schools. By 1873, when the Indiana legislature, too, was persuaded of the virtues of a county superintendency, the farmers in all the Midwestern states except Ohio were getting used to seeing their county superintendent making his rounds along their country roads as he passed from school to school on his visitations.[4]

The county superintendent's duties varied slightly from state to state, but essentially he was to keep records of the number of schoolchildren in each district and report all such figures to the state superintendent, to apportion the county and state monies among the schools according to their school population, lay out school districts, change the district boundaries when necessary, and settle district quarrels that erupted over school matters. And, as if these duties were not enough in themselves to involve the superintendent in endless controversy, he was also given the task of examining and licensing teachers, visiting schools, and making suggestions for their improvement. Eventually he also became responsible for a teacher-training program.

In the minds of the Midwestern professional educators who had pushed for the establishment of the office, the county superintendent was to standardize, elevate, and encourage education across his county, promote harmony within the districts, and bring order and efficiency to the small country school. He was, in short, to do what the superintendent of the urban school was doing. But what was possible in the cities, where the control of education was swiftly passing from the people to the educators, was impossible in the country, and for more than a decade the office of the county superintendent in the Middle West remained like a fortress under siege.[5]

City superintendents could insist that teachers have a first-grade teaching certificate and could weed out anyone who could not pass the necessary examinations. Yet when the county superintendents, particularly in the 1870s, began awarding teaching certificates only to those who passed the examinations with a reasonable mark and failing the obviously inept, the wrath of their communities fell upon them. Proud parents whose sons and daughters had been denied a certificate were outraged, and the indignation of the rejected applicants, particularly those who had been teaching for some time, was felt in every little crossroads store and village in the county. In a remarkable understatement of the situation, a Michigan county superintendent wrote in 1871 that the elimination of poor teachers there had "given dissatisfaction in many instances, as might have been predicted. Those who have been employed for years . . . in the schools," he continued, "but who were destitute of nearly every qualification to fit them for their position, and too opinionated or too indolent to consent to make any effort to improve themselves in the branches to be taught, or in methods of instruction, would, of course, complain when they found themselves set aside, and others occupying their places."[6]

County-school board members, too, were angry when they were told they could not retain a teacher they had employed because that teacher had been unable to secure a certificate. Not only did this indicate their poor judgment for all their neighbors to see, but it also seemed to them a flagrant interference with their right to manage their own schools. Nor did it soothe their irritation with the new official to know that he might be able to cut off state money to the district if they failed to comply with his demands and the law.[7]

Bad as it was, the problem of the rejected teacher was less troublesome than the controversies that swirled around the boundary lines they drew for a new school district or changed in an old district to appease dissatisfied farmers.

Rarely did a year pass before the turn of the century that the average Midwestern county superintendent was not troubled by some farmer who was unhappy with his district boundary line, either because he had been left outside a district and wanted in, or because he had been included in one and wanted out; or he might even be discontented because the lines had been drawn in such a way as to exclude or include some neighbor. Whatever his complaint, his solution was to petition his county superintendent to change the boundaries.

As often as not, a farmer requested a transfer of his property from one district to another for petty reasons. He may have fallen out with a neighbor, or lost a school election, or failed to win a point at a school meeting. Or he might wish to move into a district that had lower taxes. Then again, he might have a very good reason for asking for a change of boundaries that would put him in a new district. The other schoolhouse might actually be closer to his farm than the one in his own district. Or he might wish to avoid sending his children to school along a road on which there were dangerous obstructions—a river, perhaps, or a mill pond—which his children had to cross or walk along on their way to school.[8]

Because there often were legitimate reasons for changing boundary lines and transferring a farmer from one district to another, the Midwestern state laws provided for such changes, usually with the understanding that the transfer might take place if the farmers in each district involved agreed. But it was not often that those living in the district which the farmer wished to leave agreed. Struggling as they did each year to raise enough money to keep their school going, they fretted about the loss of tax money that would result when a farmer's property was transferred from their district to another. More than that, the mere request for a transfer was itself an affront to the farmers remaining in the district, because it implied that the farmer who wished to leave thought the school in their district was not good enough for his children.

So the farmers in the district from which a transfer had been requested usually raised their own protesting petition, thereby confronting the county superintendent with an unenviable choice. "I honestly cannot conceive," wrote a Kansas county superintendent in

1872, "of a position more . . . difficult to fill . . . than that of a county superintendent. . . . His duties and his responsibilities are . . . simply enormous. But among them all, the most embarrassing and perplexing duty, which a superintendent is called upon to perform, is the settlement of boundary lines of school districts, and the deposing of applications of various parties to be set off from one district to another. And I cannot now remember but few instances . . . in the experience of four years, when I have changed or refused to change the boundaries, or set off, or refused to set off, some party from one district to another, that dissatisfaction on the part of some has not been the result."[9]

The controversy between Districts 19 and 27 in Osborne County, Kansas, in 1897, was an excellent example of the problem.

That year a petition from District 19 requesting that G. C. Hutcherson's property be transferred from District 27 to District 19 reached Superintendent George Ruede's office. The petition was accompanied by a letter in which Hutcherson explained that the schoolhouse in District 27 was too far from his home, that he was already sending his children to the school in District 19 at a cost of three dollars a month, and that the transfer of his property would have little effect on District 27. Hutcherson's letter also spelled out what was usually merely implied. "The house [in District 27] is not in fit condition to have School in," his letter said. "The house is used for church purposes the doors are left open and Books are frequently taken I have lost some that way."[10]

The response of the farmers in District 27 to Hutcherson's request for a transfer and to the aspersions cast upon their school was not long in coming. Fifteen farmers quickly signed and sent a petition urging the superintendent to reject Hutcherson's request. Their district, they said, was small. Only twenty-two students were enrolled in its school, and each was badly needed; any loss of students would mean a loss of state money, which the district could ill afford. District 27, the petition went on, "has nothing to spare neither in the line of pupils nor property without sustaining material loss and damage to school and Patrons." On the other hand, they pointed out, District 19 was a large district; a railroad ran through it, enlarging its tax revenues; it had ample property to tax and numerous children in its school.[11]

Showing considerable courage, the county superintendent rejected Hutcherson's request for a transfer, thinking, no doubt, that District 27 would be hurt. But that did not end the matter. Hutcherson and

District 19 appealed to the Board of Commissioners, and the board reversed the county superintendent, allowed Hutcherson to transfer to District 19, and thereby alienated at least fifteen farmers.[12]

II

How to settle such issues and not make enemies? It was a question the wisest county superintendents could not answer. Still, the decisions they made on school district boundary lines and the grading of teachers were not the only irritants that jeopardized their jobs in the late nineteenth century. Their salaries, too, troubled the farmers in the 1870s and '80s. For years the superintendents were paid from three to five dollars a day for every day they served, which at first was only a few days a year. Even so, to the farmers who made so little from their days of toil, the smallest sums seemed large, and five dollars in their view was too much to pay arrogant office-holders who rode around the county in buggies wearing their Sunday suits and putting on airs.[13]

Among the Middle Border farmers the old Jeffersonian legacy of a "wise and frugal government, which shall restrain men from injuring one another, shall leave them otherwise free to regulate their own pursuits of industry and improvement" died hard. They retained through the years a natural suspicion of office-holders and wanted no more of them than absolutely necessary. Now, almost suddenly it seemed, they saw new officials in their counties who not only told them, in effect, whom they could and could not employ to teach their children, but where their district boundary lines were going to be. They snooped about the farmers' one-room schoolhouses, told the farmers their schools were inadequate, said they must have uniform textbooks, and that they needed two privies. Some of them, as is often the way with those with newly acquired authority and power, arrogantly assumed powers they did not have to make the farmers conform to their own ideas of what ought to be done.[14]

So the farmers' distaste for these sometimes-overbearing officials, who lived in the county seat and drove around the countryside at the farmers' expense telling them how they must run their schools, mounted in the 1870s, and in nearly every Midwestern state attempts were made to get rid of the county superintendent. "County superintendents are now on trial," the Nebraska state superintendent wrote in 1873, and indeed they were. In Kansas, Wisconsin, Minnesota, everywhere across the region, the question of whether to keep or eliminate the county superintendents became a topic of conversation in the general stores and little post offices, at Grange meetings, and in the state legislatures, as farmers began petitioning their legislators to get rid of the monster they had created.[15]

In Iowa a concentrated effort was made in 1872 to force the legislature to abolish the county superintendent's office, and when that failed attempts were made to reduce the superintendent's salary to a hundred dollars a year and repeal the law requiring him to visit schools. The repeal failed in Iowa, but in Illinois it succeeded in the early 1870s, so that for a time they were to visit schools there only if invited. Similar attempts were made to destroy or restrict the county superintendent's office in nearly every Middle Border state, but only in Missouri and Michigan did the farmers actually succeed in eliminating their superintendents.[16]

In Missouri the state legislature rooted out the county superintendents in 1874, leaving in their place in each county a commissioner of education whose primary function was merely to make statistical reports to the state superintendent on the status of the schools in his county. That same year the Michigan state superintendent, sensing the impending destruction of the office there, noted the growing feeling among the people that the county superintendents cost too much money, had too much power, and were trying to cover too much territory to be effective.[17]

The blow anticipated by the superintendent fell the next year. Bowing to the demands of the farmers, the state legislature eliminated the county superintendents and gave some of their duties to township superintendents. Two years later, after explaining what had happened in his annual report, the state superintendent prophesied that it would be impossible to reestablish the county superintendent's office. "There is, in Michigan, a feeling prevailing to a greater degree than in most other States," he wrote, "that abhors centralization and resents outside interference. This worked and would work against county or district supervision."[18]

In the next few years the anguished pleas the professional educators made to their state legislatures to retain the county superintendents helped save these public servants in other states, so that the eradication of the office was less widespread than it might have been. But in the end, it was not so much the professional educators that saved the county superintendents as the county superintendents themselves, who learned to become politicians first and educators afterwards.

In every state on the Middle Border where the county superintendent's office was retained, except in Indiana, county superintendents were elected by the people. More than that, they were elected every two years everywhere except Illinois, where they served four years. And like all county officers who ran for office, they had to pass through the narrows of political life. Unless they wished to run as an independent, their first step was to secure their party's nomination for the office. This was usually not easy. The competition was fierce because each section of the county sponsored its own particular candidate at the county nominating convention. When J. R. Bickerdyke, the long-time superintendent of Russell County, Kansas, sought the party's nomination in 1888, for example, he was one of four candidates, and it took four ballots to nominate him.[19]

Obviously the office was attractive in spite of the low pay and the controversies that seethed around it. For many a schoolteacher, living out his life in some small rural community and eking out a bare living in his schoolroom, the county superintendency might have seemed like a life line. It would take him from the humdrum life of teaching, launch him on a new career, and lead him on, perhaps, to greater things.

Herbert Quick, who wrote so perceptively about Midwestern rural life in the nineteenth century, probably spoke for many young men on the Middle Border when he summarized in later life the reasons he had run for the county superintendent's office of Kossuth County, Iowa, in the 1880s. First of all, he was a teacher, and if he wished to run for any office, which he did, logic suggested the county superintendency. The pay was small, to be sure, but infinitely more than he was making as the principal of a small school. But more than that, the county superintendency would take him all the way to the county seat, give him an office of his own, and place him among the county's ruling hierarchy. There he would become acquainted with the men who were on the inside of the county's affairs, men who knew before anyone else what farms could be bought for a fraction of their worth and how money was to be made from the land. All his life he had observed that county officials somehow became affluent, and who knew but what he, too, might find fortune at the end of the political rainbow. In any event, what he really wanted, as he said, was "a promotion" from the work he was in.[20]

Promotion was perhaps uppermost in the minds of those impecunious lawyers, part-time preachers, and wounded Civil War veterans who were often among the first to fill the county superintendent's office in the 1860s and '70s. Still, whatever their motives, whether they were merely trying to get ahead or whether they were primarily interested in improving education, when they ran for the office, they ran as educators, and their party newspapers magnified their educational achievements and played down those of their opponents. In the campaign for election, especially in those years after the position had become fixed, the length of a candidate's teaching career was important, as was his dedication to the profession. In the election of 1888 in Russell County, Kansas, for example, it was much to his credit that "Professor Bickerdyke," as the newspaper called him, had "devoted his whole life to the public schools."[21]

The kind of teaching certificate a candidate for the county superintendency had was important, too, and if one party's nominee held a lesser certificate than the other's, it was necessary for that party to show why and to assure the voters that its own candidate could easily secure a better one if need be. When it became known, for instance, that the Republican candidate for county superintendent in Juneau County, Wisconsin, in 1892, did not have a first-grade certificate, the editor of the Republican journal explained that the Republican candidate "had both a third and second grade certificate, never having needed a first grade did not apply for one but is thoroughly capable of securing that grade notwithstanding it has been alleged to the contrary."[22]

Like all political offices, the county superintendency could not avoid being embroiled in the political wars that were fought over local offices, and the more vicious the fight, the more bitter became the contest over the credentials of the candidate. In the 1890s, in the angry days of Populism, when passions sometimes stripped the sheath of civility from the people living on the western rim of the Middle Border, a young woman named Etta Cross, the incumbent Populist county superintendent in Osborne County, Kansas, was running for reelection. In the campaign of 1894 her Republican opponent charged that she had employed teachers from outside the county, had spent too much time with teachers' reading circles and teachers' institutes, and not enough time visiting schools. Worse than this, the Republican newspaper noted disdainfully that unlike the Republican candidate, Miss Cross did not have a first-grade teaching certificate![23]

Stung by this blot on his candidate's record, the editor of the Populist newspaper replied that "if Miss Cross wished to have a first grade [certificate] she could get it with perfect ease as far as her educational ability is concerned." As proof of this, the editor, who had access to the county superintendent's files, revealed the test scores made in the county teacher's examination by both Cross and her opponent. To the shock of the Republicans, Cross had bested her opponent in all of the ten subjects taken except reading, United States history, and Constitution. Besides that, her average grade was 90.0, while her opponent's grade was 79.8, high enough to qualify for the first-grade certificate only by the grace of the examining board.[24]

It was a bitter campaign, and charges and countercharges over the candidates' credentials continued to fill the Osborne newspapers until the election, when Cross was reelected. But at least the controversy in this case centered upon the qualifications of the candidates, which did not always happen. In 1897, when the Democratic and Populist forces fused in a local election in Saunders County, Nebraska, and the Populists agreed to support a Democrat for county superintendent, the Populist newspaper largely ignored its candidate's educational qualifications to emphasize that he had "always been on the side of the struggling masses and against the aggressiveness and oppression of corporations and trusts, and he stand[s] squarely with both his feet on the platform in favor of the free coinage of silver."[25]

Partisan politics, local as well as national, ran deeply in the rural Middle West in the late nineteenth century, and, normally, Republican candidates for county superintendent were elected in Republican strongholds, and Democratic contenders in Democratic counties. But this was not always so. Men who ran for the office of county superintendent learned very early that they could not ignore the farmers' concerns if they wished to be elected. How would the candidate settle a boundary dispute? How fair would he be in the teachers' examinations? How would he treat the school board members? All these questions would be in the minds of the farmers as they went to the polls, and the candidate who rated poorly on them could expect to be defeated.

This was a fact of life no county superintendent who wanted to be reelected could forget as he examined teachers, drew boundary lines, or drove about the county visiting schools and making suggestions. "Above all," the Minnesota state superintendent warned him "be careful not to create popular storms before which you must bend in weakness or break in obstinacy." And following this advice, the wise superintendent sought the middle way in the performance of his duties, trying as best he could to improve the quality of education in his county yet unabashedly compromising standards where it seemed necessary to promote harmony in the districts, and, not incidentally, to get himself reelected.[26]

He learned how to temper his decisions with mercy and how to suggest rather than to dictate changes to teachers and school board members. In freshly populated areas he created new school districts for almost anyone who asked, regardless of the actual need, and he gave teaching certificates away by the handful, salving his conscience with the explanation, which was true in many cases, that when the demand for teachers was so great, the normal standards could not be maintained.

III

So where the county superintendent survived on the Middle Border, he did so as a politician, not as a bureaucratic educator who ordered people about without being responsible to them, and in time he became as familiar a figure on the Midwestern rural landscape as the county sheriff. He took up residence in the county seat, and the farmers came to expect to see him in his office at the county courthouse when they paid their taxes. By the 1890s, probably most of those who saw him there had forgotten that there was ever a time when the office itself had been in jeopardy. So acceptable had the office become by 1891 that the Iowa state superintendent could write that it was a "subject for congratulation, that it is no longer necessary to address the argument in favor of retaining the county superintendency."[27]

Actually the battle had been won before 1891. The farmers, generally, had accepted the county superintendent in the 1880s, and through that decade his influence had grown. By 1891, even if he was merely a politician who led the people instead of directing them, he had become a powerful influence for the improvement of education on the Middle Border, just as the professional educators had planned.

With growing confidence in their position, the county superintendents gradually raised their teachers' academic standards. The era of the private examination, which made it more difficult for the county superintendent to fail an applicant, was already passing in the 1880s, and public examinations were becoming the rule. Young people who wished to become teachers became accustomed to the more difficult requirements and were not necessarily surprised at the more rigorous tone of the county superintendent's directions accompanying his notice in the county newspapers of the time and place of the teachers' examination. "Persons of limited attainment," the county superintendent wrote in announcing the teachers' examination for Jefferson County, Wisconsin, in 1885, "and those who have failed to conduct schools will avoid disappointment by not writing [the examinations] as our schools will [be] placed under the management of the more skilled progressive teachers. Certificates [previously given] will not be endorsed. Every person not holding a certificate and desiring to teach will be obliged to [pass] one of these public examinations and obtain a certificate upon his merits as all competent reliable teachers do."[28]

The more vigorous the testing program, however, the more work the county superintendents made for themselves. They had had no courses in tests and measurements, of course, and knew of no easy way to test. For them testing was a commonsense matter. They knew what they wanted the teachers to know, and they simply asked them if they knew it. If the teachers could do such things as parse the word *him* in a sentence, tell about the Battle of Bunker Hill, name the states touching on the Mississippi River, diagram a sentence, and write a well-organized paragraph without grammatical errors, fine; if not, they failed.

But the preparation of these lengthy examinations took time, and the grading even longer. Even giving the examinations might take several days if they were given in various parts of the county. William Scott, the superintendent of Ozaukee County, Wisconsin, in 1882, spent three of his Saturdays in March preparing the teachers' examinations, spent the week of April 11 giving the examinations in Cedarburg, Port Washington, and Waubecka, and spent the next week grading papers.[29]

Not only did the teachers' testing program become more rigorous as the county superintendents' positions became assured, but their school visits, too, became more fruitful as experience taught them what to look for and how to improve poor schools.

The county superintendents wrote much about how to make a successful school visit and discussed it at length, but there was no more agreement among them on this than upon any other pedagogical problem they discussed in those days. Some superintendents argued for the familiar, relaxed approach in visiting schools; others thought they should be reserved and dignified as they took their place in the classroom. Many believed they should conduct a class or two to show the teacher how it should be done, while others pointed out how embarrassing this might be to the teacher standing before her students. "Go to the house quickly," wrote one expert on visitations, "and without knocking enter. Make yourself at home, in a quiet cheerful way, and prepare to take notes, mentally, to be written by and by. Watch the work for a few recitations, and then ask to conduct one yourself. Do this in an easy, quiet manner without ostentation. At recess get your record of schoolhouse apparatus, fixtures, etc., but wait till after school to write up the teacher. Make all criticisms of the teacher privately to him, and no one else; say a few cheering words to the school, slip out quietly, and go about your business elsewhere."[30]

Successful visitation, however, like successful teaching, was an individual matter, and what worked for one would not necessarily work for another. But however it was done, the superintendent's visit was a major event in the lives of the teacher and the schoolchildren in those little one-room schoolhouses on the Middle Border of the past century.

If the superintendent happened to approach the schoolhouse at recess time, the children were likely to see his buggy a quarter of a mile or so down the road. "Here comes old soupbones," they would yell, as they followed his approach to the schoolhouse. They would watch him unhitch and feed his horse a bag of oats, and then follow him into the schoolhouse, where, as classes resumed, anything might happen. To shy farm children who so rarely saw a stranger, the superintendent was like a man from the "infernal regions," as one superintendent wrote, and their eyes might never leave his face. Or, to cover the awkward situation they might be rude and noisy and snap their fingers more loudly than usual.[31]

Even more disconcerting, the teacher in terror or embarrassment might forget exactly what it was she was supposed to do when the superintendent came. This was so common that one superintendent took the precaution of writing to his teachers before his visit to let them know what he expected. "I notice in my visits," he wrote, "that some of the teachers do not seem at ease. I do not wish to embarrass you in any way, and as some of you seem at a loss what to do or how to conduct yourselves during my visits, I send you this circular."[32]

But normally the teachers went on with their recitations while the superintendent observed. Sometimes he would, indeed, conduct a recitation to demonstrate how he thought it should be done, but whether he did this or not, he usually took the teacher aside at recess time to suggest to her how she might improve her teaching methods. This he tried to do as tactfully as possible in order not to discourage her, but occasionally it seemed necessary to speak bluntly. One superintendent once recalled how he had spoken to a male teacher who had difficulty controlling his school. "I told him of his faults," he related, "and suggested that some slight attention ought to be given to his personal appearance; that he should remember that the personal influence of the teacher in moulding the character of his pupils, is the most important element in their education."[33]

Before he left the school the superintendent made notes on the condition of the schoolhouse and the school apparatus, so that at a later date he could remind the directors of the needs of their school. Through the 1870s and '80s the list was likely to be long and discouraging. Joseph Funk, for example, the superintendent in Lawrence County, Indiana, filled his memorandum book with terse comments about the condition of the schools he visited in 1873 that in themselves tell a story of education in rural America. Of school after school he wrote: "Furniture poor—Small blackboard—No Map or Charts—Have no slates—Stove poor."[34]

That same year Irwin Stratton, the first superintendent of Wabash County, Indiana, found much the same thing on his tour of inspection. One of his schools sat in a barn lot, and in Stratton's view, it was the "most gloomy school, teacher and house yet visited. The teacher," he went on, "with pants in boots, dirty collar. Everything knocked, torn and kicked to pieces. 'May the curtain of charity fall over them all.' It appears to me that everybody is to blame about the failure, pupils, parents, and teacher. With such surroundings no teacher can teach and no child can learn."[35]

And yet, contrary to Stratton's conclusion and the best pedagogical theories, learning somehow seemed to be taking place under the most adverse conditions. In the majority of schools in which Funk found such poor facilities, he also found "order good," as he wrote, or "pupils . . . seemed to be at work earnestly." And Stratton himself visited a school in 1874 that must have surprised him. "Recess," he jotted in his notebook as he described the scene at the Rich Valley School. "Noise fearful—dancing, jumping, holloing—almost everything that should not be allowed. When the bell rang a dozen pupils stood around the stove and took their seats at their leisure. Hats on—floor dirty—spitting on the floor." But then came the recitations. "Small [children] geography well recited. Lesson well assigned. Pupils then asked what the lesson was. No criticisms on recitations, they were *very* good."[36]

Visiting schools was a specific duty given the Midwestern county superintendents by law, but they were also encouraged by the same laws to do whatever they could to improve and encourage education in their counties, and the enterprising among them found various ways to do this. They invited the public to attend the classes of the county teachers' institutes, and they gave evening lectures at the little district school to "willing and appreciative" audiences, as one superintendent described them, on the virtues of education. More than that, they wrote education columns for the county weekly newspapers that found their way, postage free, into so many rural homes.

The superintendents used their columns to write little homilies on the benefits of education, to point out the needs of the schools, to scold occasionally, and to remind the farmers and their families of coming educational events. But mostly they wrote of teachers and students and the everyday happenings that filled the life of the one-room schools. They wrote of students who had been neither absent from school nor tardy for a month or of those who had won some reward—for it was an age that believed in rewards—a head mark for winning a spelldown or special acclaim for memorizing Daniel Webster's "liberty and Union" speech, perhaps, or the Gettysburg Address.

There was in these columns a buoyant, optimistic outlook toward education, and parents, whose names were being spread about the county through the activities of their children, could scarcely help but be proud and take a renewed interest in the little school that obviously taught their children so much and in which their children could excel.[37]

The education column may have helped, too, to break down old barriers between the county superintendent and the country-school directors who had once resented the superintendent's interference in their affairs. Increasingly as the nineteenth century spent itself, country-school board members sought the county superintendent's advice on matters ranging from the discipline of unruly children to the employment of teachers. And in this new relationship the county superintendents grew bold enough to send the directors written instructions each year about their schools, which were to be read at the annual school meetings. "Gentleman...," they would write. "Look carefully over the school building, inside and out. See if it needs cleaning and painting.... Look carefully to the outhouses. See to it, gentlemen, that the out-houses are put in good condition long before school opens. If the old ones are too small—and nearly half of the out-houses in the county are too small—build larger.... If your school has no library, I very earnestly advise the placement of one," and in this vein they would continue until they had covered everything from directions on the employment of a teacher with a first-grade certificate to heating and ventilating the schoolhouse and beautifying the schoolyard.[38]

There seemed no end to the good county superintendent's energy, and almost no limit to which he would not go to improve rural education in his county. He worked constantly to get his schools to adopt uniform textbooks, urged teachers to hold Arbor Day ceremonies and plant trees in the schoolyards, and somewhere along the line, perhaps as a result of the Columbian Exposition in Chicago in 1893, he began collecting educational exhibits for the county fair each year. At the same time, he was busily organizing the teachers of his county into reading circles and teachers' associations at which teachers were expected to read and discuss the papers they had prepared on some aspect of their work.[39]

And by the 1890s, most Midwestern county superintendents had gone far toward grading or, as they called it, classifying their country schools.

IV

When the county superintendents began their work in the Civil War period, no Midwestern country school was graded. The teachers, still teaching as they had been taught, organized their schools around a series of readers, usually McGuffey's or copies of McGuffey's. Usually there were six readers in the series, each corresponding very loosely to a grade, so that a student in the first reader might be thought to be in the first grade.

From the first reader the teacher taught her students how to read. From those following, particularly the fourth, fifth, and sixth, she taught history from historical accounts and speeches of great men, and elocution and literature culled from the very best in the English language. Besides the readers, the teacher taught arithmetic, usually from Ray's *New Arithmetic* series and geography from James Monteith's *National Geographical* series.

In the nineteenth century no one really dignified this system by naming it, but modern educators might have called it "self-paced." Students read through the readers at their own pace, and along the way picked up as much arithmetic, geography, and grammar as the teacher could find time to give them. When they had read through the sixth reader they had gone as far as they could go, at least in reading. Many students never made it that far, and years later they would tell their children or grandchildren that they had gone through the third or fourth reader in school, which would completely mystify a generation grown accustomed to the graded school.

For bright children like Herbert Quick, whose formal education, except for some county institute work, began and ended in a one-room schoolhouse in Grundy County, Iowa, the system had certain advantages. In his first six-month term of school at the age of five, he read through the fourth reader without every being ordered to stop to wait for the slow readers to catch up. It was a system, too, that blended well into farm life, for it allowed older farm boys who were forced to be intermittent students to enter school at any time and begin in whatever reader they could read. Since there was no promotion from grade to grade, they felt no shame if at the age of twelve they were still reading in the second or third reader. It was a system, in fact, that encouraged them to get as much education as they could.[40]

Still, this loose system, as independent and individualistic as the farmers themselves, gave the students no systematic course of study, no certain place where they should be in their studies at a given time, and term after term they repeated their studies, so that it was common to ask "whoever finishes anything in a country school?" And for the professional educators, who so greatly admired the graded urban schools through which the students passed in lock-step fashion, the disorganization of the Midwestern country schools was a nightmare.[41]

"The city schools are superior [to country schools], because systematic," said one Midwestern educator in 1878, and though educators had no scientific way to prove this, the mere examination of what went on in the country schoolroom seemed proof enough. Rarely did a country teacher know at the beginning of a school term what reader to give each student, because she had no record of his previous progress. Nor could she always find out by asking. The children had either forgotten, or, for their own reasons, gave the wrong answer. "Pupils [in country schools] are promoted from book to book," complained a Kansas educator in 1887, "and from school to school at the sweet wills of the parents, teachers, and school officers and in . . . many cases, the pupils promote themselves. Studies are pursued in some sort of circular fashion. The pupil begins with a book at the beginning of the term; he goes to a certain page in the spring; he comes back, begins at the beginning of the book, and goes to the same place in the fall; he comes back next spring and begins again and goes to the same place in the fall or a few pages beyond; and so goes on and on in a circular way . . . for eight years."[42]

Like the problem of independent school districts and district school boards, this disorganization of the country schools confronted the professional educators with one more country school problem they were determined to remedy. But how? They could not hope to divide country children of different ages into separate grades as was done in the cities where each grade was taught by one teacher in one room. Neither could they reasonably expect to plan a curriculum that would apply to all country schools in one state or even one county, when one school had three months of school a year, another six, and another eight. And how could a system be built around the use of textbooks when each district had different textbooks, and some of the students within each school had different textbooks?

The Midwestern educators, however, were undaunted by such problems. With the self-assurance born of their growing expertise and professionalism, they were confident they could organize the country schools as they had the urban schools and that only they could do it. Certainly the farmers could not do it, or the country-school directors, or the teachers. Henry Clay Speer, superintendent of schools in Atchison, Kansas, in 1878, and soon to become Kansas state superintendent, thought it ridiculous to expect teachers to develop blueprints for such an organization.

In a strange speech given before the Kansas State Teachers' Association that year, he tried to show the great distance between the teachers and professional educators like himself. "it is utterly senseless to put teachers in the work of artists," he said. "Teaching is no work of genius, and a teacher need not be an inventor. . . . The best teachers are in no sense men and women of original methods or of profound convictions of the limits of education or the true line of school policies. They are, rather, men and women that have an intelligent understanding of the methods they use, and . . . they are familiar with the best tools and are constantly masters of the practical results of the science of education. This position needs no argument with school superintendents in cities where there are certain definite objects to be accomplished, and master workmen required in the several positions, not architects."[43]

In the country schools, on the other hand, Speer implied that teachers who were not geniuses were trying to draw up plans for their school's organization. This would not do. Programs for organizing country schools must be left to architects like himself, who had, as it happened, already prepared a course of study for the Kansas rural schools.

Speer's plan proposed grading, or classifying, country-school students into three divisions and specifying courses to be taught to each group on a regular basis each day. This plan would force the teacher to establish a regular schedule, so that at each hour of the day she would know what class was to recite and what all other classes would be doing. Then, at the end of the school term, the teacher might note the progress each student had made in all subjects and suggest to her successor where each student should begin in the next school term.[44]

There was nothing original in Speer's plan. Courses of study were already in use in some Midwestern states in the 1870s, and the state superintendent had even suggested one for the Kansas schools in 1871. But few schools had adopted the superintendent's program, so that Speer, ambitious and perhaps already thinking of becoming state superintendent one day, found room to promote his own plan in 1878.

Because experience had shown, not only in Kansas but across the Middle Border, how hard it was to uproot the old system and establish the new in country schools, Speer hoped to persuade the state legislature to enact legislation forcing the country schools to adopt his course of study and thus outflank those rulers of the little independent schools. "It is the duty of the state authority to outline in as great detail as is consistent with general application, the purposes in view, and to enforce the observance of the course," he said.[45]

But in Kansas, as elsewhere throughout the Midwest, the state legislature was wary of telling the farmers how to run their schools, and, in the end, the educators were forced to rely upon the county superintendents to convince the farmers that a course of study was not simply another educational fad but would provide their children with a better education than the old system.

The county superintendents, however, needed time to convince the farmers of the wisdom of this innovative method, and the farmers' hesitation drew still another blast from the professional educators against the small, independent district system that put the control of the school in the hands of ignorant men instead of educators. "You have no idea of what difficulty they have," one exasperated Kansas school official told his colleagues at a meeting in Washington in 1887, "in carrying out courses of study in the States that are cursed with the independent district system. . . . In some counties of our State we have

267, 335, and 458 school officers, and in one county 558, enough to capture a fort. Before the county superintendent can carry out the details of any particular course of study it is necessary to secure the approval, the co-operation, of 558 persons."[46]

Nevertheless, the county superintendents who were responsible for implementing the new program persisted, and as the years passed they worked hard to teach their teachers how to organize their schools around the course of study and helped them introduce it into their classrooms, often without the permission of the district school boards. "At the close of the normal institute," the county superintendent of Delaware County, Iowa, wrote in 1879, "a course of study for un-graded schools was laid out and the teachers pledged themselves to introduce it into their schools."[47]

The county superintendents were helped in all this by a popular "Red Line" series of School and Township Records, which had been prepared by W. M. Welch, an enterprising educator, in the 1880s for Midwestern schools and sold by the thousands. Included in the "Red Line" series was a Teacher's Classification Register, which had in it all the directions necessary for planning a course of study and for clas-sifying a country school, and many a country teacher on the Middle Border organized her school according to its suggestions.[48]

First, she divided her assortment of scholars into three divisions: primary, intermediate, and grammar. Then she separated those in each division into groups *A* and *B,* and worked out a schedule that called for recitations from each group in most of the eight branches of learning. Often she had more than thirty recitations in a six-hour day, which was far too many. Sometimes she reduced this number by asking an older student for help. "Mary," she would say, "would you hear the primary children," and Mary would take the small children to a corner of the room and listen to them read while the teacher went on with her other recitations. But gradually the county superinten-dents taught her to reduce the number of recitations by combining the older students, even those of different ages, into one class. In this way she might have what would amount to the third, fifth, and seventh grades in one year, and the fourth, sixth, and eighth in the next.[49]

This arrangement freed her to spend as much as two hours listen-ing to the separate recitations of the *A* and *B* primary students, whose success in education depended so predominantly on this early in-struction, and to hold longer, if fewer, recitations for the combined classes of the older children. At the Hicks School in Calhoun County, Michigan, in 1890, the teacher had so arranged her schedule that she was able to devote forty-five minutes apiece to the first and second grades in recitation time during the day, forty minutes to the combined third and fourth grades, sixty to the fifth and sixth combined, and fifty-five to the combined seventh and eighth.

This teacher had carefully spelled out what the students were to be doing when they were not reciting. While the beginners were having their reading recitation from 9:10 to 9:25, all other students were to be studying their reading lessons. And from 9:25 to 9:45, during the second-grade reading recitation, the first-graders were to be slate writing, the third and fourth were still reading, and the rest were working on their arithmetic, and so on throughout the morning. At 1:45 in the afternoon, the first and second grades were doing "busy work" at their seats, the third and fourth combined were studying spelling, the combined seventh and eighth were working on either grammar or civil government, and the fifth and sixth combined were reciting their grammar lesson. At 3:00 the lower grades were dismissed, and from 3:30 to 3:45, the upper grades—fifth through eighth—were having a spelldown.[50]

V

While the county superintendents in most Midwestern states were busily classifying their one-room schools and moving with increasing authority through their counties in the 1880s and '90s, the professional educators whose states did not have such officials looked on enviously. The Ohio commissioners of education pointed frequently through the years to the educational improvements that could be made if only the state legislature would substitute county superintendents for the three-man county boards of examiners. And in Michigan and Missouri, where the county superintendents had been abolished in the 1870s, the story was the same. As the years went by the state superintendents of those states lost no opportunity to attribute the inadequacies of their rural schools to two wants: a township district system, and a county superintendent.[51]

In 1888 the Missouri legislature did finally make it possible for counties that wanted to have a superintendent to have one, but they were not required to do so. But for years Michigan would not go that far. There the deep-seated fear of interference in local school affairs lingered on, leaving a great administrative gap between the state superintendent and the schools. "At one extreme of the system," the state superintendent said in 1878, "is the State Superintendent, at the other are one-thousand township superintendents, six thousand district boards and thirteen thousand teachers. The distance is simply disheartening."[52]

Finally, however, in 1891, the Michigan legislature, too, provided county commissioners—perhaps they dared not use the word superintendents—to be elected by the people beginning in 1893. The commissioners were given most of the duties most Midwestern county superintendents had except for examining and certifying teachers. This burdensome and sensitive problem was left with the three-man examining boards that had been established in 1881.[53]

So, at the turn of the century, all of the Middle Border states except Ohio had county superintendents, and these men and women—for there were many of the latter among them—were as near to being counterparts of the urban school superintendents as rural America would ever have. Overcoming obstacles that would have tried the patience of most urban superintendents, they did impose some order on the little country schools, and in the process some of the trappings of professionalism rubbed off on them. They formed their own associations, read papers, discussed problems that confronted them, and became as arrogant and confident of their expertise as those who ranked above them. Their reports to the state superintendents were so filled with praise for their own accomplishments that the Iowa state superintendent once admonished them "not to indulge in personal adulation" in making their reports. Furthermore, over the years, many of them adopted the prejudices of the state superintendents and other professionals toward the country schools and supported the township system in their papers and discussions.[54]

Nevertheless, few professional educators regarded their country counterparts with respect, and year by year they emphasized their weaknesses to the state legislatures. For no matter how much they had accomplished or how professional they had become, to the professional educators the county superintendents were still politicians. They were, in short, still beholden to the people who knew nothing about education, instead of to the professionals who did.

Perhaps it was not surprising in these years when civil service reform was in the air that the educators should deduce that all the weaknesses of the county superintendents sprang from politics. Politics meant elections every two years and often short terms for the best county superintendents; it meant the election of demagogues who catered to the wishes of the farmers; and it meant the election of unqualified men who were afraid to do what was necessary to improve their schools. "Ninety per cent of the superintendents of the state say this year . . . ," wrote the Wisconsin state superintendent in 1900, "that they are unable to limit the issue of certificates to people whom they believe to be thoroughly qualified for the work of teaching; that they are beset by political influence demanding that certificates shall be issued to friends or relatives of the political supporters of this officer without reference to qualification. If they fail to accede to these demands they are threatened with defeat in the next nominating convention, or at the polls."[55]

Through the years the professional educators supported a number of changes designed to correct all this. They pleaded for higher salaries for the county superintendents in the hope that this would draw a better class of men into the position. They also urged that candidates for the office be required to have a first-grade teacher's certificate or some other specific qualification. Some recommended a four-year term of office, such as Illinois had, and others proposed that at the very least the county superintendents' election be separate from the general election, so that party politics would be less important in the selection. And there were many recommendations to have the county superintendents appointed by a board of education or by the township trustees as was done in Indiana.

Some of these proposals were tried, but with less effect than the professionals desired. Higher wages did not necessarily draw better men to office, and longer terms offered the possibility that a poor superintendent would be kept in office too long. Some Midwestern states did require certain qualifications, which no doubt helped, but the proposal to have the township trustees appoint the county superintendent only transferred politics from the people to the trustees, as one observer saw in Indiana. The county superintendent, he wrote, "has come to be considered part of the spoils of politics. If the majority of the Township Trustees are Democrats the county superintendent must be a Democrat, and if a majority are Republicans, the County Superintendent must be a Republican. Qualifications are secondary to the candidate's political complexion."[56]

What most educators really wanted, of course, was to remove the county superintendents from politics completely and to be allowed to appoint them to office themselves, and they proposed various schemes for doing this. One of the most radical was that developed in Wisconsin in the 1890s.

The Wisconsin plan had been placed before the state legislature in 1892, and, when it failed, it was resurrected with much fanfare in 1899. Once more comparing country-school education to a business

that needed more effective supervision than the county superintendents could give it, the educators proposed the elimination of the
county superintendents and the creation of some one hundred and
fifteen inspectors. This small battalion of educators was to be appointed by a little group of experts composed of the professor of
pedagogy at the university, the three members of the board of
examiners for state teaching certificates, who themselves had been
appointed by the state superintendent, and the institute instructor
from each of the state's normal schools.[57]

The inspectors were to have all the duties the county superintendents had had. Their areas of responsibility, however, would not necessarily be counties but regions whose boundaries would be determined
by the same group who had appointed them to office. Moreover, each
region was to have within it, insofar as it was possible, an equal
number of school districts whose boundaries were to be the boundaries of townships, not section lines running here and there across
the countryside.

How neatly the professional educators' dreams for the centralization and control of the farmers' schools were wrapped up in this plan!
At one blow they would wipe out the educator-politicians, replace
them with their own professional men who would be responsible to
those who knew best, eliminate the little independent school districts,
and, by indirection since they could not do it directly, establish the
township district system throughout Wisconsin. No wonder the state
superintendent did not expect the project to pass the legislature.[58]

It was a scheme that flew in the face of more than a half-century's
experience with rural education. It threatened to deprive the farmers
of their right to supervise the education of their children, and they
would not have it. So the project was defeated as the state superintendent had expected, and in the years ahead only the Iowa legislature of all the Middle Border states succumbed to the importunities of
the professional educators by providing for the appointment of
county superintendents by a township board. This, however, did not
entirely eliminate the office from politics, and, in Iowa as elsewhere
across the region, the county superintendents remained politicians as
well as educators up until World War II and beyond, when the little
one-room schools themselves fell victims to improved transportation
and centralization and there was no longer any superintending to
do.[59]

Along the way, however, some changes did take place. As time went
by the county superintendent's office seemed less political. The farm-

ers tended to pay less attention to their superintendent's political affiliation and to keep him in office longer. In some ways, too, the superintendent's job was more routine and easier than in the old days. There were fewer boundary disputes to settle, for one thing, and for another, by World War I, he could move around the county in his Model T and visit more schools each year than ever before.

Finally, the burden of teacher training was gradually lifted from his shoulders and taken over by the high schools, the universities, and the teachers' colleges. This was no small change, for, during the late nineteenth century, the training of the teacher was the county superintendent's most important duty, and the one, perhaps, in which he made his greatest contribution to rural education.

9

"Teachers Are Born"

☘

I

ONE WINTER IN THE EARLY 1870S TWO SMALL BOYS, ONE FIVE AND THE
other six, began their first term of school in a one-room schoolhouse
in Burt County in eastern Nebraska. They had virtually no preparation
for this experience. Unlike many country-school beginners they did
not even know their ABC's. But when the county superintendent
visited their school only two months after they had first enrolled, he
heard them read every word from Hilliard's First Reader without a
mistake.[1]

The boys' performance was not really so unusual. Such rapid mastery of the first reader happened often in those little one-room
schools along the Middle Border in those days, but, in this case, the
county superintendent was moved to speculate on the reasons for
such progress in his report to the state superintendent. "They were
bright little fellows," he wrote; "but it was not all in the children; there
was power in the teacher. The whole school was advancing about the
same. This was a teacher teaching under a third grade certificate. My
observation impresses me with the fact that such results are not confined to teachers of the first and second grade certificates, or higher
qualifications. . . . There is more than one kind of education necessary
to make a good teacher. They are born, not altogether made."[2]

This opinion was shared by more than one Midwestern county
superintendent in the late nineteenth century. Often, as they visited
first one school then another, they found teachers teaching superbly
who had virtually no formal training, and, like the Burt County su-

157

perintendent, they concluded that good teachers had some indefinable quality, some power born in them that could not be learned.[3]

This was not quite the same thing as saying that good teachers could not be made, of course, but it suggested that born teachers did not need to be taught how to teach, and it surely implied that teaching teachers to teach had its limitations. And yet the enormous amount of time and energy the county superintendents in the Midwest spent on teacher training in the final years of the last and early years of this century made it appear that most of them really believed that almost anyone could be trained to teach.

In this they were but following the lead of the professional educators—those Midwestern state superintendents of public instruction and professors of pedagogy teaching in the region's burgeoning normal schools—who believed not only that teachers could be trained to be good teachers, but that, in fact, they must be taught how to teach even if they had a natural aptitude for it. "Natural aptitude is good as far as it goes," wrote one educator in 1898, "but it should be no more relied upon in the teacher's profession than in the medical or legal profession." A talented boy could not become a lawyer without training; neither, in the educator's view, could a natural-born teacher become a good teacher without that specialized instruction which only they were prepared to give.[4]

Already in the late 1870s the educators, eagerly elevating their discipline to a science, had convinced themselves that teaching was a science, "based on principles," as one of them wrote, "as firmly fixed, as readily determined, and capable of being as thoroughly systematized as those of either law or medicine or theology," and that good teachers were really made, not born. "The conception now gaining ground," wrote William Payne, the professor of pedagogy at the University of Michigan in 1880, "is that teaching should cease to be an empirical art and should become a rational art; that the teacher should not only be instructed in the processes but should also be taught the body of doctrine that underlies them and assures their validity. In other words, the art of teaching has outgrown its empirical stage, and is now growing into its rational or scientific stage."[5]

True, there seemed to be some uncertainty in the educators' minds over whether the body of doctrine underlying the processes of teaching was based on scientific laws or theory and whether teaching was really a science or an art. Some of their textbooks in the new science were entitled "The Art of Teaching," and even the Michigan University chair of pedagogy, established in 1879, was called "The Chair of the Science and Art of Teaching."[6]

But the Midwestern professional educators were untroubled by such ambiguities as they hurried on, certain that they were discovering the scientific laws of teaching, confident of their ability to teach teachers how to teach, and vigorous and unyielding in their demands that the great host of untrained teachers in the one-room schoolhouses in the country be taught how to teach.

Aside from the small independent school districts and the horde of school directors elected to manage them, nothing about the country school so disturbed the educators as its teachers. "Not more than one in four of the teachers of the common schools of the State is fitted for the place he occupies," the Kansas state superintendent wrote in 1874, "in respect to scholarship, methods, principles of teaching, general intelligence, ability to organize and govern a school, breadth, symmetry, and poise of character."[7]

Everywhere, from Ohio to Nebraska and from Minnesota to Missouri, the educators' view of the country schoolteachers was much the same as that of the Kansas superintendent. Country schoolteachers, they repeated endlessly, were inefficient, ineffectual, and incompetent, and in desperate need of training. The laments continued throughout the century. The Committee of Twelve called attention to the poor quality of teachers in the country schools in 1896, and a Committee of Six, studying the rural schools in Wisconsin in 1900, continued the attack. "*Poor teachers,* in so great a proportion to the whole number," so the committee's report said, "are the bane of the rural school."[8]

Those rural schoolteachers at whom these jeremiads were directed for more than half a century were mostly young women. Once, in years gone by, schoolmasters instead of schoolmistresses had presided over the country schools in the Midwest. But even in the 1870s figures already showed that in those ten North Central states, fifty-six per cent of all public schoolteachers in the region were women, and so swiftly was this calling taken over by them that in 1900 not quite twenty-seven per cent of all public schoolteachers in the region were male. And if these figures had been confined to country schools alone, the percentages would have been even more disproportionate in favor of women, for they had virtually monopolized country schoolteaching along the Middle Border by the end of the century.[9]

The Civil War had much to do with this, of course, for many a

159

young schoolmaster, patriotic and idealistic, left his classroom for the battlefield when the war came and never returned to it when he came back, if he did come back. Ohio sent five thousand or nearly half of all her male schoolteachers to the war, and Illinois furnished three thousand, among them one professor from the state normal school. In their absence the women took their place in the schoolrooms, and, when the war ended, they continued to be employed partly because they had taught successfully but mostly because they taught more cheaply than men.[10]

Why this was so was no more complicated than the law of supply and demand. Young Midwestern women, particularly those in rural America, had no position open to them in those years as satisfying as schoolteaching. Teaching gave them status in the community, educational opportunities, and wages enough to sustain themselves. Country schoolteaching, in fact, with its short terms and rapid changeover of teachers, seemed made to order for young women who had only themselves to care for, and they were quite willing to teach for modest sums.[11]

For men it was different. They could choose from a variety of occupations, and as time went on they rarely chose teaching in country schools except as a steppingstone to another profession. But even if they had wished to remain country schoolteachers, they could not easily have done so. Normally country-school boards would employ them for no longer than the winter term of three or four months. Obviously they could not make a career of such short-time employment.

More than that, as women began to dominate the field, men had a tendency to regard schoolteaching as "woman's work," and to shun it for that reason. "I wish you every success in your chosen vocation of teaching," a young Missourian wrote to his female cousin in 1905, "but I could hardly be honest to myself and tell you that I envied your choice, because the life of a pedagogue is one I have always regarded diffidently. I admit though that in the case of a girl there is a great deal of difference. People generally regard a schoolmaster as being sort of an effeminate being, while a school maam is generally given a great deal of consideration."[12]

The notion that teaching was woman's work was supported, perhaps inadvertently, by the educators themselves. For years country-school directors on the Middle Border tried to employ male teachers at least for the winter school, as they were directed to do at their annual school meeting. But when it became obvious that women teachers could always be employed for an average of ten dollars less per month than men, the necessity of employing male teachers, even in the winter term, began to dim in the directors' minds and virtually disappeared when the educators themselves began to argue, sincerely or otherwise, that women were better teachers than men.[13]

At a time when there was so much talk about the origin of the species, their various characteristics, and the differences among the races of men, almost no one was troubled when the educators pointed to the differences between men and women and suggested that woman's distinctive qualities made her man's superior in the classroom. Somehow it seemed planned that way. "If God's intents were ever visible from his works," wrote an educator in 1872, "who can doubt that He designed the female sex for this most responsible and most blessed calling? Woman is more sprightly and vivacious than man; has a larger fund of bouyancy and animal spirits at ready command. . . . Besides the school ma'am is, as a general rule less clumsy, and ponderous, and stiff than the schoolmaster; is mentally more agile and versatile than he; has fewer sharp corners; knows better how to conquer by yielding."[14]

Of course the educators did not mean that women had no deficiencies. Their voices were defective, their carriage faulty, and they lacked intellectual independence. Some even doubted that they were men's superiors in teaching. One state superintendent was so blunt as to say that he saw no difference between men and women in the classroom except the pay and suspected that that was why women were there instead of men. Moreover, at the turn of the century, a number of prominent school men began to worry about what would happen to a race of men so completely dominated by women in their early years as the American boys were.[15]

Nevertheless, the assumption that elementary education, if not the advanced grades, which women might not be able to teach because of the more complex subjects involved, was woman's peculiar domain, for which "nature," as the Minnesota state superintendent wrote in 1870, "marked her out," was widely accepted by the educators.[16]

Still, it was true that no matter how mentally agile and versatile they might be, many young women teaching on the Middle Border in those centennial years had not really mastered the subjects they were teaching.

For more than a generation following Appomattox, the average young female schoolteacher in the Midwest was likely to be a farm girl who had grown up milking cows, churning butter, picking strawberries, and husking corn, as well as doing the usual household chores. She could ride a horse, harness a team, and even plow a field when necessary. She knew what it was to rise early in the morning for the day's work, to toil in the sun, to take a bath in a tin tub beside the kitchen stove, and to use the outdoor privy on a wintry morning when the temperature had fallen below zero and the icy wind whistled eerily around it. But in the 1870s, at least, her knowledge of what to teach and how to teach it was usually limited to what she had learned and observed in the country school, and stories of her appallingly ignorant answers to questions on the teachers' examinations circulated through almost every county courthouse in the region.[17]

In the country school she might have read through McGuffey's *Sixth Eclectic Reader* if she had attended long enough, and figured her way through Ray's *Practical Arithmetic* to simple proportions or the "rule of three," as it was sometimes called. Very likely she knew how to diagram a sentence, something about diacritical marks, and how to spell an uncommonly large number of words. From Monteith's *Introduction to Geography*, she had possibly learned the names of the capitals of the states and what direction the rivers east of the Appalachian Mountains flowed.

She knew enough, in short, sometimes with the help of a kindly county superintendent, to pass the county examination for the third-grade certificate, which allowed her to teach for six months or a year without reexamination. But from the educators' standpoint, the third-grade certificate was no proof that its possessor could teach effectively. That certificate, the Nebraska superintendent once noted, was merely "the limit above *total ignorance* to be reached before a candidate [could] receive it."[18]

The young country schoolteacher could and did learn to teach on the job, of course. But that, too, had its limitations. For the most part, country schoolteachers taught only two or three years, then married and taught no more, so that each year a great wave of totally untrained teachers replaced those partially trained in a never-ending cycle.[19]

So the educators were right, of course, when they argued that the country schoolteachers needed more training. The vast majority of them did need more training in the common branches—arithmetic, grammar, geography, history, writing—to make up for what they had missed in the country school.

But were they as incompetent and ignorant as the educators made them out to be? Many of those who observed them at work more closely than the professionals did believed not. "We hear much in these days about the poor quality of instruction in the rural district schools," wrote a school inspector in Michigan in 1889. "In fact, there is a tendency to belittle the important work they do. I think that much of this opinion arises from the lack of knowledge of the quality of work that these schools actually accomplish.... Almost invariably where conditions are favorable to good school work, I have found effective and faithful teaching. I am convinced from long observation of the work of both graded and rural schools that the average rural school-teacher is as efficient as the average graded school-teacher."[20]

If this were true—and there were many testimonials to it—why did the Midwestern educators draw such a gloomy picture of the region's one-room schoolteachers? The answer was more complicated than appeared on the surface of things.

II

First was the image the educators had of the good teacher. Their model was the urban schoolteacher teaching one age group, in one grade, in one orderly classroom, supplied with the latest school apparatus. She was efficient, tidy, and effective, and beside her the rural schoolteacher, struggling to teach children aged five to twenty, in a barren, one-room schoolhouse, innocent of educational apparatus, often without standardized textbooks, appeared hopelessly disorganized and inept. Her classroom, compared with that of the urban teacher, seemed in a constant state of confusion as children passed to and from her desk in the continuous process of recitation, and her rough classification of her pupils seemed unwieldy by urban standards.

Because the urban schoolteacher looked efficient, most professionals never stopped to ask how efficient she really was. Besides, in those years of the late nineteenth century, the bustling cities—vigorous, wealthy, innovative—seemed progressive and rural America by contrast so backward. The educators absorbed the anti-rural bias of the period, which predisposed them to accept the appearances of things in the cities and look condescendingly and critically upon the farmers and the teachers they employed to teach their children.[21]

But that was not all. The professionals' passionate dislike of the small, independent school district system, which grew in direct proportion to their failures to change it, colored their thinking about country schoolteachers and warped their judgment. Convinced beyond a doubt that the small school district system was bad, they offered poor schoolteaching as proof of their contention, and through the years one of their favorite arguments for the township system was that it would somehow improve the quality of teaching in the one-room school.[22]

Finally, the Midwestern educators had a vested interest in building a case against the area's country schoolteachers. With an overweening confidence in their developing professionalism they really believed they had discovered, or were on the verge of discovering, scientific principles of teaching and that through their teacher-training programs they could cure poor teaching just as physicians cured their patients. By these programs they could wipe out the stigma attached to teaching, elevate teaching to the standard of a profession, enhance their own importance, and, not incidentally, provide jobs for themselves as teachers of teachers, which, in the 1870s, was already one of their principal occupations.

But to develop their programs and achieve the prestige they coveted, the professional educators needed state-supported professional training schools—called normal schools in those days before they became teachers' colleges—and these could be established only if the state legislatures could be convinced of the need for them. It was necessary, therefore, that they stress the weaknesses of the country schoolteachers in order to persuade their legislators of the need for training an adequate supply of good teachers. "The principles of self-preservation would justify special appropriations [by the state] for the training of common school teachers in . . . normal schools," one educator said in 1878, "if it can be shown that the law of supply and demand, acting through institutions on the voluntary principle, will not furnish teachers in sufficient numbers and with sufficient education to meet the necessities of the case"[23]

So it was left to the educators to show that there were not enough teachers with sufficient education to meet the needs, and it was not entirely accidental that the educators' somewhat exaggerated descriptions of the poor, untrained, ignorant, and ineffective teachers in the country schools went hand in hand with their pleas for the establishment of normal schools.

The Midwestern educators' efforts to found public normal schools began in Michigan with the establishment of the normal at Ypsilanti in 1852, more than a decade after the nation's first such school had opened in Massachusetts. By 1860 three more Midwestern states had built public normal schools, but the real normal school movement on the Middle Border came in the years between the close of the Civil War and the nation's centennial celebration. In that time more than a score of public normal schools were built in the area and an even greater number of private ones. By 1876 all of the North Central states except Ohio, which relied on city and private normals for teacher instruction, had at least one normal and some had more. Missouri had three and Kansas three—one at Emporia, another at Concordia, and one more at Leavenworth.[24]

It had not been easy in some states to convince the legislatures of the need for special schools to teach teachers how to teach. In Indiana it took the state teachers' association nearly ten years to persuade the legislature to establish the school at Terre Haute. And in Illinois the educators wrangled among themselves over whether the school they wished to establish at Normal should be purely a teacher-training school, a university, or partly a vocational training center before agreement was reached and the school founded. Nevertheless, near the centennial year, the normal school movement appeared to be an unqualified success in the minds of the educators, and they were writing glowing, optimistic accounts of their schools.[25]

In that very year, however, the normal schools, like so many of their other enthusiasms in these years, were already locked in a battle for existence with the farmers and their representatives in the state legislatures.

The hard times that followed the panic of 1873 and impoverished so many farmers forced a number of rural state legislators to reconsider whatever support they had hitherto given to the normal schools. So did the local jealousies that surfaced when a normal was built in one town and not in another. Nor did it help the normal schools' cause when the farmers discovered that the young people trained there, presumably to teach in country schools, regarded the country schools and the teachers who taught in them with contempt and went instead to teach in the urban schools. That this had happened even the educators acknowledged although they refused to take blame for it. "In very few cases can normal school teachers be held responsible...," protested one professional in 1886, "for any sins other than those of omission; pretensions have certainly not been encouraged; they have only not been sufficiently repressed." Perhaps. But what were young students to think when the school they attended set itself apart as a professional school, when their professors taught

165

them to believe they were learning the scientific way to teach and communicated to them, in a variety of ways, the superiority of the instruction they were receiving?[26]

Moreover, it was hard for the educators to justify their schools as time went on because they could never make them exactly what they wished them to be. Always they liked to think of their normals as professional schools like those of medicine, law, and theology, which they so greatly envied, and they had sold them to the legislatures on that basis. But, in fact, the students who enrolled in the normals had to be taught subject matter before they could be taught what the educators called their professional courses, simply because they needed to know what to teach more than they needed to know how to teach it.

This was the common sense of the matter, but the professionals themselves disagreed over what the schools should teach. Some, jealously guarding their schools' professionalism, insisted that the normals teach only professional courses and gave much greater weight to teaching than to learning what to teach. "Moreover, in awarding diplomas," said a group of Michigan educators who visited the normal school at Ypsilanti in 1879, "let ability to teach . . . be the first consideration; educational proficiency the second. The best scholar may be the poorest teacher; the poorest scholar the best teacher."[27]

But to other professionals this made little sense. William Payne, the respected professor of pedagogy at the University of Michigan, argued that methods could never be "accepted as the equivalent of scholarship," and implied that the normals had "fallen into serious error," by permitting method to usurp the place of scholarship. And a Minnesota educator sounded a similar note when he complained in 1888 of those in his profession who wanted to make the normals purely professional schools. Striking at one of the educators' cherished contentions, he noted that teaching was not really a profession, for most of those who taught were young ladies who could barely sustain themselves. The best the normals could do, he thought, was to train in any way they could those "evanescent crowds that are ever flitting into, and out of, the ranks of teachers."[28]

In the end, of course, the normals were compelled to teach subject matter whether the educators wished to or not, but this, as they had feared, weakened their argument that their schools were distinctive and therefore necessary, and made them difficult to defend before the state legislatures.

Beyond all this, however, was the farmers' skepticism about the need to teach teachers how to teach. If a person was knowledgeable and intelligent, was it necessary to teach him how to teach what he knew? No doubt the practical-minded farmers asked the question partly at least because they did not want to support the normal schools with their tax dollars. But they were joined in their question, oddly enough perhaps, by intellectuals from the universities who regarded the normal schools as "schools that were abnormal," and even by some professional educators as well. Henry Sabin, that influential Iowa superintendent of schools and author of a textbook called *Common Sense Didactics for Common School Teachers*, went so far in 1890 as to suggest that special teacher training was not indispensable. "There are," he said, "only four indispensable requisites [for teaching]— knowledge of subject-matter, uprightness of character, a desire to improve, and common sense."[29]

This was probably close to what the farmers thought. Knowing nothing about scientific principles of instruction, they made their judgments about teaching solely on the basis of common sense and observation and were likely to think, when they thought about it at all, that any intelligent person could teach what he knew without being taught how to teach it.

This opinion, so widely held "among the ignorant," as one early historian of education wrote, thoroughly exasperated the professional educators and was surely one more reason for their intemperate criticism of country schoolteachers. "The popular opinion that anybody can teach a country school [without training] is a very serious mistake," the Indiana state superintendent wrote in 1876. And to a good man like Newton Bateman, who was struggling so hard to improve education in Illinois in the 1870s, such an opinion was "a wild and dangerous assumption, contrary to all experience . . . , repugnant to reason and common sense, and of most mischievous tendency." He could not understand how thinking men could hold such erroneous views especially when "the ripest scholars and ablest educators in this country and Europe have thrown the weight of their influence and testimony in the scale, and have contributed cogent articles in support of the absolute necessity of special training for teachers."[30]

And for the opinions of educators like Sabin who ventured to suggest that teaching teachers to teach might even make a teacher a mere automaton, "crushing out spontaneity . . . by reducing everything to the dead level of certain so-called philosophical methods," most professionals had only scorn. "It was not worth while to argue," one educator said in response to Sabin's remarks, "with men who had

167

been enjoying a Rip Van Winkle slumber and were out of touch with the general educational sentiment in the country."[31]

But in the late 1870s the educators' exalted view of teacher training and training schools carried little weight with the farmers and their representatives in the Midwestern legislatures. Beginning in 1875 they launched an attack that virtually halted the building of new normal schools across the Middle Border by the end of the decade. By that time the appropriations for the normals in Minnesota had been slashed, and in 1878 the practice school associated with the normal at Peru, Nebraska, had to be dropped and salaries for new teachers could be paid only by reducing those of the older teachers. In Kansas the legislature had gone further. In 1876 it refused to appropriate any more money for the state's normal schools. Those at Concordia and Leavenworth closed their doors that same year, while the Emporia normal limped along on tuition fees alone and struggled for existence against the elements and human frailty as well as against the farmers and the state legislature. In 1877 an official embezzled nine thousand dollars of the school's money, and in April of the next year a tornado ripped through some of the school's buildings. Later, in 1878, the normal's two principal buildings were gutted by fire.[32]

As vigorous as the farmers' attacks upon the normals were, however, they never really stopped the irrepressible educators from pressing their demands upon the state legislatures, and, by the mid-1880s, the rising normal school budgets testified to the educators' persistence and to the average legislator's readiness to listen to the expert in matters educational. By that time some educators were indicating that they had won the battle and that no one really questioned the normal's right to exist any longer. "It is now no longer a question . . . ," one professional wrote in 1887, "as to the necessity of the normal school to the well-being of a system of State public schools."[33]

And so it seemed. The normals lingered on throughout the Middle Border, and a few new ones were established. And many a Midwestern farmer's daughter through the years dreamed of reaching great intellectual heights by graduating from the state normal. Even so, the normals in the Middle West never fully recovered from the blow the farmers dealt them in the 1870s, and the figures showing that the number of public normals had doubled between 1876 and 1900 were misleading. Most of the new public normals were city or county normals. The state normals, the kind that had first been established, numbered scarcely a half-dozen more in 1900 than in 1876, and in the early 1900s some observers were already predicting the end of the normals. "The old-fashioned normal school is on the road to oblivion," one educator noted in 1903, "and every earnest educator wished for it a speedy end of the journey." Yet he recognized they would be some time in dying partly because "attached to them are good-salaried positions, not only to be filled, but to hold."[34]

III

Whether for good reasons or bad, the farmers had been right about the normal schools. They had never really been needed on the Middle Border insofar as the training of country teachers was concerned, which, of course, had been the original justification for them. Except perhaps in Wisconsin and Minnesota, the normals actually trained very few rural schoolteachers. For most rural young people could no more afford to attend the normal schools than they could afford to attend the university or small college, and, in the end, the vast majority of those who taught in the Midwest's one-room schools had to be trained in teacher institutes, which were far less pretentious than the normals.

The origin of the teacher institutes in America went back to the year 1839, when Henry Barnard, the great Connecticut educator, gathered a group of young people about him to teach them how to teach. Their training consisted of attending lectures on teaching techniques and observing what was presumed to be good teaching in the Hartford schools. From there the idea passed to New York, where the training sessions were first called "institutes," and on to the Middle Border, where in years to come they would have their greatest popularity. A teacher institute was held in Jackson, Michigan, in 1846, and by 1855 both the Ohio and the Michigan legislatures had made small financial provisions for their support. At the close of the Civil War, teacher institutes were being held in nearly all of the North Central states.[35]

The first institutes were usually held by the state superintendents in four or five different places in the state each year. But these, like the normals, were not always within every aspiring teacher's reach, and in the 1870s the legislatures in many of the states began providing for teacher institutes to be held in each county. Thus began what were perhaps the most practical teacher-training programs ever devised in the nation.

The county institutes in which so many rural schoolteachers in the Midwest were trained in the last century were not all precisely alike.

169

Some were held during the school year, and some during the summer. Some were held for only a few days, and others for a month or more. In Kansas, which had one of the best programs, as if to atone for the assault on the normals, the institutes lasted four weeks. And in Indiana, besides the county institutes, township teacher institutes were also held one day each month while school was in session.[36]

But everywhere across the Middle Border the county teacher institutes were rural institutions, as unpretentious as the farmers and far more acceptable to them than the normal schools were. True, they were inspired and promoted by the educators, and in most states the professionals wrote the course outlines used to develop institute courses. Even so, they were largely what the farmers, not the educators, wanted them to be, and for that reason the educators were continually trying to change them.

The county institutes were, first of all, mostly self-supporting and so inexpensive that the poorest farmer's daughter could afford to attend them. Usually they were financed by a one-dollar tax on teaching certificates, a one-dollar institute entrance fee, and, in some states, by a modest stipend from the state government. The Kansas treasury, for example, contributed fifty dollars for each county institute, but only if that institute enrolled fifty students. The state of Nebraska, on the other hand, for years contributed nothing but encouragement to the institute work.[37]

Not only were they self-supporting and locally financed, but the institutes were, like the country schools, locally controlled as well, and it was this that bothered the educators. "I have not a particle of control over the teachers' institutes of our State," the Illinois superintendent of public instruction told a group of professionals in 1887. "I cannot dictate to them. The county superintendents suggest the subjects [to be taught], and they appoint the time; they are entirely under the control of these officers." And, indeed, they were.[38]

The county superintendents—or the county board of education, as in the case of Michigan, where there were no county superintendents—not only determined the time when the institutes would be held and what was to be taught, for the most part, but also picked the place where they were to be held and arranged the schedule of classes. But what made the professionals splenetic about the county institutes was that the county superintendents also employed the institute director, or conductor as he was called, as well as the teachers who were to help the conductor.

In the waning years of the nineteenth century the conductor of the county teacher institutes was a person of importance in the counties along the Middle Border. A day or two before the institute was to begin, he came riding into the train station at the county seat, where he was met by the county superintendent. He was whisked to the local hotel, and for the next several weeks his name was constantly before the people. The newspapers built him up as "the best in the state," and his public lectures, for which he was given an additional ten dollars, were extravagantly praised in the press and his brilliance acknowledged by townspeople and students alike.

So pleasant were these moments of fame to the educators that many of them sought the county institute positions as much to place themselves "before the public," as one shrewd observer noted, as for the stipend that went with the job, although that was not unimportant. In any case, the posts were highly desirable and the competition for them sharp. But as it turned out, those who regarded themselves as professionals and the best trained for the jobs were not always chosen to fill these places. Instead the county superintendents often employed lesser-known men and women for their conductors and teachers. Sometimes they did this for political reasons, as the educators charged, and sometimes it was done simply to give younger people a chance to earn some extra money. Probably most often it was done to save money.[39]

Whatever the reasons, when the unknowns were chosen, the older, established educators were outraged because they had been passed over and charged that the institutes were being ruined by the selection of conductors and teachers who had no reputation as teachers. "It will be sufficient proof of this," the superintendent of schools in Ann Arbor, Michigan, pointed out to a group of educators in 1886, "to run your eye over a list of institute workers for the last four or five years. We have simply to note the large number of men and women unknown beyond their immediate locality as teachers, or unknown as teachers at all."[40]

It was not just the money involved that concerned the professionals who lost out to those they regarded as their inferiors in the race for county institute jobs, though that was important. Many of them no doubt sincerely, and perhaps rightfully, believed that not to employ them was to lower educational standards, and some were so convinced of this that they refused to teach in an institute even when invited if they had to teach beside those they regarded as nonprofessionals. Once in the early 1880s, the superintendent of Cerro Gordo County, Iowa, invited both Herbert Quick, then a country schoolteacher, and

171

Carrie Lane, superintendent of schools in Mason City, to teach at the upcoming county institute. But Carrie Lane, who became Carrie Chapman Catt, the leader of the women's suffrage movement during World War I, refused because, among other things, the superintendent had invited a country schoolteacher to teach in the institute![41]

What the professional educators really wanted was to be able to control the county institute work the way they controlled the normals. Especially did they want to determine who would be chosen as workers in the institute and who would not. "We ought to have a professional corps of institute workers," the Ann Arbor superintendent said, "Comprising the best teaching talent that can be procured." And these ought to be appointed by a triumvirate of like-minded men— the state superintendent, the professor of pedagogy at the university, and the principal of the state normal school—who would be certain to select the proper professionals for the job.[42]

But this was not to be. The county institutes were the rural young people's colleges, and the state legislatures made no move to turn them over to the educators. They were left instead in the hands of the county superintendents, who were responsible primarily to the farmers who elected them, and through the years the staging of the county teacher institute was one of the county superintendent's most important responsibilities.

Because the teacher institutes were so important, the county superintendents began publicizing them well in advance of their opening. Perhaps as much as two months ahead of time, they would insert a brief announcement in the county newspaper announcing the date of the upcoming institute. With the opening of the institute still a month away they would follow this announcement with a two-column spread in which they would again give the dates of the institute and the place where it was to be held—usually in the high school at the county seat. They would instruct the students on the preparations they should make, where they might find board and room, and they would often include a thinly veiled warning that those who expected to teach in the country schools in the fall should attend the institute.

The county superintendents made every effort to make their institutes sound attractive. Nearly always they would write that the best conductor in the state had been chosen to direct the school, and more often than not they would close their blurb with the prophecy that the coming institute would be the best ever held in the county. "The school will undoubtedly be one of the most successful ever held in Dickinson County," ran the announcement of that Kansas county's institute in 1880, "as the instructors are well known for their thoroughness in the branches of study."[43]

The county superintendent's announcement of the coming teacher's institute stirred a flurry of excitement in the slow-paced life of Midwestern rural America in the late nineteenth century. It was, in effect, an invitation to the young people of those rural counties to continue their education beyond the country school, and for many shy, book-loving country boys like Herbert Quick, who attended the institute in Grundy Center, Iowa, in 1877, it offered a chance to reach beyond their rural world. "The transition from the life in Colfax Township," Quick wrote, "to the little village of Grundy Center, the plunge into the classes meeting for lectures in that old wooden schoolhouse, was the most astounding leap of my whole life."[44]

In the course of years a surprisingly large number of young people took advantage of the opportunity to continue their education whether they wished to teach or not. Some, like William Allen White in Eldorado, Kansas, drifted in and out of the institutes for want of something better to do. Others attended because they wanted not so much to make teaching a career as to make certain they could get their third-grade teaching certificate renewed so they could teach for a time. And sometimes farmers' daughters, who had just become old enough to attend their first institute and who had for years heard their older sisters tell of the good times they had had at the institutes in that distant and exciting county seat, enrolled partly at least for the fun they might have there.[45]

Serious students, too, attended the county institutes, and many a teaching career was launched from those little rural training programs. Using the money she had saved from her first teaching experience, Flora Knisely, whose widowed mother was homesteading in Dickinson County, Kansas, in 1879, attended the institute at Abilene that year, and began the training that would lead her to teach far from the little one-room schools on the Kansas frontier. And Augusta Slayton, a young Michigan woman who had grown up on a farm in Nebraska, found her life's work in a county institute.[46]

But for Augusta, as perhaps for many young Midwestern women, the decision to attend the institute was not easy. When she was sixteen her family had moved to Hillsdale, Michigan, where she had attended high school. After graduation she had drifted, and life seemed to be passing her by, when, finally, half fearful and half hopeful, she pondered the problem of attending the institute. "I've a half a notion to go," she wrote in her diary in 1907, "even if there isn't much use of my trying to pass the exams for I never could and I wouldn't know how to teach anyway but I've got to do something." A few days later she had still not made up her mind to attend although she had learned she might be able to get a job if she did. "I'd like to earn a little money," she wrote, "& I've got to do something but—well I guess I'm just a coward." At last, however, she decided to go, and when she finished she taught, as did so many, first in a little one-room school and finally in a large urban school.[47]

When the aspiring teachers had made up their minds, for whatever reason, to attend the institute, they had to make certain preparations. In the hurried round of daily chores—cooking, churning, ironing, cleaning—young women had to take time to sew a new dress or add a touch of finery to an old one. Possibly a trip to the county seat, where the institute was usually held, would be necessary to buy the necessary school supplies and make arrangements for a place to stay, for it was not always easy to find board and room at a price country people could afford to pay.

"Get your rooms and beds ready to receive the Normalites," the county newspaper would tell the townspeople as the institute was about to begin, and those who wished to have boarders would list their names with the county superintendent. But the prices they asked often seemed outrageous to country schoolteachers, who, fairly or unfairly, charged that the townspeople, knowing their need and that they had saved a little money from their salaries, took advantage of them by overcharging. The townspeople, on the other hand, regarded the rural teachers who haggled over the price as "stingy and mean."[48]

The quarrel over the price of board and room reflected the tensions between rural and small-town America that were never far beneath the surface in the late nineteenth and early twentieth centuries, and it was serious enough to draw warnings from the county superintendents. "Be Courteous To Teachers," the county superintendent of Butler County, Kansas, told the people of El Dorado in 1893, on the eve of that year's institute. She urged the townspeople to consider the teachers' meager wages when they set their prices for board and room, and implied that the site of the institute might be changed if they did not. "There is no law compelling the superintendents to hold the Institute at any certain place," she wrote.[49]

But somehow bargains were struck. The students found their places, and, for a month or so, as the long summer days ran their course, the little Midwestern towns would be filled with teachers and prospective teachers coming and going along the streets, while in the evenings the townspeople viewed from their front porch swings the passing parade of young people who would be their country school-teachers when school opened in the fall.

The gathering of young people for the county institute each year was an event of major importance in the life of those Midwestern rural communities of two generations ago, and much of the institutes' value lay in the interest in education they roused among the rural people. The county newspapers covered their institute's activities as if it were the most important happening anyplace in the world. They listed all the participants so that farmers and villagers across the county might see the names of their sons and daughters in print. They urged people to visit the institute and publicized the work being done in the classes there. "Professor Searson in history is introducing the Source method or Laboratory method," a newspaper reported of the institute in Saunders County, Nebraska, in 1896. "Today's lesson had to do with Tyre and Sidon." The paper noted too that the "vertical penmanship class was very large." And always, in that upbeat Midwestern spirit of growth and progress, there was the revelation that this year's institute was the largest ever held.[50]

The newspaper accounts were not often exaggerated, for the county institutes did, indeed, enroll large numbers of student-teachers, nearly always over one hundred and often well over two hundred, and it was not uncommon for a state to have more than eleven or twelve thousand students in its institutes in one year. Thirty-one men and one hundred five women enrolled in the Calhoun County institute in Battle Creek, Michigan, in the summer of 1890. Two girls of sixteen were the youngest students there; the oldest was a forty-five year old woman who had twenty-five years of teaching experience. Of the total number who attended, only four had teaching certificates issued from the state normal school, eight had first-grade certificates, sixteen had second-grade, and seventy-eight had third-grade certificates. Twenty-six, including the two youngest students, had no teaching experience and no teaching certificates.[51]

The scholars came to Battle Creek from all parts of the county. They came from farms and neighborhoods identified only by the name of some fourth-class post office long since abandoned; and they came from the villages and small towns, places like Albion and Bedford and Tekonsha, and even from Charlotte and Bellevue, which lay beyond the county's borders. Not all could afford to stay for the twenty days the institute lasted. One young woman who had a third-grade certificate but had already taught school for thirty months stayed only two days, while one of the sixteen-year-olds attended all the sessions but one. The average attendance for each half-day of the institute was eighty-three.[52]

Many of the young people who attended the teachers' institutes on the Middle Border did find some of the good times and the excitement they had anticipated, for the institutes were not all work. Some educators, in fact, thought there was too much entertainment associated with the "normals," as they were sometimes called, and too little work. For there were parties and ice cream socials and receptions for the students, some of which were given in the homes of the town's wealthier citizens, where the furnishings and draperies were such as some farm girls had seen before only in the pages of the Montgomery Ward catalogue.

There were flirtations, too, between the young men and women, even "in the light of open day," as the shocked young Herbert Quick recalled. "Jessie Heath and Amy are 'mashers' as they call themselves," wrote one young woman who was attending an institute in Iowa in 1884 of her boardinghouse companions. "They flirt & are so boisterous I do not care to associate with 'such.'" But that same young woman was herself not unaware of the young men at the institute. On a sultry Iowa evening as she attended a lecture entitled "Educate for Citizenship," given by an institute professor, she was deeply moved when a prominent young townsman offered her his fan. "Ah!" she confided in her diary, "*I don't see how he knew me. He is nice, too.*"[53]

The evening lectures given by the institute professors once or twice a week were favorite meeting places for the institute's students, and prominent social functions for the townspeople as well. According to the county weeklies they were almost always given "to crowded houses," and as invariably "well received." There at the Methodist church or perhaps the opera house, townspeople and student-teachers mingled to listen to lectures on topics as diverse as Longfellow and biology. But whatever the subject, the lecturers were likely to give it an inspirational or moralistic twist and above all to present it in that clear, forceful manner so pleasing to rural Americans who loved a good oration. "A fine audience assembled at the M. E. Church last evening to listen to a lecture by Superintendent Simmons," ran a newspaper's description of the Calhoun County institute lecture in 1890, "and by closest attention testified their appreciation of the entire service. The lecture was, like its author, manly, vigorous, and thoroughly enjoyable, and abounded in practical sense for every day life."[54]

And when the lecture was finished, young couples, who had sometimes only recently met, strolled hand in hand along quiet, tree-lined streets, lit here and there by the flight of an occasional firefly, to the front steps of the high school to dally for a time before making their way to their boardinghouses.[55]

When morning came, however, memory of the evening's entertainment was pushed aside. Promptly at eight o'clock, and sometimes earlier, the student-teachers met in the high school assembly hall for the day's opening exercises—a prayer, perhaps, or a Bible reading, or maybe a short inspirational talk—before they proceeded to their classes for the day's work.

IV

For years the studies pursued in the county institutes reflected the dominance of rural opinion about what should be taught. Common sense dictated that the teachers be taught what to teach before they were instructed in how to teach it. For that reason the institutes began where the country school ended, and the students' days were filled with drills in the common branches—arithmetic, grammar, reading, spelling, and so on—until they had a fair understanding of the subject matter they were expected to teach. And when the Midwestern states required the teaching of physiology and the harmful effects of alcohol upon the body, as all of them did by the 1890s, there were more drills, on human anatomy and the properties of alcohol.[56]

But the theory and practice of teaching were never completely ignored even in the early days of the institutes. John Swett's *The Method of Teaching,* published in 1880, was a great favorite of institute conductors and religiously used. Much time was spent in introducing country teachers to the "object lesson" method of teaching developed years before by the Swiss educational reformer Johann Pestalozzi, and more time in weaning them away from teaching reading by putting letters together to make words toward a "judicious combination," as Swett called it, "of the word method, phonic method, and spelling method." Besides this, hints were given the student-teachers on how to handle unruly children, how to keep school records, and how to hold class recitations, or, as they put it, "how to manage the school."[57]

Yet as the years went by more and more institute time was taken up in teaching how to teach, and some county superintendents even boasted that their county institutes were no longer teaching anything but professional courses. Even so, most of those professional courses centered upon teaching methods and for that reason were more utilitarian than theoretical. At the institute in Allegan County, Michigan, in 1890, for example, the students were told how to get travel books for geography classes and how to teach that subject by the "trip" method. They were shown how to illustrate the relation of the moon, earth, and sun at various seasons by constructing a mechanism from croquet balls, wire, and boards. Simple experiments for teaching the effects of alcohol on the body were demonstrated, and ways of finding original problems for arithmetic drills were discussed. The student-teachers were even shown new methods of instructing their pupils in government, money, and taxes.[58]

Methods, methods, methods! Many of the professional educators in the 1880s and '90s seemed mesmerized by them. At one time or another, perhaps most of those who taught in the institutes had hit upon a way of teaching a particular subject that they supposed was original, and had apparently convinced themselves, in the absence of proof to the contrary, that their method of teaching that subject was superior to any other. So at the institutes they expounded at length on methods, their own especially, but others as well, until some of the professionals themselves complained that they had gone too far and that teaching methods was not enough. "The cry for methods in our time has amounted almost to a craze," said one disgruntled professional in 1886. "It has come to be a substitute for thinking. Genuine teaching is not imitation." What he wanted was more instruction in psychology. "The best educational thought of our time," he continued, "affirms that true teaching is based on the laws of the mind—is a science, and this must not be forgotten in the institute.... Methods not consciously based on principles will speedily wear out—but psychology is fundamental and will work out its own methods."[59]

And with ever-increasing frequency educators began including in their institutes lectures on what they believed were scientific principles derived from psychology.

By the beginning of the nineteenth century, English and European philosophers had been speculating for two centuries or more about how the mind perceived reality, but it was not until the nineteenth century that psychology left the realm of philosophy and became a science that was, through the nineteenth century, especially concerned with the various faculties of the mind. Faculty psychology, as it was called, divided the mind into various faculties to explain how the mind received sensations and converted them into perceptions of reality. It had been developed by Thomas Reid, among others, a Scots Presbyterian philosopher, near the middle of the eighteenth century, but it was, inadvertently, a German anatomist named Franz Joseph Gall who helped popularize the faculty theory of psychology in the nineteenth century.[60]

Borrowing Reid's ideas about the faculties, Gall theorized that the mind was divided into thirty-seven faculties, each with its own particular place in the brain, and if any one of these faculties—the faculty of combativeness for example—was overdeveloped, a bump or protrusion would appear in the skull directly above the area where that faculty was located. From this theory came the practice of phrenology, or reading a person's character by feeling the bumps on his head.

The science of phrenology, as it was referred to, swept through America like a whirlwind in the years before the Civil War and claimed among its converts many learned Americans including Horace Mann. Still, many scientists and even many anatomists never accepted phrenology, and in the post–Civil War period its popularity waned in part, at least, because phrenologists multiplied like fortunetellers. They appeared at county fairs and medicine shows and other public gatherings, until the practice of phrenology lost whatever academic respectability it had had.[61]

Yet the idea that the brain was divided into faculties that governed the intellect, the emotions, and the will lived on. It seemed to explain how the mind was put together and how it worked, and in the late nineteenth century the American educators embraced it with the ardor of lovers. And no wonder! For faculty psychology was wrapped in the mantle of science. By associating their discipline with it, the educators could claim that education was truly a science, and science was the necessary ingredient to support the academic pretensions of the educators and elevate them to the professional ranks. "In truth," wrote Gabriel Compayre, that prolific French scholar whose books on education were read by thousands of country schoolteachers in the light of smelly kerosene lamps that burned into the night in farm homes across the Middle Border, "the rules for teaching are but the laws of psychology applied, transformed into practical maxims, and tested by experience."[62]

For the purposes of education, then, all that was needed was to transform the laws of psychology into practical maxims or scientific principles of teaching, and this became one of the new roles of professional educators. "It [psychology] names the faculties to be exercised, but it does not tell how to exercise them," wrote one educator in

1887, and his book was only one of a large number stamped out by the presses in the closing two decades of the last century trying to explain just how it was that the faculties should be trained.[63]

The faculties, the educators believed, could be exercised like muscles and developed by performing certain tasks and by studying certain subjects, and the results of that training would be transferred to other activities. According to this theory, then, certain academic subjects were valuable, not necessarily for their subject matter, but for their power to train the faculties. Arithmetic, for example, trained the reason, which when developed by this training could be used to solve many of life's problems.

But it was not only the intellectual faculties—the perceptive, expressive, and reflective faculties—that were to be trained. The moral faculty, too, must be exercised, and for many a professional educator, troubled by the great changes taking place in the rising industrial nation and anxious to raise the nation's moral standards, this training was the most important of all. The state superintendent of Illinois insisted in 1888 that the moral faculties can and must be trained. "Indeed," he wrote, "no faculty . . . is more concerned with the important interests of our lives than this. . . . If the annals of nations teach us anything, they teach that all vice is enfeebling, and that virtue alone is fearless and strong. And I cannot shake off the impression that in the near future our own nation is to illustrate the same law, either by a triumphant mastery of the evils that threaten it, or by a dismal surrender to them."[64]

So the faculties must be trained and the principles underlying that training taught to teachers, and almost no county institute was complete in the 1890s that did not have at least one class on the training of the faculties. In lengthy lectures and with detailed outlines on the blackboard, the institute instructors listed the faculties, divided them into those relating to the intellect, the emotions, and the will, and took their young students through the order in which they should be trained. The faculties, they would say, must be trained simultaneously even though, like runners in a race, they would not all advance at the same pace. And they warned against the excessive training of one faculty over another. "The independent culture of each faculty should not make us lose sight of the final aim," proclaimed a leading textbook on the subject, "which is the harmony and equilibrium of all the faculties."[65]

Just how the teachers in the one-room schools were to apply all this to teaching their students the multiplication tables and the rudiments of reading was never really made clear, and how much of it the young country girls fresh from the country schools understood is uncertain. But no matter. Dutifully they filled their notebooks with the rules, goals, methods, and faculties their instructors gave them, with the expectation, perhaps, that someday they would make sense. "One thing needful is a high aim," one Minnesota girl wrote in her notebook, "and a strong faith in the infinite possibilities which lie hidden in a child's nature." And there, along with the listing of the faculties, she had copied some definitions:

> Why we teach—To awaken the moral and intellectual faculties
> Whom we teach—Children and youth
> What we teach—Matter
> How we teach—Method or way.[66]

Still, the time spent on faculty psychology and even on methods was usually limited, because, finally, most county institutes had to prepare the teacher-students for the county teacher examinations. These usually came at the close of the institute, and because they emphasized subject matter more than teaching theory, the institute instructors were forced to teach subject matter no matter how much they preferred to talk about methods and first principles derived from faculty psychology.

Like so much that the county institutes did, this was in keeping with the rural view of things. Farmers would surely have been as puzzled as their daughters doubtless were about the connection between faculty psychology and the three R's, and their attitude toward instruction in the theory and practice of teaching was close to that of the critic from Tekonsha, Michigan, who complained in 1886 because the graduates of the normal school did not have to take the county teacher examinations. "It may be urged," he wrote, "that the State Normal prepares students practically for the work of teaching, training them in theory and practice. All of which can be admitted, and yet the fact remains that theoretical knowledge itself seldom leads to success in any profession. The assumption that Normal graduates, of all others, are best qualified for the profession is false, as well as unjust to teachers of knowledgeability and success who never followed the ruts of the Normal."[67]

But if the farmers, like this critic, were skeptical of the value of training in the theory and practice of teaching, they did know the value of the three R's, and insofar as they wanted to know anything about their teacher's ability to teach, they wanted to know how well she could spell, figure, write, and maintain discipline. Most of this information was provided by the county teacher examinations, and, at least until near the turn of the century, the educators themselves thought these tests necessary in order to keep the quality of teaching from further deterioration.[68]

The county teacher examinations taken by the Midwestern country schoolteachers in the fading years of the nineteenth century were nothing if not thorough, and unlike anything given to contemporary graduates from the nation's schools of education. The students sometimes began at six o'clock in the morning and for two days they reasoned their way through lengthy arithmetic problems, diagrammed sentences, parsed numerous nouns and verbs in the sentences, wrote detailed essays on the Constitution or perhaps on the Revolutionary War, and named the important lakes, rivers, and mountains of North America and Europe. In the 1890s they were examined on the human anatomy, the properties of alcohol, and, by the turn of the century, on the theory and practice of teaching.

Naturally such examinations sometimes brought student complaints. "There was a general complaint among the students that the studies and examinations were very hard," the newspaper in Russell County, Kansas, reported in 1893 following the close of the institute. And once in Walworth County, Wisconsin, an irate student who had just been through the examinations for a third-grade certificate wrote a testy letter to the newspaper in Whitewater. "Is a third grade teacher expected to be acquainted with every little rock in the sea...?" he asked. "Should a teacher understand all about the age of the earth and zoological classes of animals and the location and nature of paxy-waxy [sic], to pass in physical geography?"[69]

Still, the examinations continued in spite of such complaints, and the students accepted the fact that they had to take them and that they would be difficult. And as they prepared for them in the closing days of the institute they seemed grateful for the opportunity the institute had given them and even a little nostalgic about its close.

Their mood was reflected in the resolutions their committee on resolutions drew up and published in which they thanked the townspeople for their hospitality, praised the county superintendent for his work, complimented the institute conductor and his assistants, and ended on a note of determination and bittersweet sadness. "As we separate," ran the eighth resolution of the institute committee in Osborne County, Kansas, in 1893, "perhaps never to meet again in this

182

Interior of a one-room school in District 8, Berrien Township, Berrien County, Michigan. (From the *Sixty-first Annual Report of the Michigan Superintendent of Public Instruction* [Lansing, 1898], pp. 50–51.)

Typical country-school library from a school in Springfield Township, Clark County, Ohio. (Ohio Historical Society.)

Interior of a one-room school in Iowa, 1909, showing typical seating arrangement. (State Historical Society of Iowa.)

"Live to Learn. Strive to Excel." Interior of the Arbor Vitae Summit School, District 7, Oneida Township, Delaware County, Iowa. (State Historical Society of Iowa.)

Lunchtime in a one-room school in Iowa, 1909. Students with their teacher. (State Historical Society of Iowa.)

A part of a rural eighth-grade graduating class, Page County, Iowa, ca. 1911, with the county superintendent of schools, Sarah Huftalen, in the last row, center. (State Historical Society of Iowa.)

Jesse Field, county superintendent of schools in Page County, Iowa, 1912.
(State Historical Society of Iowa.)

A meeting of country schoolteachers in Postville, Iowa, ca. 1895. (State Historical Society of Iowa.)

Transporting country children to a consolidated school, ca. 1904, Trumbull County, Ohio. (Ohio Historical Society.)

Teachers' Institute at Valentine, Cherry County, Nebraska, 1889. (Nebraska State Historical Society.)

Children walking to school in the winter on the Illinois prairie. (From the *American Monthly Review of Reviews*, vol. 26 [1902], p. 704.)

Horse-drawn van used for bringing children to a consolidated school in the Longdon District, Minnesota. (From *American Schoolhouses*, Bulletin no. 5 [1910], U.S. Bureau of Education.)

The Herbert Quick School. Moved from a farm to Grundy Center, Iowa, and restored. (State Historical Society of Iowa.)

District School No. 19, Frontier County, Nebraska. (Nebraska State Historical Society.)

Typical sod-house school with children and homesteaders in 1881, Osborne County, Kansas. (Kansas State Historical Society.)

Last log schoolhouse built in Barry County, Missouri. Built in 1894. (State Historical Society of Missouri.)

McStay School, Osborne County, southwest of Downs, Kansas, ca. 1900.
(Kansas State Historical Society.)

Children playing outside a one-room school in Wisconsin, ca. 1918. (State
Historical Society of Wisconsin.)

One-room school near Hill City, Aitkin County, Minnesota, 1911, in a time of dwindling country-school enrollments. (Minnesota State Department of Education.)

Arbor Vitae Summit School, District 7, Oneida Township, Delaware County, Iowa. (State Historical Society of Iowa.)

Brick country scholhouse in Indiana, typical of many in that state in the late nineteenth century. (Indiana State Library.)

Center Consolidated School, Knox, Indiana, ca. 1900. (Indiana State Library.)

The Ise Schoolhouse, District 37, Osborne County, Kansas, in 1981.

life, and depart to our several fields of labor, let us go forth determined to put into practice the lessons we have learned, and to do all in our power for the moral as well as the intellectual advancement of all who may come in reach of our influence."[70]

At such moments the students forgot for the time the difficulties of the examination, and, with goodbyes and promises to see one another again, they scattered to their homes about the county to wait for the superintendent's letter that would tell them whether they had passed or failed, and, in effect, whether they would teach or not.

As the years passed, the news when it came was bad for an ever-increasing number of them. By the late 1880s and early '90s, everywhere across the Middle Border the teachers' examinations were being read with greater care and graded with more severity, and students who once might have passed with mediocre performances could do so no longer. In Indiana in the early 1890s—and Indiana was no exception—the county superintendents became accustomed to failing more students than they passed, even when they sometimes needed more teachers than they had available. From 1890 to 1893, for example, 234 applicants were given their teaching certificates in Brown County, Indiana, and 279 were rejected; and in Boone County, Indiana, 531 received certificates and 562 failed.[71]

To be sure, the county examinations did not eliminate all poor teachers from the Middle Border's one-room schools any more than the Master of Education degree would separate all inept teachers from the urban schools in a later period. But at the very least, they did indicate what the teacher knew about the three R's. They served to eliminate those who were hopelessly lost in subject matter, and they did give some assurance to those who passed and to the school boards who employed them that they could teach a country school.

The results of the examinations also made clear, of course, that the county teacher institutes wrought no miracles. They had not been able to teach all those who attended them the fundamentals of grammar and arithmetic, the configuration of their native land, and the story of the American past. Nor were they able to make all those who passed the examinations good teachers, for there was much truth, in fact, in the Nebraska county superintendent's observation that teachers are born, not made. "We have learned . . .," said one educator looking back on the 1880s and '90s, "that no one can be a good teacher without a native aptitude for teaching. The teacher is as truly born and not made as the poet." For it was one thing to teach a

183

teacher that one of the scientific principles of teaching was to interest the student, and another to put a spark in the teacher's eye, enthusiasm in her voice, and a cheerful confidence in her manner.[72]

Even so, the county institutes made an immense contribution to education of Midwestern country children in the years before the new century. Rooted in the practical, commonsense environment of rural America, they stripped teacher-training to its bare essentials and prevented, for the most part, the addition of bloated, unnecessary courses to the training curriculum. They gave rural young people a chance to continue their education beyond the country school with little expense; and finally, they sent out to the little white schoolhouses across the Middle Border thousands of farm, village, and small-town girls who were able, as a rule, to teach effectively and to lift some three generations of rural Americans to a standard of literacy unequaled by any other region in the nation.

10

"As Is the Teacher..."

※※

I

On a sunday afternoon in april 1872, mary bradford and her parents drove west from Kenosha, Wisconsin, in the family's two-seated buggy on their way to a farm which sat near the boundary line between Kenosha and Racine counties, some fourteen miles from Kenosha. The owner of the farm was an acquaintance of Mary's father, and his son was the clerk of the school board of Joint District 2 of Paris and Yorkville townships, where Mary was to teach the summer school term from April to July.

At the farmer's home, where Mary was to spend the night, her parents visited briefly, and then with a hasty farewell started back to Kenosha. With a sinking heart Mary watched them go, saw the buggy disappear behind a grove of trees, emerge again, then pass over a hill and beyond her sight, leaving her alone with strangers.

Mary was then sixteen years old, and she had never felt so desolate. Until she was thirteen she had lived on a farm in Paris Township and had attended the District 5 school there. After the family moved to Kenosha, she had gone for only a short time to the high school there before the family's financial situation forced her to begin earning her own living. Without further instruction of any kind, she had taken the county teacher's examination, received a third-grade certificate, and had somehow managed to secure the position in Joint District 2.

That evening, after the lamps had been lit, Mary signed a contract agreeing to teach for three months for twenty-five dollars a month and was shown how to keep the school records in the clerk's big black book. She was told of homes in the district where she might find room and board and was given a little school bell and a big iron key to the schoolhouse door. And, since she had no watch of her own, and the schoolhouse had none, her host loaned her his to use until she could buy one.

Early the next morning, dressed in a neat calico dress and loaded down with the school bell, the key, the watch, a tin lunch pail, and sundry articles, Mary walked the half-mile from the farm where she had spent the night to the schoolhouse and was completely unprepared for what she saw. Unlike the country school she had attended, this schoolhouse had no beauty the eye could see. The doorstep was broken and the schoolroom itself was a shambles. Ashes and paper were strewn across the floor, tobacco quids spotted the area around the stove, and clods of dried mud lay scattered about. In answer to her questions of what had taken place in the room, a student replied: "They held spring caucus here."[1]

Prim and neat, Mary felt compelled to clean the schoolhouse, and not until she and the children had swept and dusted the room, and she had made herself as presentable as possible, did she ring the little bell to bring the students to their seats and take their names and ages. And this brought another shock. For among her sixteen students of various sizes and ages was a girl of nineteen who wanted to study algebra, a subject Mary had just begun before her high school career had been interrupted![2]

Mary Bradford's experiences were little different from those of thousands of other young farm and village girls who left their homes to teach in the country schools along the Middle Border in the late nineteenth century. Loneliness, homesickness, uneasiness in strange surroundings, worry over a place to board, even cleaning the schoolhouse on the first day—all these and more—were the common experiences of nearly every teacher who taught a Midwestern rural school in those years.

Young and inexperienced, with only a minimum of training in the county institute or high school, and often, as in Mary's case, with none at all, such girls entered their classrooms to confront a student body that, in most instances, would have challenged the most experienced teacher.

Sometimes, in the early morning of a clear, crisp, autumn day, standing alone at a window of her quiet schoolroom, the country schoolteacher of two generations ago watched her students walking along the country road or cutting across the harvested grain fields in groups of twos or threes, swinging their lunch pails and laughing and shouting as they made their way to school, and something of what she saw can still be seen in the hundreds of school photographs taken in that era before schools became too large for group pictures.

If the young people who peer from the old photographs at the contemporary observer felt deprived in any way, it does not show in their faces. They stand there smiling for the camera or squinting into the sun, apparently proud and pleased to have their pictures taken and seemingly unaware that the one-room schoolhouse behind them is not the finest school anywhere. They appear to be a homogeneous group of white, Anglo-Saxon, Protestant children, and none seems more prosperous than another. The girls, with their hair swept back from their faces and falling in braids behind their backs, are dressed in homemade calico dresses that button up the back and black stockings that emerge from beneath their skirts to disappear into ankle-top button shoes. And the boys, sometimes wearing their Sunday suits but more often dressed in overalls or loose-fitting homemade trousers and white suspenders to anchor them in place, stand in male clusters and look confidently into the camera.

But these are surface impressions, for there were as many differences as similarities among the children in the one-room schools in the Middle West. One, which is immediately apparent in the photographs, is the difference in the sizes and ages of the scholars. The little ones stand in front and the large ones in back, according to the photographer's instructions, and the difference in their ages might be as much as fifteen years. And the teacher, standing among her older students, is often indistinguishable from them, for, in fact, she was often the same age as they were.

Furthermore, the backgrounds of those children were likely to be as diverse as their sizes and ages, so that many times when the teacher took the roll she found more than enough German, Scandinavian, and Bohemian names to match the Smiths and Joneses.

Frequently this meant that her school, if not exactly a tower of Babel, was, nevertheless, filled with children who spoke different languages, and many a German and Scandinavian child entered the little white school by the side of the road unable to speak a word of English. Only German children attended the first school Herbert Quick taught in Iowa in his youth, and no English whatever was spoken on the school grounds or in school except when the children addressed the teacher.[3]

But even the English-speaking children spoke a dialect filled with quaint expressions which their parents used, sometimes merely because the parents did not wish to appear "stylish." If they were doubt-ful about something, the children might say they were "jubus," and if they spoke of avoiding someone they would say they would "get shet of him." A disagreement between two boys might be described as a "little striffen," and if the quarrel deepened, one boy might say he was "worse-outed" with his antagonist than ever. A person might be "dauncy" if he did not feel well, and a girl the "very spit" of her mother if she resembled her.[4]

Religion, too, separated one child from another in the Midwestern country schools. William Allen White once wrote that they "were all little Protestants" in his school in Eldorado, Kansas, in the 1870s, but that was by no means true everywhere across the Middle Border. For if many country schoolchildren came from religious Protestant homes where the Bible was read each morning and grace said at every meal, there were also many from Catholic homes and not a few whose irreligious parents sprinkled their conversation with profanity and vulgarities that were carried to school on the tongues of their chil-dren. "I have learned," an Iowa teacher once wrote of a young girl whose language she had corrected on the schoolyard, "that the lan-guage in her home is very coarse and profane so the child is not to blame. It is miraculous for a teacher to lead a pupil beyond home influence which is fairly breathed into the very life and existence of the child."[5]

Besides all this, there were major differences in the culture of the homes of the Midwestern rural schoolchildren in spite of the appar-ent economic equality among them. Some children were from homes where the farm papers and the county weekly piled up on the library table in the family parlor along with the latest circulars, bulletins, and the yearbook from the Department of Agriculture. "We boys [have] gotten our American Agriculturist," Curtis Downer, a schoolboy in DeKalb County, Illinois, wrote in his diary in 1873, and in such homes as his near the turn of the century there might also be stereopticon pictures of faraway places to look at and a piano or even a Windsor organ to practice on. On the other hand, there were those in the little schools from homes where no newspapers or magazines were taken and where no pictures or artistic objects of any kind were to be seen.[6]

Whatever their differences, nearly all children who made their way to the one-room schools in the Middle West in the late nineteenth and early twentieth centuries were forced by circumstances to be inter-mittent students. Sometimes it was the weather that kept them home. Winter temperatures commonly fell to forty degrees below zero in the region, and gales filled the roads with snow from fence to fence, so that farm boys and girls must either stay at home or wade in the bitter cold a mile or more to school through snowdrifts that were sometimes as high as their heads. "I went to school and froze my ear coming home," Curtis Downer wrote in January of 1873. "We are having a terrible storm. The fire in the hard coal stove won't burn worth a cent." And an Iowa teacher noted in her journal on January 4, 1884, that the temperature stood at forty-two below zero that day, that she had only two scholars in school, and that she, too, had frozen an ear.[7]

Illness also accounted for much of the absenteeism in the country school each year. Especially was this true in the winter. Because the water dipper was shared and the little schoolroom was shut so tightly against the cold that no fresh air could penetrate, illness spread from pupil to pupil until frequently the school would have to close until the epidemic ran its course. Once in April and early May of 1893 the little Sanford School in Michigan had to close for nearly a month because of scarlet fever.[8]

But mostly it was work that kept the children, particularly the older ones, from regularly attending school, for when spring came to the Midwestern farms and the ground warmed there was always so much to do that all able hands were needed. Curtis Downer recorded in his diary that he had completed the winter school term in the little schoolhouse near his home in March of 1873 and that a new school term had begun on May 5, 1873. But he had not gone, and subsequent entries explained why. He was busy hauling manure to the fields, killing gophers, cultivating, and dragging the plowed fields. Not until the tenth of June did he begin school again, but he was fortunate to attend even then. Most farm boys of working age could never attend summer school.[9]

These, then, were the children fate had thrown together in the little schoolhouses of the hills and valleys and plains of the Middle Border. They were to be taught in one room, by one teacher, usually young and female, who was expected to teach them not only the three R's, but spelling, history, geography, physiology, and civil government, cultivate in them a love of country, beauty, and truth, improve their manners, and above all raise their moral standards to make them citizens worthy of their great nation. And all this she was to do in an environment that seemed to the educators to be completely hostile to learning.

The teacher's classroom was likely to be uncomfortably warm in summer and suffocatingly hot in winter, at least around the stove.

189

Away from that, it was often drafty, so that the children nearest the stove were too warm and those farthest away were cold. Aside from a few charts, possibly a map, and maybe a globe, she had no school apparatus, no visual aids to help her explain difficult points to her students. Until the 1890s or so, she usually had no clock on the wall and commonly no janitor, except herself, to clean the floors, wash the blackboards, and make fires on a cold winter day. Indeed, for years she did not even have a dictionary in the schoolroom and, of course, no uniform textbooks.

As often as not her school had no well, and each day the snapping of fingers and confusion in the room indicated it was time to send two boys to the nearest farm for water. When the water was brought, the boys carrying the bucket walked down the aisles giving each student a drink from a single dipper, or they set the water bucket in the back of the room where the students went in an endless parade during the day ostensibly to get a drink but principally to burn up excess energy.[10]

II

Under the circumstances it was no wonder that the Midwestern professional educators despaired of rural education in the late nineteenth century and compared it so unfavorably with urban education. Against the background of a fine, large, centrally heated schoolhouse with rooms filled with the latest school apparatus, encyclopedias, dictionaries, uniform textbooks, and uniform classes, the country school seemed ineffably bleak and backward.

Compare that large urban school, for example, with the little one-room school in Boyd County, Nebraska, near the South Dakota border, that an inspector of rural schools and the county superintendent visited in 1903. The schoolhouse, the inspector observed, was so humble "we could look out through the roof and see the sun and sky. We could see out the door without opening it. Some of the window lights were out. There were holes in the floor which was laid almost on the earth—just two by two scantlings under it."[11]

Yet here in this unlikely place, fourteen students, some of them terribly poor, were being educated in a rigorous fashion. When the inspector and the county superintendent entered the schoolhouse unannounced, "there was no one staring at us," the inspector noted, "no laughing at us, no uncomplimentary remarks. Every pupil kept at his work. Classes were called and dismissed in good order." The spelling class they listened to was composed of five little girls and a boy named Dick, "freckle-faced, shabbily dressed . . . who took his place at the head of the class. As he came to the recitation," the inspector continued, "he pushed one foot along over the rough floor. At first we thought he was lame. But a glance told the cause and we looked the other way. He was wearing an old shoe that would hardly hang on his foot. . . . Had he lifted his foot the old shoe sole would have flapped . . . as he walked. . . . But Dick held his place at the head of the class," and the inspector could see the "proud sparkle in his eyes, the bright gleam on his face," when he heard the teacher announce: "Dick wins the head mark today."[12]

Such scenes as this were repeated hundreds, even thousands of times daily throughout the region, and the educational progress of the Midwest's rural schoolchildren was charted, at least indirectly, by statistics gathered by the census bureau. By 1910, in six of the ten North Central states, the percentage of illiterate rural people ten years of age and older was less than that of the urban areas. Only in Indiana, where the township school district system prevailed, and in Wisconsin, Minnesota, and Missouri was the reverse true. Moreover, in the region as a whole, a region overwhelmingly rural, where the one-room school was the rule and not the exception, the illiteracy rate of the population was reduced from 9.3 to 4.2 per cent between 1870 and 1900, and in Kansas, Iowa, and Nebraska it fell below 3.0 per cent.[13]

No other section of the nation had done as well. Even the North Atlantic division, with a predominately urban population in 1900 and large, impressive schools, had reduced its illiteracy rate only from 7.6 to 5.9 per cent in the same period. True, the North Atlantic Division had sustained a massive influx of immigrants in the period, many of whom were illiterate. But so had the Midwest. Nearly two million immigrants, only eight per cent fewer than entered the North Atlantic area, had moved into the North Central states in those years.[14]

Obviously, magnificent school buildings, expensive school apparatus, and tightly administered schools systems, like teacher training, were not necessarily essential to learning. What contributed most to the success of any school, finally, was the teacher, as many county superintendents and even some of the more professionally minded educators saw. "Expensive schoolhouses, costly apparatus, intelligent supervision, and the cordial support of school boards, will not compensate," the superintendent in Dodge County, Wisconsin, wrote in 1880, "for a lack on the part of the teachers, of tact, education, or the adaptability to the discharge of the practical duties of the school room." The educators had a saying which was rooted in the rural experience, that "as is the teacher, so is the school," and on this much, at least, the farmers probably agreed with the educators.[15]

Perhaps this was not so clear in the cities, where the large school and graded system tended to shield the incompetent teacher and where supervisors were always at one's elbow to give directions. In the rural Midwest, however, where the teacher in the one-room school had the sole responsibility for what took place there, it was obvious to the most casual observer that the teacher made the school. Yet, as true as this was, it was also true that whatever success the country teacher on the Middle Border enjoyed was attributable in some measure to her own rural background and especially to the rural school system which the educators tried so hard to change.

Years after she had retired from teaching, a country schoolteacher in Nebraska recalled how she had gone in 1916 to teach in School District 148 in Cherry Creek County. The schoolhouse was made of sod and possessed an old organ, a pendulum clock, and not much else. The farmers were homesteaders and very poor. Neither school nor children had textbooks, and the county was so big that the county superintendent did not discover her until she was in her second term of teaching.[16]

For various reasons—the numerous schools in a county, poor roads, bad weather, epidemics—Midwestern county superintendents rarely visited all the schools in their counties in a single term, and a rural teacher might even teach an entire year without a visit from the superintendent. It was a condition greatly deplored by the professional educators, who supposed that if they who knew so much about teaching could only be on hand to direct the country teacher, rural education would somehow be greatly improved.

Supervision, they always said, was necessary in business, and therefore it must also be in education. "No man engaged in business in any industrial enterprise where any considerable number of men are employed and any large expenditures made," said the Wisconsin superintendent's report for 1900, "thinks of carrying it on without providing for close and effective supervision at every stage in the progress of the work. . . . It must be evident that sound business principles demand that in the expenditure annually of $3,171,000 for any purpose of such vital importance as the education of the citizens of the state, there must be careful, and effective supervision of the persons employed to do the work."[17]

But was there no point at which supervision became regimentation that stifled the teacher's creative impulses? By the 1890s there were some critics of the urban schools who believed there was, and Lorenzo Dow Harvey, who was the Wisconsin state superintendent when the above report was written, was himself an excellent example of what happened when a principal supervised his teachers too closely. As a principal in the urban schools in Wisconsin, he was so determined, according to those who knew him well, to force his teachers to teach by his four fundamental principles of teaching that he subordinated learning to method and "tended to regiment everyone under his methodology."[18]

This kind of supervision, at least, the country schoolteacher on the Middle Border escaped. Without a principal to supervise her, she was her own principal. She could organize her school and teach her students as she thought best, and, in the rural tradition of self-help, she was free to make herself a very good teacher or, of course, a very poor one. "In the work of the rural schoolteacher," remarked a Michigan school inspector who observed the country teacher's freedom in the 1880s, "there is less that is perfunctory, less of routine, more flexibility in the classification and more adaptation to the instruction of the individual needs of the pupils [than in the urban schools]."[19]

This flexibility was especially noticeable, as the Michigan inspector observed, in the way the teacher classified her students.

By the 1890s, thanks to the perseverance of the county superintendents, most Midwestern country schoolteachers had learned to use a course of study and to classify their students into what corresponded very roughly to the grades in urban schools. So rapidly had this process taken place, in fact, that the professional educators had begun to quarrel among themselves over the wisdom of trying to grade the country schools. The disagreement was passionate enough to find its way in a refined manner into the report of the Subcommittee on Instruction and Discipline made to the Committee of Twelve in 1896. "Your subcommittee would call special attention . . .," the report said, "to the evil results that come from the attempt to remedy the defects of the country school by forcing on it a system of classification found in the cities."[20]

The author of this report was the prominent educator and United States commissioner of education William T. Harris, and what troubled him was the grouping together of children, even for the sake of efficiency, who were as much as two years apart in their educational

193

advancement. This, he reasoned, yoked students of such unequal ability together that it could result only in holding back the brightest students or humiliating the slower ones who could not keep up.

Harris had found that even in the cities where students of similar age and advancement were grouped together in one room in one grade, the brightest were often forced to mark time for the slowest in order that all might advance together in efficient, lock-step fashion, so that the next grade might fill the room left by the promotion of the other. The situation, he thought, would be far worse in the country schools. For his part, he preferred the older individualistic method of country schoolteaching and organization even if it meant using older students in the classroom to teach the younger.

But the other two members of Harris's subcommittee thought Harris had exaggerated the dangers involved in classifying rural schools. Both believed it was better to try to grade country schools, for what was lost in slowing the good students or humiliating the poor ones, which they agreed occurred even under ideal circumstances, was gained in efficiency. "Grant all cases of individual hardship that the report truly affirms of misguided pupils," one committee member wrote, "yet the total loss of efficiency is immeasurably less than where no grading is attempted."[21]

Harris's opponents had the last word, for the commissioner of education could no more stop the educators across the Midwest from urging the classification of country schools than he could stem the torrent of new educational theories they advanced as time went on. By the early part of the twentieth century, even the school boards of many Midwestern country schools were telling their teachers exactly how they wished to have their school graded. In its meeting on March 1, 1906, the school board of the Hicks School, for example, drew elaborate specifications for classifying their school into eight grades and even provided for one course per term for the ninth grade.[22]

As it turned out, classification in the Midwestern rural schools was never as rigid as it was in the cities, and the country teachers were rarely as unresponsive to the capabilities and needs of their students as Harris feared they might be. True, it did happen that some students fell by the way. The Iowa state superintendent reported in 1889 that some students had been so humiliated by their failure to keep up with where they were supposed to be that they stopped coming to school. But for the most part adjustments were made to fit the pupil's needs, for many things were possible in the small country schools that were impossible in the large, impersonal urban schools.[23]

In the first place, in that one-room schoolhouse students in the lower classes could not help but hear the recitations going on in the higher grades, and so they were somewhat prepared for advanced work when they reached the upper levels. Of more importance, however, was the fact that the teacher in the one-room school, acting on her own authority, could classify her students as she wished and shift them about until they were reciting in most subjects with those most closely approximating their own educational advancement regardless of age.

The Teachers' Classification Registers, in which the country schoolteachers kept records of their students' progress and standing in their class for the succeeding teacher, showed how the adjustments were made for fast and slow learners.

In the Ise School in Kansas in the spring of 1889 the ages of the students in the Intermediate *B* class, arranged largely according to their academic ability, ran all the way from nine to fifteen. But in that class were three students, aged ten, twelve, and thirteen, who were reading ahead of their class and were reciting in that subject with the more advanced students in the Intermediate *A* class. And two students in Intermediate *A* were reciting with the next higher class, Grammar *B*. On the other hand, one ten-year-old boy in the Intermediate *B* class recited in both arithmetic and geography with the primary class, and the teacher's note to her successor said that he should be "demoted to the Primary Grade." Adjustments were also made for a student in the Grammar *B* grade. Because the textbook she had been using in grammar had been replaced, she was behind in that one subject and was reciting with the Intermediate *A* class, which was the next lower grade.[24]

All these notations were made along with numerous remarks that would guide the new teacher when she began the next term of school. The names of the textbooks used, the number of pages covered in each class in each book, which students needed help and which could be moved into the next higher grade—all these matters were recorded in the classification register. In 1893 the teacher at the Ise School noted that one student, who happened to be Henry Ise's daughter, was "away ahead of her mates and should be given every advantage." Another student should be encouraged but not pushed, and still another was described as "ambitious but timid." The teacher thought that one student "should be kept back," but noted that another, who was only eight years old and in the primary class, could already "read in the fourth reader."[25]

So the strengths and weaknesses of the students in the country school were labeled according to the teacher's best judgment, and accommodation made for each student's capabilities insofar as that was possible.

III

Not all country teachers learned to classify their students successfully, of course. Nor were all teachers on the Middle Border able to take advantage of that freedom from supervision which the country school gave them to improve their teaching. Often they stopped teaching before they learned to find their own way. And sometimes they were so overwhelmed by what their professor had taught them at the institute that they could not see that the teaching methods they had learned were not really scientific and that they did not have to be followed to the letter. Then, there were always those who did not have the aptitude or the energy to teach a country school or become a good teacher. "This teacher has not enough life to be successful," the county commissioner of Mecosta County, Michigan, wrote of a teacher in one of his schools in 1899; and of others he observed that they were tied too closely to the textbook or that they too often failed to make the students think to be successful teachers.[26]

Still, there were many, perhaps a majority of those who taught for any length of time, who did profit from the lack of supervision, who learned to modify what they had been taught at the institute to fit their own situation and to implement their county superintendent's suggestions in their own way, so that their schools took on an individuality that would have been frowned upon in the urban schools, where teachers were so often intimidated by the hovering principal. One teacher who learned all this was Sarah Gillespie Huftalen.

Sarah Huftalen was raised on a farm in Iowa in the 1870s, educated in a country school, and trained in the county institutes, so that the road she followed to teaching in a one-room school was no different from that followed by thousands of other Midwestern schoolteachers. But unlike so many of them, she continued to teach after her marriage, and shortly after the turn of the century she won state-wide and even national acclaim as a teacher of Subdistrict 7, a little one-room school in Oneida Township, Delaware County, Iowa, which she and her pupils named the Arbor Vitae Summit School.[27]

Like most country teachers in the Middle West, Huftalen classified her students as she thought best and drew up her own teaching schedule. But she never permitted her schedule to dominate her. As the days sped by, she varied her program as she wished, so that on some days her students would be ciphering down at the board instead of reciting, or preparing for a spelldown, or memorizing a poem or an oration, or drawing a map of DeSoto's march for history and geography, or writing invitations to their parents to visit school on parents' day for their grammar lesson.

Since she was free to improvise as she went along, Huftalen was able to take advantage of unusual situations that occurred in the community to put her students to work on different assignments. When it was announced in the spring of 1908 that a Chautauqua was to be held in Delaware County, she had her students write essays on Chautauquas as a part of their geography, grammar, and spelling lessons. And she never missed an opportunity to do something different on special days of which there were always a large number in the country schools, such as the birthdays of Washington, Lincoln, and Longfellow, Arbor Day, and Thanksgiving. Usually she prepared programs for these days in which each pupil was given a special assignment. For Thanksgiving in 1906, for example, her pupils gave twenty-three recitations, one reading, two class performances, three songs, and one dialogue.

Huftalen's records make no mention of those special winter days such as the one Hamlin Garland described in his *Boy Life on the Prairie,* when the teacher took her students in sleighs over snow-packed roads to a neighboring school where a young boy won resounding applause for his recitation of "Lochiel's Warning." But when Oneida Township had a spelling contest at the Rector School some distance from Subdistrict 7 in the spring of 1908, she did get two farmers to take her students in their surreys through the rain to the contest.[28]

This Iowa teacher, moreover, worked so hard to teach her students to appreciate beauty and growing things that her weariness still issues from the pages of her journal.

Most Midwestern rural teachers were teaching beauty in the 1890s by decorating their schoolrooms with pictures and the art work of their own students, and sometimes in the spring they arranged bouquets for their rooms from the wildflowers the children picked along the roads as they made their way to school. But Huftalen went beyond all this. In the four years she taught at Subdistrict 7 she and her pupils transformed a barren, hilly schoolyard into a lush grove of trees, shrubs, grass, and flowers. Together they planted a wide variety of trees, nine of them arbor vitae, laid out flower beds, and even built an arbor and planted vines to grow about it.[29]

Through the years the teaching of cleanliness, which was so important to the training and discipline of those country children of three generations ago who were growing up in homes where soap was a luxury, occupied much of the country teachers' time on the Middle Border, and, left to their own devices, they worked out their own ways to teach this. One teacher taught her children to wash their hands and clean their fingernails by casually doing this in front of them; and another made her children aware of a problem they did not know they had by writing "dirty hands" on the blackboard. Sarah Huftalen's approach was more direct. "I have compelled them to be clean," she wrote of the children of one family in her school, "at the price of eternal vigilance." And when she learned that the boys were soiling their toilets, she lectured them on the virtue of cleanliness and not only exacted a promise from them not to soil their toilet seats but forced them to clean them when they failed to fulfill their promise.[30]

But if cleanliness was next to godliness, as they said on the Middle Border, morality was godliness itself, and this, too, the country schoolteachers taught in their own ways.

The teaching of morality, by which they generally meant the teaching of middle-class Protestant values, was another of those problems the Midwestern professional educators wrestled with in the late nineteenth century, and perhaps no group in the land, except the ministers, talked more about the necessity of uplifting the nation's moral standards than they. Rarely did they gather at a professional meeting in which there was no paper read or speech given on this subject. Again and again they reported on the necessity of feeding the child's spirit as well as his mind, and emphasized the catastrophe that awaited the nation that failed to do this. "The leading object in the organization of any school system," the Indiana state superintendent wrote in 1872, "should be the moral culture of children. That system of education that aims at the development of the intellectual faculties and the neglect of the moral is exceedingly deficient." He warned, as so many of his colleagues were to do, that "nations that lose their virtue, lose their freedom."[31]

The professionals were heirs of the men who had preached morality on the Middle Border before the Civil War in the fight for free public education, and like them, they, too, were worried about the changes in the world about them. To the migration of immigrants into their region, which had so troubled their predecessors, and which was continuing at an accelerated pace, were added new problems—the rapid growth of cities, unemployment, radicalism, vice, and the rise of crime. Scarcely six months after the Haymarket Square riot in Chicago and the roundup of eight anarchists there, the president of the Michigan State Teachers' Association warned his audience of the dangers that lurked in the American society. "For many decades the tide of immigration has set against our shores with almost un-diminished vigor. The gates of every nation on the globe have been opened outward, and there has burst out a living throng with faces set toward the promised land. . . . The ignorance of this vast throng of people of our peculiar customs and theory of government; their lack of acquaintanceship with our language and proper appreciation of the duties of citizenship; and finally their clannish instincts have filled the larger cities and many sections of the country with great colonies as separate and distinct from American civilization as though planted on an island in a far away sea. In the low moral state, the limited in-tellectual development, and erroneous views of civil liberty of this people, lies the danger."[32]

To alleviate this danger Midwestern educators offered two solu-tions: the English language and moral instruction. "The first requi-site . . .," said the Minnesota state superintendent in 1888, "is that they [the schools] teach thoroughly the English language as the language of the country. . . . Other languages are necessarily un-American (not anti-American) carrying with them the traditions, associations, and national spirit of other governments and civilizations."[33]

Neither solution was easy to effect. In Wisconsin and Illinois, where in the 1880s the illiteracy rate was rapidly rising, a furious fight broke out in 1890 over legislation that forced teachers to instruct schoolchil-dren only in the English language. The trouble was not so much the use of the English language as it was the feeling of immigrant groups that the laws were meant to destroy their parochial schools. In any case, in states like Minnesota and Wisconsin concessions had to be made to the idea of bilingualism. In Minnesota in the 1890s, for example, the school law provided that all schoolchildren were to be taught in English; however, a school board might permit a teacher who was able "to speak a language that is the vernacular of a pupil" to use "that language to aid in the teaching of English words." Such a teacher might also, with the board's permission, "give instruction in that language for one hour or less a day."[34]

Though such compromises were made, most Midwestern states did require, either directly or indirectly, that instruction in the common schools be given in English so that, in effect, one of the educators' goals was reached. The teaching of morality was another matter.

It was easy to see from the Minnesota school law what the educators had in mind when they spoke of morality. That law provided that as a part of a school's daily exercise, "the elements of social and moral science, including industry, order, economy, patience, cleanliness, honesty, self-reflection" might be taught. The problem was how to teach all this. Throughout the years the educators wrote about morality at length but never really found a method of teaching it, and the rural schoolteacher, inspired by the professor's exhortations at the institute, was left to teach it the best way she could.[35]

For years she taught morality as she had been taught. Sometimes she opened her school with a prayer or a hymn, or possibly the reading of the scriptures. But in states where court decisions ruled against such practices because they seemed to violate the principle of the separation of church and state, she found other ways to teach morality. The schoolbooks she used, books like the McGuffey Readers, were full of moral lessons, of course, and she needed only to emphasize the points they made. She learned, too, as an Indiana educator wrote, that "children have a natural desire to imitate some great character in life," and in those days before the antihero, she had a number of lives, like that of Washington or Lincoln, with whom Midwestern rural children could easily identify, from which to draw a moral lesson. Besides this, when it was necessary to discipline any of her students, she often used the occasion to lecture them on right and wrong.[36]

Few teachers worked harder to teach morality than Sarah Huftalen. The programs she prepared for special days such as Arbor Day, Thanksgiving, and Christmas, the poems and orations she had her students learn were saturated with moral principles. For the graduation exercises in her little school in 1907 she had one of her students recite a solemn oration on "The Purpose of Life," and on another occasion one of her students memorized an oration on the "Physical Effects of the Use of Alcohol," which began "Wine is a mocker, strong drink is raging, and whosoever is deceived thereby is not wise. Be not among wine-bibbers or riotious [sic] eater of flesh."[37]

Nor would she permit her students to use unseemly language on the playground. Once, when she heard one of the older girls in her school say "g-o-s-h," as she wrote in her journal, she warned all the children against the use of such language. "When school [was] called," she wrote, "I said I was sorry to have it necessary to speak about language on the school-grounds but that although it had been over a year and a half since we had to correct this thing we could again if we had to, and we would do as we had done—that was those who persist in use of swear words or vulgarity could not be allowed to play with the other pupils and would be detained in their seats until they had overcome it."[38]

For the most part, however, the country schoolteacher taught morality by example. In her high-buttoned shoes and long skirt, black apron and shirtwaist fringed with celluloid collar and cuffs, she was expected to be and she was a symbol of rectitude there on the Middle Border and the major figure in the educators' moral uplift movement in the late nineteenth century. She was frequently a Sunday school teacher, as Sarah Huftalen was, and regular in her church attendance, and her daily life was above reproach. Unlike her male counterpart, she virtually never had her teaching certificate rescinded for immorality. Indeed, it said much about her character and the moral code of Midwestern rural America that her indiscretions with the opposite sex were as rare as sexual assaults made upon her, even though she taught male students of her own age in isolated schoolhouses where such attacks might easily have occurred.[39]

IV

The confidence these largely unsupervised Midwestern rural teachers developed in their ability to teach in their own way and by their own methods was reflected in the programs of their teachers' associations that had been formed among them by their county superintendents in the late 1880s and '90s. Throughout the school terms, they met in various corners of their counties to read and discuss the papers they had prepared on such problems as how to teach fractions, what to do about tardiness, and how to keep small children busy. Sarah Huftalen even worked out her own method of teaching reading, and in the fall of 1908 her students demonstrated her method to teachers' groups in her own and neighboring townships. And the seriousness with which she and others like her took their jobs was suggested by the "resolves" she made in her journal as she planned a school term's work: "Go slower: not crowd 1st and 2nd nos. . . . Explain more. . . . Make our school home beautiful this year."[40]

Whatever methods they developed, however, to keep little children quiet or to teach reading, the teachers in the one-room schools on the Middle Border never wandered far from either the traditional purposes of teaching the three R's or the tested methods of teaching, partly because, being unsupervised, they were not forced to accept the educational fads that came and went with the seasons in those years that spanned the two centuries.

Country teachers taught through the use of recitations and drills. Day in and day out they drilled their students in subject matter and put a heavy burden on the memory. The multiplication tables, poems, speeches, names, dates, cities, islands, rivers, mountain chains—all were memorized and asked for in the recitations.

No doubt the theory behind the drills and memorization had its roots in the desire to train the faculties. Memory, it was believed, was trained by memorization, and the faculty of reason and logic by arithmetic, and so on. And possibly the rigor and discipline involved in this kind of training was reinforced by the stern, Calvinistic theology Americans had inherited from their Puritan ancestors. At least, this was the view of some professional educators.[41]

But all this was lost on the average country schoolteacher, who rarely ventured into the ethereal realms of educational philosophy. Even when she was introduced to the mind's faculties at the county institute, she scarcely knew more about them than the order in which they were to be trained and would have been surprised to learn that she was merely training faculties or that the Calvinistic theology had anything to do with her drills and recitations.

No, she drilled her students and taught them to memorize because that was the way she had been taught, and because, in her common-sense way, she believed that unless a student remembered what he had learned and could say it, he had not learned it. Her opinion on this coincided exactly with that of the county superintendent of Dickinson County, Kansas. "A lesson is not thoroughly learned until it has been recited," he wrote in 1885. "The mere act of telling a thing will impress it upon the mind. It is no excuse for a pupil to say 'I know but I can't tell.' If he knew he could tell. It is not clear in his own mind when he cannot tell. . . . Review," he told his teachers, "until pupils can tell what they know."[42]

This was so uncomplicated that the poorest teacher could understand it. So the country teacher reviewed her students and drilled them over and over, and when they failed to learn their lessons, which usually meant memorizing them, she was prone to insist that they do so. "Roy said 'I' in Geog[raphy] was *too hard, could not do it*," Sarah Huftalen wrote in 1907. "It was to name the countries of S. A. . . . I insisted he must which he did in a very few minutes."[43]

Good teachers, of course, used the recitations to probe and explore and further their students' understanding of the subject, and many country teachers did just that. One man in Indiana recalled how hard

202

his teacher had tried to get the students to understand what they were reading. That teacher, he wrote "wanted us to actually see in our minds [*sic*] eye, the 'lowing herd winds slowly o'er the lea,'" and would ask what "lowing" meant and what the "lea" was.[44]

Yet there were many rural teachers who used the recitation more to find out what the students had memorized than to learn how much they understood, so that memorization became an end in itself and the recitation a dreary exercise in which the student did little more than repeat what he had memorized.

How such recitations were conducted was described by an Illinois county superintendent in the 1880s. He wrote that shortly after his entrance into one schoolroom, he heard the teacher say to the leader of the fifth-reader class: "Mary, your class may read." Whereupon, Mary, followed by four girls and a boy, moved to a crack in the floor that served as a recitation line. There they faced the school and each read a stanza from the "Mariner's Dream." When the students stumbled over a word the whole class pronounced it aloud, but when the class was finished reading no questions were asked and no explanations given. At that point the county superintendent took over and asked one of the girls to begin at a certain point and read to the first period. Instead, almost without stopping to catch a breath, she read to the end of the paragraph and the boy's hand went up to correct her. "She did not stop at 'Hindoostan,'" he said.[45]

Another Illinois superintendent, writing in 1883, recalled how he had listened while a class read through a history lesson on the Civil War. After one student read that "it was feared that the rebels would obtain command of the heights commanding Washington," he stopped the reading to ask what that meant. No one answered. Finally, one student said she thought it meant that "Washington commanded." And still another superintendent, when asked to examine a geography class that the teacher thought was well prepared, looked at the lesson and asked: "What is the most populous state in the Union?" In unison the class replied: "Ohio is the most populous state in the Union," but when the superintendent asked what *populous* meant, everyone was silent until one boy ventured that it meant "Ohio raised more wheat than any other state."[46]

The educators had many such stories to tell and told them frequently to illustrate the inadequacies of country schoolteachers and to emphasize the need for teacher training. It was just such stories as these, stories of teachers walking about their classrooms, textbook in hand, asking questions, and demanding the exact wording of the textbooks for answers, that so exasperated Illinois' Newton Bateman and made him a crusader for teacher training.[47]

Still, men like Batemen wanted primarily to encourage teachers to improve their recitations so that students would understand what they were memorizing; they did not necessarily want to do away with drills and memorization and textbooks. But in the 1890s other professional educators were attacking memorization and drills with such vehemence that it appeared they believed learning could take place without memorization at all. At the very moment when hundreds of Midwestern educators were still laboriously trying to teach country teachers at the county institutes about the faculties, their colleagues, presumably the most advanced among them, were already scoffing at faculty psychology and deriding the notion that each faculty could be trained separately. "The attempt to train a single faculty . . . is inevitably futile," the superintendent of schools in St. Paul, Minnesota, pronounced in 1895, "but in so far as it succeeds at all it distorts the soul and renders it one-sided, incapable of viewing whole truths, unfit for life."[48]

This astounding discovery and the ideas that flowed from it captured the soaring imaginations of many American professional educators in the 1890s, and catapulted them into another educational utopia they called the "new education," which was derived in large measure from the ideas of Johann Herbart, the German philosopher and educator of the early nineteenth century. And from their new vista the new educators heaped contempt upon the old education they had so lately championed.

The old education, they said, with its emphasis upon memory and drill and the training of the faculties, had "been the key note and curse of education for more than a century." It centered upon the school, not the child, and snuffed out the child's interest in education, so that, according to the St. Paul superintendent, many a child, "fresh from its mother has had the light of life crushed out of him in the hard, heartless, grind of the schoolroom." It was, in a way, what was wrong with the nation in that era of big business and high finance. "The typical successful man," the superintendent continued, "the narrow, hard, unsympathetic, tricky contractor, or speculator is the natural product of our school systems and of the ideas upon which they are based."[49]

On the other hand, the new education, the educators argued, focused on the child, produced a new kind of moral training, and above everything else, made learning interesting.

From antiquity to Shakespeare's "whining schoolboy, creeping like a snail unwillingly to school," to the late nineteenth century, some children had always found school dull and forbidding. And perhaps educators had always searched for that magic formula which would make learning fun. But probably not even Herbart, whose great aim was to interest students, was as confident he had found the answer to this old problem as the American educators were in the 1890s.[50]

Their prescription for making learning interesting was shrouded in language so vague and diffuse that they themselves could not always understand one another. "Much of the present conflict of opinion in pedagogy," wrote an Ohio educator in 1896, "is largely due to the fact that those who differ do not understand each other, and it is doubtful if each one always understands himself." But what emerged through the mist was their insistence upon deemphasizing the three R's and the drill and memory work by which these had been taught. Instead they planned to integrate these old subjects, which in their view were only tools for learning, into courses that were more naturally interesting and relevant to the students. In this way, while they were studying the courses they liked, students would be painlessly learning reading, writing, arithmetic, and all those things they had formerly been taught separately. The three R's, as one educator summarized it, "should be taught incidentally merely, as need for them actually comes up in the course of learning by the help of the senses the interesting things of science, history, and poetry."[51]

The new education never fulfilled the promises made in its name, of course, but it did stir a furious debate among the educators. In the first place, the opponents of learning made easy noted the practical limitations to teaching literature, history, science, and even the three R's in a course on nature study, which, in that time of galloping urbanization at the turn of the century, was the feature attraction of the new educators' course of study. The problem was, one educator suggested, that "nine-tenths of the important facts of nature can not be hitched to a poem."[52]

A more serious objection to the new education than this, however, was its implication that the students should study only what interested them. To this that nay-sayer of educators, William T. Harris, protested vehemently. Not even in the face of the argument that children were different and that adjustments had to be made for some, and not even for the sake of the child's interest in learning, would Harris give up the necessity of teaching the five branches of study—grammar, literature, arithmetic, geography, and history—and those separately taught. The training of a child's character and civilization itself, he thought, would be in jeopardy if children studied only what interested them.[53]

In the early twentieth century some of the principles of the new education would find their way into the school curricula of the Midwest's one-room schools, as the educators sought to improve country life. Country schoolteachers were sometimes taught the five formal steps of teaching so dear to the hearts of the new educators, and a few would even try to combine the teaching of various subjects in one overarching lesson. Sarah Huftalen caught the spirit of the new education when her school celebrated Longfellow's birthday in 1908. The reading classes read from his works, and the language lesson centered on the punctuation, rules, and expression in "The Village Blacksmith." Portland, Maine, and Cambridge, Massachusetts, places where Longfellow had lived, were studied in geography, and the spelling lesson words were taken from the poet's poems.[54]

But for the most part the Midwestern country schoolteachers left the new education to the educators and went on teaching as they always had, partly because they had no supervisor to order them to deemphasize the three R's, and partly because their common sense told them these subjects were important and could not be learned by some osmotic process while the children studied only what interested them. Improvising where they had to and modifying their methods as they went along, the one-room teachers continued to drill their students and exercise their memories by making them learn the multiplication tables, a substantial number of poems, orations, historical facts, and places on the map.

And, in time, some of the professional educators themselves became disenchanted with the new education and urged a return to vigorous training in the basic studies from which the country teachers had never really departed. Complaining that for a generation the value of "reading, writing, spelling, arithmetic . . . grammar, and geography," had been minimized and emphasis given to "basket weaving, sewing, cooking, drawing, nature study, juvenile literature, paper folding," the Wisconsin state superintendent in 1906 called for a return to "a mastery of the most essential things in every subject that is taught," and to the "old-time" thoroughness in school work. "The mastery to which I refer," he wrote, "is a mastery of such homely and old-fashioned matters as, for instance, the multiplication tables. There are some who are so pessimistic as to believe that the art of memorizing is a lost art, but I cannot believe that the art is permanently lost. The fact that pupils once in years gone by learned tables of various kinds, even including addition tables, leads me to believe that with a sufficiently strenuous effort, it may even now be accomplished. I shall go so far as to say that I believe in some back woods places such results are reached today. To use the memory vigorously is *work*. Ordinarily it is uninteresting, and that which is uninteresting must, now-a-days, be eliminated from the class room, at least so thinks the up-to-date teacher. . . . No plea is here made for the uninteresting teacher, but the teacher who thinks that to be interesting she must relieve her pupils from strenuous effort, makes an egregious and fatal blunder. The light intellectual calisthenics of the modern school room as compared with the heavy gymnastics of the best schools of a quarter of a century ago, is a form of degeneration, from which reaction should speedily come."[55]

V

Probably the average country teacher in the Midwest was no more aware that what she taught and the way she taught it were again in vogue than she was that she had ever been out of step in the first place. Isolated and largely unsupervised, she had gone her own way, but her job had been made easier through the years by the fact that she usually came from a rural background. "Our schools were created by the society they served," Herbert Quick observed of Iowa's country schools. "Our teachers were our own boys and girls." They had no one else to choose from, of course, but it can scarcely be doubted that rural elementary education in that vast area profited from the situation.[56]

Occasionally, of course, there did appear among the rural Midwesterners a teacher from the normal school or from a large town who sniffed at rural ways and tried without much subtlety to change the farmer's life style. That a Kansas newspaper columnist felt compelled to warn rural teachers against overdressing suggests the pretensions some country teachers had. "The teacher," the columnist wrote, "who meets her pupils on the first morning of school, attired in a plain dress of substantial material . . . will make a far better impression upon her pupils than one who meets them dressed in costly silk and with many ornaments."[57]

Usually, however, the teacher who taught the farmers' children was no interloper attempting to change the farmers' ways. Born to rural ways, she knew what could and could not be done in rural communities and found it easy to adapt to her schoolhouse and to her students and their parents. She thought nothing of riding a horse or walking to school, building a fire in the stove on a cold morning, or cleaning her schoolroom when the day was done. She could even cope, when it was necessary, with the fact that her school had no privy, or perhaps only one. And who but one accustomed to farms and farmers could have stood so well the close, ill-ventilated schoolroom on a winter's day when the fire roared in the big stove and the odors from the boys' barnyard boots and the asafetida bags the girls wore about their necks filled the room?[58]

Because the little community she taught in was isolated from the rest of the world during much of the school year by impassable roads, the Midwestern country teacher was forced to board in the district even though her father's farm or her village home might be no more than five or six miles away. But even the prospect of boarding in some farmer's cramped home held no terrors for her. Often she was not used to much more. When Flo Knisely taught her first school in Kansas in 1879, she boarded in a one-room home that was home for the farmer, his three children, and two hired men. And Mary Bradford, forced to share a bed with the farmer's daughter where she taught her first school that spring of 1872, learned on her first trip home that her hair had become a haven for lice. Even as late as 1919, the average Midwestern country schoolteacher in Nebraska was still boarding in a home that had no indoor toilet, lived in a room that was not heated, and had to use washbowls, tin washbasins in the kitchen, and, as one teacher reported, a "teacup and a handkerchief" for bathing.[59]

Uncomfortable as it sometimes was, boarding in the district, like the lack of supervision, worked to her advantage. At the farmer's supper table she heard much about the community she served and quickly learned what she must do and must not do. And on winter nights and spring evenings she attended oyster suppers in the community, prayer meetings, or perhaps a singing school or debate at the schoolhouse where she met her students and their families socially. By living in the community she was also able to visit her students' parents as the textbooks on teaching instructed her to do and so enlarge her understanding of the problems her students had at school, and some of this information she was able to pass on to her successor. The sympathy and understanding the teacher at the Hicks School in 1905 had for the Benson children, for example, were reflected in the notations she left for the next teacher. Gladys Benson, she noted in her remarks, was a "fair student," but "she lacks the necessary books. This hinders progress." Her sister, too, the teacher continued, was a "good and faithful student," who "had to leave school to work."[60]

The country teacher found also that visits to the homes of her most unruly children could sometimes solve some of her worst discipline problems.

There had been a time on the Middle Border, just before and just after the Civil War, when maintaining discipline in the country school had been an awesome problem. In those days "driving the teacher out" was a popular pastime, and only male teachers seemed capable of teaching the older boys in the winter school. Perhaps this was to be expected on the raw frontier where civilization had barely taken root, but even later, when the frontier had given way to peaceful farms and small towns, violence in the one-room schoolhouse was not unknown. In 1882 a schoolmaster in a country school in Guernsey County, Ohio, stabbed to death two of his students who attacked him after he insisted that they study their grammar lessons. And not far from the little village of Elm Creek in Buffalo County, Nebraska, in 1894, when the teacher of the little country school sent two boys home for throwing cartridges into the stove, they returned, battered down the door, and attacked her. Only the timely intervention of the other students saved her from a severe mauling or worse.[61]

These were bizarre incidents, of course, but there was never a time when the Midwestern country schoolteacher had no discipline problems. Even Sarah Huftalen, who studied pedagogical principles religiously and tried so hard to improve her school, was troubled by discipline problems. "I can think of nothing like [his behavior]," she wrote of one of her students in 1907, "except a calf that lays back in the halter and has to be dragged by main force. That's the way Roy has been all day. . . . Not taking up studies when the rest do, or when told to until the second or third time. Placing excuses not to wash pen when told to. . . . So one thing followed another all day. Kicked Harry Hoag at recess." And once in defiance of her rule not to soil the toilets, she heard him say: "I will soil it and I won't help clean it either."[62]

The professional educators wrote learnedly about how to maintain discipline, for it seemed clear to everyone, to farmers, educators, and the teachers too, that no learning could take place without it. "The means of discipline are as various as the instincts of human nature," wrote a leading authority on pedagogy in 1890. "Children may be led by different mobiles, which are connected with three or four principal groups: 1. the personal feelings, as fear, pleasure, and self-love; 2. The affectionate sentiments, as the love of parents and affection for the teacher; 3. Reflective interest, such as the fear of punishment and the hope of reward; 4. The idea of duty."[63]

Following these observations was a lengthy discourse on rewards and punishments and how to use them in disciplining recalcitrant students. The essay was filled with suggestions, including the notion of that popular English educational theorist, Herbert Spencer, who believed there should be no punishment of children except that which the child received from the mistake itself, such as when he placed his hand on a burning coal.[64]

Unfortunately none of these was very useful to the teacher facing a concrete problem, for it was difficult to remember the "mobiles" the children were led by when students were throwing cartridges into the stove. There was more help for the country teacher in the less learned but more direct advice the county superintendent in Dickinson County, Kansas, gave his teachers in 1885: "Grant no request during the progress of a recitation . . .," he wrote. "Do not dismiss a class until you have assigned the next lesson. . . . Always treat your pupils politely; then you can expect the same treatment from them. . . . Govern your school with kindness but firmness. Do not *govern the life out of it.* Never tell a pupil he shall do anything that you are not sure you can make him do if he refuses, and be sure to see that he does it."[65]

Yet no one could really teach the teacher how to discipline her students, and how well she governed her school finally depended on her own inner resources and personality. Many tried to rule with the rod, others with kindness, and some with a system of rewards and punishments. And sometimes when everything failed, the country teacher visited her willful student's parents and tried to get them to share the responsibility for their child's behavior.

The response she received from her refractory student's parents was not always as helpful as she hoped for, but her visit was rarely completely wasted. At the very least she had called the farmer's attention to the school, and if at the same time she had in any way aroused his interest in the school, she had performed another of what were considered to be her duties.[66]

For many years the Midwestern country schoolteachers were expected to be missionaries who preached the virtues of education to the farmers in their districts and tried to enlist their support for it. "It is no less the duty of the teachers to *preach* than to *teach* school," the Kansas state superintendent wrote in 1873, and that obligation lingered for years among the rural teachers. The reason for this was that the Midwestern country schools were not, for the most part, shored up by laws compelling people to do this or that. They operated insofar as possible on the voluntary principle, and from the Civil War to World War I, school attendance at the country school was largely voluntary.[67]

To be sure, by the early 1900s, all the North Central states had laws compelling children to attend school. But these laws were slow in coming to all the Middle Border states, and when they did come, they were passed to take the children off the streets of the cities—those "recruiting places for the idle, the vicious, and lawless portions of the community," as the Wisconsin state superintendent wrote in 1872. In rural areas of the Middle West they were regarded as an infringement on the parents' right to send or not to send their children to school, and they remained in force in those states largely because they were unenforced in rural areas.[68]

So, even though the compulsory education laws were on the books, it continued to be the rural teacher's task to maintain the farmers' interest in their schools to make certain they would send their children regularly, and it was in part a tribute to her success that the North Central states, mostly rural, largely filled with one-room schools, and largely dependent upon voluntary attendance, led the nation in the percentage of their schoolchildren enrolled in school through most of the last three decades of the nineteenth century. Iowa, for example, had no compulsory education law even as late as 1897, yet in that very year she was second only to Kansas in the nation in the percentage of her schoolchildren enrolled in school, partly because of the vigorous activity of her teachers. "During the past year," the county superintendent of Butler County, Iowa, wrote in 1879, "the general cry among the farmers and business men has been 'hard times;' yet notwithstanding all this, our educational interests have prospered. Our teachers as a class have done better work . . . ; they have done more visiting among the patrons of their schools, and the result has been that the patrons have taken more than usual interest in the schools."[69]

In her missionary efforts the Midwestern country teacher had the vigorous support of the larger community—the newspapers, the clergy, and other articulate groups, and even of most of the farmers themselves whose interest in the education of children, at least elementary education, was profound. But this support would have been less important if the teacher had not learned how to take advantage of it. Besides visiting around the district, she sent information about her school to the county newspaper, so that farmers could see their children's names in print, and sometimes she even wrote a column for the newspaper. And in the final week of any school term she worked doubly hard to teach her students poems, orations, and songs to be given on the last day of school at the school exhibition, which was itself designed primarily to stir the farmers' interest in the schools.

School exhibitions were as much a part of the country-school curriculum on the Middle Border as the three R's and almost as necessary. They gave the farmers and their wives an opportunity to see their children perform in the presence of their neighbors. It made them proud to hear their children recite poems and deliver orations filled with words they themselves sometimes might not have been able to define. Often the performances were reported in the county newspapers and the children praised for their parts, so that the exhibition might be remembered and talked about in the community for weeks. "Miss Belle Sellers closed a very successful school term last Friday with an entertainment in the evening and a dinner and social gathering during the day," the newspaper in Russell County, Kansas, reported in March of 1890. "We would like to give a full report of the entertainment but time, space and inability will not permit.... It consisted of songs, declamations, dialogues, select readings, and historical essays. 'Welcome Song' was well rendered by Miss Dora Anshutz and Miss Lizzie Miller," the reporter continued. "A declamation entitled Naughty Ned was well rendered by Clyde Tobin and received great applause.... The ABC song was very well rendered by seven little boys and girls. It was a great success and will be long remembered by those present."[70]

Through the years the rural people responded to these exhibitions with enthusiasm. On cold winter evenings, at Christmas time or at the close of the winter term of school when the snow still blanketed the schoolyard, they crowded into the little schoolhouse and watched their children perform by the light of kerosene lamps that cast shadows and an almost eerie orange light about the room. And for the school picnic and exhibition that closed the spring term of school, they brought an abundance of food to the schoolhouse or the grove of trees by the river for the noonday meal and prepared to spend the day talking to their neighbors and watching the exhibition in the afternoon. But no exhibition so aroused their interest or was so important to them as the county eighth-grade graduation ceremonies that were being held in most counties in the Middle West by the 1890s.

VI

The practice of giving county-wide examinations to country school-children in the Midwest had begun in the 1880s, and by the next decade almost everywhere in the area county superintendents, or sometimes the state superintendents, were preparing examinations based on whatever course of study had been adopted for the country schools and holding county-wide graduation ceremonies, usually at the county seat, for all those who passed the examinations.

The examinations were usually given in the eight common branches—orthography, reading, writing, arithmetic, geography, history, grammar, and physiology—and sometimes in civil government and other subjects as well, and they were not easy. Avis Carlson, who took the examinations in Chautauqua County, Kansas, in the early 1900s, recalled that she had ten questions for each subject. For spelling she not only had to spell such words as *abbreviated, obscene, elucidation,* and *assassination,* but also to make a table showing the different vowel sounds and to divide into syllables and mark diacritically words like *profuse, retrieve, rigidity,* and *propagate.* In arithmetic she was asked to find the interest on an eight per cent note for nine hundred dollars running for two years, two months, and six days, and to reduce three pecks, five quarts, and one pint to bushels. She had to tell what she knew about the writings of Thomas Jefferson for her reading examination and to define *zenith, deviate, misconception,* and *panegyric,* among other words; and for physiology she wrote a two-hundred-word essay on the evils of alcoholic beverages.

Her examinations in geography, history, and grammar were equally thorough. In history she had to give a brief account of the colleges, printing, and religion in the colonies before the Revolution, and to "name the principal political questions which have been advocated since the Civil War and the party which advocated each." She had to give, among other things, the names of two countries that produced large quantities of wheat for her examination in geography, and to name three important rivers in the United States, three in Europe, three in Asia, three in Africa, and three in South America. And in grammar she was asked to "analyze and diagram" the sentence: "There is a tide in the affairs of men, which taken at the flood, leads on to fortune," and parse the words *tide, which, taken,* and *leads.*[71]

Her reward for the successful completion of these examinations was a trip to the county seat, twenty miles from her father's farm, which she remembered vividly through the years, as doubtless most country schoolchildren did who passed through the rigors of those examinations and experienced the thrill of a county graduation ceremony. "When my family took me on an overnight trip to the county seat...," she wrote, "the evening ceremony of diploma-bestowal seemed to me a blaze of lights and glory."[72]

Clearly not all who attempted these examinations could pass them even after two or three attempts. In 1900 in Nebraska, 9,912 pupils took the examinations, but only 5,026 received free high school certificates which would entitle them to go on to high school. And of the 55 students who took the county examinations in Racine County, Wisconsin, in December of 1907 and April of 1908, only 35 passed.[73]

Like most such examinations given throughout the Midwest, those in Racine were rigorous. They included tests in orthoepy, agriculture, and civil government, as well as those in the regular subjects, so that altogether the children had to take eleven examinations, a trial of endurance that made it all but impossible for the younger students to pass them. The average age of those who took the examinations in Racine County was thirteen. Some of the students were as young as eleven, but only one of that age, a girl from District 17 of Caledonia Township, passed. Two who took the examinations were sixteen, young men who probably had gone to school through the years only as farm work permitted but who were determined to get the best education they could. One managed to pass with an average of 75 in the eleven subjects, but the other took only four examinations, and though he did well in those, he failed to get a diploma.[74]

Besides stimulating the interest of rural people in their schools, the county examinations gave the country teachers a new purpose in their teaching, and nothing better reflected their versatility, the strenuousness of their task compared with that of urban teachers, and their progress as teachers than their work in preparing their students for the eighth-grade examinations. Lacking in almost everything the professional educators thought necessary for good teaching—sufficient training, supervision, apparatus, scientific methods—they taught their pupils everything from partial payments to the parts of speech, from the causes of the Revolutionary War to the location of European rivers, and from the bones of the body to samplings from Shakespeare, to prepare them for the most searching examinations, at the same time as they were teaching their smallest students their numbers and how to read.

They did this, too, with a fair amount of success. Eleven teachers had worked through the year to prepare the fifty-five students who took the examinations in Racine County that winter and spring of 1907 and 1908, and though it was true that a large number failed, a larger number passed and some with excellent records. Several students had an average of ninety in the eleven subjects and one had a ninety-one average. But most had averages in the eighties and high grades in some of the difficult subjects. As a whole the students' grades suggested that, of the basic subjects—arithmetic, reading, geography, grammar, and history—the eleven teachers had been most successful in teaching reading and geography and the least successful in teaching history and grammar, which followed a pattern educators had noted from time to time. Those who were awarded the eighth-grade diploma had an average grade of 86.00 in reading and geography, 83.00 in arithmetic, 82.42 in grammar, and 82.14 in history. The successful students had even done one full point better in civil government than they had in history.[75]

The students' records showed, too, that there were varying degrees of success among the eleven teachers, as was to be expected. The teacher in District 13 of Waterford Township had only four passing students out of nine. On the other hand, nine of the eleven students taught by the teacher in District 17 of Caledonia Township were successful, including the eleven-year-old girl who passed with an average of eighty-four.[76]

This might have meant, as the records suggest, that the teacher in District 17 was a better teacher than the one in District 13, but not necessarily. For seldom did a teacher in the Midwestern one-room schools ever stay in any one school long enough to make more than a passing contribution to any student's success or failure on the eighth-grade examinations. Through the late nineteenth century and even into the twentieth, country schoolteachers moved from school to school as if they were playing musical chairs, and the newspaper items, in noting that they had just completed teaching a school term in one school, announced at the same time that they would be teaching the next term at another. "Miss Dora Barnhard closed her winter term of school at Harrison Center last Friday," an Iowa newspaper in Adair County reported in 1886, "and begins a spring term at Jefferson Center next Monday."[77]

215

Sometimes a teacher was not rehired simply because the farmers found her unsatisfactory. And occasionally she was not asked to come back because she had been involved in some way in a community quarrel. Even such a reputable teacher as Sarah Huftalen fell victim to a dispute· that split the little community of Oneida in Delaware County, Iowa, where she had taught so successfully.

She had been teaching at the Arbor Vitae Summit School for three years, an exceptionally long time for a teacher to stay at one school, when she was elected Sunday school superintendent in the village of Oneida. Unknown to her, she had defeated a man who wanted to be superintendent, and the community used this incident to take sides against one another over old festering sores that seemed only partially related to her. Caught in the middle of the fight, she watched the neighborhood controversy deepen through the school year of 1908 and 1909, saw the Sunday school disintegrate, and sensed that this would be her last year there, as it was. "I have been weaning myself away from my beloved 'Arbor Vitae Summit' all the year," she wrote in May of 1909 when she knew she would not be returning to it. "In the early mornings before the children came I have gone from window to window & looked out long & silently on my little yard and trees. I planted my love in their rootlets. I felt sad but brave not to show it."[78]

There were times, of course, when the teacher herself chose not to remain at a certain school even though the farmers were fond of her and wanted her to remain. The farmers in Subdistrict 3, Orient Township, in Adair County, Iowa, thought so much of their teacher that when she could not be persuaded to stay in the spring of 1886, they adopted and published a resolution praising her. "Whereas Miss Ida Speaker is about to close her fourth term of school in this sub-district," read the resolution, "and we the patrons regret her leaving the school, Be it resolved, that we the patrons in subdistrict meeting assembled do say we are highly pleased with the manner in which our school has been conducted by her as a teacher, knowing that the scholars have been well instructed and that she has done all in her power to make the school both pleasant and progressive, Do resolve that a copy of this resolution be presented to Miss Speaker at the close of her school."[79]

But whether they liked or disliked their teacher, whether she had been successful or unsuccessful, the usual rule throughout the Midwest was for the school boards to employ their teachers for only one term or at most for two.

At the turn of the century this custom had been followed so long that the farmers themselves perhaps did not know its origin or why they continued it. Possibly it had started with the practice of employing a male teacher in the winter and a female in the summer. But more likely it was rooted in the farmers' abiding reluctance to keep any public official in office very long. "There is an unhealthy sentiment in our western communities which demands frequent changes in all officials in government, in school, in church," complained the Michigan state superintendent of schools in 1897. "Rotation in office in congress, legislature, council schoolboards, teaching force, and pulpit, is in too many minds the panacea for corruption and stagnation. Change for change sake," he argued, "is too common. Like most social customs this one flies two-winged, a blessing and a curse; it turns out the poor as well as the good."[80]

The practice of removing teachers each term or so did fly "two-winged," as the Michigan superintendent said, which meant that it was not altogether bad. Teachers were removed before they stayed long enough to build up loyalties that might eventually divide the community. Moreover, since teachers did not normally expect to be rehired, bad teachers were easily gotten rid of by following the traditional practice of not rehiring. At the same time, one teacher's removal opened the way to bring in a perhaps better and in any case different teacher, to whom the children might respond more enthusiastically. Then, too, the new teacher was less likely to become bored with her school and take her students for granted when she stayed so short a time. Indeed, the very fact that she did not teach anywhere very long tended to make her more enthusiastic about her work while she did teach than those urban teachers who had taught so long that teaching had become a habit, not a vital, creative act. So obvious had this become in some city schools, that critics were suggesting that teachers be limited to ten years of teaching.[81]

Still, the great turnover of teachers that took place each school term in the Midwest did seem excessive, and to the professional educators it was wasteful, inefficient, and unbusinesslike. Some of them estimated that a change of teacher meant "a loss of at least one-fourth of the year," and year after year they railed against the farmers' custom of changing teachers each school term. And by the early 1900s school boards were, as a general rule, employing their teachers for longer periods. But by this time, the educators had another new enthusiasm called "consolidation," which they believed would be the remedy not only for the teacher turnover problem, but for all the ailments of rural education they had complained of for more than forty years.[82]

11

Consolidation

❧❧

I

THE FLEETING YEARS BETWEEN THE TURN OF THE CENTURY AND WORLD War I marked the Indian summer of rural America. For that brief period old agrarian America flourished as it never had before. The desperate years of the 1890s, when money was so scarce the farmers had been forced to shorten their school terms, had gone, and in their place came unprecedented prosperity. Farm prices rose to such heights between 1909 and 1914 that in the years to come they would be taken as a standard against which to measure farm prosperity, and even the weather, in spite of some cold winters, contributed to the production of bumper crops and the farmers' well-being.[1]

Moreover, everywhere throughout the Middle West there were sure signs of progress. Men from the Post Office Department were hastily laying out rural mail routes so farmers might have their mail delivered to their homes each day, and country roads were rapidly being improved. Telephone lines were being strung along highway right-of-ways; here and there farm homes were being modernized; and new one-room schoolhouses were displaying for the first time in two generations a new style of architecture. And now and again, an occasional automobile, the harbinger of unimaginable changes, shattered the country quiet as it rumbled past solitary farmhouses.

Yet rural America had the feel of autumn about it. The songs that looked back to the "good old summer time," and to "the shade of the old apple tree," the books that were written, even the "back-to-the-farm" movement were redolent with nostalgia for an older, quieter rural world that Americans sensed was giving way to a hurrying urban

218

civilization. And indeed it was. For neither prosperity nor improvements in rural life had slowed the cityward drift of Americans that had been going on steadily for nearly a century. Each year more and more Americans, old and young alike, forsook the quiet country roads for the city's busy streets. In 1900 sixty per cent of the nation's people lived in rural places; by 1910 only fifty-four per cent still lived there, and it was obvious to those who observed such things that the balance between the rural and the urban populations would soon be broken in favor of the cities.[2]

In the Midwest one poignant reminder of the great exodus from the countryside was the declining enrollments in the area's little one-room schools. At the turn of the century there were already forty-two thousand one-room schools with fewer than twenty students in them in Indiana, and between 1906 and 1916 the percentage of Wisconsin schoolchildren enrolled in such schools dropped from fifty to thirty-six per cent. What such figures meant could be seen even more dramatically in individual schools like the Hicks School in Calhoun County, Michigan. In the winter term of 1875 and 1876, that little school, still strong and vigorous after more than a quarter of a century's existence, enrolled forty students, nearly half of whom were from pioneer families in the district. By the winter of 1899 and 1900 only seventeen students were going to school there, and of these only five came from families whose residence in the area stretched back to the pioneer days.[3]

This migration of people from country to city was a nineteenth-century phenomenon common to all the western world, but it was regarded more seriously in the United States, perhaps, than in any other western nation. For this had always been a nation of farmers and farm people. Its institutions, government, traditions, and ideals, even the very character of its people had been shaped in a rural environment, and thoughtful Americans were fearful of what might happen to their nation when the majority of its people had been torn from their natural roots and transplanted in the city.

No one seemed more concerned about this in the early 1900s than the President—Theodore Roosevelt. "I warn my countrymen," he wrote in 1909, "that the great recent progress in city life is not a full measure of our civilization; for our civilization rests at bottom on the wholesomeness, the attractiveness, and the completeness, as well as the prosperity, of life in the country." And in that same message he affirmed one of the nation's oldest traditions. "The men and women on the farms stand for what is fundamentally best and most needed in our American life. Upon the development of country life rests ultimately our ability . . . to continue to feed and clothe the hungry nations; to supply the city with fresh blood, clean bodies, and clear brains that can endure the terrific strain of modern life."[4]

So concerned, indeed, was the president with the drift of rural men and women to the cities that he appointed a Country Life Commission in 1908 to find out why farmers were leaving the farms for the cities and to suggest ways to make farm life so attractive that young people would remain there, so that the "most precious part of the state," as Jefferson had called the farmers, would be preserved.[5]

Through the remainder of the year the commission, under the leadership of Liberty Hyde Bailey, professor of agriculture at Cornell University and one-time Michigan farm boy, who had lived in such isolation that he had not seen a railroad until he was eighteen, held thirty hearings in twenty-nine states and received over a hundred thousand responses to questionnaires sent to selected farmers around the country to find out what was wrong with farm life. And across the land thousands of farmers gathered in their little schoolhouses in the fall of 1908 to discuss their problems and write their own reports on what life was like in rural America.[6]

The commission found, as it set out to do, that in spite of the unprecedented rural prosperity there was much wrong with life in agrarian America. Intemperance, poor sanitation, poor roads, poor communication facilities, poor leadership, and a poor social life, all these, the commission reported, were responsible for the declining farm population. But nothing was as much to blame as rural education. Based on the voluminous testimony they had gathered, the commissioners wrote that "the schools were held to be largely responsible for ineffective farming, lack of ideals, and the drift to town."[7]

It was the ministers, teachers, and lawyers—those professional groups in the villages and small towns of rural America—who were the most convinced that the schools were to blame for the depopulation of the countryside. But even the farmers themselves, or at least a majority of those who spoke at all on the subject, seemed to agree. Some sixty-two per cent of the farmers and their wives whose responses to the commissioners' question on education were tabulated indicated that they, too, believed that their one-room schools were to blame for the exodus of their young people from the farm.[8]

Yet this did not mean that farmers felt their schools had not given their children a good education in the three R's, for they had not been questioned about this. They were asked instead to answer a question for which the commissioners probably already had an answer. "Are the schools in your neighborhood," the Commissioners asked, "training boys and girls satisfactorily for life on the farm?" It was to this question that the majority of more than fifty thousand farmers and their wives responded negatively, not necessarily because they thought their schools were poor schools, but because they believed their schools had, in fact, encouraged their children to leave the farm and seek more advanced positions in life than farming.[9]

Nevertheless the commission's report, which laid the blame for the declining rural population squarely upon the country school, seemed to confirm the professional educators' long-standing contention that education in the one-room school was poor education. And this impression was supported by the commission's recommendations that country-school education had to be redirected, even revolutionized, if the great cityward migration was to be slowed. Borrowing from the ideas of John Dewey, the philosopher and educator, who ridiculed the notion that "social efficiency" could ever be achieved by a "return to the barren discipline of the traditional formal subjects, reading, writing, and the rest," the commission urged that rural education have a "relation to living, that schools ... express the daily life, and that ... they ... educate by means of agriculture and country life subjects."[10]

II

Obviously, the Country Life Commission's recommendations on rural education marked a victory for the new educators, for the argument that rural education must be related to living in order to keep farm boys and girls on the farm was invaluable support for eliminating drills and memorization and for integrating the teaching of the three R's into courses in nature study and agriculture in the country schools.

Courses in nature study had been in vogue for more than a decade by the time the Country Life Commission made its report in 1909, and few subjects ever attained such popularity in such a short time or drew such glowing praise from the educators. "Even the plain road has its lessons," exclaimed a Michigan educator ecstatically as he read a paper on the subject in 1897. "Now for us [who study nature] the sun shines, the wind blows, the rain falls, the birds sing, the crickets chirp, the brook murmurs, the flowers bloom, the grass grows, the trees clap their hands, and the children shout, 'I'm glad I'm alive.'"[11]

With its emphasis on the study of plants and animals and the wonders of the great outdoors, and with frequent trips through parks to observe the natural world, nature study seemed an excellent course for acquainting urban children with growing things as well as the perfect vehicle for developing the principles of the new education. Not only would it stimulate the children's interest, but, as one educator wrote, "instruction about plants and animals and insects may easily and naturally be connected with exercises in composition and in numbers, which will bring into practical use from day to day what the child is learning about the English language, arithmetic, or geography."[12]

It had been more difficult, of course, to find reasons for teaching nature study to country children who saw the world's natural wonders each day on every hand; but the educators had argued that country children did not appreciate the natural world about them and must be taught to do so. Furthermore, some professionals saw nature study as an introduction to the study of agriculture, a subject they came to believe should be taught in every rural school.

As far back as the late 1870s, following the Centennial Exposition in Philadelphia, where the European manual training exhibits had drawn so much attention, some American professional educators had emphasized vocational training in the schools, and by the late 1880s some of them were already trying to interest the rural schools in such studies. But vocational training in rural schools then seemed as irrelevant as a class in wood chopping. "There does not seem to be any need for a special system of manual training in the schools of a purely agricultural community," one Illinois county superintendent wrote in 1888. "The everyday work which the children are necessarily required to do in the great majority of families well fits them for the duties of life. As it has proved in the past, the boy and the girl of the farms of to-day will stand in the front row in all the professions . . . for years to come."[13]

But in the early 1900s, and especially in the aftermath of the Country Life Commission's report, the professional educators, bent on relating education to living, grafted nature study and agriculture onto the courses of study used in rural schools throughout the Middle West with such fervor that many of them must truly have believed that nature study alone would keep country children on the farm. And because they believed so firmly that "all real teaching builds upon past experience," as one of them wrote in 1912, they worked to relate old subjects like arithmetic and geography to rural experience as well.[14]

Besides revising the curriculum of country schools to stimulate student interest in the farm, the educators and country life planners also urged the farmers to use their one-room schoolhouses as community centers where they might gather for social evenings and form social clubs to promote efforts to make farm life attractive. The old, natural, haphazard use of the schoolhouse as a community center, which had been so much a part of rural life, would no longer do. Now they must organize and even have constitutions for their social clubs! "Make your schoolhouse a neighborhood gathering place and help make country life worth while," wrote Nebraska's state superintendent in 1913. "The proper use of a schoolhouse as such a social center will bring about a change for the better in the general management and course of study, and increase the efficiency of the school."[15]

If enthusiasm alone could have done it, the educators would have solved the country problem, for their efforts to restore a dying countryside in the Middle West were, in some instances, heroic. Across the region country schoolhouses were turned into community centers where meetings were held—24,308 in Wisconsin alone between 1914 and 1915—and social clubs were formed like the Ladies' Social Civic Club at the little Uphoff School in Dane County, Wisconsin, which served refreshments at the annual school meetings. And here and there schools were changed to fit the educators' precise prescription for keeping boys and girls on the farm.[16]

Jessie Field, for example, county superintendent of Page County, Iowa, who believed that "we must teach the country child in terms of country life," had gone far by 1912 in redirecting the country schools in her county. When a journalist visited her county that year he found children reading compositions on "Why I Like to Live in the Country," and "How to Make a Bed." The school he visited one morning had for its nature study lesson the identification of weeds the children had brought from the roadsides as they made their way to school and a drill in the recognition of various kinds of apples. The superintendent, he leaned, had even written an arithmetic book for the children in her county, which stressed the kinds of problems country children would have to solve in their daily life.[17]

Perhaps the most famous of all such efforts to redirect rural education in the Middle West in those years of reform was the experiment conducted at the Porter School near Kirksville, Missouri. Here, in

1912, an expert country teacher, Marie Turner Harvey, took charge of a neglected one-room schoolhouse and transformed it into a progressive school that drastically changed the life of the community. Under her direction and insistence, a new basement was built under the schoolhouse, and the schoolhouse itself, twenty years old, dilapidated, and a nighttime haven for hoboes, as many rural schoolhouses were, was repaired. The outdoor facilities were rebuilt and the school grounds beautified.

More importantly the school's curriculum was redirected to focus on agriculture. Home economics and agriculture were taught, and the teaching of the three R's completely revised. Finally, the schoolhouse was made a community center. New kinds of programs were held there the first year, and the second year the Farm Women's Club of Porter Community, which was to be involved in important community functions, was organized at the school. "Porter stands out," wrote the biographer of this little school in 1919, "throughout the state of Missouri as an example of the possibilities for growth and achievement that are latent in every country community, and which need only the guidance of a sympathetic and public-spirited teacher to be harnessed to progressive and constructive work."[18]

Yet enthusiasm and successful experiments like the one at the Porter School were not enough to alter fundamentally rural education throughout the Middle West. There were not enough teachers like Mrs. Harvey to revolutionize rural education, for one thing. But more than that, the farmer's natural conservatism made him wary of changes in his school's curriculum. As early as 1901, an educator in the Department of Agriculture had observed that "the greatest obstacle to the...movement to introduce nature study into the rural schools, aside from the lack of competent teachers, is to be found in the conservatism of the patrons of the schools. Reading, writing, and arithmetic they understand, but what, forsooth, is this new-fangled nature study?"[19]

The question was not as ridiculous as the educator tried to make it appear. Some professional educators themselves, particularly those not associated with the new education, were, in effect, asking much the same question partly because the course seemed to hav no structure. But the farmers were skeptical of it because, in their view, school was where their children were to learn the three R's, poems, orations, grammar, history, and geography—subjects they could not learn outside the classroom. "There was a time when reading, writing, spelling, arithmetic, and geography were the five fundamental principles of learning," an Illinois State Grange committee reported in 1906. "We believe they are as truly so to-day—they are the essentials of all learning. All higher branches must rest upon these fundamental elements and there must be something wrong with an educational system that produces high school graduates who cannot spell."[20]

Grangers, it was true, perhaps like most farmers, were ambivalent about the kind of education they wanted their children to have. Midwestern state Granges sometimes passed resolutions in support of the three R's and sometimes in support of nature study and agriculture. But the fact was that a significant number of them did not care to have the curriculum in their one-room schools related to farm life if it meant a deemphasis of the three R's. In the twentieth century some of them were not even anxious to have their children remain on the farm. It was mostly the educators and country planners who wanted that, and this so mystified one farmer that he wrote to ask the Country Life commissioners why they wanted rural boys and girls to stay on the farm when they themselves had left it. Farmers generally wanted their children to have the same kind of education as their "city kinsmen" had, as an Illinois State Grange resolution expressed it, for the educators themselves had taught the farmers that a good education was the key to advancement in life, and they often wanted their children to advance beyond the farm. It was for this reason, indeed, that farm parents who could afford it sometimes sent their children to the village schools.[21]

In one of his novels, Herbert Quick, who knew farm people well, captured one prevalent rural attitude toward education precisely. The hero of his story was a young country schoolteacher who was determined to relate education to life. Caught up in the principles of the new education and the country life movement, he began using agricultural bulletins for reading and language classes, utilizing arithmetic to solve farm problems, having the children debate the merits of various kinds of corn, and, in effect, discarding the textbooks.

But his students' parents objected to this study of "corn and wheat, and hogs and the like," as one mother put it, "instead of the learnin' schools was made to teach." When the teacher protested that the children must be taught to make a living, one immigrant mother, whose tongue still bore the inflections of the old country, replied: "Haakon and I will look after the making of a living for our family. . . . We want our children to learn nice things and go to high school, and after a while to the Juniwersity." Nor would she relent from her position in the face of the possibility that her children might be happy with the teacher's new approach to teaching. "I don't send them to school to be happy, Yim," she replied. "I send them to learn to be higher people than their father and mother. That's what America means!"[22]

So the farmers often objected to the redirection of the curriculum of their one-room schools. But even where education was related to rural life in the most thorough fashion, as in Page County, Iowa, there is little evidence to show that this revision slowed the drift of young people from the farms to the cities, for the fact was that education in the one-room school was not, as the Country Life Commission thought, the reason young people left the farm.

III

Because rural America seemed an ideal place for the new educators to put their theories into practice, to demonstrate that school was "not a preparation for life," as the saying went, but life itself, and to prove how well education could be used to achieve whatever social goals seemed desirable, their failure to keep young people on the farm by relating education to rural life was perhaps a disappointment to some of them. Yet, in retrospect, it is clear that most professional educators in the Midwest who were involved in rural education were much less interested in relating the country school curricula to life than in controlling rural education, as they had so long tried to do. Using the nation's concern over the loss of farm population, they moved energetically in various directions to take the control of the rural schools from the farmers, and in the new mood of the country they found the state legislatures more receptive to their suggestions than they had been before.[23]

Now, for the first time, the professional educators were better able to manage those educator-politicians in the county superintendent's office. They secured legislation in most Midwestern states not only requiring the county superintendents to have certain qualifications to hold office, but also stripping those officials of their control over certifying teachers. By 1911 the laws of the Midwestern states provided that teachers' examinations were to be prepared only in the state superintendent's office, not by the county superintendent, and in some cases the tests had to be graded in the state office. Iowa had even gone a step beyond this. In that state all teaching certificates, including those for country teachers, were issued only by the state superintendent's office, and it seemed obvious that it would not be long before teacher certification would be completely in the hands of state offices throughout the Middle Border.[24]

Furthermore, by the time the United States entered World War I, a part of the county superintendent's work had been parceled out to teaching supervisors and rural inspectors in some Midwestern states. In 1916 Wisconsin had eighty-one teaching supervisors spread throughout the country districts to supervise rural teachers, and a number of rural inspectors who in some ways superseded the county superintendents. They had the power, for example, to condemn schoolhouses they thought unsuitable, and between 1914 and 1915, they condemned 479 schoolhouses throughout the state. In Missouri rural inspectors had the authority to visit the country schools, just as the county superintendents did; to meet with the school boards of the little schools; and even to make suggestions to the county superintendents about how to improve their schools. And because they were appointed rather than elected, they could afford to be more independent in their judgments as the educators had long wanted the county superintendents to be.[25]

The Midwestern educators also had much success in the early 1900s in developing what they called standard schools for which they, and not the farmers, set the standards. A standard school in Missouri in the century's early years, for example, was one in which school was held for eight months, and which had a library, was well disciplined, and employed a teacher who had at least a second-grade teaching certificate and was paid as much as forty dollars a month. Points were given by the state superintendent's office for each of these requirements, and any school scoring eighty points or better received a handsome lithographed certificate signed by the state superintendent and stamped with the seal of his office. One of the first schools in Missouri to receive this award was the Peavine School in Carroll County, which had a library of 145 volumes, a schoolhouse that cost seven hundred dollars, and a teacher who made forty-five dollars a month.[26]

In other states, however, farmers were lured into raising their schools to certain standards not with certificates but with money. A law passed in Wisconsin in 1907 promised fifty dollars to any school that properly heated and ventilated its schoolhouse, purchased readers, dictionaries, card catalogue cases, and suitable blackboards. This law enticed the farmers in many little districts like one above the Sugar River in Dane County to consider the improvement of their building. "The heating and ventilating system was talked over thoroughly ...," ran the minutes of the district's special meeting in July 1908. "It was made unanamous [sic] to except [sic] the plans and the school board to make the necessary improvements so as to receive additional state aid."[27]

Through all this, however, the great goal of Midwestern educators was, as it had always been, to make the one-room schools as much like urban schools as possible, and in the early twentieth century nothing offered so much promise of doing this as something they called "consolidation." By this they meant eliminating all one-room schools in a given area and transporting the children from those schools in wagons to one large, centrally located school.

Consolidation, like so many of the nation's educational innovations, originated in Massachusetts. In 1869, worried about the state's declining rural population and the high cost of maintaining small rural schools, the Massachusetts General Court passed a law permitting school districts to use school money to transport their children to larger schools if they wished. Five years later the town of Quincy, acting under this law, began closing its small rural schools and so became the first to consolidate and to wagon its children to one large school.[28]

It was years after this, however, before consolidation reached the Middle Border, and when it did, it came almost as much by accident as by design. In 1892 the school officials in Kingsville Township in Ashtabula County, Ohio, were debating whether or not to build a new schoolhouse for Subdistrict 4, when the principal of the Kingsville School suggested closing Subdistrict 4 and sending the children to the Kingsville School. The plan was welcomed by the township school officers, but before it could be implemented legislation was needed to permit the township to use public education money to transport the pupils to the school.

So touchy was the business of legislating for rural schools, that it took two years before the Ohio legislature gave its carefully restricted permission to use school money in this way, and another year before Subdistrict 4, and subsequently other township schools which asked to be included in the plan, closed their schools and began sending their children to the Kingsville School. Shortly thereafter the Ohio legislature passed another law permitting any township in the state to close its township schools and convey its children to a centralized school, and by 1900 several Ohio townships had gone to the consolidated system. By then Indiana had consolidated schools, and so, too, did Iowa. That same year, Ollie Jerome Kern, the county superintendent of Winnebago County, Illinois, wrote an enthusiastic account of the Ohio experiment and drew the attention of educators to this new method of centralizing country schools throughout the Middle West.[29]

IV

One-time high school teacher, county superintendent, writer, and gadfly, Ollie Kern was among the most enthusiastic of Midwestern educators. Like Jessie Field, he redirected education in the rural schools in Winnebago County, where, before he began his remarkable revision of the curriculum, according to one journalist, the children were being educated "to be as helpless in a world of busy competition as the farmer without horses is in a world of farm machinery." He worked hard to relate education to country living, to have the children raise gardens, beautify their school grounds, and improve their dilapidated schoolhouses in order to make school interesting and keep farm children on the farm.[30]

But Kern was also interested in the organization of rural schools. He had been in the county superintendent's office only a short time when, in the autumn of 1900, he made a tour through the rural areas of Ohio's Western Reserve country to see for himself the operation of the consolidation plan he had heard about. He had gone first to Perry in Lake County to talk to the principal of the high school who had been the driving force behind Ohio's first consolidation experiment at Kingsville, and then on to Kingsville itself, a little rural village that sat about a mile and a half from the nearest railroad.

In that little village Kern spoke to the school principal and the town clerk and inspected the schoolhouse. He talked to the teachers; he stood in the schoolyard at the close of a beautiful October school day and watched the children rush from the schoolhouse and climb aboard the wagons that were waiting to take them home; and he was deeply impressed. Here, at least, it seemed, was a school system that promised to equalize the education of rural and urban children.

Kingsville, however, was a small village where a large schoolhouse had been built even before consolidation had been attempted, and Kern was anxious to see the plan put into operation in the open country where it had started from nothing and where a large, centrally located building had to be built purely for the purposes of consolidation. So he hurried on, thirty-five miles south of Kingsville, to Trumbull County and Gustavus Township.

There, in the very center of that rural township, where only a town

229

hall, a post office, a church, and a few homes had stood, he inspected the four-room schoolhouse the farmers had built at a cost of three thousand dollars to take the place of nine little one-room school-houses. He learned that the township had nine wagons to carry children from all over the township to and from the central schoolhouse. The wagons picked the children up at their farm gates and arrived at the schoolhouse each morning at 8:45. Promptly at 3:45 in the afternoon they were at the schoolhouse to return pupils to their homes.

On the advice of the principal of the Gustavus School, Kern drove five miles west of Gustavus to Green Township to see another consolidated schoolhouse that had been built in a township so isolated it was eleven miles from one railroad and six miles from another. Here he found a beautiful new six-thousand-dollar schoolhouse with six classrooms, a room for a library, another for an office, and a basement that ran the length of the building which could be used for a gymnasium or laboratory. To this school, children were brought across the township in eight wagons.[31]

Everywhere he went during those October days, in Lake County, through Ashtabula and Trumbull counties, Kern found the new consolidation system working flawlessly, and the people lavish in their praise of it. At one farmhouse he stopped to ask a wagon driver if he had had trouble with any of the children on his wagon, and was told that he had not. Farther along the way he talked to a public-spirited and prosperous farmer about the new centralized system and was assured that the people would never return to the old one-room schoolhouse system. Even those who had at first been the bitterest foes of the system were now, he found, "its most enthusiastic supporters."[32]

Kern was so impressed by these remarkable experiments that he could not repress his enthusiasm as he wrote of his trip to the people in Illinois. Of Green Township's six-room schoolhouse, he was almost lyrical in his praise. "We never saw the like before in the country, to take the place of miserable box-car 1-room structures," he wrote. "And the possibilities of such a school, who can measure it?" And standing inside the Gustavus schoolhouse, he had reflected on the significance of consolidation. "Anyone who stands in that building," he continued in his report, "and looks at those children and wagons, must be convinced that here is the solution to the country-school problem."[33]

Kern's report appeared at approximately the same time that Indiana's consolidated schools were also drawing public attention, and the enthusiastic accounts of the movements in both states led nearly all influential Midwestern educators, almost overnight, to embrace consolidation as the wave of the future. And why not? The arguments for it seemed irrefutable, and proof of its success was apparently already at hand. In both Ohio and Indiana, large, well-lighted, properly ventilated schoolhouses had been built to replace the one-room buildings that had served the people so long. The new schools had, or would have, libraries, the best educational apparatus available, and even room for laboratories for conducting agricultural experiments. They were completely graded and thoroughly supervised by a principal who watched over four or five teachers who were much better prepared than any teacher the little school districts could afford.[34]

The student bodies of these consolidated schools were large enough to give life to the schools, make them interesting, and provide competition that was thought to be a necessary stimulant to the learning process. Here the schoolchildren's social life could be broadened by a wider acquaintance with their peers throughout the township, their intellects could be sharpened, and, in place of having scarcely enough boys to play "two-cornered cat," they could have enough in time to have organized athletics. "Think what it is," Kern wrote, "to get all the boys of a township, country boys, I mean, on one playground. There will grow up a unity. Each boy, having played and studied with other boys of the entire township, will be the stronger for it."[35]

Besides all this, there were the advantages of transporting the children to school. Experience showed, the educators said, that transporting children to school had ended truancy, and increased school attendance—as much as fifty to a hundred fifty per cent in Kingsville. Furthermore, the children were never tardy, never had wet feet or wet clothes, and had far fewer colds and illnesses than they had had when they walked to school. And not the least important advantage of transportation was that riding in the wagons provided a more moral and wholesome environment for the children than walking along the roads, because they were supervised by the drivers.

In both Indiana and Ohio the educators had insisted on employing good men to drive the school wagons. The drivers had signed contracts agreeing to furnish their own wagons and to enclose them in the winter, to provide lap robes, soapstones, and even stoves to keep the children warm. They had also agreed not to use profane or obscene language, spiritous liquors, or tobacco while the children were in their care, and the educators argued that such drivers would prevent the immoralities among the children that had occurred in their own days when, as they remembered, they had walked by "two's and four's and larger groups" along the roads unattended.[36]

Wagoning children to school, it was pointed out, was also taking care of that old problem of children hanging around the schoolhouse after school instead of going home to do the chores. And finally, looking to the future, some educators saw the time coming when barges, as the wagons were called, would take the children's parents to school in the evening for a play, school meeting, or simply for a social gathering, just as they took the children to school by day.[37]

Yet the best part of all this, according to the enthusiastic school men, was that consolidation actually cost less than the one-room schools had cost, even after the cost of transportation had been added in. By eliminating the need for so many teachers and the wasteful upkeep of seven or eight schools, consolidation in Ohio, it was argued, had actually reduced the cost of education. School authorities in Kingsville claimed they had actually saved a thousand dollars in three years by the new system, and the officials at one of the Lake County schools produced figures to show that consolidation there had reduced the tuition per pupil from $16.00 to $10.48.[38]

In short, the consolidated schools, economical and efficient, were as good as urban schools, and yet they could be established in the pure open country as the experiments in Gustavus and Green townships had proven. And, in addition to all other benefits, so the educators argued, they were just the schools to keep farm children on the farm. "What should we do to be saved from our great cities?" asked the Nebraska state superintendent as he argued for consolidation in 1904. "Shall we permit the decay and destruction of our pure country life, or shall we endeavor to bring some of the great comforts and conveniences and advantages of city life into the country?"[39]

Clearly, there was only one answer to that, and the way to be saved from the great cities, in his view, was to wipe out the little one-room schoolhouses and the small quarrelsome school districts along with them, and send the children to large, urbanlike schools.

So the case for consolidation—from conveyance, to cost, to the conservation of country life—was made, and in no place did it receive a more enthusiastic reception than among the Midwestern educators who had tried for so long to solve the problem of rural education. Hailing consolidation as the new ultimate solution to the country-school problem, they wrote hundreds of pieces about its virtues, pushed their state legislatures to enact laws supporting it, and pleaded with county superintendents, school directors, and farmers to abandon their small schools and transport their children to large, graded schools. And where transportation was clearly out of the question, they urged farmers whose schools lay close to one another to send their children to the most centrally located school when it was within walking distance and abandon the others.[40]

Supported by the businessmen in the little rural towns who saw in consolidation a chance to include the countryside in assessing taxes for their town schools and possibly increased trade to their stores as well, the educators seemed never to tire of their efforts, and often went directly to the people to urge them to consolidate and give their children as good an education as the town children received. The superintendent of the Marathon schools in Buena Vista County, Iowa, even took a leave of absence in 1903 and drove through Poland Township for three weeks trying to sell the farmers on the idea of closing their schools and sending their children to Marathon to school. "The favorite conference room," he recalled, "was the kitchen with the farmer on one side and his wife on the other and the map and drawings on the kitchen table."[41]

And in the wake of their relentless campaign, consolidation inched forward through the Middle West in the early 1900s. By 1903 nearly all the states in the region had enacted laws making it legal to use public funds for wagoning farm children to school and establishing procedures for obtaining consolidated schools, and by that time a number of states had taken advantage of the laws. Consolidation continued to spread throughout Ohio and was being tried in twenty-eight counties in Iowa and twenty-one in Nebraska. But no state had gone as far as Indiana. Consolidated schools had been created in two-thirds of that state's counties by 1903. From Montgomery County in the west to Delaware County in the east, and from LaGrange in the north to Washington County in the south, large central schoolhouses had been built, and 181 wagons were carrying 2,599 students to school at public expense.[42]

V

But it was easier for the educators to establish consolidated schools in Indiana, where the township district system had long before deprived the people of much of the control of their schools, than it was in those states where the small independent district system prevailed. There, petitions had to be signed and elections held before consolidation could take place, and the elections usually revealed that, in spite of the educators' arguments in behalf of consolidation, the farmers were as adamantly opposed to it as they had been to the township district system years before.[43]

Unfortunately, the records of the farmers' opposition were compiled largely by the educators who, because of their burning enthusiasm for their new solution to the country-school problem, tended to make the farmers' reasons for rejecting consolidation appear absurd. According to them, the farmers opposed the new plan because they were either irrational, ignorant, and selfish, or simply too conservative to make needed changes. In part, of course, they were right. School directors and rural teachers, too, did oppose consolidation for selfish reasons, for both groups believed they would lose their positions in a new consolidated district. And surely the farmers' natural resistance to change had something to do with their refusal to build a large, consolidated school in their midst.[44]

But the farmers had reasons for opposing consolidation that merited more understanding and sympathy from the educators than they received.

The controversy between the farmers and the educators over consolidation was a replay of their fight over the township district system. At issue in that battle, as in this, was the question of who was to control rural education: the farmers or the educators. To the farmers consolidation meant not only the loss of the little school down the road to which they were sentimentally attached, but also the loss of their ability to control their children's education for which they had to pay. This was their principal objection to the new system.

Often the educators referred contemptuously to the farmers' fear of "destroying the sacred 'little red schoolhouse,'" and their aversion to witnessing the disappearance of familiar landmarks. "People seem to be against the plan," the county superintendent of Muscatine County, Iowa, reported in 1901. "The real objection is a sentimental love for 'our little red schoolhouse,' and the people are opposed to its removal from the neighborhood." Always the implication in such observations was that the farmers were plainly unreasonable to want to save their homely little schoolhouse when they could have a beautiful consolidated building with many rooms and an abundant supply of school apparatus.[45]

And perhaps they were. But the educators rarely seemed to understand that abandoning a one-room schoolhouse that had been standing in the countryside for half a century or more was much different from rearranging urban schools. To close a country school was to destroy an institution that held the little rural community together. It was to wipe out the one building the people of the district had in common and, in fact, to destroy the community, which, in those years, so many were trying to save and strengthen. Even more important, as far as the farmers were concerned, the destuction of their school meant that their power to set the length of the school terms, to employ their teacher, and to determine how much they would spend for education would be taken from them and given to some board far removed from their community and their control.

When the farmers voted on the question of consolidation, its cost was always a part of their calculations and not the least of the reasons they usually opposed it. For, contrary to the claims of the educators, the farmers never believed that they could build large new schoolhouses, equip them with the finest school apparatus, and employ an experienced teacher for less than they spent to operate their one-room schools, and experience proved them right, as one farmer in Buffalo Township in Winnebago County, Iowa, found. Asked what he thought of consolidation in his township, he spoke for many farmers who were not misled by the educators' argument about the cost. "It has given us the great privilege of furnishing 45 per cent of the pupils," he said, "and of paying 65 per cent of the cost of the school, and having two of the five directors out in the country." In time, the educators saw that the farmers were right and changed their argument from the idea that consolidation cost less to the proposition that consolidation gave them more.[46]

Yet it was not only the closing of their own schoolhouse and the loss of control over their school's affairs, or even the cost, that troubled the farmers about consolidation. They worried, too, about the schoolhouse to which their children were being transported each day. No more than their descendants in the suburbs of modern cities did the farmers of the early 1900s wish to see their children, especially their younger children, wagoned out of their communities each day. And particularly was this so if the school to which they were taken was, as most consolidated schools were, in the village or town where, as one man explained, "the good country boys [were thrown] into association with the uncouth, cigarette smoking boys of the village."[47]

A few educators had seen this danger early in the consolidation movement and had emphasized the need to build the new consolidated schools in the open country. Writing in support of consolidation in his own state in 1901, the Indiana state superintendent warned against building centralized schools in towns and cities lest the rural values be lost. "The very strong movement which leads to centralizing schools in towns and cities is to be deplored and should be avoided if possible," he wrote. "The preservation of the conservatism of the farms; the simplicity of its manners and dress; the ruggedness of its life; the peace, quiet, and contentment of its homes; its formation of good habits; its absence of vice; its opportunities for physical development, and its making of men and women of clear consciences are items which argue eloquently for rural life and make its preservation of vital necessity to the welfare of the nation."[48]

In practice, however, the consolidated school to which most farm children were taken each day was a town school where life was different from that which they had known. In part, of course, the difference was only in the minds of the parents, for village boys may or may not have been less pure than the country boys. Other differences, however, were not imaginary. Parents of farm children now felt forced to dress their children better than they had when they sent them to the district school; more money was needed, too, for school supplies; and many a farmer worried about how his children would do in a consolidated school when they could not work at their own pace as they had been able to do before. Would they fail? Or, worse still, would they be pushed along with everyone else without really knowing how to spell or read?[49]

And often there was the fear, unspoken but nevertheless real, of proud farm parents who worried that the town children would make their own feel inferior to them because of their shy, country ways, and their poorer circumstances, and in the end make farm children ashamed of their home and family.[50]

Beyond all this, the transportation of the children itself turned out to be less idyllic than Kern had pictured it in his story of the Ohio consolidation, and many farmers objected to having their children ride the wagons. At certain seasons of the year the Midwestern roads were "20 feet wide and two feet deep," as one Indiana county superintendent put it, and there were days when the wagons could not make their rounds at all. Then there was the long ride. Often children were forced to ride as much as five miles to and from school, and sometimes as much as nine miles. This meant that they left home at an early hour, and even if the wagon traveled at five miles an hour as it was supposed to do in some places, the children did not return home until late in the evening, sometimes not until after sundown on a winter day, which left them to complete their daily chores in the gathering darkness.[51]

Nor did the wagons always pick the children up at their farm gates as the planners had originally intended. Often the pupils had to walk a considerable distance to catch the wagon, and if, as sometimes happened, they had to wait in the cold so that their feet and clothes were wet when they finally climbed into it, they were as likely to catch cold and develop sore throats as if they had walked to their district school. The fact that the Ohio legislature found it necessary to enact a law permitting the establishment of depots along the wagon routes where the children might wait indicated how far the transportation system had strayed from the ideal.[52]

Finally, the picture that Kern drew of the good wagon driver happily transporting the children in his charge without trouble and keeping them from unruly conduct proved to be more fanciful than factual in many cases. The drivers often did, in fact, have trouble with the students, and even the drivers themselves turned out to be something less than the good men the educators had wanted for the job. Indeed, in some places, in order to cut the expenses of transportation, the wagons were actually driven by the older students themselves.[53]

In spite of all their objections to consolidation, however, farmers might have been more sympathetic to the idea had the educators been less arrogant in their efforts to get them to vote for the new system. But in their enthusiasm for the new solution the educators not only made unsupportable claims for consolidation, but they continually told the farmers how bad their schools were until, like the people on the Country Life Commission, who angered the farmers by telling them how to improve rural life, thereby suggesting that something was terribly wrong with it, they stirred resentment of the farmers who did not have much use for the expert anyway. "You may be doing well under the conditions," the Nebraska state superintendent once wrote in a plea for the consolidation of schools, "but what are the conditions? How could they be worse? Poor battered old schoolhouses, sometimes lacking paint, with cannon ball stoves, and cheerless yards; while in our cities we are building modern, scientific structures, correctly heated, ventilated, lighted and seated, often built of brick, sometimes with stone foundations and with beautiful surroundings."[54]

Such attacks scarcely helped the cause of consolidation. They were more likely to lead the farmers to defend their little schools as the Iowa State Grange did in 1908. In a series of resolutions the Iowa Grangers praised their country schools for being near their children and for placing the responsibility for running the schools in the hands of those most interested in them, and they ended their resolutions by noting that in these and many other ways "our sometimes much maligned little white school house helps smooth the way to knowledge and wisdom for the child, and, at the same time to school his parents in the principles of free government, taxation, and neighborliness."[55]

So the farmers had their reasons for disliking consolidation, and when they met in their annual meetings in those years surrounding World War I and voted on whether to consolidate or not, they usually voted no. The farmers at the Gravel Hill School in La Prairie Township in Rock County, Wisconsin, voted emphatically, sixteen to two, not to consolidate when the proposition came up at their annual meeting in July of 1917. That same year in the same township the farmers in District 3 had a strong inducement to vote for consolidation, for their schoolhouse had been condemned. But after two annual meetings the farmers voted to repair it rather than abandon it. And in some places like Joint District 16 in Caledonia and Mt. Pleasant townships in Racine County, Wisconsin, there were attempts to end consolidations that had already taken place and return to the one-room schools.[56]

To be sure, consolidations continued to be made here and there across the Middle Border in the early 1900s. But by the end of the new century's first decade it was obvious the movement had not caught fire, and the educators began returning to their state legislatures for new laws that would make establishing consolidated schools easier and financially more attractive.

In this effort they were partly successful. In Indiana, where consolidation was already proceeding rapidly, the state legislature made it mandatory in 1907 for the township trustees to close any school with twelve or fewer students, and gave them authority to close those with fifteen or fewer if they saw fit. Elsewhere throughout the region legislation was enacted designed to lure the farmers by monetary rewards into consolidating their schools.

One such law, called the Holmberg Act, was passed by the Minnesota legislature in 1911 and provided monetary help for three kinds of consolidated schools: four-room, three-room, and two-room schools. To the first, the law promised $1,500 a year, to the second $1,000, and to the third $750. Similar laws were passed in Missouri and Iowa in 1913, although neither was quite so generous.[57]

These laws did spur the growth of consolidated schools throughout those states. Especially was this true in Minnesota and Iowa. In 1910 and 1911 there had been only nine consolidations in the entire state of Minnesota. Within one year after the passage of the Holmberg Act, sixty consolidations had been made. And in Iowa in 1920, at the height of the consolidation movement there, thirty-three consolidated districts were formed in the month of March alone![58]

The price the farmers paid, however, for these consolidations, which were so heavily subsidized by the state, was the loss of much of the control of their school. Consolidated schools receiving financial aid in Iowa were obligated to add vocational courses to their curriculum so that education might be related to life. And in Minnesota a new consolidated district created under the Holmberg Act had to permit the state superintendent to establish the standards for the school building and school apparatus and to write the regulations for the transportation of the schoolchildren. Moreover, the principals of the four-room schools had to have diplomas from a state normal school, and the teachers of consolidated schools had to have teaching certificates issued by the state, not the counties.[59]

Yet even with the very substantial aid given in these and other Middle Border states to school districts that would abandon their small schools and build larger ones, the number of consolidations fell off dramatically throughout the Middle West in the mid-twenties, and this at the very time when roads were being improved and motor buses were providing better transportation for the children. The farmers' declining income in this period probably had much to do with their waning interest in consolidation. But in the 1920s much that rural Midwesterners held dear was under attack. Tensions between rural and urban America rose, and every issue had its rural and urban side. So the farmers' aversion to consolidation may have been partly attributable to their greater determination to retain control of their schools in these years when so much else was changing.[60]

In spite of the decline in consolidations, some Midwestern educators were still writing glowing accounts of the advantages of consolidation and were as optimistic as ever about its future. A professor of education at Ames, Iowa, wrote in 1922 that "the little white schoolhouse" was "no longer regarded as the symbol of intellectual freedom," and would soon disappear. Yet even as he wrote, other educators in the region were already reappraising consolidation, and were, in fact, beginning to wonder whether education in the poor, battered one-room schoolhouse was, after all, as bad as they had always thought.[61]

VI
One of the popular fads of the professional educators in the 1920s

was the educational survey, in which they attempted to compare rural and urban education by reducing to concrete figures the number of teachers with college degrees in each kind of school, the teachers' salaries, the school facilities, length of school terms, school attendance, and so on. In most of these surveys they labored over the obvious and came up with the obvious: rural teachers had less training than urban teachers; school facilities were poorer in country schools; and school terms in one-room schools were shorter than in urban schools.[62]

The crucial test of a school, however, was not to be found in the number of teachers it had with college degrees but in what the children who attended the school had learned. In the nineteenth century there had been no way to measure this except in a general way by examining the statistics on illiteracy. But in the early 1900s intelligence and standardized achievement tests were developed, and with these new tools the professional educators rushed to measure the students in the one-room schools against those in graded urban and consolidated rural schools to prove that what they had been saying for so long about the superiority of large graded schools was true.

From World War I through the early 1920s, most of the tests, but by no means all, comparing one-room schoolchildren with those in the graded schools on the Middle Border indicated, indeed, that the students in the graded schools did better than those in the one-room schools. In one subject the pupils in the graded schools might be a year or even two years ahead of those in the one-room schools; in another they might be only a half-year ahead, and in still another there might be no difference at all. But in nearly all comparisons there were test scores that did not fit this pattern, and in few cases were the differences between the pupils in one-room and graded schools as overwhelming as the educators had expected. Clearly they were puzzled by the results.[63]

The educators reacted to their findings in various ways. Some ignored the ambiguities in their statistics and emphasized only the superior test scores of the graded schoolchildren or found reasons why there were fewer differences than expected. One educator suggested that the failure of the graded schoolchildren to do better than those in the one-room school in an English composition test he had given was due to the fatigue of the graded pupils. Another educator's answer to the perplexing scores he found in a study in Ohio was to write that those subjects in which the rural children surpassed or equaled the urban children were subjects, such as spelling, in which

240

instruction was unimportant! And a Kansas educator concluded in 1923 that a study made in that state proved conclusively that one-room schools were inferior to graded schools, that because of the inferior instruction in the one-room schools it would do no good to lengthen their school terms to make them equal to the graded schools, and that "the one-teacher school system as an instrument of instruction has outlived its usefulness, stands impeached in every essential detail of its operation, and is totally unworthy of a place in the educational system of any energetic, fairminded commonwealth."[64]

But other educators could not so easily overlook the fact that the differences in scores of the two groups were not as large as they had expected; that in some subjects there was no difference at all; and that in others the pupils in the one-room schools actually did better than those in the graded schools. A major study of city, village, rural graded, and one-room schools made in Wisconsin between 1920 and 1922, for example, showed that in reading, the superior ten per cent of students in the one-room schools surpassed the superior students from all other schools. From this and other tests, the examiner concluded that "the differences between the one-room rural schools and other schools are in general less than would have been expected."[65]

This conclusion was confirmed by a massive investigation of one-room and consolidated schools undertaken for the National Education Association in the early 1920s. Nineteen states, which included selected Midwestern as well as southern states, were involved in this study of the achievement scores of children in both kinds of schools. It was the largest project of its kind ever made to that date and required an enormous amount of time and energy. The investigators began their work in 1920 and finished in 1922, and examined more than fifteen thousand children from 135 consolidated schools and 374 one-room schools.[66]

The results of this investigation were published in 1923, and, as in other tests of its kind, showed that in each of the five subjects in which the children were tested—reading, arithmetic, language, spelling, and writing—the pupils from the consolidated schools ranked ahead of those from the one-room schools. Converted into terms of yearly progress, the grade achievement differences indicated that the students in the consolidated schools were anywhere from eighteen to forty per cent ahead of those in the one-room schools. The median difference was twenty-seven per cent.[67]

Nevertheless the scores were a great disappointment to the professional educators who had expected to find the achievement of the children in the consolidated schools overwhelmingly superior to that of the one-room students. Instead they discovered that the differences were, after all, minimal. It was sobering for them to consider that after all the claims they had made for consolidation—after all the money that had been spent in building large schoolhouses, equipping them with the best apparatus, employing experienced teachers, and lengthening school terms—the children in the consolidated schools in grades three through eight were only fifty-six days ahead of those in the one-room schools.[68]

The questions the investigative committee appended to its report indicated how the results had jarred the educators' confidence in their professional wisdom. "Have we not," the committee asked, "erected costly buildings, installed elaborate equipment, and set up extensive organizations, and *assumed* that they would produce superior classroom results?" Clearly, the committee's faith in consolidation had been shaken. "The movement for consolidation contemplates the *abandonment* of the one-teacher school and the transportation of *all* pupils to the central school," the report continued. "Would it be wise in the light of the report, to recommend some modification of the program?"[69]

The committee's findings, as one educator wrote, raised two questions: were the consolidated schools as good as the educators had believed; and were the one-room schools as bad as they had thought. To these two questions the educators had two answers.

Some professionals believed the study had proved the worth of the one-room schools and were unwilling to see them abandoned. On the basis of this study and others as well, Charles Everett Myers, who had been trained in the Midwest but who was professor of education at Pennsylvania State College, wrote in 1924 a stout defense of the one-room school in which he attacked many of the assumptions Midwestern educators had had about rural education for more than half a century. He maintained that the ability to organize schools like businesses had not been perfected; that competition in the classroom was not necessary to the learning process; that a large number of children in the classroom was unnecessary for socializing purposes; and that the close supervision of teachers, an idea borrowed from industry, was neither necessary nor helpful, for it stifled their freedom and individuality. "According to such measurements as are available at present," the professor concluded, "it would seem that the miserable one-teacher school is as efficient, day for day, as the better staffed, better financed, graded school in so far as school achievement tests can show."[70]

Other educators, of course, interpreted the results of the tests differently. Obviously exasperated and admittedly disappointed over the test results of the survey of fifteen thousand children, the supporters of consolidation looked for reasons why the "data presented," as they wrote, did not "seem to give the final answer" to whether or not the educators had made a mistake about consolidation. They stressed the fact that, after all, the schoolchildren in the consolidated schools had done better in every test than those in the one-room schools. Furthermore, they argued, the consolidated schools used in the study were not the best consolidated schools. They were small, and their teachers, though obviously better trained than those in the country schools, still had only limited experience.[71]

Finally, one professional concluded that the reason there had not been a greater difference between the consolidated and one-room children's test scores was that the children had been tested only in the five basic subjects. "Isn't it a fact," he asked, "that the untrained teacher most frequently found in the one-room schools doesn't know that school teaching consists of anything more than hammering away at the fundamental arts of reading, spelling, writing, and numbers?" On the other hand, he continued, the teacher in the consolidated school seeks to educate the children in the "beauties of nature and the elementary sciences, in the rich content of geography, history, and civics, in music and art."[72]

He may have been right. The Midwestern farmers had no philosophy of education to confuse them about the purposes of education. They had never expected much more from their little schools than that they teach their children to read, write, figure, and spell, and this they did. Indeed, in the lower grades, one through six, the one-room schools were quite as good as the more costly consolidated schools, and with a lengthened school term might even have been superior, for learning, as Professor Myers observed, was an individual process, and the small number of students in the one-room school forced the teacher and pupils to work with one another as individuals. This, it seemed, was one important lesson to be learned from the test scores comparing children from the consolidated schools with those from the one-room schools.[73]

The test scores also taught, contrary to the educators' expert opinion, held through more than half a century, that the organization of the school did not really matter very much insofar as learning was concerned. This much, at least, even one supporter of consolidation indirectly conceded when he asked, after the disappointing results of the study of fifteen thousand children, what reason they had "to assume that a form of organization which is only a means to an end would itself guarantee better results?" What reason indeed! Unfortunately they had been misled by following form rather than substance, theory rather than fact. And if they had no real reason to believe that organization was the key to successful learning before the tests were given, neither did they have much reason to believe it afterwards. The test scores at best were scarcely a mandate for consolidated schools.[74]

But whether the results of the tests were a vote for consolidation or for the one-room school made little difference to many of the influential Midwestern educators who continued to urge consolidation as the solution to the country-school problem. "In a number of States," wrote the school expert in the Bureau of Education in 1928, "the consolidation movement has for years been presented as a State policy and may be said now to have gained such momentum that relatively little additional stimulation or promotion is necessary." And in Indiana and Ohio, and other sections of the nation that appeared to be true. Between 1918 and 1936 the percentage of schools with one room fell in Indiana from 67.2 to 39.1 per cent, and in Ohio from 72.6 to 39.8. Moreover, from the East Coast through the South and out to the Far West, the process of consolidation went forward so rapidly that by 1936 the number of one-room schools in twenty-seven states was less than half the total number.[75]

But with the exception of Indiana and Ohio, on the Middle Border, where the small, independent school district system was so deeply rooted and where the farmers had fought so long to retain control of their schools, the one-room school lingered on as one familiar landmark by which the farmers could chart their course in a changing world. In 1936 Illinois still had 9,925 one-room schools, more than any state in the nation, and Iowa was second with nearly as many. Then came Missouri, Minnesota, Kansas, Wisconsin, and Nebraska in that order, all with one-room schools that numbered more than seventy per cent of the total in each state. Together the ten states of the Middle West had among them forty-six percent of the 131,101 one-room schools left in the nation by that year.[76]

So the farmers in the heartland of the nation were able to keep their little schools from the clutches of the educators to the eve of World

War II. But what the educators had been unable to do, the declining rural population did in the years following that war. Even as early as 1935, the end of the one-room school on the Middle Border had been in sight. That year Iowa enrolled only 26.1 per cent of her schoolchildren in her 9,115 one-room schools, and in Illinois nearly ten thousand such schools were serving only 12.8 per cent of the school population. Then, when the war was over, many who had left the farm during that upheaval never returned, and some who had remained gradually drifted from the farm until hundreds of one-room schools had but one or two students and some had none at all. Moreover, comfortable yellow buses, speeding along recently blacktopped country roads, were easily able to transport the few children left in the countryside to larger schools.[77]

No longer, then, could the farmers withstand both the educators' demands for change and the loss of population, and through the 1950s the one-room schoolhouses were abandoned one by one. In time many of them were torn down, so that in places like District 40 in Saunders County, Nebraska, nothing remains to mark the small hilltop where the schoolhouse stood for so long. Elsewhere they were remodeled or replaced with other buildings. A house now occupies the site above the Sugar River in Montrose Township in Dane County, Wisconsin, where the schoolhouse William Morehead served so many years was located, and both the Sanford schoolhouse in Lenawee County, Michigan, and the Tri-County schoolhouse near Whitewater, Wisconsin, have been made into homes.

But here and there across the Midwest's back country roads, one-room schoolhouses can still be found. The little Austin schoolhouse in Dodge County, Wisconsin, across from the Catholic church, and the Ise schoolhouse near Downs, Kansas, were still standing in 1981. With their broken windows and peeling paint, and weeds and underbrush grown up about them, they are quaint reminders of an educational system that once promoted democracy, strengthened community life, unabashedly taught generations of Midwesterners the three R's, and made the Middle Border the most literate part of the nation through the years.

Schools Most Often Mentioned

❧❧

IOWA
District 7, Oneida Township, Delaware County
(Arbor Vitae Summit School)

KANSAS
District 37, Osborne County
(Ise School)

MICHIGAN
District 1, Pennfield Township, Calhoun County
(Hicks School)
District 5, Woodstock Township, Lenawee County
(Sanford School)

NEBRASKA
District 40, Saunders County
(Eureka School)

WISCONSIN
District 3, Blooming Grove Township, Dane County
(Nichols School)
Joint District 9, Dunn Township, Dane County
(Uphoff School)
District 3, Montrose Township, Dane County
(Moorehead School)
District 2, Elba Township, Dodge County
(Austin School)
District 2, La Prairie Township, Rock County
(Gravel Hill School)

Sources

ꙮ

A NUMBER OF PERCEPTIVE BOOKS HAVE BEEN WRITTEN IN RECENT years on the history of urban education, but the education of rural children in the nineteenth and twentieth centuries has been largely ignored by the historians. This essay is designed not only to summarize the original sources on which this study has been based but to suggest to the interested scholar the vast amount of material available for further investigations of rural education and country life.

As the Notes show, much of the material for *The Old Country School* has been drawn from the reports of the state superintendents of public instruction of the ten Midwestern states upon which the study focused. These reports are filled with useful statistics, reprints of educational papers on various subjects, and year-by-year summaries of the status of education in each state. Also included in these volumes are the county superintendents' accounts of the year-by-year progress of the one-room schools over which they had jurisdiction, together with various insights into aspects of rural life. These were invaluable sources for this work.

No less important than the state superintendent reports for the overall picture of the country schools were the Annual Reports of the United States commissioner of education. In these reports are to be found a wealth of statistical information, historical sketches of education in the Midwest, digests of the state laws on education, synopses of professional educators' meetings, reports of various committees appointed to study different aspects of education in the nation, and brief accounts of current contemporary opinion on a wide range of educational topics. Brief summaries of the Midwestern state superintendents' reports are also included in the commissioner of education reports from 1870 to the early 1890s. Besides these annual reports, the Bureau of Education, established in 1867, also published a steady stream of circulars and bulletins, many of which were especially concerned with rural education.

Aside from these easily accessible sources, an enormous amount of material, largely untouched by historians, relating to country schools in the Midwest has been preserved in the state historical societies and state libraries in each Midwestern state and in the area's county historical societies as well. Diaries, journals, memoirs, and the correspondence of teachers and public school officials are included in this material. The correspondence of the Indiana state superintendents, as well as many reports from the county superintendents, for example, is on microfilm in the Indiana State Historical Library in Indianapolis. Chapters 3, 4, and 5 are based primarily on the records of the one-room schools themselves—the minutes of the annual school meetings, school board meetings, and special school meetings. Especially rich collections of these valuable but little-used sources are to be found in the Michigan Historical Collection (MHC) at the University of Michigan in Ann Arbor, in the Wisconsin State Historical Society (WSHS) in Madison, in the Iowa State Historical Society (ISHS) in Iowa City, and in the Minnesota State Archives in St. Paul.

Because the farmers rarely wrote directly or at length about education in their diaries or other papers, their view of their schools, teacher education, the county superintendents, and education generally has been drawn in this study from the records of their one-room schools; the weekly columns of the county newspapers, which were written by farm people; the educators' comments about the farmers' opinions; the minutes of Grange meetings; and the farmers' correspondence with their county superintendents. Especially helpful in this respect were the school records of Kansas, which, with the disappearance of the county superintendents, were turned over to the register of deeds in each county.

A vast amount of periodical literature on the country schools in the Midwest fills many shelves in the libraries of Midwestern universities. Each state had its own educational journals, and numerous national educational journals were published as well. Particularly useful for the chapters on the professionals, teacher training, and the teacher in the classroom in this study were the *Proceedings of the National Education Association* and *Education,* a periodical that began publication in 1881.

Few books were written about the country schools until after the turn of the century when, during the consolidation movement and the movement to keep the young people on the farm, a spate of books on the subject appeared. These were not really histories of the country schools but books that dealt with the problems of rural education and solutions to those problems. O. J. Kern, *Among Country Schools,* and Mabel Carney, *Country Life and the Country School,* published in 1906 and 1912, respectively, are typical of most of those published in the period. These, together with numerous articles published in the popular magazines, such as *World's Work, Outlook,* and the *American Monthly Review of Reviews,* and professional journals such as the *Journal of Rural Education,* were helpful in rounding out the story of the consolidation movement in the Midwest.

Notes

۞

CHAPTER ONE

1. Newton [Ill.] *Mentor-Democrat,* Mar. 27, Apr. 17, and July 24, 1947; See also Byron [Ill.] *Tribune,* Aug. 29, 1947.

2. Adell Krebs, "Saga of a Country School," Manuscript Division, Wisconsin State Historical Society, Madison. Hereafter referred to as WSHS. Neither did educators make a real effort to find out, before they developed their new education, what students had found profitable in their education in their mature years.

3. See, for examples, J. H. Patterson, *Of Me I Sing; or, Me and Education* (Napanee, Ind., 1940), 5–6, 9; Frank T. Clampitt, *Some Incidents in My Life: A Saga of the "Unknown Citizen"* (Ann Arbor, Mich., 1935), 15–16; Herbert Quick, *One Man's Life: An Autobiography* (Indianapolis, 1925), 153–55.

4. Hamlin Garland, *A Son of the Middle Border* (Lincoln: Bison Press, 1979), 95.

5. For one who did complain, however, see Patterson, *Of Me I Sing,* 6–8.

6. Quick, *One Man's Life,* 71–79; Garland, *Son of the Border,* 132–36; Avis Carlson, *Small World—Long Gone: A Family Record of an Era* (Evanston, Ill., 1976), 80–82.

7. Carl Seashore, "The District School," *The Palimpsest* 23 (Mar. 1942): 105; see also Patterson, *Of Me I Sing,* 9.

8. E. E. Byrum, *Life Experiences: Containing Narratives, Incidents, and Experiences in the Life of the Author* (Anderson, Ind., 1928), 34–35.

9. W. H. Morton, "Pioneers Who Believed in Children First," *Journal of the National Education Association* 21 (Dec. 1932): 286.

10. Patterson, *Of Me I Sing,* 6.

11. Quick, *One Man's Life,* 145, 153–54, 223; Carlson, *Small World,* 74, 78; J. W. Crabtree, *What Counted Most* (Lincoln, 1935), 6.

12. Ray Stannard Baker, *Native American* (New York, 1941), 26; Patterson, *Of Me I Sing,* 6; Carlson, *Small World,* 68.

13. Nancy Weberg Younggren, "My Early Memories," 17, Manuscript Division, WSHS; Byrum, *Life Experiences,* 34.

14. Quick, *One Man's Life*, 241; Garland, *Son of the Border*, 209.

15. Crabtree, *What Counted Most*, 7–8.

16. Byrum, *Life Experiences*, 45; Carlson, *Small World*, 68; Baker, *Native American*, 31; Orange Judd Laylander, *The Chronicles of a Contented Man* (Chicago, 1928), 16; Younggren, "Early Memories," 7; Clarence Darrow, *The Story of My Life* (New York, 1932), 10–11.

17. Garland, *Son of the Border*, 109. On the routine of farm life, see Clampitt, *Some Incidents in My Life*, 16–17, 31–33; Younggren, "Early Memories," 7.

18. Laylander, *Chronicles*, 17.

19. Garland, *Son of the Border*, 171. But, on community, see also Clampitt, *Some Incidents in My Life*, 23; Marshall A. Barber, *The Schoolhouse at Prairie View* (Lawrence, Ka., 1953), 79; Quick, *One Man's Life*, 154–55; Crabtree, *What Counted Most*, 5–6; Mary Bradford, *Autobiographical and Historical Reminiscences of Education in Wisconsin, Through Progressive Service from Rural School Teaching to City Superintendent* (Evanston, Wis., 1932), 79–80.

20. Garland, *Son of the Border*, 77–78. See especially Quick, *One Man's Life*, 115–28; W. N. Davis, "Out of the Past," Jackson [Ohio] *Herald*, Jan. 19, 1968, Installment 33; Barber, *Prairie View*, 5–7, 24.

21. A number of writers recalled that their fathers served on the school board. See, for example, Quick, *One Man's Life*, 223–24; Seashore, "The District School," 102; Bradford, *Reminiscences*, 44; Barber, *Prairie View*, 16.

22. Byrum, *Life Experiences*, 35–37; W. N. Davis, "Jackson County Reminiscences," Jackson [Ohio] *Herald*, Aug. 18, 1967, Installment 11; Barber, *Prairie View*, 51–56; Albert Mock, "Christmas in Old District School," Indianapolis *Star*, Dec. 22, 1940.

23. Clampitt, *Some Incidents in My Life*, 15; Carlson, *Small World*, 76–77; Cyrenus Cole, *I Remember, I Remember* (Iowa City, 1936), 87–88; Barber, *Prairie View*, 28–29.

24. Quick, *One Man's Life*, 143–44.

25. Ibid., 100; John Ise, *Sod and Stubble* (Lincoln: Bison Press, 1967), 231–32.

26. Bradford, *Reminiscences*, 64; Quick, *One Man's Life*, 29–30.

27. W. N. Davis, "Jackson County Reminiscences," Jackson [Ohio] *Herald*, Aug. 1, 1967, Installment 9; Laylander, *Chronicles*, 29–30; Crabtree, *What Counted Most*, 12–13.

28. Crabtree, *What Counted Most*, 16–21.

29. Quick, *One Man's Life*, 158–60; Barber, *Prairie View*, 31. See also William McGuffey, *McGuffey's Pictorial Primer*, repr. ed. Johnsburg, N.Y.: Buck Hill Associates, 1965), 28.

30. Darrow, *The Story of My Life*, 18.

31. Seashore, "The District School," 101; Quick, *One Man's Life*, 78–79, 224–25; Patterson, *Of Me I Sing*, 12–13; C. W. Perry, "Autobiography," Joseph R. Funk Papers, Lilly Library, Indiana University, Bloomington; Laylander, *Chronicles*, 31.

32. Barber, *Prairie View*, 30–38. On the study of physiology, see W. N. Davis, "Out of the Past," Jackson [Ohio] *Herald*, Jan. 23, 1968, Installment 34.

33. W. N. Davis, "Jackson County Reminiscences," Installment 9; Larkin L. Beeman, "Reminiscences: Rural Life in and around School District No. 3,

Marion Twp., Boone Co., 1876–1900," Taped Interview, Manuscript Division, Indiana Historical Society, Indianapolis; Bradford, *Reminiscences*, 51. For the new method of teaching reading, see William T. Harris et al., *Appletons' School Readers: The First Reader* (New York, 1884), 1–3. This book was copyrighted in 1878 and by the next year even the revised edition of the McGuffey Readers gave instruction on the new reading methods. See *McGuffey's First Eclectic Reader*, rev. ed. (New York, 1879), ii. See also *McGuffey's Pictorial Eclectic Primer*, 8.

34. Seashore, "The District School," 105; Bradford, *Reminiscences*, 81–88; Carlson, *Small World*, 75–78.

35. W. N. Davis, "Out of the Past," Jackson [Ohio] *Herald*, Feb. 6, 1968, Installment 36; James L. Hill, *My First Years as a Boy* (Andover, Mass., 1927), 183; Barber, *Prairie View*, 36.

36. Barber, *Prairie View*, 41; Bradford, *Reminiscences*, 86.

37. Barber, *Prairie View*, 41.

38. Carlson, *Small World*, 78; Hill, *First Years*, 183–84; Barber, *Prairie View*, 30–31. The arithmetic textbook used by so many of them was Joseph Ray, *Ray's Arithmetic, Third Book: Practical Arithmetic, by Induction and Analysis*, 1,000th ed. improved (New York, 1881). This famous text had first been published in 1857 and provided thousands of country schoolchildren with an excellent grasp of arithmetic. As one man wrote: "It was a great joy to me when I came to the realization that I could solve every problem in Ray's Third Part, including 'The One Hundred Examples.'" See also Laylander, *Chronicles*, 29. For an excellent description of the study of arithmetic in the district schools, see W. N. Davis, "Out of the Past," Jackson [Ohio] *Herald*, Feb. 13, 1968, Installment 37.

39. W. N. Davis, "Jackson County Reminiscences," Jackson [Ohio] *Herald*, Feb. 13, 1968, Installment 10; Bradford, *Reminiscences*, 82–85; Hill, *First Years*, 199–200; Barber, *Prairie View*, 32–33.

40. Barber, *Prairie View*, 50–51.

41. Garland, *Son of the Border*, 113. For the rules on articulation, etc., see especially Lewis B. Monroe, *The Fifth Reader* (Philadelphia, 1871), 13–34; *McGuffey's Fifth Eclectic Reader*, rev. ed. (New York, 1879), 9–33.

42. Laylander, *Chronicles*, 28.

43. Carlson, *Small World*, 78; Garland, *Son of the Border*, 112.

44. Seashore, "The District School," 105. On Seashore, see J. McKeen Cattell, Jacques Cattell, E. E. Ross, eds., *Leaders in Education: A Biographical Directory*, 2d ed. (1941), 903. Seashore did admit, however, that not all children could memorize rapidly, and spoke of individual differences. On Becker, see Burleigh Taylor Wilkins, *Carl Becker: A Biographical Study in American Intellectual History* (Cambridge, 1961), 3, 14. Becker's biographer made the point that Becker had been placed a grade above his age level in the Waterloo School even though "he had come from an inferior rural school," to show Becker's precosity. It says much about the way country schools have been interpreted that the biographer should have made this observation without really entertaining the possibility that Becker might actually have learned more in his country school than students of his age were learning in the Waterloo schools. For another account of what was learned in the country

schools and how successfully students made the transition from a one-room school to a town school, see Mary R. Luster, *The Autobiography of Mary R. Luster* (Springfield, Mo., 1935), 96, 102.

45. Darrow, *The Story of My Life*, 22–23.

46. Barber, *Prairie View*, 48.

47. Laylander, *Chronicles*, 27.

48. W. N. Davis, "Jackson County Reminiscences," Installment 9; Barber, *Prairie View*, 47–48.

49. For a general account of McGuffey, his readers, and his influence, see the excellent chapter in Mark Sullivan, *Our Times: America Finding Herself*, 5 vols. (New York, 1926–35), vol. 2, chap. 2. See also Cole, *I Remember*, 86; Hill, *First Years*, 193–95; W. N. Davis, "Jackson County Reminiscences," Jackson [Ohio] *Herald*, Aug. 25, 1967, Installment 12.

50. Garland, *Son of the Border*, 112.

51. Quick, *One Man's Life*, 163.

52. Garland, *Son of the Border*, 112–13.

53. Quick, *One Man's Life*, 159–163; Barber, *Prairie View*, 46; Byrum, *Life Experiences*, 38. See also O. J. Felton, "Pioneer Life in Jones County," *Iowa Journal of History and Politics* 29 (Apr. 1931): 254.

54. Byrum, *Life Experiences*, 39; Garland, *Son of the Border*, 206–7.

55. Hill, *First Years*, 187; Barber, *Prairie View*, 34–35.

56. Byrum, *Life Experiences*, 34; Laylander, *Chronicles*, 28.

57. Carlson, *Small World*, 78–79; Hill, *First Years*, 184–85.

58. W. N. Davis, "Jackson County Reminiscences," Installment 10.

59. Sara Gillespie Huftalen, "School Days of the Seventies," *The Palimpsest* 27 (Apr. 1947): 127–28; Barber, *Prairie View*, 14–20; Beeman, "Reminiscences"; Younggren, "Early Memories," 18. One unique sport was chasing flying squirrels. See W. N. Davis, "Jackson County Reminiscences," Jackson [Ohio] *Herald*, July 28, 1967, Installment 8.

60. Huftalen, "School Days," 127; Garland, *Son of the Border*, 96–97; Barber, *Prairie View*, 14; Younggren, "Early Memories," 18.

61. Younggren, "Early Memories," 18; Garland, *Son of the Border*, 112; Clampitt, *Some Incidents in My Life*, 22; Barber, *Prairie View*, 17–18.

62. Garland, *Son of the Border*, 111. See also Patterson, *Of Me I Sing*, 9–10; Barber, *Prairie View*, 4–5.

63. Patterson, *Of Me I Sing*, 10.

64. Huftalen, "School Days," 126; Hill, *First Years*, 189.

65. Laylander, *Chronicles*, 33.

66. Barber, *Prairie View*, 20–21; W. N. Davis, "Out of the Past," Installment 33. See also Carlson, *Small World*, 85; Quick, *One Man's Life*, 143–46.

67. Barber, *Prairie View*, 33.

68. Patterson, *Of Me I Sing*, 6. Patterson also felt the pangs of discrimination because he was Irish in a German neighborhood. Carlson, *Small World*, 79.

69. Quick, *One Man's Life*, 100; Carlson, *Small World*, 84.

70. Seashore, "The District School," 101.

71. Quick, *One Man's Life*, 106.

72. Carlson, *Small World*, 75; Patterson, *Of Me I Sing*, 7; Laylander, *Chronicles*, 33; Younggren, "Early Memories," 17.

73. Bradford, *Reminiscences*, 86.

74. Quick, *One Man's Life,* 161. The method by which reading was taught was apparently not the principal deciding factor in how well one learned to read. Quick and others mastered the art very quickly; others had difficulty. See Quick, *One Man's Life,* 99–100; Bradford, *Reminiscences,* 50–51; Clampitt, *Some Incidents in My Life,* 14.

CHAPTER TWO

1. *Historical Statistics of the United States: Colonial Times to 1970,* pt. 1 (Washington, 1975), 22; James Bryce, *The American Commonwealth,* 2 vols. (New York, 1897), 2:311. North and South Dakota, although included in the North Central division, are omitted from this study because they did not become states until 1889.

2. For the composition of the Midwestern population, see Henry Clyde Hubbart, *The Older Middle West, 1840–1880: Its Social, Economic and Political Life and Sectional Tendencies before, during, and after the Civil War,* reissue (New York, 1963), 3–8; John Murray, ed., *The Heritage of the Middle West* (Norman, 1958), 3–26, 121–51. See also Bryce, *Commonwealth,* 2:309–11.

3. *Report of the Commissioner of Education for 1886–87* (Washington, 1888), 54.

4. Henry Steele Commager, ed., *Documents of American History,* 2 vols., 6th ed. (New York, 1958), 1:128–32. For the various state constitutions, see Francis Newton Thorpe, ed., *The Federal and State Constitutions, Colonial Charters and Other Organic Laws of the States, Territories, and Colonies, Now or Heretofore Forming the United States of America,* 7 vols. (Washington, 1909).

5. Timothy Flint, *The History and Geography of the Mississippi Valley ...,* 2 vols., 2d ed. (Cincinnati, 1832), 1:336; U. S. Grant, *Personal Memoirs,* 2 vols. (New York, 1885), 1:24–25.

6. Benjamin Thomas, *Abraham Lincoln* (New York, 1952), 12.

7. Carlyle Buley, *The Old Northwest,* 2 vols. (Bloomington, 1962), 2:349, 362; W. L. Pillsbury, "Early Education in Illinois," *Sixteenth Biennial Report of the Superintendent of Public Instruction of the State of Illinois, 1884–86* (Springfield, 1886), cvii; *Fifty-Fourth Annual Report of the Public Schools of the State of Missouri for the School Year Ending June 30, 1903* (Jefferson City, n.d.), 99; *Forty-Fourth Annual Report of the Superintendent of Public Instruction of the State of Michigan, with Accompanying Documents, for 1880* (Lansing, 1881), 310, 312.

8. Theodore Clark Smith, *The Life and Letters of James Abram Garfield,* 2 vols. (New Haven, 1925), 1:14–15; *First Annual Report of the Association for the Promotion of Schools in Indiana, 1833,* Pamphlets: Education, vol. 1, no. 3, Indiana State Historical Library, Indianapolis, 6.

9. Commager, *Documents,* 123–24; Buley, *The Old Northwest,* 2:352–54. See also B. A. Hinsdale, "Documents Illustrative of American Educational History," *Report of the Commissioner of Education for 1893,* 2 vols. (Washington, 1895), 1270–71.

10. On the development of school funds, see A. D. Mayo, "Original Establishment of State School Funds," *Report of the Commissioner of Education for 1895,* 2 vols. (Washington, 1896), 1505–11; *An Address in Relation to Free Common Schools by a Committee of the State Education Convention, May 26, 1847,*

Pamphlets: Education, Indiana State Historical Library, Indianapolis, 1847, 6.

11. Rate Bill, Oct. 25, 1850, District 1, Pennfield Twp., Calhoun Co., Mich., School Records, Michigan Historical Collection, University of Michigan, Ann Arbor, Michigan. Hereinafter referred to as MHC.

12. Ibid., and Anson DePuy Van Buren, *Pioneer Collections: Reports of the Pioneer Society of the State of Michigan, Together With Reports of County, Town, and District Pioneer Societies* (Lansing, 1880), xiv, 287.

13. Pillsbury, "Early Education in Illinois," cvii; Mary Hinsdale, "A Legislative History of the Public School System of the State of Ohio," *Report of the Commissioner of Education for 1901,* 2 vols. (Washington, 1902), 140–41.

14. See A. D. Mayo, "Education in the Northwest during the First Half Century of the Republic," in *Report of the Commissioner, 1895,* 2:1535–39, 1544–48, for a general account of what happened in the area in the early period. See also *Fifty-Fourth Report, Missouri, 1903,* 99–101.

15. *First Report of the Association, Indiana, 1833,* 5; Pillsbury, "Early Education in Illinois," cviii; William T. Coggeshall, "History of the Common Schools in the State of Ohio," *American Journal of Education 6* (Mar. 1859): 86–87.

16. Maximilian of Wiede, *Travels in the Interior of North America,* in *Western Travels,* ed. Reuben Gold Thwaites, 32 vols. (Cleveland, 1904–7), 22:179; Schoolcraft quoted in Walter Williams and Floyd Calvin Shoemaker, *Missouri: Mother of the West,* 5 vols. (Chicago, 1930), 1:298.

17. Newton Edwards, *The School in the American Social Order: The Dynamics of Education* (New York, 1947), 298–319. For the great migration west, see Francis S. Philbrick, *The Rise of the West* (New York, 1965), 303–19.

18. As quoted in Louis Filler, ed., *Horace Mann on the Crisis in Education* (Yellow Springs, Ohio, 1965), 18.

19. B. A. Hinsdale, "The Western Literary Institute and College of Professional Teachers," in *Report of the Commissioner of Education for 1899,* 2 vols. (Washington, 1900), 1:704–45, suggests the cosmopolitan character of the reformers. Individual biographical studies of the leaders in this organization indicate the predominance among them of New England backgrounds.

20. Ibid. For a contemporary description of the best people, see Fredricka Bremer, *Letters of Fredricka Bremer,* ed. Adolph B. Benson (London, 1924), 249.

21. See, for example, *First Report of the Association, Indiana,* 13–17; Francis W. Shearman, ed., *System of Public Instruction and Primary School Law of Michigan . . .* (Lansing, 1852), 226.

22. Charles Allen Dinsmore, "Lyman Beecher," *DAB;* Lyman Beecher, *Plea for the West* (Cincinnati, 1835), 29–30. For an arresting essay on the spirit of the age, see John Higham, *From Boundlessness to Consolidation: The Transformation of American Culture, 1848–1860* (Ann Arbor, 1969), especially pp. 8–15.

23. Edward Dwight Eaton, "Calvin Ellis Stowe," *DAB;* Richard D. Mosier, *Making the American Mind: Social and Moral Ideas in the McGuffey Readers* (New York, 1965), 17–26.

24. Hinsdale, "The Western Literary Institute," 740.

25. A. D. Mayo, "The Development of the Common School in the Western States from 1830 to 1865," in *Report of the Commissioner, 1899,* 1:363; *First*

Report of the Association, Indiana, 5–6; Hinsdale, "The Western Literary Institute," 740; *Union Agriculturist and Western Prairie Farmer* 2 (Nov. 1842), hereinafter cited as *Prairie Farmer.*

26. *Statistical View of the United States . . . Being a Compendium of the Seventh Census* (Washington, 1854), 347. Cincinnati, the largest of the Midwestern cities, had a population of 115,435; for the Midwestern population, see *Historical Statistics of the United States,* 22.

27. *Prairie Farmer* 2 (Nov. 1842): 92; Russell Anderson, "John Wright," *DAB.*

28. James Albert Woodburn, *The Common School System of Indiana,* Bulletin No. 10 (Washington: Bureau of Education, 1891), 50–51; for Caleb Mills, see *The National Cyclopedia of American Biography.*

29. *Congressional Globe,* 27 Cong., 1 Sess., 105 (June 30, 1841); James H. Lanman, "Agricultural Commerce of the United States," *Hunt's Merchants' Magazine* 5 (Sept. 1841): 203–4. For the perception of the Midwestern farmer in the American mind, see Henry Nash Smith, *Virgin Land* (Cambridge, 1950), 123–44.

30. The literature on the character of the pioneer Midwestern farmer is abundant and contradictory. For first-hand accounts of their independence and other characteristics, see James Hall, *Letters from the West* (Gainesville: Scholars' Facsimile Reprints, 1967), 115–31; James H. Lanman, "The Progress of the Northwest," *Hunt's Merchants' Magazine* 3 (July 1840): 37–39; "The Mixed Up Farmer," *Prairie Farmer* 10 (Mar. 1849): 89. For a survey of the Midwestern character see Francis S. Philbrick, *The Rise of the Middle West* (New York, 1965), chap. 14.

31. Bryce, *Commonwealth,* 1:294.

32. On the farmer's antiintellectualism as it related to "book-farming" and education, see Richard Hofstadter, *Anti-Intellectualism in American Life* (New York: Vintage, 1963), 272–82; Earl W. Hoyter, *The Troubled Farmer, 1850–1900: Rural Adjustment to Industrialism* (De Kalb, 1968), 3–11; Merle Curti, *The Growth of American Thought* (New York, 1943), 265–70.

33. The farmers' apparent indifference to education was pointed out in numerous publications. See "Educational Department," *Prairie Farmer* 2 (Mar. 1842): 32, and 4 (June 1844): 130; Mayo, "Development of the Common School, 1830–1865," 362–63.

34. Woodburn, *The Common School System of Indiana,* 64. An interesting quarrel between the professor and the practical farmer may be followed in *Prairie Farmer* 8 (Oct. 1843): 305ff.

35. The Southerner's attitude toward free public education can be seen in Pillsbury, "Early Education in Illinois," cxxxii; Edward Eggleston, *The Hoosier Schoolmaster* (New York: Hill and Wang 1957), 22. See Timothy Flint, *Recollections of the Last Ten Years* (New York: DeCapo, 1968), 32–37, for an account of the Southerner's dislike of the Yankee.

36. Paul H. Johnstone, "Old Ideals Versus New Ideas," *Agricultural Yearbook, 1940* (Washington, 1940), 121 and 136–37. For the farmer's interest in education on the Middle Border, see Buley, *The Old Northwest,* 2:329.

37. *Prairie Farmer* 3 (July 1843): 164–65, shows how one mother taught her own children.

38. The arguments both for and against free public schools as they appeared to farmers and others in Michigan in 1850 can be found in Shearman, *System of Public Instruction,* 212–40.

39. *Prairie Farmer* 5 (June 1845): 148.

40. For the relationship between taxes and school laws in Ohio, see Mary Hinsdale, "Legislative History of Ohio," 136.

41. See *Prairie Farmer* 3 (Oct. 1843): 232–33, on some problems of taxation.

42. Woodburn, *The Common School System,* 51–54; *Prairie Farmer* 4 (Sept. 1844): 211, and 5 (June 1845): 137; Mayo, "Development of the Common School, 1830–1865," 362.

43. Mary Hinsdale, "Legislative History of Ohio," 144; *Forty-Fourth Annual Report, Michigan,* 322; Pillsbury, "Early Education in Illinois," cxlvii–viii and cxc.

44. Mary Hinsdale, "Legislative History of Ohio," 147–348; W. C. Whiford, *Early History of Education in Wisconsin,* in *Report and Collections of the State Historical Society of Wisconsin,* ed. Lyman C. Draper, 20 vols. (1903–15), 5:342–43; Mayo, "Development of the Common School, 1830–1865," 375, 439–40; Pillsbury, "Early Education in Illinois," cxvii; Clarence Ray Aurner, *History of Education in Iowa,* 2 vols. (Iowa City, 1914), 50.

45. Williams and Shoemaker, *Missouri,* 2:523; *Forty-Fourth Annual Report, Michigan,* 320.

CHAPTER THREE

1. District Boundary Records, 1850–1900, La Prairie Twp., Rock Co., Wis., Rock County Historical Society, Janesville, Wis. Hereinafter cited as RCHS.

2. See *Combination Atlas Map of Rock County, Wisconsin* (Chicago, 1873), 35; Ruth Hughes, "Memoirs," Manuscript, RCHS.

3. Orrin Guernsey and Josiah Willard, eds., *History of Rock County and Transactions of the Rock County Agricultural Society and Mechanics Institute* (Janesville, Wis., 1856), 94.

4. For an account of the origin of the district system, see Wellford Addis, "The Social Unit in the Public School Systems of the United States," *Report of the Commissioner of Education for 1895,* 2 vols. (Washington, 1896), 2:1457–67.

5. Ibid., 1458.

6. Ibid., 1460. See also Lawrence Cremins, *The American Common School* (New York, 1951), 133–35.

7. Mary Hinsdale, "Legislative History of Ohio," 1:132. There were some ninety thousand rural schoolhouses in the ten Midwestern states in 1899. See *Report of the Commissioner of Education for 1899,* 2 vols. (Washington, 1900), 1:lxxx.

8. Miscellaneous Papers, Joint District 1, Koshkonong Twp., Jefferson County, Wis., School Records, WSHS, Madison. For the location of the Tri-County School, see *Illustrated Atlas of Jefferson County, Wisconsin, Containing Maps of Every Township in the County with Village and City Plats* (Chicago, 1887), 87. For some general rules on establishing a district, see, for example, *Third Annual Report of the State Superintendent of Public Instruction, to the Governor of Nebraska for the Year Ending Dec. 31st, 1871* (Des Moines, Ia., 1872), 23–24.

9. As quoted in Bryce, *American Commonwealth,* 1:603.

10. See, for example, *Illustrated Atlas of Jefferson County, 1887.*

11. Within recent years much has been written on the role of community in American life, but the school district community has been neglected. In his appraisal of the speculative farmer on the Great Plains, Richard Hofstadter, *The Age of Reform* (New York, 1955), overlooked the school district community when he wrote that "the frequent movements, the absence of village life, deprived the farmer and his family of the advantages of community" (pp. 45–46). Merle Curti, *The Making of an American Community: A Case Study of Democracy in a Frontier County* (Stanford, Calif., 1959), also failed to see the importance of the country-school district and slighted its role as a training ground for democracy (p. 382). For other important studies of community, see Park Dixon Goist, *From Main Street to State Street: Town, City, and Community in America* (New York, 1977); R. Jackson Wilson, *In Quest of Community: Social Philosophy in the United States, 1860–1920* (New York, 1968); Jean B. Quandt, *From the Small Town to the Great Community: Social Thought of the Progressive Intellectuals* (New Brunswick, N.J., 1970); Thomas Bender, *Community and Social Change in America* (New Brunswick, N.J., 1978).

12. Nebraska laws governing a school district are typical of most Midwestern states. See *The School Laws of Nebraska, As Amended in 1875, with Forms for the Use of School Officers* (Omaha, 1875).

13. Ibid. 5–12, 24ff. See also *The General School Laws of Michigan* (Lansing, 1901), 14–15. The Indiana school laws did not follow this pattern, and the laws of Ohio, Iowa, Illinois, and Missouri varied somewhat from the description given here. See Addis, "The Social Unit in the Public School Systems" 1465–66.

14. The dates of the annual school meetings were changed by the state legislatures from time to time, but see *School Laws of Nebraska, 1875,* 9; *The Illinois School Law, 1889–1901: An Act to Establish and Maintain a System of Free Schools, Approved May 21, 1889* (Springfield, Ill., 1901), 40; *The General School Laws of Michigan,* 11; *Handbook for Rural School Officers: Comprising the Revised Laws for Minnesota to 1905, And All Subsequent Laws and Amendments, Together with Annotations of Decisions of the Supreme Court, and Opinions of the Attorney General* (Minneapolis, 1910), 19–20.

15. Minutes of the Annual Meeting, Sept. 8, 1877, District 3, Blooming Grove Twp., Dane Co., Wis., School Records, WSHS; Minutes of the Annual Meeting, Sept. 3, 1883, District 5, Woodstock Twp., Lenawee Co., Mich., School Records, in possession of Merton Dillon, Jerome, Mich.

16. Minutes of the Annual Meeting, Nov. 1, 1881, District 3, Blooming Grove Twp.

17. Minutes of the Annual Meeting, July 5, 1897, Joint District 1, Koshkonong Twp., Wis., School Records, WSHS.

18. Minutes of the Annual Meeting, Apr. 5, 1886, District 40, Saunders Co., School Records, Nebraska State Historical Society, Lincoln. Hereinafter referred to as NSHS.

19. Minutes of the Annual Meeting, Sept. 3, 1883, District 5, Woodstock Twp.

20. District Treasurer's Reports, Jan. 5, 1882, July 20, 1885, July 6, 1886, July 1, 1889, and Minutes of the Annual Meeting, July 5, 1892, District 3, Montrose Twp., Dane Co., Wis., School Records, WSHS. For the location of

the school, see *Plat Book of Dane County, Wisconsin* (Chicago, 1890), 55.

21. Minutes of the Annual Meetings, Aug. 21, 1863, Sept. 28, 1863, Sept. 2, 1878, Sept. 1, 1879, Nov. 1, 1881, Aug. 15, 1884, July 18, 1885, District 3, Blooming Grove Twp. For the location of the school, see *Plat Book of Dane County, Wisconsin: Drawn from Actual Surveys and County Records* (Minneapolis, 1890). One reason for the inability to secure a quorum for the meetings in District 3 may be the great influx of immigrants into the district. When the district was formed in 1851, the names of those directing school affairs were all Anglo-Saxon. But during the 1850s and '60s, large numbers of immigrants moved into the area, and the votes on building the schoolhouse reflected the change. Of the five persons who voted for the new building, all were men with apparently Anglo-Saxon names; the ten votes against the proposition were cast by men with Irish, German, or Norwegian names. See Minutes of the Special Meeting, Aug. 21, 1863, Blooming Grove Twp. On the influx of immigrants into the district, see Michael P. Conzen, *Frontier Farming in an Urban Shadow: The Influence of Madison's Proximity on the Agricultural Development of Blooming Grove, Wisconsin* (Madison, 1971), 52–53.

22. Minutes of a Special Meeting, Jan. 17, 1870, and Minutes of Annual Meetings, 1870–90, District 1, Pennfield Twp., Calhoun Co., Mich., School Records, MHC, Ann Arbor. See also *Atlas of Calhoun County* (Chicago, 1873), Pennfield Twp., for the location of the school.

23. Minutes of the Annual Meeting, July 23, 1893, District 37, Osborne Co., Ka., School Records, Kansas State Historical Society, Topeka. Hereinafter referred to as KSHS.

24. The records of District 1, Pennfield Twp., Calhoun Co., Mich., furnish a good example.

25. Anson Buttles, Diaries, 1856–1906, Sept. 27, 1858, Manuscript Division, WSHS; Minutes of the Annual Meeting, June 5, 1882, District 3, Blooming Grove Twp.; *School Laws of Nebraska, 1875*, 13.

26. Minutes of the Annual Meeting, July 6, 1891, District 4, La Prairie Twp., Rock Co., Wis., School Records, RCHS; Minutes of the Annual Meeting, Sept. 2, 1889, Fractional District 1, Tecumseh Twp., Lenawee Co., Mich., School Records, MHC.

27. Minutes of the Annual Meeting, Oct. 1, 1875, District 3, Blooming Grove Twp.; Minutes of the Annual Meeting, Sept. 26, 1870, Joint District 9, Dunn Twp., Dane Co., Wis., School Records, WSHS.

28. Minutes of the Annual Meetings, Apr. 7, 1879, District 40, Saunders Co.

29. Minutes of the Annual Meetings, Sept. 7, 1885, to Sept. 1, 1890, District 11, Pennfield Twp. For Joshua Webb, see *Biographical Review of Calhoun County, Michigan, Containing Historical, Biographical, and Genealogical Sketches of Many of the Pioneer Citizens of Today and Also the Past* (Chicago, 1904), 670–71.

30. Minutes of the Annual Meeting, Sept. 2, 1889, District 11, Pennfield Twp.

31. Minutes of the Annual Meeting, Sept. 20, 1872, Joint District 13, Lancaster Twp., Grant Co., Wis., School Records, WSHS.

32. Petition, July 31, 1884, and Minutes of a Special Meeting, July 31, 1884, District 40, Saunders Co.

33. Treasurer's Reports, 1892–1900, District 2, La Prairie Twp.

34. *Plat Book of Dodge County, Wisconsin* (Minneapolis, 1890), 44; Columbus [Wis.] *Democrat,* July 9, 1886.

35. Minutes of the Annual Meetings, July 5, 1886, and July 5, 1887, District 2, Elba Twp., Dodge Co., Wis., School Records, WSHS.

36. Minutes of the Annual Meetings, Sept. 1, 1884, Sept. 7, 1885, Sept. 6, 1886, Minutes of a Special Meeting, Oct. 5, 1884, Report of the District Board, Sept. 10, 1887, District 5, Woodstock Twp. For the location of this school, see Atlas, Lenawee County, Mich. (Chicago, 1893), Woodstock Twp.

37. Adrian [Mich.] *Weekly Times and Expositor,* Sept. 11, 1891; Minutes of the Annual Meeting, Sept. 7, 1891, District 5, Woodstock Twp.

38. Minutes of the Annual Meetings, July 5, 1910, and June 7, 1915, District 3, Albion Twp., Dane Co., Wis., School Records, WSHS.

39. State of Indiana, Department of Public Education, *Nineteenth Biennial Report of the State Superintendent, for the School Years Ending July 31, 1897, and July 31, 1898* (Indianapolis, 1898), 207.

CHAPTER FOUR

1. *Wisconsin State Journal,* Sept. 17, 1890.

2. Ibid.

3. Vachel Lindsay, *Collected Poems,* rev. ed. (New York, 1955), 74.

4. State of Indiana, Department of Public Education, *Nineteenth Biennial Report of the State Superintendent, for the School Years Ending July 31, 1897, and July 31, 1898,* 26.

5. *Fourteenth Annual Report of the Department of Public Instruction of the State of Kansas, 1874* (Topeka, 1874), 39; *Twenty-Eighth Report of the Superintendent of Public Instruction of the State of Indiana, Being the Eleventh Biennial Report and for the Years Ending August 31, 1881, and August 31, 1882* (Indianapolis, 1882), 114–15; and *Tenth Annual Report of the State Superintendent of Public Instruction to the Governor of Nebraska for the Year Ending December 31, 1878* (Lincoln, 1878), 11–14.

6. *Twenty-Fourth Report of the Superintendent of Public Instruction of the State of Indiana, Being the Eighth Biennial Report, and for the Years Ending August 31, 1875, and August 31, 1876* (Indianapolis, 1876), 95.

7. Minutes of the Annual Meeting, Oct. 30, 1869, and Treasurer's Report, 1869, Joint District 9, Dunn Township.

8. Notice of a Special Meeting, July 6, 1880, District 2, Elba Twp.

9. Minutes of Special Meetings, Aug. 21, 1863, Apr. 13, 1868, and Apr. 17, 1869, District 3, Blooming Grove Twp.; *History of Dane County, Wisconsin: Containing an Account of Its Settlement, Growth* . . . (Chicago, 1890), 1078–79.

10. Minutes of a Special Meeting, Jan. 3, 1870, District 1, Pennfield Twp.

11. Minutes of Special Meetings, Jan. 16, 1870, and Jan. 17, 1870, District 1, Pennfield Twp.

12. *Fourth Annual Report of the State Superintendent of Public Instruction to the Governor of Nebraska for the Year Ending December 31, 1872* (Des Moines, 1872), 8.

13. Minutes of Special Meetings, Apr. 16, 1873, May 31, 1875, and May 12, 1877, Minutes of the Annual Meeting, Apr. 5, 1875, District 40, Saunders Co.

14. Minutes of Special Meetings, July 15, Sept. 3, and Sept. 16, 1889, Notice

of Special Meeting, Sept. 7, 1889, District 2, Elba Twp.; Columbus (Wis.) *Republican,* July 20, 1889; Columbus (Wis.) *Democrat,* June 21, 1889. For some reasons for improving the schoolhouse, see Marion Kirkpatrick, *The Rural School from Within* (Philadelphia, 1917), 81–83.

15. Minutes of the Annual Meetings, Sept. 6, 1880, and Sept. 9, 1882, Minutes of a Special Meeting, Sept. 14, 1880, District 5, Woodstock Twp.

16. Minutes of the Annual Meetings, Aug. 31, 1875, Aug. 25, 1879, Aug. 31, 1880, and Aug. 31, 1881, Joint District 1, Koshkonong Twp.

17. Minutes of a Special Meeting, Dec. 17, 1883, District 5, Woodstock Twp.

18. Ibid.

19. Receipt, July 9, 1873, District 40, Saunders Co.; Proceedings of the District Board, Nov. 11, 1889, District 2, Elba Twp.; Accounts presented to the District Board, Dec. 10, 1884, District 5, Woodstock Twp.

20. James Johonnot, *School Houses: Architectural Design* (New York, 1871). Johonnot's book first appeared in 1858. For an example of a state superintendent's report on architecture, see *First Annual Report of the State Superintendent of Public Instruction to the Legislature of Minnesota, 1861* (St. Paul, 1861), 19–38. See also T. M. Clark, *Rural School Architecture with Illustrations,* Circular of Information No. 4 (Washington: Bureau of Education, 1880), 7–106.

21. Minutes of a Special Meeting, Dec. 17, 1883, District 5, Woodstock Twp.; Specifications for Schoolhouse, n.d., Subdistrict 1, Scott Twp., Henry Co., Ia., School Records, Iowa State Historical Society. Hereinafter referred to as ISHS.

22. Minutes of a Special Meeting, Mar. 4, 1884, Woodstock Twp. See also Minutes of a Special Meeting, May 10, 1873, District 40, Saunders Co.

23. Specifications for Schoolhouse, Subdistrict 1, Scott Twp.; Treasurer's Reports, July 31 to Dec. 10, 1884, District 5, Woodstock Twp.; Osborne County [Ka.] *Farmer,* May 3 and June 7, 1883; Minutes of the Annual Meeting, Aug. 26, 1878, District 3, Montrose Twp.

24. Contract for Building Schoolhouse, Mar. 1, 1884, Subdistrict 1, Scott Twp. District 40, Saunders Co., employed a contractor from Lincoln to build its school. See Building Contract, May 24, 1873, and "Brief History of District 40," School Records, NSHS.

25. Clark, *Rural Architecture,* 17–18.

26. *Biennial Report of the State Superintendent of the State of Wisconsin for the Two Years Ending June 30, 1888* (Madison, 1888), 161; *Sixteenth Biennial Report of the Superintendent of Public Instruction of the State of Illinois, July 1, 1884–June 30, 1886* (Springfield, 1886), lxv.

27. Clark, *Rural Architecture,* 33.

28. Specifications for Schoolhouse, Subdistrict 1, Scott Twp.

29. Clark, *Rural Architecture,* 20. For the Greek Revival in the Midwest, see Talbot Hamlin, *The Greek Revival Architecture in America: Being an Account of Important Trends in American Architecture and American Life prior to the War between the States* (New York: Dover, 1964).

30. Rural schoolchildren were sometimes frightened, however, for they had rarely seen a strange face. See Herbert Quick, *One Man's Life,* 106.

31. For the quote on the Populist meeting, see Osborne County [Ka.] *Farmer,* Oct. 4, 1894. Ruth Hughes, Janesville, Wis., recalled the Christmas

play in the early 1900s. In Saunders Co., Nebr., in what was once District 40, a schoolhouse, now two rooms, is still used as the precinct's polling place. Interview with Francis Beaman, summer 1977. See also Adair County [Ia.] *Reporter,* June 24, 1886, for voting at the schoolhouse. The Osborne Co. *Farmer,* Feb. 27, 1879, has one of thousands of notices about prayer meetings and church to be held in the schoolhouse.

32. Marshall [Mich.] *Statesman,* Feb. 12, 1886.

33. See, for example, Minutes of the Annual Meeting, Oct. 5, 1872, District 36, Olmstead Co., Minn., School Records, Olmstead County Historical Society, Rochester, Minn. Hereinafter referred to as OCHS.

34. W. N. Davis, "Jackson County Reminiscences," Installment 8; Minutes of the Annual Meeting, Aug. 30, 1875, Joint District 9, Dunn Twp.

35. *Report of the Superintendent, Ill., 1884–86,* lxv. See also Ise, *Sod and Stubble,* 121.

36. Minutes of the Annual Meeting, July 5, 1893, District 2, Elba Twp.; Minutes of the Annual Meetings, July 1, 1907, and July 6, 1909, Joint District 9, Dunn Twp.

37. State of Indiana, Department of Public Education, *Nineteenth Biennial Report of the State Superintendent of Public Instruction for the School Years Ending July 31, 1897, and July 31, 1898* (Indianapolis, 1898), 719; State of Indiana, Department of Public Education, *Twentieth Report of the State Superintendent of Public Instruction for the School Years Ending July 31, 1899, and July 31, 1900* (Indianapolis, 1901), 156.

38. Nat Brandt, "To the Flag," *American Heritage* 22 (June 1971): 73; Minutes of the Annual Meeting, July 6, 1896, District 3, Montrose Twp.; Minutes of the Annual Meeting, July 1, 1895, Joint District 9, Dunn Twp.

39. *Sixty-First Annual Report of the Superintendent of Public Instruction of the State of Michigan, with Accompanying Documents, for the Year 1897* (Lansing, 1898), 52.

40. *Report of the Committee of Twelve on Rural Schools,* Bulletin of Information No. 3. Issued by J. Q. Emery, State Superintendent of Public Instruction, Wisconsin (Madison, 1898), 74, an opinion borrowed from the *Massachusetts State Report, 1895;* and Eldorado [Ka.] *Educational Advance,* Apr. 1, 1893.

41. Miscellaneous Papers, District 1, Pennfield Twp.; Minutes of the Annual Meeting, June 1, 1914, Joint District 9, Dunn Twp.; Montgomery Ward & Co., *Catalogue and Buyers' Guide,* no. 57, Spring and Summer *1895* (New York: Dover Publications, 1969), 551.

42. Box social report, Apr. 12, 1918, Joint District 1, Koshkonong Twp.

43. *Annual Report of the Superintendent of Public Instruction of the State of Wisconsin, for the School Year Ending August 31, 1878* (Madison, 1879), 32.

44. Minutes of the Annual Meetings, Sept. 9, 1882, Sept. 7, 1896, and Sept. n.d., 1897, and Catalogue of Books in District Library, District 5, Woodstock Twp.

45. Minutes of the Annual Meeting, July 3, 1905, Joint District 9, Dunn Twp.; District Librarian's Book, District 9, Fulton Twp., Rock County, Wis., School Records, RCHS.

CHAPTER FIVE

1. Minutes of the Annual Meeting, July 27, 1893, District 37, Osborne Co.; Osborne County [Ka.] *Farmer,* July 27, 1893; Downs [Ka.] *Times,* July 27, and Aug. 3, 1893.

2. Minutes of the Annual Meeting, July 27, 1893, District 37, Osborne Co.

3. Ibid., and Downs [Ka.] *Times,* July 27, 1893.

4. See, for examples, C. G. Schulz, ed., *Handbook for Rural School Officers: Comprising the Revised Laws of Minnesota to 1905, and All Subsequent Laws and Amendments, Together with Annotation of Decisions of the Supreme Court, and Opinions of the Attorney General* (Minneapolis, 1910), 24–38; *The Illinois School Laws, 1889–1901; An Act to Establish and Maintain a System of Free Schools, Approved May 21, 1889* (Springfield, 1901), 39–47; Fred M. Warner, ed., *The General School Laws of Michigan* (Lansing, 1901), 15–33.

5. For William Hicks, see "Ephraim H. Hicks," *Portrait Biographical Album of Calhoun County, Michigan: Containing Full Page Portraits and Biographical Sketches of Prominent and Representative Citizens of the County Together with Portraits and Biographies of All Presidents of the United States and Governors of the State* (Chicago, 1891), 267. For Lewis Sanford, see *Portrait and Biographical Album of Lenawee County, Michigan* (Chicago, 1888), 1129. See also Ise, *Sod and Stubble,* 10–11. For the opinion, often given, that the character of the school depends upon the character of the school officers, see *Annual Report of the State Superintendent of Wisconsin, for the School Year Ending August 31, 1880* (Madison, 1881), 23. For leadership in pioneer communities, see Stanley Elkins and Eric McKitrick, "A Meaning for Turner's Frontier: Democracy in the Old Northwest," *Political Science Quarterly* 69 (Sept. 1954): 321–53.

6. See "Ephraim H. Hicks," 267, and *Combination Atlas of Rock County, Wisconsin* (Chicago, 1873), 18, for examples.

7. Adrian [Mich.] *Weekly Times and Expositor,* Jan. 22, 1886.

8. Register of District School, 1866–1902, District 5, Woodstock Twp.; Minutes of the Annual Meetings, 1870 to 1900, District 3, Montrose Twp. That school board members were chosen again and again meant, of course, that many farmers remained in the community in which they had pioneered throughout the rest of their lives, which is in contrast to the picture one historian drew of restless, capitalistic, speculative farmers who moved rapidly across the frontier, never developed community life, and had no real agrarian values. See Hofstadter, *The Age of Reform,* 42–46. For the studies on the persistence rates of pioneer farmers, see Allan Bogue, *From Prairie to Corn Belt: Farming on the Illinois and Iowa Prairies in the Nineteenth Century* (Chicago, 1963), 25–28, and Merle Curti, *The Making of An American Community: A Case Study of Democracy in a Frontier County,* 65–67.

9. Minutes of the Annual Meeting, Sept. 7, 1885, District 1, Pennfield Twp.; "Ephraim Hicks," 267.

10. J. M. McKinzie, "Work to Be Done at the Annual District School Meeting," n.d., in District 40, Saunders Co., School Records, NSHS.

11. C. S. Taylor to J. R. Bickerdyke, July 31, 1890, Correspondence of the County Superintendent, Russell Co., Ka., School Records, Register of Deeds Office, Russell, Ka.

12. On the Grange as a training ground for school board members, see

Journal of Proceedings: Twentieth Session of the Illinois State Grange, Patrons of Husbandry . . . , Dec. 1891 (Peoria, n.d.), 69. For the view that the farmers did not choose their best men for their school boards, see *Report of the Superintendent, Wisconsin, 1880*, 23.

13. Minutes of the Annual Meeting, Sept. 5, 1887, Fractional District 1, Tecumseh Twp.

14. For an unfriendly description of the school directors, see *Tenth Biennial Report of the Superintendent of Public Instruction of the State of Illinois, 1873–1874* (Springfield, 1874), 64–65. The quarrels among the school board members and the dismissal of one of them may be followed in the Adrian [Mich.] *Weekly Times and Expositor,* Sept. 9, Oct. 28, Dec. 9, 1887, and Jan. 20, 1888, in the Thurber column. For confusion on the appointment of a teacher, see Marshall [Mich.] *Statesman,* Mar. 10, 1886.

15. Marshall [Mich.] *Statesman,* Apr. 16, 1886.

16. J. M. McKinzie, "Work to Be done at the Annual School Meeting," 1.

17. *Biennial Report of the State Superintendent of Wisconsin, for the Two Years Ending June 30, 1888* (Madison, 1888), 20–21; Marion Kirkpatrick, *The Rural School from Within* (Philadelphia, 1917), 72–73.

18. Minutes of the Annual Meeting, Sept. 1, 1890, District 1, Pennfield Twp.; Minutes of the Annual Meetings, Sept. 29, 1873, Sept. 7, 1874, and Aug. 26, 1875, Joint District 1, Koshkonong Twp.

19. See, for example, *The General School Laws of Michigan,* 24.

20. Annual School Report for 1890, District 62, and Annual School Report for 1890, District 63, Russell Co., Ka., School Records, Register of Deeds Office, Russell, Ka.

21. Clerk's Annual Report for the Year Commencing September 1st 1881 and Ending May 31st 1882, and Teacher's Contract, Nov. 3, 1868, Joint District 1, Koshkonong.

22. For a statement on embezzlements of the district treasurers, see *Eighteenth Biennial Report of the Superintendent of Public Instruction to the General Assembly of the State of Iowa, 1877–1879* (Des Moines, 1879), 99. For the honesty of the treasurers, see *Biennial Report of the Superintendent of Public Instruction of the State of Iowa, 1885–1887* (Des Moines, 1887), 10.

23. *Biennial Report of the Superintendent of Public Instruction to the Seventeenth General Assembly of the State of Iowa, 1875–1877* (Des Moines, 1876), 82; *History of Dane County; Biographical and Genealogical* (Madison, 1906), 34–35; Minutes of the Annual Meeting, July 7, 1902, District 3, Montrose Twp.

24. Annual Report of the Treasurer, July 2, 1888, District 3, Montrose Twp.

25. Record of the Doings of District School Board, Sept. 1896 to May 1897, District 5, Woodstock Twp.

26. Montgomery Ward & Co., *Catalogue and Buyers' Guide,* 35–37, 509.

27. Annual Report of the Treasurer, July 6, 1885, District 3, Montrose Twp.

28. See the Annual Reports of the Treasurer, 1885 to 1890, and 1896, District 3, Montrose Twp.

29. Minutes of the Annual Meetings, July 2, 1894, and July 6, 1896, District 3, Montrose Twp.

30. *Eleventh Biennial Report of the Superintendent of Public Instruction: State of*

Minnesota, for the School Years Ending July 31, 1899 and 1900 (St. Paul, 1900), 5; *Report of the Superintendent, Iowa, 1875–77,* 80, 97; "Report of the Committee of Six on Rural Schools," in *Biennial Report of the State Superintendent of the State of Wisconsin, for the Two Years Ending June 30, 1900* (Madison, 1901), 27.

31. "Normal Institute," Eldorado [Ka.] *Educational Advance,* Apr. 1, 1893; Lillie Gasman to H. Kraemer, July 6, 1896, District 2, Redwood Co., School Records, Minnesota State Archives, St. Paul. Sometimes the school boards advertised for teachers. See Records of Transactions by Trustees, Sept. 17, 1881, District 2, Redwood Co.

32. The laws on teachers' qualifications were much alike in all Middle Border states. See *The General School Laws of Michigan,* 19–20; Minutes of the Annual Meeting, Apr. 3, 1876, District 40, Saunders Co.

33. Minutes of the Annual Meeting, July 5, 1893, Proceedings of the District Board, Feb. 8, 1894, Ella Burns Teacher's Contract, Feb. 6, 1894, Tessie Cullen Teacher's Contract, Apr. 16, 1894, District 2, Elba Twp. For the farmers' comments on teachers, see Employed in the District, District 5, Woodstock Twp.; and Teachers, 1881–1897, District 5, Twp. 6, Range 9, Jasper Co., Ill., School Records, Manuscript Division, Illinois State Historical Library, Springfield.

34. Proceedings of the District Board, Feb. 13, July 22, 1895, July 29, 1896, Mar. 20, 1897, July 8, 1898, Ella Burns Teacher's Contract, Feb. 6, 1894, Mary Roche Teacher's Contract, Oct. 20, 1894, District 2, Elba Twp.

35. "The Text-Book Question," in *Annual Report of the Superintendent of Public Instruction of the State of Wisconsin, For the School Year Ending Aug. 31, 1874* (Madison, 1874), xxxii–xli.

36. James A. Blodgett, "Digest of Laws Relating to Text-Books, Their Selection and Supply," *Report of the Commissioner of Education for 1898, 2 vols.* (Washington, 1899), 1:893–908.

37. For the problem in Kansas, see Abilene [Ka.] *Reflector,* July 9, 1885.

38. Rules and Regulations Adopted by the District School Board, May 18, 1881, District 5, Woodstock Twp.; Proceedings of the District Board, Apr. 21, 1882, Joint District 1, Koshkonong Twp.

39. *School Board Journal* 6 (May 1894): 10.

40. For a good account of the disreputable salesmen, see *Twelfth Annual Report of the State Superintendent of Public Instruction to the Governor of Nebraska, for the Year Ending December 31, 1880* (Lincoln, 1880), 11–12.

41. *Annual Report of the State Superintendent of the State of Wisconsin, for the School Year Ending August 31, 1880* (Madison, 1881), 37.

42. Minutes of a Special School Meeting, Aug. 5, 1878, Meeting of the District Board, Aug. 10, 1878, and Minutes of the Annual Meeting, Sept. 2, 1878, Blooming Grove Twp.

43. As quoted in *Report of the Commissioner of Education for 1883* (Washington, 1884), 51.

44. Most of the arguments for and against free textbooks, by farmers as well as others, are summed up in "Free Text-books—Benefits, Objections, and Cost," *Report of the Commissioner of Education for 1902,* 2 vols. (Washington, 1903), 1:632–40.

45. Minutes of the Annual School Meeting, Sept. 2, 1889, District 5, Woodstock Twp.

46. See Minutes of the Annual Meetings, Sept. 5, 1871, Sept. 24, 1877, July 5, 1886, July 22, 1894, and Maggie Garvoille Teacher Certificate Second Grade, Sept. 1894, District 3, Montrose Twp.; Minutes of the Annual Meetings, Sept. 8, 1877, Aug. 26, 1878, and July 2, 1894, District 3, Blooming Grove Twp.

47. See Schulz, *Handbook for Rural School Officers,* 31.

48. Visitors' Register, District 37, Osborne Co., Ka.

49. Proceedings of the District Board, Apr. 20, 1882, Joint District 1, Koshkonong Twp.

50. School Board Meeting, Feb. 2, 1894, District 4, La Prairie Twp.

51. For the balloting in District 4, see Minutes of the Annual Meeting, July 5, 1897, District 4, La Prairie Twp. For McIntyre's defeats, see Minutes of the Annual Meeting, July 2, 1888, July 1, 1889, and July 7, 1890, Joint District 1, Koshkonong Twp.

52. A. C. Monahan, *Consolidation of Rural Schools and Transportation of Pupils at Public Expense,* Bulletin No. 30 (Washington: Bureau of Education, 1914), 15.

53. *Journal of Proceedings, Twentieth Session of the Illinois State Grange, Patrons of Husbandry . . . December, 1891* (Peoria, n.d.), 69.

CHAPTER SIX

1. *Report of the Committee of Twelve,* 7–11; Chicago *Daily Tribune,* Nov. 19 and 21, 1896.

2. *Report of the Committee of Twelve,* 52.

3. Elbert J. Benton, "Burke Aaron Hinsdale," *DAB.*

4. As quoted in George H. Genzmer, "Newton Bateman," *DAB.* For some distinctions between educators before and after the Civil War in New England, see Paul Mattingly, *The Classless Profession: American Schoolmen in the Nineteenth Century* (New York, 1975), 134–39. Mattingly distinguishes between two generations of professional educators in the nineteenth century, but his book, like most recent significant studies of education, deals almost exclusively with New England and the East. The Middle West has been largely ignored by historians of education, and Midwestern educators do not appear to follow in all particulars the pattern Mattingly has sketched.

5. Chicago *Daily Tribune,* Nov. 19, 1896.

6. Much work has recently been done on the development of professionalism in the nation in the late nineteenth century. Thomas L. Haskell, *Emergence of Professional Social Science: The American Social Science Association and the Nineteenth Century Crisis of Authority* (Urbana, Ill., 1977), is especially good in developing both the intellectual and the material changes in American life out of which professionalism grew. See particularly his chapters on "Interdependence" and "Antebellum Origins." *The Culture of Professionalism: The Middle Class and the Development of Higher Education in America* (New York, 1977), by Burton J. Bledstein, is a provocative study developing the relationship between the rise of a new middle class in America and professionalism, especially in the field of higher education. On various aspects of professionalism, see also Robert Wiebe, *The Search for Order, 1877–1920* (New York, 1967), chap. 5; John Higham, Leonard Krieger, and Felix Gilbert,

History (Englewood Cliffs, N.J.: Spectrum Books, 1965), 6–11; Michael B. Katz, *Class, Bureaucracy, and Schools: The Illusion of Change in America* (New York, 1971), 36–37, 56–73.

7. W. H. Payne, "The Aspects of the Teaching Profession," *Education* 2 (Mar. 1882): 327.

8. Ibid., 332.

9. Ibid., 338.

10. Wellford Addis, "The Inception and Progress of the American Normal School Curriculum to 1880," *Report of the Commissioner of Education for 1889*, 2 vols. (Washington, 1891), 1:276. Natural science had taken the lead in establishing the authority of the professionals, and so successful were they, according to one historian, that "by the end of the century the word 'scientific' seemed to epitomize the very essence of well-founded authority." See Haskell, *The Emergence of Professional Social Science*, 65–66.

11. John M. Gregory, "Is There a Science of Education?" *Education* 1 (Mar. 1881): 384–85.

12. Gabriel Compayre, *The History of Pedagogy*, tr. W. H. Payne (Boston, 1886), 535. Thirteen years after the first article appeared in *Education* asking if education were a science, another appeared in the same periodical asking the same question and finding the same answer. See Heber Holbrooke, "Is There a Science of Education?" *Education* 14 (Jan. 1894): 280.

13. The National Education Association traced its origins to the National Teachers' Association formed in 1857. It was perhaps reflective of the new image the educators had of themselves that they changed the name in 1870. See Stephen B. Weeks, "A Preliminary List of American Learned and Educational Societies," *Report of the Commissioner of Education for 1894*, 2 vols. (Washington, 1896), 2:1639–40. For the processes of professionalism, see Haskell, *The Emergence of Professional Social Science*, 25; Bledstein, *The Cult of Professionalism*, especially pp. 83–92.

14. The best recent work of the development of education is David B. Tyack, *The One Best System: A History of American Urban Education* (Cambridge, 1974). See especially parts 2 and 3. Recently historians have argued that American educators imposed educational reforms which reflected their own middle-class fears and perceptions of social deficiencies upon the lower classes in order to inculcate them with middle-class values and make them productive factory workers. See Michael B. Katz, *The Irony of Early School Reform: Educational Innovation in Mid-Nineteenth Century Massachusetts* (Cambridge, 1968), 87–88, 131. Katz's study, however, is concerned mainly with urban education in Massachusetts in the first flush of urbanization and industrialization. Professional educators in the Midwest, while no less eager to teach middle-class morality, were certainly not interested in making docile or productive factory workers of farm children. Beyond their sincere hope of improving rural education, their motives in attempting to reform rural schools appeared to be in part an effort to extend their authority and professional expertise over every aspect of education.

15. Tyack, *The One Best System*, 147–76.

16. "Discussions of Educational Questions, Chiefly by School Officials," in *Report of the Commissioner of Education, 1889*, 1:643.

17. *Fifth Annual Report of the State Superintendent of Public Instruction, To the*

Governor of Nebraska, for the Year Ending December 31st, 1873 (Lincoln, 1873), 12.

18. *Tenth Biennial Report of the Superintendent of Public Instruction of the State of Illinois, 1873–1874* (Springfield, 1874), 61; Genzmer, "Newton Bateman."

19. *Report of the Superintendent, Ill., 1873–1874,* 62.

20. Ibid., 63–64.

21. Ibid., 63.

22. "Qualifications of School Officers," *The Illinois Schoolmaster* 7 (Apr. 1875): 130; "Report of the Committee of Six," 27.

23. *Report of the Committee of Twelve,* 71.

24. Ise, *Sod and Stubble,* 120–21.

25. "In the Matter of Alicia Thompson, Appellant, and O. O. Stearns, Appelle[e]," June 18, 1886, Ladd Papers, Manuscript Division, WSHS; J. H. Moon to Newton Bateman, Apr. 17, 1874, W. H. Downy to Newton Bateman, Apr. 21, 1874, John B. Ward to Newton Bateman, July 20, 1874, in Newton Bateman Papers, Illinois State Historical Library. For a lengthy statement on Bible reading in the schools, see *Sixteenth Biennial Report of the State Superintendent of Public Instruction to the Governor of the State of Nebraska, January 1, 1901* (n.p., n.d.), 27–36.

26. *Annual Report of the Superintendent of Public Instruction of the State of Wisconsin, For the School Year Ending August 31st, 1870* (Madison, 1870), 113.

27. *Report of the Superintendent, Ill., 1873–1874,* 65; *Report of the Committee of Twelve,* 46–47.

28. *Report of the Committee of Twelve,* 46–48; "Report of the Committee of Six," 25–33.

29. Mary D. Bradford, *Memoirs: Autobiographical and Historical Reminiscences of Education in Wisconsin, Through Progressive Service from Rural School Teaching to City Superintendent* (Evansville, Wis., 1932), 190.

30. O. J. Kern, *Among the Schools* (New York, 1906), 235.

31. *Report of the Committee of Twelve,* 30. See also "Report of the Committee of Six," 30.

32. *Report of the Committee of Twelve,* 30.

33. *Annual Report of the Superintendent of Public Instruction of the State of Wisconsin, For the School Year Ending Aug. 31, 1874* (Madison, 1874), lxix; "Report of the Committee of Six," 31.

CHAPTER SEVEN

1. *Forty-Third Annual Report of the Department of Public Instruction of the State of Michigan with Accompanying Documents for the Year 1879* (Lansing, 1879), xxiii.

2. *Report of the Committee of Twelve,* 42 and 52. Some educators' views on the township system may be found in "Discussions of Educational Questions, Chiefly by School Officials," *Report of the Commissioner of Education, 1889,* 1:642–44. In a general way, the educators' drive for centralization may be found in Jonathan Sher, ed., *Education in Rural America: A Reassessment of Conventional Wisdom* (Boulder, Colo., 1977), 11–42. The problem of the district system as it related to the establishment of high schools in Massachusetts before the Civil War was touched upon by Katz, *The Irony of Early School Reform: Educational Innovation in Mid-Nineteenth Century Massachusetts,* 50–56.

3. *Massachusetts: Tenth Annual Report of the Board of Education, together with the Tenth Annual Report of the Secretary of the Board* (Boston, 1847), 130.

4. The story of these developments may be followed in *The Sixth Annual Report of the Superintendent of Public Instruction for the State of Indiana* (Indianapolis, 1857), 6–7; Mary Hinsdale, "Legislative History of Ohio," 1:147–48; and Clarence Ray Aurner, *History of Education in Iowa*, 5 vols. (Iowa City, 1914–1920), 1:250–57.

5. As quoted in the *Report of the Commissioner of Education for 1873* (Washington, 1874), 310–11.

6. *The Seventh Annual Report of the Superintendent of Public Instruction for the State of Indiana* (Indianapolis, 1858), 5.

7. For these changes, see Aurner, *History of Education in Iowa*, 1:250–57.

8. "Rural Schools," *Eleventh Biennial Report of the Department of Public Instruction of the State of Wisconsin, July 1, 1902, to June 30, 1904* (Madison, 1904), 3–25.

9. *Biennial Report of the Superintendent of Public Instruction, to the Fifteenth General Assembly of the State of Iowa, 1871–1873* (Des Moines, 1874), 34; *Report of the Secretary of the Board of Education, to the Board of Education and the Eighth General Assembly of the State of Iowa for 1859* (Des Moines, 1860), 10; Aurner, *History of Education in Iowa*, 1:250–57.

10. *Report of the Secretary, Iowa, 1859*, 34; Aurner, *History of Education in Iowa*, 1:255.

11. *Sixth Annual Report of the Superintendent of Public Instruction for the State of Indiana* (Indianapolis, 1857), 54.

12. *Report of the Superintendent, Iowa, 1871–1873*, 34; *Biennial Report of the Superintendent of Public Instruction of the State of Iowa, 1881–1883* (Des Moines, 1883), 27–28.

13. Aurner, *History of Education in Iowa*, 1:265; *Report of the Superintendent, Iowa, 1881–1883*, 28.

14. *Report of the Superintendent, Iowa, 1881–1883*, 28; *Biennial Report of the State Superintendent of Public Instruction to the Nineteenth General Assembly of the State of Iowa for the Period Ending September 30, 1889* (Des Moines, 1889), 104.

15. For the role of the subdirectors, see Henry Sabin, *Hand-book for Iowa Teachers* (Des Moines, 1890), 7.

16. As quoted in *Report of the Commissioner of Education, 1889*, 2:711 and 738.

17. *Forty-First Annual Report of the State Commissioner of Common Schools [Ohio] for the Year Ending August 31, 1894* (Norwalk, 1895), 5; *Forty-Fifth Annual Report of the State Commissioner of Common Schools to the Governor of the State of Ohio, for the Year Ending August 31, 1898* (Norwalk, 1898), 5.

18. As quoted in *Report of the Commissioner, 1873*, 99. Confusion over the appointment of teachers in Indiana through the years may be seen in the correspondence of Samuel Rugg, state superintendent 1862–65, Correspondence of the Superintendent of Public Instruction, State of Indiana, Indiana State Library, Indianapolis.

19. As quoted in *Report of the Commissioner of Education for 1888*, 2 vols. (Washington, 1889), 2:1100.

20. *Report of the Commissioner, 1873*, 97; *State of Indiana: Department of Public Education: Nineteenth Biennial Report of the State Superintendent, for the School Years Ending July 31, 1897, and July 31, 1898* (Indianapolis, 1898), 447–48.

21. Adele Marie Shaw, "From Country School to University," *World's Work* 8 (May 1904): 4795.

22. *Report of the Commissioner of Education for 1887* (Washington, 1889), 72–73.

23. *State of Indiana: Thirty-Ninth Report of the Superintendent of Public Instruction, Being the Sixteenth Biennial Report and for the Years Ending July 31, 1891, and July 31, 1892* (Indianapolis, 1893), 7; *State of Indiana: Fortieth Report of the Superintendent of Public Instruction, Being the Seventeenth Biennial Report and for the Years Ending July 31, 1893, and July 31, 1894* (Indianapolis, 1895), 71; "Discussions of Educational Questions, Chiefly by State Superintendents," *Report of the Commissioner, 1888,* 1:157–78.

24. *Report of the Commissioner, 1887,* 52.

25. Averages are based on school statistics drawn from the annual reports of the commissioner of education between the years 1892 and 1900. See, for example, *Report of the Commissioner of Education for 1901,* 2 vols. (Washington, 1902), 1:lxxi–xcv. For the quote from the commissioner, see *Report of the Commissioner of Education for 1892,* 2 vols. (Washington, 1894), 1:47.

26. For the growth of Indiana's urban population, see *Thirteenth Census of the United States: Population: 1910,* 2 vols. (Washington, 1913), 1:57.

27. *State of Indiana: Department of Public Instruction: Twentieth Biennial Report of the State Superintendent of Public Instruction for the School Years Ending July 31, 1899, and July 31, 1900* (Indianapolis, 1901), 430–32.

28. *Report of the Commissioner of Education for 1907,* 2 vols. (Washington, 1908), 2:564–65. Indiana's educational progress was also retarded a number of years by a decision of the state supreme court holding that raising taxes at the township level for educational purposes other than building schoolhouses was unconstitutional, since it violated the principle requiring uniformity of all public schools. Without adequate taxes for education, through which uniformity was to be achieved, education languished until 1867, when the state legislature passed a law allowing townships to tax for all educational purposes. This was later approved by the supreme court. See Emma Lou Thornbrough, *Indiana in the Civil War Era, 1850–1880: The History of Indiana,* 4 vols. (Indianapolis, 1965–1971), 3:467–75.

29. *Report of the Commissioner of Education for 1890,* 2 vols. (Washington, 1893), 1:24; *Report of the Committee of Twelve,* 34.

30. *Biennial Report of the Superintendent of Public Instruction to the Eighteenth General Assembly of the State of Iowa for the Period Ending September 15, 1879* (Des Moines, 1879), 88; *Fourteenth Biennial Report of the Superintendent of Public Instruction of the State of Illinois, 1880–1882* (Springfield, 1883), 321.

31. The money was spread evenly across the township, but the equality was not state-wide; some townships were richer than others. See *Twenty-Sixth Report of the Superintendent of Public Instruction of the State of Indiana, Being the Ninth Biennial Report, and for the Years Ending August 31, 1877, and August 31, 1878* (Indianapolis, 1879), 45.

32. *Report of the Commissioner, 1890,* 1:22 and 26. The rest of the money for Iowa and Kansas came largely, of course, from the state permanent school fund.

33. For comparison with Iowa, see *Report of the Commissioner, 1901,* 1:lxxxii and lxxxvii.

34. J. A. Piper to John Bloss, May 6, 1884, Correspondence of John Bloss, Correspondence of the Superintendent of Public Instruction, Indiana State Library.

35. *Thirty-Fourth Report of the Superintendent of Public Instruction of the State of Indiana, being the Thirteenth Biennial Report, and for the Years Ending August 31, 1885, and August 31, 1886* (Indianapolis, 1886), 190–94.

36. *Report of the Commissioner of Education for 1902*, 2 vols. (Washington, 1903), 2:2314–26.

37. Ibid.

38. *Supplementary Analysis and Derivative Tables: Twelfth Census of the United States: 1900* (Washington, 1906), 344.

39. *Report of the Commissioner, 1901*, 1:lxxi and lxxxix; *State of Iowa: Department of Public Education, 1899–1901* (Des Moines, n.d.), 23.

40. Sabin, *Hand-book for Iowa Teachers*, 6–7; Minutes of School Board Meeting, Mar. 21, 1887, Fairview Twp. See also Aurner, *History of Education in Iowa*, 1:249.

41. See Minutes of the School Board Meetings, Mar. 15, 1886, Oct. 15, 1887, and Mar. 19, 1888, Fairview Twp.

42. Appeal to the State Superintendent, Aug. 23, 1870, Sugar Grove Twp., Dallas Co., Ia., School Records, ISHS.

43. Minutes of the School Board Meeting, Mar. 21, 1887, Fairview Twp.

44. Minutes of the School Board Meetings, Nov. 5, 1886; Sept. 19, 1887; and Mar. 18, 1889, Fairview Twp.

45. *Report of the Commissioner, 1901*, 1:lxxxv.

46. Ibid., lxxxii, lxxxvii, and lxxxix; *Report of the Commissioner, 1902*, 2:2314–15.

47. *Forty-Third Annual Report of the State Commissioner of Common Schools, to the Governor of the State of Ohio, for the Year Ending August 31, 1896* (Norwalk, 1897), 66; *Twenty-First Biennial Report of the State Superintendent of Public Instruction to the Governor of the State of Nebraska, 1909–1911* (n.p., n.d.), iii–iv.

48. *Sixty-Fourth Report of the Superintendent of Public Instruction of the State of Michigan with Accompanying Documents for the Year 1900* (Lansing, 1901), 7.

49. *Report of the Committee of Twelve*, 44. On the turnover in state superintendents, see, for example, *Seventeenth Biennial Report of the Superintendent of Public Instruction to the Governor of the State of Nebraska, Jan. 1, 1903*, 2 vols. (1903), frontispiece; and W. C. Kampschroeder, ed., *Kansas Educational Progress, 1858–1967* (Topeka, 1967), 16ff.

CHAPTER EIGHT

1. Anson W. Buttles, Diaries, 1856–1906, Nov. 7, 8, and Dec. 30, 1865, Manuscript Division, WSHS.

2. Ibid., Apr. 5 and Oct. 6, 1859, Nov. 7, 1860, and Nov. 4, 1861.

3. "Common Schools: Historical Sketches," in *Forty-Fourth Annual Report of the Superintendent of Public Instruction of the State of Michigan, with Accompanying Documents, for the Year 1880* (Lansing, 1881), 312, 328.

4. Aurner, *History of Education in Iowa*, 1:51; *Report of the Commissioner of Education for 1885–1886* (Washington, 1887), 90; *Report of the Commissioner of Education for 1873* (Washington, 1874), cxvii and cxx–xxiii; *Thirty-Eighth An-*

nual Report of the Superintendent of Public Instruction of the State of Michigan, with Accompanying Documents for the Year 1874 (Lansing, 1875), lxxxvi.

5. *Proceedings of the Department of Superintendence at the National Education Association, at Its Meeting at Washington, D.C., Feb. 18–20, 1880,* Circular of Information No. 2 (Washington: Bureau of Education, 1880), 96–97.

6. *Thirty-Fifth Annual Report of the Superintendent of Public Instruction of the State of Michigan, with Accompanying Documents for the Year 1871* (Lansing, 1872), 11. See also M. S. Hopkins to David M. Geeting, Aug. 7, 1895, Correspondence of David M. Geeting, Correspondence of the Superintendent of Public Instruction, State of Indiana, Indiana State Library.

7. For the farmers' attitude toward county superintendents' interference, see *Report of the Superintendent, Michigan, 1874,* lxxv and 44; John McDonald, "The Lights and Shadows of the County Superintendent's Work," *Western School Journal* 9 (Sept. 1893): 211–13.

8. Reasonable reasons for a transfer from one district to another may be found in O. R. Pomeroy, Appellant, vs. The Supervisors of the Towns of Fulton and Porter, County of Rock, State of Wis., Nov. 28, 1891, Miscellaneous Papers, Porter Township, Rock County, Wis., RCHS.

9. *Twelfth Annual Report of the Department of Public Instruction, of the State of Kansas, 1872* (Topeka, 1872), 131.

10. Petition from District 19, Nov. 13, 1897; S. W. Smith [for G. C. Hutcherson] to Geo. Ruede, n.d., Records of the County Superintendent, Register of Deeds Office, Osborne Co., Osborne, Ka.

11. Petition from District 27, n.d., Records of the County Superintendent, Osborne Co., Ka.

12. S. W. Smith [for G. C. Hutcherson] to Geo. Ruede, n.d., and Notice of Alteration of School District Boundaries, Dec. 11, 1897, Records of the County Superintendent, Osborne Co., Ka.

13. *Report of the Commissioner, 1873,* cxx–xxiii.

14. *Thirty-Seventh Annual Report of the Superintendent of Public Instruction of the State of Michigan, with Accompanying Documents for the Year 1873* (Lansing, 1874), 8.

15. *Fifth Annual Report of the State Superintendent of Public Instruction, to the Governor of Nebraska, for the Year Ending December 31st, 1873* (Lincoln, 1873), 47.

16. Aurner, *History of Education in Iowa,* 2:64–81; *Ninth Biennial Report of the Superintendent of Public Instruction of the State of Illinois, 1871–1872* (n.p., n.d.), 130. See also *Annual Report of the Superintendent of Public Instruction for the State of Minnesota, for the Year Ending September 30, 1874* (St. Paul, 1875), 24–33.

17. *The Ninth Annual Report of the Superintendent of Public Schools of the State of Missouri, 1874* (Jefferson City, n.d.), 6; *Report of the Superintendent, Michigan, 1874,* lxxxiii.

18. *Thirty-Ninth Annual Report of the Superintendent of Public Instruction of the State of Michigan, with Accompanying Documents for the Year 1875* (Lansing, 1876), lxxxi–ii, and *Forty-First Report of the Superintendent of Public Instruction of the State of Michigan, with Accompanying Documents for the Year 1877* (Lansing, 1878), xxiv.

19. *Report of the Commissioner, 1873,* cxx–xxiii; and Russell [Ka.] *Journal,* Aug. 22, 1888.

20. Quick, *One Man's Life*, 309–11.

21. Russell [Ka.] *Journal*, Oct. 24, 1888. For the character of early county superintendents, see *Third Annual Report of the State Superintendent of Public Instruction to the Governor of the State of Nebraska, for the Year Ending December 30, 1871* (Des Moines, 1872), 33.

22. Mauston [Wis.] *Star*, Oct. 20, 1892.

23. Osborne County [Ka.] *News*, Aug. 30 and Sept. 27, 1894, and Osborne County [Ka.] *Farmer*, Sept. 20, 1894.

24. Osborne County [Ka.] *News*, Sept. 27, 1894.

25. Osborne County [Ka.] *Farmer*, Oct. 4, 11, 25, 1894; and Wahoo [Nebr.] *Semi-Weekly New Era*, Sept. 17, 1897.

26. *Sixteenth Annual Report of the Superintendent of Public Instruction, State of Minnesota, for the Year Ending Sept. 30, 1875* (St. Paul, 1876), 27.

27. *Biennial Report of the Superintendent of Public Instruction of the State of Iowa for Period Ending September 30, 1891* (Des Moines, 1891), 23.

28. Whitewater [Wis.] *Register*, July 25, 1885.

29. William Scott, Diaries, 1875–1886, Mar. 11, 18, 25, 1882, Apr. 10–14, 1882, Manuscript Division, WSHS.

30. *Twenty-Sixth Report of the Superintendent of Public Instruction of the State of Indiana, Being the Ninth Biennial Report, and for the Year Ending August 31, 1877 and August 31, 1878* (Indianapolis, 1879), 142.

31. Interview with A. L. Markley, July, 1977, Luray, Ka.; Irwin Stratton, Notebooks, Oct. 13, 1873, Manuscript Division, Indiana State Library.

32. J. L. Robertson, "Problems of the County Superintendent: Effective County Supervision," *County Superintendent Monthly* 4 (Feb. 1903): 323.

33. *State of Indiana: Thirty-Ninth Report of the Superintendent of Public Instruction, Being the Sixteenth Biennial Report and for the Years Ending July 31, 1891, and July 31, 1892* (Indianapolis, 1893), 71.

34. Joseph R. Funk, Memorandum Books, Aug. 26, 1872–Jan. 1874, School Visits, Oct. 22–30, 1873, Joseph Funk Manuscripts, Lilly Library, Indiana University, Bloomington.

35. Stratton, Notebooks, Dec. 28, 1873.

36. Ibid., Jan. 12, 1874; Funk, Memorandum Books, Oct. 22–30, 1873.

37. For one such column, see Abilene [Ka.] *Reflector*, June 11, 1885. See also Lea P. Harlan, "Duties and Difficulties of the New Superintendent," in *Thirty-Second Report of the Superintendent of Public Instruction of the State of Indiana, Being the Thirteenth Biennial Report and for the Years Ending August 31, 1885, and August 31, 1886* (Indianapolis, 1886), 94–96.

38. S. J. Race, Co. Supt., Notice to School Trustees and Voters, To Be Read at the Annual Meeting, n.d., School Records, Redwood Co., Minn., Minnesota State Archives, St. Paul.

39. A County superintendent's activities in Kansas in the 1890s may be followed in the Eldorado [Ka.] *Educational Advance*, a monthly paper published by the county superintendent of Butler Co., Ka.

40. Quick, *One Man's Life*, 99–100.

41. J. W. Holcombe, "A System for Grading of County Schools," *Proceedings of the Department of Superintendence of the National Educational Association*, Circular of Information No. 3 (Washington: Bureau of Education, 1887), 139.

42. Ibid., 150; H. C. Speer, "A Course of Study for Common Schools," *Programme and Proceedings of the State Teachers' Association, of Kansas, and the Papers Read at the Session of the Association* (Topeka, 1878), 22.

43. Speer, "Course of Study," 23.

44. Ibid., 23–25.

45. Ibid., 23.

46. Holcombe, "A System for Grading Schools," 150.

47. *Biennial Report of the Superintendent of Public Instruction, to the Eighteenth General Assembly of the State of Iowa, 1878–1879* (Des Moines, 1879), 74.

48. See *Teacher's Classification Register,* District 37, Osborne Co., Ka., School Records, KSHS.

49. Mrs. Arthur Dundas, "Reminiscences of Education, Pioneer Life, etc.," Taped Interview by Robert Warner, Aug. 24, 1956, MHC; and Holcombe, "A System for Grading Schools," 141–43.

50. Daily Programme of Study and Recitation, Winter, 1890–1891, School Records, District 1, Pennfield Twp., Calhoun Co., Mich., MHC.

51. *Report of the Commissioner of Education, 1889,* 2:738.

52. *Forty-Second Annual Report of the Superintendent of Public Instruction of the State of Michigan, with Accompanying Documents for the Year 1878* (Lansing, 1879), 28; and *Report of the Commissioner of Education, 1889,* 2:728.

53. *Fifty-Fifth Annual Report of the Superintendent of Public Instruction of the State of Michigan, with Accompanying Documents for the Year 1891* (Lansing, 1892), 9–10.

54. For examples of county superintendent conventions, see *Fourteenth Annual Report of the State Superintendent of Public Instruction to the Governor of Nebraska, for the Year Ending December 31, 1882* (Lincoln, 1883), 35–41; *Report of the Superintendent, Iowa, 1878–1879,* 65.

55. *Biennial Report of the State Superintendent of the State of Wisconsin, for the Two Years Ending June 31, 1900* (Madison, 1901), 71–72.

56. *State of Indiana: Fortieth Report of the Superintendent of Public Instruction, Being the Seventeenth Biennial Report for the Years Ending July 31, 1893, and July 31, 1894* (Indianapolis, 1895), 226. For the various efforts to upgrade the county superintendents, see the *Sixteenth Biennial Report of the State Superintendent of Public Instruction: Minnesota, For the School Years Ending 1909–1910* (Minneapolis, 1910), 8–9; and Ellen B. McDonald, "The Curse and Cure of the County Superintendency," *Journal of Rural Education* 1 (Apr. 1922): 366–67.

57. *Superintendent's Report, 1899–1900, Wisconsin,* 73–5; Conrad E. Patzer, *Public Education in Wisconsin* (Madison, 1924), 60–61.

58. *Report of the Superintendent, Wisconsin, 1899–1900,* 75.

59. *Biennial Report of the Department of Public Instruction to the Governor of Iowa, For the Period Beginning July, 1912, and Ending June 30, 1914* (Des Moines, 1914), 19; William R. Hood, ed., *Digest of State Laws Relating to Public Education in Force June 1, 1915,* Bulletin No. 47 (Washington: Bureau of Education, 1916), 91–105.

Chapter Nine

1. *Fourth Annual Report of the State Superintendent of Public Instruction to the Governor of the State of Nebraska, for the Year Ending December 31st, 1872* (Des Moines, 1872), 193.

2. Ibid.

3. *Fifth Annual Report of the State Superintendent of Public Instruction to the Governor of the State of Nebraska, for the Year Ending December 31st, 1873* (Lincoln, 1873), 11; Ex County Superintendent, "Sermons from the West," *County Superintendent Monthly* 4 (Aug. 1902): 132.

4. *Fifteenth Biennial Report of the State Superintendent of Public Instruction to the Governor of the State of Nebraska, December 1, 1898* (Lincoln, 1898), 13; R. D. Bailey, "The Summer School a Necessity," in *Sixty-First Annual Report of the Superintendent of Public Instruction of the State of Michigan, with Accompanying Documents for the Year 1897* (Lansing, 1898), 166.

5. *State of Indiana: Thirty-Eighth Report of the Superintendent of Public Instruction, Being the Fifteenth Biennial Report for the Years Ending July 31, 1889, and July 31, 1890* (Indianapolis, 1891), 110. Payne's quote is found in *Report of the Commissioner of Education, 1889*, 1:275.

6. David Salmon, *The Art of Teaching* (New York, 1898). For the establishment of the chair of the science and art of teaching, see *Report of the Commissioner of Education for 1881* (Washington, 1883), cxxxii.

7. As quoted in the *Report of the Commissioner of Education for 1874* (Washington, 1874), 125.

8. *Report of the Committee of Twelve*, 19; "Report of the Committee of Six," 26. See also *Fifteenth Biennial Report of the State Superintendent of Public Instruction to the Governor of Nebraska, Dec. 1, 1898* (Lincoln, 1898), 12.

9. *Report of the Commissioner of Education for 1901*, 2 vols. (Washington, 1902), 1:lxxxiv.

10. *Report of the Commissioner of Education, 1889*, 1:319.

11. *Annual Report of the Commissioner of Education for 1870* (Washington, 1871), 58–60; Mabel Purcell Clarke, Taped Interview, Manuscript Division, Indiana State Library.

12. James Ezell to Sallie Ezell, June 17, 1905, Belwood-Ezell Papers, Folder 33, Missouri Historical Collection, University of Missouri, Columbia.

13. For the differences between the wages of male and female teachers, cf. *Report of the Commissioner of Education for 1900*, 2 vols. (Washington, 1901), 1:xviii and lxxiii.

14. D. L. Leonard, "Women as Educators," *The Chicago Schoolmaster* V (Oct. 1872): 272. See also *Third Biennial Report of the State Superintendent for the School Years Ending July 31, 1881, and July 31, 1882, Kansas* (Topeka, 1882), 126.

15. Leonard, "Women as Educators," 272; *Report of the Commissioner of Education for 1888* (Washington, 1889), 121; and *Seventeenth Biennial Report of the State Superintendent of Public Instruction to the Governor of the State of Nebraska, January 1, 1903*, 2 vols. (Lincoln, 1903), 1:131–32.

16. *Annual Report of the Superintendent of Public Instruction for the State of Minnesota, for the Year Ending September 30, 1870* (St. Paul, 1871), 67.

17. For the life of one country schoolteacher, see Flo Menninger, *Days of My Life* (New York, 1939). In Wisconsin, as late as 1921, 94.00 per cent of the

rural schoolteachers were women, and 67.57 per cent of them had been born on the farm. See C. J. Anderson, *The Status of Teachers in Wisconsin,* Department of Public Education, Wis., 1921–1922 (Madison, n.d.).

18. *Report of the Superintendent, Nebraska, 1872,* 24.

19. "Report of the Committee of Six," 26. Each year in Nebraska in the early 1870s, one-third of the teachers quit. See *Report of the Superintendent, Nebraska, 1873,* 81.

20. As quoted in *Report of the Commissioner of Education, 1889,* 1:590.

21. For the presumed efficiency of the urban schoolteachers, see *Report of the Commissioner of Education for 1871* (Washington, 1872), 173. For the difficulties of the country teacher's classification system, see *Report of the Committee of Twelve,* 94–98. For the educators' view of the differences between urban and rural schools, see "Report of the Committee of Six," 25–26. Occasionally, an educator did see that urban and rural teachers were, in effect, judged by different standards. See Gertrude Dobson, "Discussions—Is the High School Graduate Prepared to Teach?" *Sixty-First Annual Report of the Superintendent of Public Instruction of the State of Michigan, with Accompanying Documents for the Year 1897* (Lansing, 1898), 151.

22. "Report of the Committee of Six," 32–36; *Report of the Committee of Twelve,* 42.

23. As quoted in *Report of the Commissioner of Education for 1877* (Washington, 1878), lxxiii. See also Thomas Hunter, "Normal Schools: Their Necessity and Growth." *Education* 5 (Jan. 1885): 237ff.; Grace C. Bibb, "The Education of the Public with Reference to Normal Schools and Their Work," *Education* 1 (July 1881): 574–81.

24. For a perceptive account of the rise of normal schools in New England, see Paul H. Mattingly, *The Classless Profession,* chap. 7. The development of normal schools on the Middle Border may be followed in J. P. Gordy, *Rise and Growth of the Normal School Idea in the United States,* Circular No. 8 (Washington: Bureau of Education, 1891), 5–97; M. A. Newall, "Contributions to the History of Normal Schools in the United States," *Report of the Commissioner, 1900,* vol. 2, especially pp. 2355–98. For Kansas and Missouri normals, see *Report of the Commissioner of Education for 1875* (Washington, 1876), 131–32, 247.

25. *Report of the Commissioner, 1875,* 104, 131–32, 226; *Report of the Commissioner of Education for 1876* (Washington, 1877), 101.

26. *Report of the Commissioner of Education for 1871–1872* (Washington, 1873), xxx; and Bibb, "The Education of the Public," 581.

27. *Forty-Third Annual Report of the Superintendent of Public Instruction of the State of Michigan, with Accompanying Documents for the Year 1879* (Lansing, 1879), 37.

28. "Normal School Curriculum," *Report of the Commissioner of Education, 1889,* 1:297; W. H. Payne, "The Normal School Problem," *Education* 5 (Mar. 1885): 389–90; *Fifth Biennial Report of the Superintendent of Public Instruction, State of Minnesota, for the School Years Ending August 31st, 1887–1889* (St. Paul, 1890), 87–89; *Fourteenth Annual Report of the State Superintendent of Public Instruction to the Governor of Nebraska for the Year Ending December 31, 1882* (Lincoln, 1883), 46; *Report of the Commissioner of Education for 1889–1890,* 2 vols. (Washington, 1891), 2:1178. See also D. L. Kiehle, "The True Place of the Normal School," *Education* 4 (Mar. 1883): 428–32.

29. *Report of the Commissioner, 1890,* 2:1177. For another view of intellectual opinion, see Mary R. Alling, "Some Causes of Failure among Teachers," *Education* 3 (Sept. 1882): 84.

30. James A. Woodburn, *Higher Education in Indiana in Contributions to American Educational History,* ed. Herbert B. Adams, Bulletin No. 10 (Washington: Bureau of Education, 1891), 193; *Tenth Biennial Report of the Superintendent of Public Instruction of the State of Illinois, 1873–1874* (Springfield, Ill., 1874), 60; *Twenty-Fourth Report of the Superintendent of Public Instruction of the State of Indiana, Being the Eighth Biennial Report for the Years Ending August 31, 1875–1876* (Indianapolis, 1877), 85.

31. *Report of the Commissioner, 1890,* 2:1177.

32. For the action of the Grangers in Minnesota, see D. L. Kiehle, "The True Place of the Normal School in the Education System," *Education* 3 (Mar. 1883): 429–32; *Tenth Annual Report of the State Superintendent of Public Instruction to the Governor of Nebraska, for the Year Ending December 31, 1878* (Lincoln, 1879), 33; *Report of the Commissioner, 1876,* 126; *Report of the Commissioner of Education for 1878* (Washington, 1879), 77.

33. "Training of Teachers," *Report of the Commissioner of Education for 1887* (Washington, 1888), 396.

34. Cf. *Report of the Commissioner, 1876,* 550–54, and *Report of the Commissioner, 1900,* 2:2098–2107. See also Julius Abernathy, "The Passing of the Normal School," *Education* 23 (Feb. 1, 1903): 325–29.

35. *Fifty-Fourth Annual Report of the Superintendent of Public Instruction of the State of Michigan, with Accompanying Documents, for the Year 1890* (Lansing, 1891), 124ff.; Carl Ruediger, *Agencies for the Improvement of Teachers in Service,* Bulletin No. 3 (Washington: Bureau of Education, 1911), 10–11. For the status of the county teacher institutes in 1873, see the pertinent pages in the abstracts from school officer reports in *Report of the Commissioner of Education for 1873* (Washington, 1874), 79–423.

36. *First Biennial Report of the Department of Public Instruction, State of Kansas, for the School Year Ending July 31, 1877 and 1878* (Topeka, 1879), 12; *Report of the Superintendent, Ind., 1889–1890,* 99. For the difference among the various states, see the appropriate pages in "Summary of State School Laws," *Report of the Commissioner of Education for 1885–1886* (Washington, 1887), 77–190.

37. *Report of the Commissioner, 1886,* 94 and 123.

38. *Proceedings of the Department of Superintendence of the National Education Association,* Circular of Information No. 3 (Washington: Bureau of Education, 1887), 163.

39. Abilene [Ka.] *Weekly Democrat,* May 13, 1880, and July 15, 1880. For meeting the conductor and expenses involved, see Racine County, Wis., Institute Fund Ledger, July 3, 1905, Country School Records, WSHS. For charges against the county superintendents in making political appointments, see *Twelfth Biennial Report of the State Superintendent of Public Instruction to the Governor of the State of Nebraska, for the Biennium Ending December 31, 1892* (Lincoln, 1893), 16–17; *Biennial Report of the State Superintendent of the State of Wisconsin for the Two Years Ending June 30, 1900* (Madison, 1901), 85–104.

40. H. King, "How Can County Institutes Be Made More Profitable?" in *Forty-Eighth Annual Report of the Superintendent of Public Instruction of the State of*

Michigan, with Accompanying Documents for the Year 1886 (Lansing, 1887), 279; see the discussion on this paper.

41. Quick, *One Man's Life,* 277.

42. King, "How Can Institutes be More Profitable?" 275–80. For a conductor's comments on having professional educators control the institutes, see Records of County Teacher Institutes, Isabella Co., Mich., July 28 to Aug. 6, 1890, School Records, MHC. See also *Report of the Superintendent, Wis., 1900,* 85–92.

43. Russell [Ka.] *Record,* July 3, July 10, 1890. See also Lafayette Co. [Wis.] *Democrat,* Aug. 25, 1882; Adair [Ia.] *County Reporter,* Mar. 4, 1886. For the quotation, see Abilene [Ka.] *Weekly Democrat,* May 13, 1880.

44. Quick, *One Man's Life,* 241.

45. William Allen White, *The Autobiography of William Allen White* (New York, 1946), 97; Alice Jensen Larson, "County Institute, Brown County, Nebraska," in *The Sway of the School Bells: Schools and Histories of Brown, Keya Paha, and Rock Counties, Nebraska,* comp. by Ainsworth Area retired teachers (n.p., 1977), 92.

46. Menninger, *Days of My Life,* 199.

47. Augusta Slayton, Diary, July 14, 17, 23, 1907, Augusta Slayton Diaries, 3 vols., 1889–1900, 1903–1909, and 1906, MHC.

48. Sara Gillespie Huftalen, Diary, June 30, July 3, 23, 1883, Sara Gillespie Huftalen Papers, ISHS; Adair County [Ia.] *Reporter,* Mar. 4, 1886; Eldorado [Ka.] *Educational Advance,* Feb. 1, 1893.

49. Eldorado [Ka.] *Educational Advance,* Feb. 1, 1893. So badly were the teachers treated in one Iowa town in the 1860s that one school official wondered if they would ever attend another meeting there. See *Biennial Report of the State Superintendent of Public Instruction to the Twelfth Regular Session, Held at Des Moines, Jan. 2, 1867* (Des Moines, 1868), 82.

50. Wahoo [Nebr.] *New Era,* June 18, 1896. See also Russell [Ka.] *Record,* Aug. 3, 1893; Abilene [Ka.] *Reflector,* July 30, 1885.

51. *Biennial Report of the Superintendent of Public Instruction to the Eighteenth General Assembly of the State of Iowa, 1877–1879* (Des Moines, 1879), 56; County Teacher Institute Records, Calhoun Co., Mich., July 21–Aug. 15, 1890, MHC.

52. Teacher Institute, Calhoun Co., Mich., 1890.

53. *Report of the Superintendent, Iowa, 1877–1879,* 19; Eldorado [Ka.] *Educational Advance,* July 1, 1893; Abilene [Ka.] *Reflector,* Aug. 20, 1885, 4; Quick, *One Man's Life,* 242; Huftalen, Diary, Aug. 14, 1884.

54. See clipping from Battle Creek [Mich.] *Journal,* in County Institute Records, Calhoun Co., Mich. See also Adrian [Mich.] *Weekly Times and Expositor,* Aug. 31, 1885.

55. White, *Autobiography,* 97. See also Lewis Atherton, *Main Street on the Middle Border* (Bloomington, Ind., 1954), 179–80.

56. For the laws on teaching the harmful effects of alcohol, see *Report of the Commissioner of Education for 1895,* 2 vols. (Washington: 1896), 2:1833.

57. Minneapolis [Ka.] *Normal Institute Record,* July 18, 1878. On teaching reading according to the word method, see *Sixth Annual Report of the State Superintendent of Public Instruction to the Governor of the State of Nebraska, for the Year Ending December 31st, 1874* (Lincoln, 1874), 17; John Swett, *Methods of*

Teaching: A Hand-Book of Principles, Directions and Working Models for Common School Teachers (New York, 1880), 123. For an outline of course studies to be pursued, see *Report of the Superintendent, Michigan, 1879,* 76–105.

58. County Institute Records, Allegan Co., Mich., 1890, MHC.

59. King, "How Can County Institutes Be Made More Profitable?" 280.

60. Edward G. Boring, *A History of Experimental Psychology,* 2d ed. (New York, 1950), 205–9. See also Morris L. Bigge and Maurice P. Hunt, *Psychological Foundations of Education,* 2d ed. (New York, 1968), 112–13, which traces faculty psychology to Christian Wolff, a German philosopher of the eighteenth century.

61. Boring, *Experimental Psychology,* 51–58; John D. Davis, *Phrenology Fad and Science: A 19th Century American Crusade* (New Haven, 1955), 62–64, 65–75, and 172–74.

62. Gabriel Compayre, *Lectures on Pedagogy: Theoretical and Practical,* tr. W. H. Payne (New York, 1890), 7–8.

63. Francis B. Palmer, *The Science of Education* (New York, 1887), 7.

64. *Seventeenth Biennial Report of the Superintendent of Public Instruction of the State of Illinois, July 1, 1887–June 30, 1888* (Springfield, 1888), ccii. The heavy emphasis on morality may be seen in a study of schoolbooks used in the nineteenth century. See Ruth Miller Elson, *Guardians of Tradition: American Schoolbooks of the Nineteenth Century* (Lincoln: Bison Press, 1964).

65. For the teaching of psychology in the institutes, see County Institute Records, Gennessee Co., Mich., 1890, MHC. For the quote, see Compayre, *Lectures on Pedagogy,* 60–61.

66. Personal Papers of Lucy Stewart Herrick, Notebooks, School Records, Olmstead Co., Minn., Olmstead County Historical Society, Rochester, Minn.

67. Marshall [Mich.] *Statesman,* Feb. 5, 1886.

68. *Biennial Report of the State Superintendent of the State of Wisconsin, for the Two Years Ending June 30, 1892* (Madison, 1892), 23. Toward the end of the century, however, some educators thought the examinations too hard and were in favor of dropping them. *Report of the Superintendent, Nebr., 1898,* 51.

69. Copies of the teachers' examinations may be found in *Report of the Superintendent, Nebr., 1892,* 144–46; *Sixtieth Annual Report of the Superintendent of Public Instruction of the State of Michigan with Accompanying Documents for the Year 1896* (Lansing, 1897), 111–60; Russell [Ka.] *Record,* Aug. 31, 1893; Whitewater [Wis.] *Register,* Apr. 30, 1885. For beginning at six o'clock each morning, see Eldorado [Ka.] *Educational Advance,* July 1, 1893.

70. Osborne County [Ka.] *Farmer,* Aug. 31, 1893. See also Adair County [Ia.] *Reporter,* Apr. 1, 1886; Abilene [Ka.] *Weekly Democrat,* July 29, 1880.

71. Reports of the County Superintendents of Boone and Brown Counties, Indiana, 1890–1893, and Reports of the County Superintendent of Schools to the Superintendent of Public Instruction, Indiana, Archives Division, Indiana State Library, Indianapolis.

72. Abernathy, "Passing of the Normal School," 329.

CHAPTER TEN

1. Bradford, *Autobiographical Reminiscences,* 128–33.
2. Ibid., 134.

3. Quick, *One Man's Life*, 249.

4. Ibid., 179; Joseph R. Funk, Memorandum Book, Aug. 26, 1872, to Jan. 7, 1874, Joseph R. Funk Papers.

5. White, *The Autobiography of William Allen White*, 38; Huftalen, Journal, Dec. 1906–Sept. 1908, 11.

6. H. C. Downer, Diary, Jan. 29, 1873, Illinois State Historical Library, Springfield.

7. Ibid., Jan. 8, 1873; Huftalen, Diary, Jan. 4, 1884.

8. Adrian [Mich.] *Daily Times and Expositor*, May 19, 1893.

9. Downer, Diary, May 5, 1873, and June 10, 1873.

10. Belle Cushman Bond, "Early Wisconsin School Teachers," *Wisconsin Magazine of History* 23 (Sept. 1939): 59.

11. *Twentieth Biennial Report of the State Superintendent of Public Instruction to the Governor of Nebraska, 1907–1909* (n.p., n.d.), 206.

12. Ibid.

13. *Report of the Commissioner of Education for 1902*, 2 vols. (Washington: 1903), 2:2314–15; A. C. Monahan, *The Status of Rural Education in the United States*, Bulletin No. 8 (Washington: Bureau of Education, 1913), 18.

14. *Report of the Commissioner, 1902*, 2:2320–21.

15. *Annual Report of the Superintendent of Public Instruction of the State of Wisconsin for the School Year Ending August 31, 1880* (Madison, 1881), 25; *Report of the Commissioner of Education for 1891*, 2 vols. (Washington, 1892), 2:1051.

16. Frances Sherman, "Teaching School in the Sandhills," in *Telling Tales Out of School: Teachers of Nebraska*, ed. Alma Ashley, etc. (Lincoln, 1976), 38.

17. *Biennial Report of the State Superintendent of the State of Wisconsin, for the Two Years Ending June 30, 1900* (Madison, 1901), 71.

18. Joseph Shafer, "Sketch of Lorenzo Dow Harvey," in Lorenzo Dow Harvey Papers, Manuscript Division, WSHS.

19. As quoted in *Report of the Commissioner of Education for 1899*, 2 vols. (Washington, 1891), 1:590; E. C. Hewett, "Teaching in Country Districts," *The Educationist* 3 (Mar. 1881): 76–78.

20. *Report of the Committee of Twelve*, 99. See also Harris's comments on the rural classification in *Report of the Commissioner, 1891*, 2:1055.

21. *Report of the Committee of Twelve*, 112, 114–19.

22. Proceedings of the District School Board, Mar. 1, 1906, District 1, Pennfield Twp., Calhoun Co., Mich., School Records, MHC.

23. *Biennial Report of the Superintendent of Public Instruction of the State of Iowa for Period Ending September 30, 1889* (Des Moines, 1890), 73.

24. Teachers' Classification Record, Spring Term, Mar. 4 to May 24, 1889, District 37, Osborne Co., Ka., School Records, KSHS.

25. Ibid.

26. See reports on District 1, Colfax Twp., and District 8, Big Rapids Twp., in Record of Visits to Schools of Mecosta Co., Mich., Sept. 7, 1899–July 1, 1900, School Records, MHC.

27. See Huftalen, Diaries and Journals and Miscellaneous papers for her background. For the naming of the school, see newspaper clippings, Sept. 1908, in her papers.

28. For the variety of her program, see Huftalen, Journal, Dec. 1906 to Sept. 1908, and clippings in her papers; Hamlin Garland, *Boy Life on the*

Prairie (Lincoln: Bison Books, 1961), 377–78. Garland's account of the sleigh ride as a common occurrence on the Middle Border was supported by many newspaper stories of such rides.

29. Huftalen, Journals, especially April 26, 1907.

30. Huftalen, Journal, Dec. 1906 to Sept. 1908, 3 and 9; Oberlin [Ka.] *Times,* Oct. 6, 1893. See also Wayne E. Fuller, "Country Schoolteaching on the Sod-House Frontier." *Arizona and the West,* 17 (Summer 1975), 121–140.

31. *Twentieth Report of the Superintendent of Public Instruction of the State of Indiana, Being the Sixth Biennial Report, and for the Years Ending August 31, 1871 and August 31, 1872* (Indianapolis, 1873), 89–90.

32. *Forty-Eighth Annual Report of the Superintendent of Public Instruction of the State of Michigan with Accompanying Documents for the Year, 1886* (Lansing, 1887), 204–5. For a typical discussion of morality see "Discussions of Educational Questions, Chiefly by School Officials," *Report of the Commissioner of Education, 1889,* 1:622–34.

33. As quoted in *Report of the Commissioner of Education for 1888* (Washington, 1888), 165.

34. *Report of the Commissioner of Education for 1894,* 2 vols. (Washington, 1896), 2:1211. The fight over the so-called Bennett law and the problem in Illinois may be followed in Richard Jensen, *The Winning of the Midwest: Social and Political Conflict, 1888–1896* (Chicago, 1971), 122–53.

35. *Report of the Commissioner, 1894,* 2:1211.

36. *State of Indiana: Department of Public Instruction: Nineteenth Biennial Report of the State Superintendent, for the School Years Ending July 31, 1897, and July 31, 1898* (Indianapolis, 1898), 463.

37. Huftalen, Journal, Dec. 1906–Sept. 1909, 21, and Clipping, May 6, 1908.

38. Huftalen, Journal, Dec. 1906–Sept. 1909, 10.

39. J. B. Blount, "Revocation of Licenses, etc.," *Twenty-Sixth Report of the Superintendent of Public Instruction of the State of Indiana, Being the Ninth Biennial Report, and for the Years Ending August 31, 1877 and August 31, 1878* (Indianapolis, 1878), 129–31.

40. Huftalen, Journal, Dec. 1906–Sept. 1909, 25.

41. C. B. Gilbert, "The New Education," *Education* 16 (Sept. 1895): 43.

42. Abilene [Ka.] *Reflector,* Jan. 29, 1885.

43. Huftalen, Journal, Dec. 1906–Sept. 1909, 1.

44. Larken J. Beeman, Reminiscences: Rural Life in and around School Dist. #3, Marion Twp., Boone Co., Ind., 1876–1900, Taped Interview, Manuscript Division, Indiana State Library.

45. John Trainer, *How to Teach a Country School* (Decatur, Ill., 1887), 15.

46. James P. Slade, "Country Schools," *Education* 3 (Jan. 1883): 239.

47. On Bateman, see *Report of the Commissioner of Education for 1872* (Washington, 1873), 81–87. See also H. H. Snowdon, "Discussion—Should the Summer School Be Made an Institute and Thus Be Free to Teachers," *Sixty-First Annual Report of the Superintendent of Public Instruction of the State of Michigan with Accompanying Documents for the Year 1897* (Lansing, 1898), 175.

48. Gilbert, "The New Education," 41.

49. Ibid., 41.

50. C. B. Gilbert, "The New Education, Part II," *Education* 16 (Oct. 1895): 99.

51. As quoted in *Report of the Commissioner of Education for 1896*, 2 vols. (Washington, 1897), 1:930, 937.

52. Ibid., 933.

53. Ibid., 934–38, has an interesting discussion of the opposing views of Charles Eliot and William T. Harris with respect to education which involved differing views of civilization itself. For Harris's opposition to the Herbartian position of the training of will, see "Editorial," *Education* 16 (Nov. 1895). For Harris's broader views on elementary education and disagreements with him see "Report of the Committee of Fifteen, II," *Report of the Commissioner, 1894*, 1:489–541.

54. Huftalen, Clipping, Feb. 1908.

55. *Twelfth Biennial Report of the Department of Public Instruction of the State of Wisconsin, July 1, 1904, to June 30, 1906* (Madison, 1907), 5–6, 8, 10.

56. Quick, *One Man's Life*, 154.

57. Oberlin [Ka.] *Times*, Oct. 6, 1893.

58. Curtis G. Shake, Reminiscences, Transcript, Taped Interview, 1968, Manuscript Division, Indiana State Library.

59. Menninger, *Days of My Life*, 198–99; Bradford, *Autobiographical Reminiscences*, 136; *The Rural Teacher of Nebraska*, Bulletin No. 20 (Washington: Bureau of Education, 1919), 49.

60. Teacher's Register for 1905–6, District 1, Pennfield Twp.

61. Noble County [Ohio] *Republican*, Dec. 14 and 28, 1882, and Jan. 4, 1883, and *School Board Journal*, 6 (Jan. 1894), 8.

62. Huftalen, Journal, Dec. 1906–Sept. 1907, 2, 6.

63. Gabriel Compayre, *Lectures on Pedagogy*, 447.

64. Ibid., 448–62.

65. Abilene [Ka.] *Reflector*, Jan. 29, 1885.

66. See Ise, *Sod and Stubble*, 237–38, for one notable failure.

67. *Report of the Commissioner of Education for 1873* (Washington, 1874), 117.

68. *Annual Report of the State Superintendent of the State of Wisconsin, for the School Year Ending August 31st, 1872* (Madison, 1872), 26. For a survey of the laws on compulsory education, see *Report of the Commissioner of Education for 1897*, 2 vols. (Washington, 1898), 2:1525–26. On the problem of enforcement, see *Fifty-Third Annual Report of the Department of Public Instruction of the State of Michigan with Accompanying Documents for the Year 1889* (Lansing, 1889), 10–17.

69. *Report of the Commissioner, 1897*, 1:lviii; *Biennial Report of the Superintendent of Public Instruction of the State of Iowa for the Period Ending September 15, 1879* (Des Moines, 1880), 67.

70. Russell [Ka.] *Record*, Mar. 27, 1890.

71. Carlson, *Small World*, 82–84.

72. Ibid., 84.

73. *Sixteenth Biennial Report of the State Superintendent of Public Instruction to the Governor of the State of Nebraska, January 1, 1901* (n.p., n.d.), v; Superintendent's Record of Examinations, Dec. 1907 and Apr. 1908, Racine Co., Wis., School Records, WSHS.

74. Superintendent's Record of Examinations, Dec. 1907 and Apr. 1908, Racine Co., Wis.
75. Ibid.
76. Ibid.
77. Adair County [Ia.] *Reporter,* April 15, 1886.
78. Huftalen, Miscellaneous Papers, May 1909 and Apr. 1959.
79. Adair County [Ia.] *Reporter,* Mar. 11, 1886.
80. *Report of the Superintendent, Michigan, 1897,* 43.
81. David B. Tyack, *The One Best System: A History of Urban Education* (Cambridge, 1974), 82.
82. *Report of the Superintendent, Michigan, 1897,* 46.

CHAPTER ELEVEN

1. Theodore Saloutos and John D. Hicks, *Twentieth Century Populism: Agricultural Discontent in the Middle West, 1900–1939* (Madison, 1951), 20–21 and 478. See also *Report of the Secretary of Agriculture for 1912* (Washington, 1913), 11; but see *Report of the Secretary of Agriculture for 1911* (Washington, 1912), 13–14.
2. *Statistical Abstract of the United States, 1938* (Washington, 1939), 6.
3. Frank L. Jones, "Transportation of Pupils in Indiana," *Report of the Commissioner of Education for 1901,* 2 vols. (Washington, 1902), 1:185; *Education in Wisconsin, 1914–1916: A Two Year Analysis of Educational Problems and Progress in the State of Wisconsin* (Madison, 1917), 18–19; Teacher's Daily Register, Nov. 15, 1875, to Mar. 17, 1876, and Nov. 20, 1899, to Mar. 23, 1900, District 1, Pennfield Twp., Calhoun Co., Michigan, School Records MHC.
4. "Report of the Country Life Commission," *S. Doc.,* 705, 60 Cong., 2 Sess., 9.
5. Ibid.
6. Ibid. For the complete story of the Country Life Commission, see William L. Bowers, *The Country Life Movement in America, 1900–1920* (Port Washington, N.Y., 1974). On Bailey, see Clayton S. Ellsworth, "Theodore Roosevelt's Country Life Commission," *Agricultural History* 30 (Oct. 1960): 5.
7. "Report of the Country Life Commission," 14–15.
8. Bowers, *Country Life Movement,* 109.
9. "Report of the Country Life Commission," 26.
10. John Dewey, *Moral Principles in Education* (New York, 1909), viii; "Report of the Country Life Commission," 53. The goals of the commission, however, seem only distantly related to those of the new educators who, as one historian argued, sought to suppress the individualism of urban schoolchildren and teach them to cooperate in order to produce men and women for the needs of the corporate state. See Joel H. Spring, *Education and the Rise of the Corporate State* (Boston, 1972), 1, 44–61.
11. *Sixtieth Annual Report of the Superintendent of Public Instruction of the State of Michigan with Accompanying Documents for the Year 1896* (Lansing, 1897), 270. For a good summary of nature study, see James Ralph Jewell, *Agricultural Education, Including Nature Study and School Gardens,* Bulletin No. 2 (Washington: Bureau of Education, 1907), 9–70. See also William A. Bullough, "It Is

Better to Be a Country Boy: The Lure of the Country in Urban Education in the Gilded Age," *The Historian: A Journal of History* 35 (Feb. 1973): 183–95, for the failure of nature studies. Bullough's argument that educators thought the country school was "superior simply because it was in the country," p. 185, obviously does not agree with my findings.

12. A. C. True, "Some Problems of the Rural Common School," *Yearbook of the Department of Agriculture, 1901* (Washington, 1902), 149.

13. *Seventeenth Biennial Report of the Superintendent of Public Instruction of the State of Illinois, July 1, 1886–June 30, 1888* (Springfield, 1889), 176.

14. Mabel Carney, *Country Life and the Country School* (New York, 1912), 240.

15. *Twenty-Second Biennial Report of the State Superintendent of Public Instruction to the Governor of the State of Nebraska, for the Biennium Beginning January 5, 1911, and Ending January 9, 1913* (n.p., n.d.), 11. For a constitution of a rural social club, see *Sixty-Fifth Report of the Public Schools of the State of Missouri, Year Ending June 30, 1914* (Jefferson City, n.d.), 23.

16. *Education in Wisconsin: 1914–1916*, 55; Minutes of the Annual Meeting, June 1, 1914, Joint District 9, Dunn Twp.

17. W. K. Tate, "Country Schools for Country Children," *World's Work* 24 (May 1912): 102–7.

18. Evelyn Dewey, *New Schools for Old: The Regeneration of the Porter School* (New York, 1919), 52–72, 222, 293–321.

19. True, "Some Problems of the Rural Common School," 149.

20. For a critical comment on nature study, see Burke Hinsdale's remarks in *Report of the Superintendent, Michigan, 1896*, 277–78; *Journal of Proceedings of the Thirty-Fifth Annual Session of the Illinois State Grange, Patrons of Husbandry . . . 1906* (Peoria, n.d.), 49.

21. *Journal of Proceedings: Twenty-Eighth Session of the Illinois State Grange: Patrons of Husbandry . . . 1899* (Peoria, n.d.), 48; Bowers, *Country Life Movement*, 121. For the Grange endorsement of nature study, see *Journal of Proceedings of the Thirty-Third Session of the Illinois State Grange: Patrons of Husbandry . . . 1904* (Peoria, n.d.), 34.

22. Herbert Quick, *Brown Mouse* (Indianapolis, 1915), 92–93.

23. For social goals of rural education, see Carney, *Country Life and the Country School*, chap. 7. On the necessity and the utility of relating education to life, see John Dewey, *The School and Society*, rev. ed. (Chicago, 1961), chap. 1.

24. Harlan Updegraff, *Teacher Certificates Issued under General State Laws and Regulations*, Bulletin No. 18 (Washington: Bureau of Education, 1911), 28–54, 57–59, 62–65, 86–89, 128–29; N. William Newsom, *The Legal Status of the County Superintendent*, Bulletin No. 7 (Washington: Bureau of Education, 1932), 35–37.

25. *Fourteenth Biennial Report of the Department of Public Instruction of the State of Wisconsin, July 1, 1908, to June 30, 1910* (Madison, 1910), 11–12; *Education in Wisconsin: 1914–1916*, 55; *Fifty-Ninth Report of the Public Schools of the State of Missouri, School Year Ending June 30, 1908* (Jefferson City, n.d.), 19–20. The development of rural school supervisors to 1930 may be traced in Annie Reynolds, *Supervision and Rural School Improvement*, Bulletin No. 31 (Washington: Bureau of Education, 1930), 1–42.

26. *Sixty-First Report of the Public Schools of the State of Missouri, School Year Ending June 30, 1910* (Jefferson City, n.d.), 24, 40–52.

27. *Report of the Superintendent, Wisconsin, 1908–1910,* 11; Minutes of the Special Meeting, District 3, Montrose Twp.

28. "The Conveyance of Children to School," *Report of the Commissioner of Education for 1895,* 2 vols. (Washington, 1896), 2:1469–82.

29. O. J. Kern, "A Visit to the Centralized Schools of Ohio," *Report of the Commissioner, 1901,* i.

30. J. McKeen Cattell, Jacques Cattell, E. E. Ross, eds., *Leaders in Education: A Biographical Directory,* 2d ed. (New York, 1941), 558; Adele Marie Shaw, "Common-Sense Country Schools," *World's Work* 8 (June 1904): 4881–94.

31. Kern, "A Visit to Schools of Ohio," 161–70.

32. Ibid., 161–62.

33. Ibid., 165, 168.

34. For consolidation in Indiana, see "The Rural Schools," *State of Indiana: Department of Public Instruction: Twentieth Biennial Report of the State Superintendent of Public Instruction for the School Years Ending July 31, 1899, and July 31, 1900* (Indianapolis, 1901), 520–57; Kern, "A Visit to Schools of Ohio," 165–70. The arguments for consolidation were passed from one educator to another and copied in report after report. For a good summary, see *Eighteenth Biennial Report of the State Superintendent of Public Instruction to the Governor of Nebraska, for the Biennium Ending Nov., 1904* (York, Nebr., 1905), 227–29.

35. Kern, "A Visit to Schools of Ohio," 165, 170.

36. Ibid., 165. For a contract made with the wagon driver in Indiana, see "Rural Schools," *State of Indiana: Department of Public Instruction: Twenty-First Biennial Report of the State Superintendent of Public Instruction for the School Years Ending July 31, 1901, and July 31, 1902* (Indianapolis, 1903), 745; *Eleventh Biennial Report of the Department of Public Instruction of the State of Wisconsin, July 1, 1902, to June 30, 1904* (Madison, 1904), 16.

37. A. A. Upham, "Transportation of Rural School Children at Public Expense," *Ninth Biennial Report of the State Superintendent of the State of Wisconsin, for the Two Years Ending June 30, 1900* (Madison, 1901), 23–24.

38. Edward Erf, "The Kingsville Plan of Education," *Arena* 22 (July 1899): 61–67. See also Kern, "A Visit to Schools of Ohio," 165.

39. *Report of the Superintendent, Nebraska, 1904,* 231. For a general survey and bibliography of the consolidation movement to 1914, see A. C. Monahan, *Consolidation of Rural Schools and Transportation of Pupils at Public Expense,* Bulletin No. 30 (Washington: Bureau of Education, 1914), 5–108.

40. Monahan, *Consolidation of Rural Schools,* 5–108.

41. George May, "Iowa's Consolidated Schools," *The Palimpsest* 37 (Jan. 1956): 16–17, 23, 40.

42. "Consolidation of Schools and Transportation of Pupils," *Report of the Commissioner of Education for 1903,* 2 vols. (Washington, 1905), 2407–14; "Rural Schools," *Report of the Superintendent, Indiana, 1901–02,* 729. Missouri did not have a law allowing public funds for transportation until 1910. See *Sixty-Second Report of the Public Schools of the State of Missouri, School Year Ending June 30, 1911* (Jefferson City, n.d.), 35.

43. For the complicated process of consolidating schools in Nebraska, see *Report of the Superintendent, Nebraska, 1902–04,* 235.

44. Erf, "The Kingsville Plan," 63. See also, Monahan, *Consolidation of Rural Schools,* 15.

45. *State of Iowa: Department of Public Instruction: Biennial Report Ending 1901* (n.p., n.d.), 63; "Rural Schools," *Report of the Superintendent, Indiana, 1899–1900,* 540; *Report of the Superintendent, Nebraska, 1903–04,* 256.

46. John F. Riggs, "Present Status of Consolidation," in *Conditions and Needs of Iowa Rural Schools* (Des Moines, 1905), 44, 49. See also May, "Iowa's Consolidated Schools," 41. The question of cost was apparently not a major objection to consolidation in Indiana where the township system prevailed and where townships relied heavily on state aid. But see "Rural Schools," *Report of the Superintendent, Indiana, 1900–02,* 739, for one view. For the change in the educators' argument on cost, see Monahan, *Consolidation of Rural Schools,* 55–56.

47. "Rural Schools," *Report of the Superintendent, Indiana, 1899–1900,* 539; May, "Iowa's Consolidated Schools," 38–39.

48. "Rural Schools," *Report of the Superintendent, Indiana, 1899–1900,* 526.

49. Ibid., 527; Riggs, "Present Status of Consolidation," 49.

50. For a survey of the arguments against consolidation, see *Report of the Superintendent, Nebraska, 1903–04,* 229–30. The farmers' feeling that they were regarded as inferior by townspeople was often expressed in their meetings. See *Journal of Proceedings, Eighteenth Session of the Illinois State Grange . . . 1889* (Peoria, n.d.), 13.

51. Jones, "Transportation of Pupils in Indiana," 189, 192, 201; Riggs, "Present Status of Consolidation," 43, 46–47, 54.

52. *Report of the Superintendent, Nebraska, 1903–04,* 229. See also Monahan, *Consolidation of Rural Schools,* 45–46. For the Ohio law requiring depots, see *Report of the Commissioner of Education for 1915,* 2 vols. (Washington, 1915), 1:10.

53. Upham, "Transportation of Rural School Children at Public Expense," 22; Riggs, "Present Status of Consolidation," 43; Jones, "Transportation of Pupils in Indiana," 201–2. A good survey of the problems of transportation after it had been tried for a number of years can be seen in *State of Indiana: Department of Public Instruction: Twenty-Sixth Biennial Report of the Superintendent of Public Instruction for the School Years Ending July 31, 1911, and July 31, 1912* (Indianapolis, 1913), 113.

54. *Report of the Superintendent, Nebraska, 1903–04,* 231.

55. *Proceedings of the Thirty-Ninth Annual Session of the State Grange: Iowa . . . 1908* (Council Bluffs, 1909), 45–46.

56. Minutes of the Annual Meeting, July 2, 1917, District 2, LaPrairie Twp.; Minutes of the Annual Meeting, July 3, 1916, and July 2, 1917, Minutes of Special Meeting, July 18, 1916, District 3, LaPrairie Twp.; Application for the Alteration of Joint District #16 Towns of Caledonia and Mt. Pleasant, Racine Co., Wis., July 7, 1914, School Records, WSHS.

57. *Report of the Commissioner of Education for 1913,* 2 vols. (Washington, 1914), 1:176–78. See also May, "Iowa's Consolidated Schools," 28–30; *Sixty-Sixth Report of the Public Schools of the State of Missouri, School Year Ending June 30, 1915* Jefferson City, n.d.), 36–37.

58. *Report of the Commissioner, 1913,* 1:177; May, "Iowa's Consolidated Schools," 33. See also *Minnesota: Department of Public Education: Nineteenth Biennial Report, 1915–16* (St. Paul, 1916), 35.

59. *Report of the Commissioner, 1913,* 1:177; May, "Iowa's Consolidated Schools," 29.

60. For the decline in consolidations in Iowa, see May, "Iowa's Consolidated Schools," 55–61.

61. Forest Ensign, "Consolidated Schools in Iowa," *American City* 27 (Dec. 1922): 513.

62. For examples of these surveys, see "A Comparative Study of City School and Rural School Attendance," *Studies in Education from the Department of Education of the State University of Iowa,* Bulletin 2, Vol. 1 (Iowa City, 1912); Francis A. Threadgold, "A Survey of Rural Schools in Michigan," *American Schoolmaster* 15 (June 1922): 228–30; M. S. Pittman, et al., *A Rural School Survey of Oakland County, Michigan* (Ypsilanti, Mich., 1923); Hans C. Olsen, "Some Shortcomings Revealed by a School Survey of a Typical Rural County," *Journal of Rural Education* 1 (June 1922): 456–63; Burt Loomis and Earle C. Duncan, *Survey of Gentry County Public Schools* (Marysville, Mo., 1927); Harvey C. Lehman, "A Comparison of the Play Activities of Town and Country Children," *Journal of Rural Education* 5 (Jan.–Feb. 1926), 253–59; C. W. Odell, "A Few Data Concerning the Comparative Efficiency of One-Room and Two-to-Four-Room Rural Schools," *School and Society* 19 (May 1924), 530–32.

63. See, for example, Charles McCracken; J. Cayce Morrison; and Ward G. Reader, *A Comparative Study of Certain Phases of the Fairfield County, Ohio, School System,* University Studies, No. 4, Vol. 2, Ohio State University (Columbus, Ohio, 1925); F. P. O'Brien and T. J. Smart, "Schooling in One-Teacher Schools," *Journal of Rural Education* 1 (Nov. 1921), 106–19; Crosby J. Chapman and H. L. Eby, "A Comparative Study, By Educational Measurements of One-Room Rural School Children and City School Children," *Journal of Educational Research* 2 (Oct. 1920), 636–46; W. J. Osborn, "Educational Measurements in the Rural Schools of Wisconsin," *Journal of Rural Education* 1 (June 1922): 441–46; S. M. Thomas (prep.), "Educational Tests and Measurements in Wisconsin," in *Education in Wisconsin: Biennial Report, 1920–1922* (Madison, 1922), 87–105; Theo. Irion and Fred C. Fischer, "Testing the Intelligence of Rural School Children," *American Schoolmaster* 14 (June 1921): 221–23. Tests given outside the region indicated much the same thing. See Frank T. Wilson, "Achievement in Fundamental Subjects in Some Rural Schools in Connecticut," *Journal of Rural Education* 3 (Sept. 1923): 19–27.

64. O'Brien and Smart, "Schooling in One-Teacher Schools," 117; Crosby and Eby, "A Comparative Study, By Educational Measurement of One-Room Rural School Children and City School Children," 644; C. E. Rarick, "Selling Rural Education to the Public in Kansas," *National Education Association of the United States: Addresses and Proceedings of the Sixty-First Annual Meeting* (Washington, 1923), 833.

65. Thomas, "Educational Tests and Measurements in Wisconsin," 90.

66. John M. Foote, "A Comparative Study of Instruction in Consolidated and One-Room Schools," *Journal of Rural Education* 2 (Apr. 1923): 337–51.

This study appeared also in *NEA Proceedings, Sixty-First Meeting,* 812–26.

67. Foote, "A Comparative Study of Instruction," 350–51.

68. Leo M. Favrot, "Discussion of the Report of the Committee on a Comparative Study of Instruction in Consolidated and One-Teacher Schools," *Journal of Rural Education* 3 (May–June 1924): 434.

69. Foote, "A Comparative Study of Instruction," 351.

70. Favort, "Discussion of the Report of the Committee," 434; Charles Everett Myers, "The One-Teacher School, Front and Center," *Journal of Rural Education* 3 (May–June 1924): 439–49. For a sketch of Myers, see Cattell, *Leaders in Education,* 742.

71. F. P. O'Brien, "On the Report of Mr. Foote's Committee," *Journal of Rural Education* 3 (Sept. 1923): 27–29.

72. Favrot, "Discussion of the Report of the Committee," 435.

73. Myers, "The One-Teacher School, Front and Center," 439.

74. F. P. O'Brien, "On the Report of Mr. Foote's Committee," 28. For an excellent recent survey of the inadequacies of consolidation and centralization, see Jonathan P. Sher, ed., *Education in Rural America: A Reassessment of Conventional Wisdom* (Boulder, Colo., 1977).

75. Katherine M. Cook, "Rural Education," *Biennial Survey of Education, 1926–1928,* Bulletin No. 16 (Washington: Bureau of Education, 1930), 111; W. H. Gaumnitz, *Are the One-Teacher Schools Passing? Eighteen Years of History,* Pamphlet No. 92 (Washington: Bureau of Education, 1940), 17.

76. Gaumnitz, *Are the One-Teacher Schools Passing?* 12–13.

77. Ibid., 15.

Index

Absenteeism, pupil, 188–89
Adams, Oliver, school record book of, 85, 87
Adrian Weekly Times and Expositor, 81
Agents, book, 95
Agriculture, study of, 222
American Economic Association, 103
Arbor Day: ceremonies on, 76, 197; county superintendents and, 147; origins of, 76
Arbor Vitae Summit School. *See* Oneida Township, Delaware County, Iowa
Arithmetic: book of, 223; degree of success in teaching, 215; examination in, 231; faculty psychology and, 180; instruction in, 11
Austin School. *See* Elba Township, Dodge County, Wis.

Bailey, Liberty Hyde, 220
Baker, Ray Stannard, 6
Baldwin, George (school board clerk), 86
Barber, Marshall (malariologist): schooling of, 7; and memorization, 15–18
Barnard, Henry (educator), 169
Bateman, Newton (superintendent of public instruction, Ill.): attacks

small school districts, 107–8; criticizes school directors, 108; and Protestant values, 102; supports teacher training, 167, 204
Becker, Carl, 15, 255 n.44
Beecher, Lyman, on need to educate, 33, 103
Bellamy, Francis, 76
Belleville, Wis., 49, 87, 89
Berrien Township, Mich., schools in, 79
Bible, reading of, 5–6, 39, 110, 177, 188, 200
Bickerdyke, J. R. (county superintendent, Kans.), 139, 140
Blooming Grove Township, Dane County, Wis.: building of school in, 50, 63; disputes in, 51; length of school terms in, 52–53, 97; location of, 50; postponed meetings in, 50, 262 n.21; selection of textbooks in, 95–96
Bonds, for building schools, 65–66, 69
Bradford, Mary (educator): education of, 9, 23; teaching experiences of, 185–86, 208
Branches of learning, common: easy grasp of, 14–15; subjects included in, 11; taught in county teacher institutes, 177; teachers and, 162

293